Other Power-glide Products:

How to Reach Us:
Web Page: www.power-glide.com
e-mail: jimb@power-glide.com
Phone: 801-373-3973
Fax: 801-343-3912

CD-ROM for Spanish:

This interactive CD-ROM supplements the current cassette and book based Spanish program. The CD-ROM will greatly enhance some of Power-glide's most popular features.

Power-glide's interactive CD includes three levels, easy, medium and hard, comes with an electronic dictionary and includes nine tests. Power-glide's CD is available for IBM compatible computers running Windows.

Teacher's Guide/Test Book:

Each book includes both a teacher's guide, 12 tests, answer keys, and a listening cassette. The Teachers' Guide has objectives for every lesson, ideas for teaching, games, tips, and quizzes. The tests will prepare students for high school and college credit exams.

Extra Workbooks:

If you have more than one learner, you may wish to purchase extra workbooks.

We offer courses in:

Spanish   French   German   Japanese   Russian

And soon others. *Check with us!*

Send in this card to register your product and receive a free, one year subscription to our newsletter. Each issue is filled with tips, ideas, games, announcements, contests and updates. It's one way we help to ensure you succeed with your new language. Please fill out this card completely and send it in today!

CUSTOMER SUPPORT REPLY CARD

We at Power-glide Language Courses want you to get the most out of our programs. To do this, we are developing valuable helps to further <u>your</u> success. Please fill out this information reply card and mail it to us *today*!

- What language are you learning? _____
- Where did you purchase your course? _____
- Where will you use the course? _____
- How many people will be using this course? _____
- What are the ages of those users? _____
- Name _____
- Address _____

_____
State   Zip

- Phone _____

Thank You!

Power-glide Language Courses
988 Cedar Avenue
Provo, Utah 84604-2862

This project would not have been possible without the assistance of many people. The help of those mentioned below was invaluable.

Editorial, Design, and Production Staff

Project Coordinator: James Blair

Cover Design: Darren Albertson

Editors: Troy Cox, C. Ray Graham, Richard Tice

Editorial Assistants: Julia Blair, Dell Blair, James Blair, Margaret Young, Ingrid Farmer, Andy Bay, Ben Blair

Head Compositor: Troy Cox

Translators: Robert Blair, Dell Blair, Raquel Decker

Voices, Audiocassettes: Dell Blair, James Blair, Julia Blair, Robert Blair, Raquel Decker, Carlos Ramirez, Julio Salazar, Margaret Young

Musicians: Paul Anderson, Marty Hughes, Scott Mills

Recording Engineers: Bruce Kirby, John Brady

Printed in the United States of America

10   9   8   7   6   5   4   3   2   1

Table of Contents

Introduction

WHAT MAKES A POWER-GLIDE LANGUAGE COURSE UNIQUE?

Our course is developed by linguists, not marketing strategists. Many commercial language companies promise a super shortcut. They put together a selection of useful words, phrases, and dialogues that simulate situations a tourist might face. They have you listen to natives deliver the lines and repeat what they say. And that's it. However, such little scraps aren't enough to get to the core of a language, to develop a strong sense of how it works and feels, and to build the habits, skills, and strategies that make efficient learning possible. This Power-glide language course gives you real language learning—the kind where you actually internalize the language, and begin to use it as your own. And with the capability you will have after completing the course, you can readily acquire the special language you need for business or other purposes.

Dr. Robert Blair, Ph.D. in Contrastive Linguistics and author of Innovative Approaches to Language Learning, is the developer of Power-glide languages courses. His methods are informed by current language acquisition theory and rooted in the work of world-renowned language teaching innovators such as Burling & Lentolay, Lozanov, Asher, and Curran. These pioneers created holistic, nonlinear models focused on the learner, the learning process, and on natural acquisition strategies. Dr. Blair has adapted their contributions to his own creative work to make superb language courses.

This course is fun and engaging because it gives rich experience in communication; it does not rely on mazes of grammar rules, rote memorization, and mind-numbing drills. Instead, you'll find:

- Music

- Stories

- Memory aids

- Diglot weaves

- You-are-there adventures

- Kinesthetic, visual, and audio activities

- Pictographs

What's more, Power-glide language courses can be used...

- with or without a teacher.

- in groups or individually and self-paced.

- for many different learning styles and aptitudes.

PHILOSOPHY

Power-glide courses cover grammar without emphasizing it. Our approach lets students gradually soak up the language. The course has exercises designed to help students discover the grammar for themselves. They learn grammar by listening to and seeing the language, much like small children do. Power-glide students have two main objectives: understanding, and speaking & writing. It's critical that they follow the learning methods.

How to Use this Course

- **Understand** the text.
- **Say it** and **write it**.

To **understand**, students should:

1. Look over the material and compare the Spanish to the English.
2. Listen to the tape while following the written text.
3. Listen to the tape a couple of times *without* looking at the written text.

Don't be shy: Use the pause button to stop the tape for a moment if you want a bit more time.

To **say** it, do this:

1. Read the story or material out loud in chorus with the tape, and keep the meaning in mind.
2. Turn the tape off, read each Spanish sentence out loud, and then look away and say it. Think of the meaning.
3. Now cover up the Spanish, look at the first English sentence, and try to say it in Spanish. Check to see if you did it right. Do that for all of the sentences.
4. Play the recording of the text, but pause the tape after each English sentence and say the Spanish.
5. Using notes of key words only, try to say the Spanish sentences the best you can.

To **write it**, do the same as above, but write your sentences instead of speaking them.

TEACHING SUGGESTIONS

Here are some ideas that will help you learn the language better.

General Tips

1. Use the course daily. Ten minutes per day is far better than an hour once a week. Sporadic use leads to lower retention and motivation. Students may forget previous material, have difficulty developing crucial habits, and eventually become frustrated.
2. Follow the instructions carefully. Use the advice given in the How To Use this Course. It will result in greater understanding, faster learning, and better retention of the material. If your students do not follow the prescribed order, they will not only not learn well— they will not learn *how* to learn.
3. Give weekly quizzes. This will encourage them to study and take responsibility for their learning. It will also give the teacher an indication of student needs and help keep students on the schedule you've created for them.
4. Pause and review as needed. Although it's not necessary to know everything perfectly before moving on, it's also not necessary to hurry through the course. Take some time to review, and play and replay the audio tapes as often as needed. The more exposure to the target language, the better.

Tips for Groups

1. Encourage creativity. Let students dramatize or act out their exercises as much as possible. Use games, role-plays, songs, poetry, or any other ideas that get students to immediately apply what they've learned.

2. Encourage a high level of interaction among students. Give students some time to help each other, to talk to each other in the language, and to otherwise support each other in their learning.

3. Allow students some personal learning time. This will let them absorb the material in their own particular way. Student's strengths vary greatly, so some will take longer or do better than others for certain kinds of activities.

4. Help students learn the steps given in the How to Use This Course section. Write them on the board, or on a poster. Review them often and make sure students follow them whenever they work on an exercise.

5. Give frequent positive feedback. Don't worry that the kids are having too much fun for learning to happen. The more fun they have, and the more positive encouragement they receive from their teacher, the better they will do.

Tips for Young Students

1. Emphasize listening and positive exposure to the language. Younger children need extra reinforcement.

2. Skip the more complex grammar ideas. Focus instead on stories, games, role-plays, ditties, and songs. Give them as much exposure to the language as possible. Kids learn grammar by listening and speaking, not by consulting grammar books.

3. Try some of these activities:

   a. Diglot Weaves (Tape 1, Side A & B)

   b. Well-known stories such as *The Three Bears* (Tape 4, Side A) and *Little Red Riding Hood* (Tape 4, Side B)

   c. Points, Lines, and Figures (Tape 1, Side A)

NEW SUPPLEMENTARY MATERIAL AVAILABLE!

You can now buy a Teacher's Supplement that contains:

1. Clear objectives for every exercise. Now you'll know what you're supposed to learn and when you have accomplished the objective—so you can confidently move on to the next section.

2. A package of twelve tests: pre- and post-tests, listening comprehension tests, and suggestions for quizzes to keep kids on their toes.

3. Tests at the end of each side of your cassette tape.

If you have questions, please contact us at (801) 373-3973.

Answers to your questions may be on our web page: www.power-glide.com, or you may email us.

The symbol ▣ is used to indicate that the text is tape-on, whereas ▣ indicates that the text is off the tape. The symbol ⊙ CD ROM indicates that a supplementary activity is available on CD ROM.

1

▣ Mission to *isla de Providencia*

(Day One—05:15 hours)

It is just before dawn, April 2, 1997. You and your companion are intelligence officers assigned to parachute onto *Isla de Providencia,* a tiny island in the Western Caribbean. It has been seized by invaders from an unknown place of origin. Your mission is to discover why this tiny island was singled out for capture. What is there on the island that is of such value? A submarine is to pick you up in ten days at midnight at the north point of the island.

You are to be met by three agents, code-named "Margarita," "Burrito," and "Tequila." You were given the code name "Rumpelstilskin" and your fellow officer the name "Stumpelrilskin." The people of the island speak Spanish. You and your fellow officer, "Stump," have never studied the language, but you know that English has taken in hundreds of words from Spanish, like *amigo, macho, siesta, adiós* and such. From just living in America, you've picked up phrases like *yo también* (me too), *más o menos* (more or less), *un poco* (a little), *(yo) no hablo español* (I don't speak Spanish), *¡perdón!* (pardon!), *sí señor* (yes sir), *no señora* (no ma'am), *¿qué pasó?* (what happened?), *(yo) no comprendo* (I don't understand), *por favor* (please), *muchas gracias* (thanks a lot), *buenos días* (hello/good day), *hasta la vista* (so long).

You review these, working on saying them smoothly and rapidly: *yo también, más o menos, un poco, no hablo español, ¡perdón!, sí señor, no señora, ¿qué pasó?, no comprendo, por favor, muchas gracias, buenos días, hasta la vista.*

Just before departure you are given four new phrases and some pronunciation helps:

You speak English?	*¿Usted habla inglés?*	oosted avla inglace
What is this?	*¿Qué es esto?*	resembles "K. S. S-toe"
I don't know.	*No sé.*	rhymes with José
How does one say this?	*¿Cómo se dice esto?*	resembles "Como say thee-say S-toe"

You review these, working on saying them smoothly and rapidly: *¿Usted habla inglés? ¿Qué es esto? No sé. ¿Cómo se dice esto?*

▣ Review all the above expressions until you can say the Spanish.

▣ You jump into the dark ahead of "Stump" and land just fifty yards off shore. You hide behind some rocks. Stump is nowhere to be seen. You wait for dawn, worried about him, hoping he landed nearby. As it begins to get light, you see a woman walking up the beach toward you. With her are two Russian wolfhounds. As she comes near, you take a chance. You step out of hiding and

1

ask, «*Perdón, Señora, ¿Usted habla inglés?*» Startled, she hesitates but then answers, «*¿Inglés? No...español...Yo hablo español y francés.*» Then she extends her hand and says, «*Buenos días, señor, yo soy la señora Quintana.*» Pointing to the dogs, she adds with a smile, «*Y éste es Burrito... y ése es Tequila.*»

Recognizing the dogs' names as the code names *Burrito* and *Tequila*, you figure this lady is your contact. «*¿Margarita?*» you ask. «*Sí, señor. Yo soy Margarita. Y usted es el señor...*»

You give her your code name. She nods, then, looking up and down the beach, asks, «*¿Y el otro...Stumpelrilskin?*» You shake your head. She motions you to follow: «*Por favor, señor, venga conmigo.*» You take it to mean "Please, sir, come with me."

As you follow her up to her beach house, you reflect on her words *conmigo* "with me," *venga conmigo* "come with me," then on her words *yo hablo español* "I speak Spanish," contrasting it with *¿Usted habla español?* and *¿Usted habla inglés?* You deduce that "I speak English" would be *yo hablo inglés* and that "I am Spanish" would be *yo soy español*, but you're unsure how to pronounce *yo soy American*. You comment, «*Yo soy...American.*» She nods. «*Mmm, usted es americano. Sí, yo sé.*» Of course she knows.

You race through these expressions, playing with them, concentrating mainly on increasing fluency:

Venga conmigo, señor.	*Sí, yo sé.*	*Y éste es Burrito.*
Por favor, venga conmigo.	*No, yo no sé.*	*Y ése es Tequila.*
¿Usted es americano?	*¿Usted habla inglés?*	*Buenos días, señora Quintana.*
Sí, yo soy americano.	*No, yo no hablo inglés.*	*¿Habla usted inglés?*
Yo no soy español.	*Perdón, ¿Usted es Margarita?*	*Usted habla inglés un poco, ¿no?*
Yo hablo inglés.	*Perdón, señor, no comprendo.*	*Burrito y Tequila, ¿qué pasó?*
Yo no hablo español.	*¿Es usted Margarita?*	
Yo sé.	*Oh, sí, yo soy la señora Quintana, yo soy Margarita Quintana.*	

 Practice saying these expressions, always keeping the meaning in mind. Don't worry about having the expressions memorized. Just be familiar with them.

 Arriving at the door, *la señora* Quintana bids you enter: «*Por favor, pase.*» You bid her go ahead of you, saying, «*Señora, por favor, pase usted.*» She smiles and goes in, expressing thanks with «*Gracias, muchas gracias.*» Practice saying these new expressions.

As you enter, you meet a gentleman who bids you welcome with «*Bienvenido*»—sounds a bit like "B.M. B'Knee though"—and then introduces himself, «*Yo soy el señor Quintana, Gustavo Quintana.*» You ask him, «*¿Usted habla inglés?*» He replies, «*No, señor, pero usted habla español. Usted habla español bien. Usted es americano, ¿no?*» Before you can respond, a girl comes in and speaks with the man and lady of the house. In a moment they excuse themselves and leave. The girl introduces herself as Mariela and offers to help you. Together you work on pronunciation and spelling. You work on pronouncing fluently the following list of expressions:

Yes, please.	*Sí, por favor.*
This is Tequila; that is Burrito.	*Este es Tequila; ése es Burrito.*
Go ahead.	*Pase. Pase usted.*
Thanks, sir.	*Gracias, señor.*
Welcome!	*¡Bienvenido!* ("B.M. B'Knee though")

Do you speak Spanish?	¿Habla usted español?
I am English.	Yo soy inglés (or just: Soy inglés).
I am not French.	Yo no soy francés.
You are American.	Usted es americano.
Are you American?	¿Es usted americano?
I am American.	Yo soy americano (or just: Soy americano).
I speak English.	Yo hablo inglés (or just: Hablo inglés).
I am Spanish.	Yo soy español.
I speak English a little.	Yo hablo inglés un poco.
Come with me.	Venga conmigo.
Mr. Gustavo Quintana	El señor Gustavo Quintana
And the other?	¿Y el otro?
I know.	Yo sé.
I don't know.	Yo no sé.

* Note: When an accented letter is capitalized, the accent is left off: *éste/Este.*

You also prepare a list of your previously learned expressions.

Me too.	Yo también.
more or less	más o menos
a bit, a little	un poco
Thanks much.	Muchas gracias.
I don't speak Spanish.	No hablo español.
Pardon.	Perdón.
Yes, sir.	Sí, señor.
How does one say...?	¿Cómo se dice...?
in English	en inglés
in Spanish	en español
What is this?	¿Qué es esto?
I don't understand.	No comprendo.
Hello (good day).	Buenos días.
So long.	Hasta la vista.

After practicing your pronunciation, cover the English column. How many of the Spanish words do you recognize? Don't get caught up trying to memorize the words. You will see them often throughout the course. As you see them used in different contexts, you will gradually acquire their meaning.

▦ As you and Mariela sit, lacking words with which to communicate, you initiate some language exploration. Pointing to the door you ask, «¿Qué es esto?» She says what sounds like "la puerta," and you relate it to the word port or sea port, a door to a country. She writes it, "the door" = la puerta and then asks, «¿Cómo se dice «la puerta» en inglés?» You tell her. In a moment, you've each acquired several new words:

	Spelling	Helpful hints
foot	pie	(sounds a lot like P.A.)
hand	mano	(related to manual, handbook)
head	cabeza	(not caboose-ah but cabase-ah)
mouth	boca	("Put a coca in your boca!")

⏺ While you're arranging these words into your memory storage, *la señora* Quintana comes in with a concerned look on her face. She looks at you and says something you don't understand about Stumpelrilskin. You guess she's made contact with him.

⏺ Review the previous section until you feel comfortable with the Spanish phrases.

SELF-TEST

How many of the Spanish phrases can you recognize? See if you can match the English and the Spanish phrases. The answers are in the appendix.

1	_____	*¡Buenos días!*	a. And you?
2	_____	*Señor, por favor, pase.*	b. Do you speak English?
3	_____	*Gracias.*	c. Do you speak Spanish?
4	_____	*¿Habla usted inglés?*	d. Good day!
5	_____	*No señor.*	e. I am Margarita.
6	_____	*¿Usted habla español?*	f. I am Spanish.
7	_____	*Si, yo hablo español.*	g. No sir.
8	_____	*Yo soy español.*	h. Please, sir, go in.
9	_____	*Yo soy Margarita.*	i. Thanks.
10.	_____	*¿Y tu?*	j. Yes, I speak Spanish.

11.	_____	*Yo soy Rumpelstilskin.*	a. And the other?
12.	_____	*Yo soy americano.*	b. Come with me.
13.	_____	*Sí, yo sé.*	c. Hello Burrito and Tequila.
14.	_____	*¿Usted es americano?*	d. I am American.
15.	_____	*¿Y el otro?*	e. I am Rumpelstilskin.
16.	_____	*Yo no sé.*	f. I don't know.
17.	_____	*Venga conmigo.*	g. That is Tequila.
18.	_____	*Este es Burrito.*	h. This is Burrito.
19.	_____	*Ese es Tequila.*	i. Yes, I know.
20.	_____	*Hola Burrito y Tequila.*	j. Are you American?

21.	_____	*Por favor, señor.*	a. Good-bye, sir.
22.	_____	*Gracias.*	b. How does one say "king" in Spanish?
23.	_____	*Muchas gracias.*	c. How does one say *"señorita"* in English?
24.	_____	*Adios, señor.*	d. How does one say?
25.	_____	*¿Como se dice?*	e. I don't understand.
26.	_____	*En español.*	f. In English.
27.	_____	*En inglés.*	g. In Spanish.
28.	_____	*¿Como se dice "king" en español?*	h. Please, sir.
29.	_____	*¿Como se dice "señorita" en inglés?*	i. Thanks a lot.
30.	_____	*No comprendo.*	j. Thanks.

End of Episode One

2

📼 Episode Two: The Secret Discovered

Day One—09:00 hours

Your reception has taken a strange twist. The invaders are searching the area, so you are led down to a hiding area in the basement. There you are shown a large notebook, a tape player, and some cassette tapes. When the heavy door slams shut behind you, you are left alone to find what these contain. You open the notebook and find this note:

> Hidden deep inside this island is a treasure of incalculable value. It is this the invaders came for. They don't know its location, but if they find it, our world will pay a terrible price. They seek the map to the treasure. Hidden in this room are the keys to the vault where the map is kept. Three keys and two persons are needed to open the vault. To obtain the keys, you must first work this puzzle. Once you have the map in hand, you will find out what the treasure actually is. And then begins the real adventure, the race to obtain the treasure. Good luck!

You decide to go as far as you can on your own, so you proceed to work the puzzle, hoping "Stump" will soon join you.

Tape off. Work carefully on the three-part puzzle that occupies the next five pages. Then after you take the self-test, listen to the puzzle sentences on the tape. Following that, you will make your next critical move in the adventure game.

📼 THE PUZZLE

This tape-off exercise continues several pages. The next tape-on section begins with "Listening to a reading of the puzzle sentences."

The purpose of this puzzle is to make you prove your ability to tackle the language on your own, figuring out by yourself some fundamental things about the language. Working the puzzle will help you see that learning Spanish is a fascinating and delightful experience. In the process of "breaking the code," you will learn quite a bit about how Spanish works to convey meaning, and you will discover how to form a great number of novel sentences of considerable complexity. Keep alive the information you gain from this challenging exercise and use that information in learning more Spanish.

Puzzle Part 1

Instructions: Below, you will find sentences in normal Spanish, but with no spaces in between the words. Your first task is to figure out where the word breaks are. Do this by comparing the Spanish phrases and their English translation. Don't worry about pronunciation. Mark with pencil or pen the word breaks that you hypothesize. Then do the following:
• Compare the right vs. wrong columns.
• Study the examples and explanations in the help section.
• Fill in the blanks.
When you have finished you can check your answers in the appendix.

    1. *PabloyMaría*   Pablo and Maria

2. *Pabloesunmuchacho.*	Pablo is a boy.
3. *Maríaesunamuchacha.*	Maria is a girl.
4. *Pablotienedoshermanas.*	Pablo has two sisters.
5. *Maríatienetreshermanos.*	Maria has three brothers.
6. *PabloeselhermanodeMaría.*	Pablo is Maria's brother.
7. *MaríaeslahermanadePablo.*	Maria is Pablo's sister.
8. *EllaesunadelashermanasdePablo.*	She is one of Pablo's sister.
9. *LamadreyelpadredePabloyMaría*	The mother and the father of Pablo and Maria
10. *LashermanasyloshermanosdePablo*	The sisters and the brothers of Pablo

Compare Right with Wrong

	Right	Wrong
one sister/one brother	*una hermana/un hermano*	*un hermana/una hermano*
the brothers/the sisters	*los hermanos/las hermanas*	*las hermanos/los hermanas*
Pablo is the brother.	*Pablo es el hermano.*	*Pablo es la hermano.*
Maria is the sister.	*María es la hermana.*	*María es el hermana.*
one of the sisters	*una de las hermanas*	*una de los hermanas*

Help Section

1. In English, we use the word the in all cases. In Spanish, however, there are different ways of saying the:

   el hermano, la hermana, los hermanos, las hermanas

   Similarly, "a brother," "a sister," but *un hermano, una hermana*

2. English has several ways to show possession: the father of the girl = the girl's father. Spanish lacks the 's option, having only the one way: *el padre de la muchacha.*

Exercise 1

Instructions: Fill in the translation equivalents. Leave spaces between your words. You can check your answers in the appendix.

a father ____ _____   a boy _____ _____

the father ____ _____   the boy _____ _____

a mother ____ _____   a girl _____ _____

the mother ____ _____   the girl _____ _____

a brother _____ _____   he has ___ _____

the brother ____ _____   she has _____ _____

the brothers _____ _____   one of (the sisters) _____ ___ _____ _____

a sister _____ _____   Pablo's/of Pablo ____ _____

the sister _____ _____   Maria's/of Maria ____ _____

the sisters ____ _____

Puzzle Part 2

Instructions: Continue as before, marking the word breaks and figuring out the patterns. Check your answers in the appendix.

1.	*Estemuchachoesalto...muyalto.*	This boy is tall...very tall.
2.	*Elotronoestanalto.*	The other is not so tall.
3.	*Esteesrico;eltienemuchodinero.*	This one is rich; he has much money.
4.	*Elotronoesrico;elnotienedinero.*	The other one is not rich; he has no money.
5.	*Estahermananoesrica.*	This sister is not rich.
6.	*Peroellaesmuybonita.*	But she is very pretty.
7.	*Esa (laotrahermana) noestanbonita.*	That one (the other sister) is not so pretty.
8.	*Peroellatienemásencanto.*	But she has more charm.

Help Section

1. Many adjectives have four forms:
rich = *rico, rica, ricos, ricas*
tall = *alto, alta, altos, altas*

Many adjectives (like "tall," "rich") have four forms in Spanish to match a single form in English: The vowel o indicates masculine; a indicates feminine. Adjectives are pluralized just like the nouns they describe.

The tall boy.	The tall girl.	The tall boys.	The tall girls.
El muchacho alto.	*La muchacha alta.*	*Los muchachos altos.*	*Las muchachas altas.*

Which of the forms is selected depends on the gender (masculine or feminine) and number (singular or plural) of the noun that the adjective goes with. Stated in traditional terms, Spanish adjectives agree with or reflect the gender and number of the noun they modify.

2. Negative words always precede the verb; they never follow as in English.
Pablo <u>is not</u> rich. *Pablo <u>no es</u> rico.*

Compare Right with Wrong

	Right	Wrong
this boy	*este muchacho*	*esta muchacho*
this girl	*esta muchacha*	*este muchacha*
this tall girl	*esta muchacha alta*	*esta muchacha alto*
The brother is rich.	*El hermano es rico.*	*El hermano es rica.*
The sister is not so rich.	*La hermana no es tan rica.*	*La hermana no es tan rico.*
The boy is not tall.	*El muchacho no es alto.*	*La hermana es no alto.*

Exercise 2

Instructions: Translate the following. Leave space between words you have identified. Check your answers in the appendix.

this girl _____

that boy _____

(She is) tall and rich _____

He is not very rich. _____

(He is) tall and rich. _____

She is not so tall. _____

Pablo's money _____

He has much money. _____

7

Your success at solving the puzzle thus far entitles you to the first clue to the location of the first key: Below is a chart of 12 sets of keys. The key you need has the shape of the last key in the fourth set on this chart. Eventually you'll be told which key it is.

Puzzle Part 3

Instructions: Continue as before, marking the word breaks and figuring out the patterns. Check your answers in the appendix.

1.	*Estaserpiente. Esapaloma.*	This snake. That dove.
2.	*Estasserpientesyesaspalomas.*	These snakes and those doves.
3.	*Unaserpiente. Laserpiente. Laotraserpiente.*	A snake. The snake. The other snake.
4.	*Unasserpientes. Lasotrasserpientes.*	Some snakes. The other snakes.
5.	*Laspalomas. Unasotraspalomas.*	The doves. Some other doves.
6.	*Unasserpientesduermenmucho.*	Some snakes sleep a lot.
7.	*Unasserpientesnoduermen.*	Some snakes don't sleep.
8.	*Estapalomaduerme;esaserpientecome.*	This dove sleeps; that snake eats.
9.	*Estaspalomasduermen;esasserpientescomen.*	These doves sleep; those snakes eat.
10.	*Cuandolasotraspalomasduermen...*	When the other doves sleep...
11.	*Unaserpiente<u>las</u>ve.*	A snake sees (watches) <u>them</u>.
12.	*Silaserpienteduermelaspalomas<u>la</u>ven.*	If the snake sleeps, the doves see (watch) <u>it</u>.
13.	*Laserpienteoyelapaloma.*	The snake hears the dove.
14.	*Perolaspalomasnooyenlaserpiente.*	But the doves don't hear the snake.
15.	*Laspalomas<u>la</u>venperono<u>la</u>oyen.*	The doves see <u>it</u> but don't hear <u>it</u>.
16.	*Laspalomas<u>las</u>oyenperono<u>las</u>ven.*	The doves hear <u>them</u> but don't see <u>them</u>.

Compare Right with Wrong

	Right	Wrong
these snakes	*estas serpientes*	*esta serpientes*
the snakes	*las serpientes*	*la serpientes*
some snakes	*unas serpientes*	*una serpientes*
The dove eats.	*La paloma come.*	*La paloma comen.*
The doves eat.	*Las palomas comen.*	*Las palomas come.*
The snake hears the dove.	*La serpiente oye la paloma.*	*La serpiente la paloma oye.*
The snake hears it.	*La serpiente <u>la</u> oye.*	*La serpiente oye <u>la</u>.*

8

Help Section

1. Ordering of subject, verb, and object.

The normal order of sentence parts in Spanish is the same as in English:

Subject	Verb	Object
1	2	3
The snake	hears	the doves.
La serpiente	*oye*	*las palomas.*

However, to say "the snake hears them" (where the object is a pronoun), the Spanish sentence order changes to:

Subject	Object	Verb
1	3	2
The snake	them	hears.
La serpiente	*las*	*oye.*

2. Verb forms change with singular and with plural subject.

The snake eats. The snake<u>s</u> eat.

La serpiente come. Las serpientes come<u>n</u>.

3. Negative words go before the verb and before the object.

This snake sees doves.	*Esta serpiente ve palomas.*
That snake doesn't see doves.	*Esa serpiente <u>no ve</u> palomas.*
This snake sees them.	*Esta serpiente las ve.*
That snake doesn't see them.	*Esa serpiente <u>no las</u> ve.*

Verb Practice

Instructions: Give the Spanish verb form that goes with subject. The answers are in the appendix.

(It) sleeps   *duerme*

1. eats   _____
2. hears   _____
3. sees   _____

(It) doesn't sleep   *no duerme*

4. eat   _____
5. hear   _____
6. see   _____

(They) sleep   *duermen*

7. eat   _____
8. hear   _____
9. see   _____

(They) don't sleep   *no duermen*

10. eat   _____
11. hear   _____
12. see   _____

(It) eats it   *la come*

13. hears   _____
14. sees   _____

(It) doesn't eat it   *no la come*

15. hear   _____
16. see   _____

3

Self-Test

UNDERSTANDING BASIC SENTENCES

Can you get the meaning of the following sentences? Check your comprehension in the appendix.

1. *La paloma come cuando la serpiente duerme.*

2. *Si las serpientes comen, las palomas duermen.*

3. *Esas palomas no oyen las serpientes.*

4. *Pero estas serpientes ven las palomas y las oyen.*

5. *Unas palomas duermen cuando las serpientes comen.*

6. *Si esta paloma no oye, esa serpiente no ve.*

7. *Si unas palomas duermen, las serpientes las ven.*

8. *Si estas palomas no duermen, las serpientes ven las otras.*

9. *Unas serpientes y unas palomas comen mucho, pero estas serpientes y esas palomas no comen mucho.*

If you understand *less* than six of the nine test sentences, go back and review, then test yourself again. When you can correctly understand at least six of the nine test items, you will earn the second clue to the location of the first key:

> Look back at the key chart—the twelve sets of keys. The key you need is *the fourth key from the right* and *the fourth key from the bottom* in the twelfth set of keys (bottom-right corner). The actual key corresponding to this chart is hidden behind the topmost brick in the north wall. It will open only the outside door of the vault. To open the inside door, two persons and two keys will be required.

You're wondering again what happened to "Stump" when suddenly he appears out of nowhere. You are as pleased to see him as he is to find you. You tell him what you've discovered and point to the place where the key is located. Together you remove the brick and find a dozen keys, one of which matches the description given.

LISTENING TO A READING OF THE PUZZLE SENTENCES

Part 1

1. *Pablo y María.*
2. *Pablo es un muchacho.*
3. *María es una muchacha.*
4. *Pablo tiene dos hermanas.*
5. *María tiene tres hermanos.*
6. *Pablo es el hermano de María.*
7. *María es la hermana de Pablo.*
8. *Ella es una de las hermanas de Pablo.*
9. *La madre y el padre de Pablo y María.*
10. *Las hermanas y los hermanos de Pablo.*

Part 2

1. *Este muchacho es alto...muy alto.*
2. *El otro no es tan alto.*
3. *Este es rico; el tiene mucho dinero.*
4. *El otro no es rico; el no tiene dinero.*
5. *Esta hermana no es rica.*
6. *Pero ella es muy bonita.*
7. *Esa (la otra hermana) no es tan bonita.*
8. *Pero ella tiene más encanto.*

Part 3

1. *Esta serpiente. Esa paloma.*
2. *Estas serpientes y esas palomas.*
3. *Una serpiente. La serpiente. La otra serpiente.*
4. *Unas serpientes. Las otras serpientes.*
5. *Las palomas. Unas otras palomas.*
6. *Unas serpientes duermen mucho.*
7. *Unas serpientes no duermen.*
8. *Esta paloma duerme; esa serpiente come.*
9. *Estas palomas duermen; esas serpientes comen.*
10. *Cuando las otras palomas duermen...*
11. *Una serpiente las ataca.*
12. *Si la serpiente duerme, las palomas la atacan.*
13. *Pero si la paloma muere, la serpiente vive.*
14. *La serpiente come la paloma.*
15. *Pero las palomas no comen la serpiente.*
16. *Las palomas la atacan pero no la comen.*
17. *Las palomas las atacan pero no las comen.*

With your successful completion of the three-part puzzle, you may now be told the location of the vault. Remove the bottom-most brick in the north wall, and you will find a button. Press it, and the east wall will open, revealing the vault. Take this notebook and the tapes with you into the vault.

You remove the brick, press the button, and watch as the wall opens up, disclosing the vault. You unlock the steel door, swing it open, and switch on the light. The two of you step into the vault. The door shuts behind you. Your next task requires two keys. The notebook tells you that one is in deposit box 47 on your right, the other is in 93 on your left.

4

Speed Learning

 (This section has a supplementary activity on the Powerglide CD ROM. The symbol will be used throughout the course to indicate when activities have CD ROM counterparts.)

BASIC QUESTION WORDS

Here are some question words. Listen to them, then take the twenty-minute workshop.

¿Entiende?	Do you understand?
Entiendo.	I understand.
¿Cómo?	How?
¿Cuánto?	How much?
¿Dónde?	Where (at)?
¿Cuándo?	When?
¿Cuál?	Which one?
¿Quién?	Who?
¿Qué?	What?
¿Por qué?	Why? (for what [reason])

Tape off. Proceed on your own.

A TWENTY-MINUTE WORKSHOP

Among the most important words in conversation are question words like "where," "when," "how," etc. The leading question is "Do you understand?" We'll start with that one. You already know *¿comprende?*. The more common way to ask "Do you understand?" sounds like N.T.N.-day (en-tee-EN-day). The stress is on the second "en": "en-tee-EN-day." Say it rapidly, speeding up the second syllable so it's "en-tyEN-day." It is written *¿entiende?*. Say it rapidly several times, with its meaning in mind. Pretend you are asking someone if they understand.

Equally important is to learn to say "I understand." It sounds like N.T.N.-dough (spelled *entiendo*). Say it rapidly, speeding up the second syllable so it's "en-tyEN-dough." Now put your hands in front of your face, like two puppets facing each other. Have one puppet ask the other: «*¿Entiende?*» And have the other answer: «*Si, entiendo*».

Five Question Words

Now for more question words. Give these your full concentration, and you will absorb them within minutes. First a set of five.

¿Cómo? (as in Perry Como)—How?
    "*Cómo* did you get here?" "*Cómo* can I thank you?"

¿Cuánto? (as in squanto minus the s-, but as always, the *t* has a distinct t-sound)—"How much?"
    Related to our word <u>quant</u>ity (just think of asking "What <u>quant</u>ity of money?").
    "*Cuánto* is this?" "*Cuánto* are the shoes?" "*Cuánto* do I owe you?"

¿Dónde? (as in Doan-day)—"Where?"

> Sounds like Doan-day. "Where's Mr. Doan-day?" "It's dark. *Cómo* can I see *dónde* I am?"

¿De dónde? (put "day" in front of *dónde*)—"From where? Whence?"

> "*¿De dónde* are you?" "*¿De dónde* are you coming from?"

¿A dónde? (put "ah" in front of *dónde*)—"To where?"

> "*¿A dónde* are you going?"

Review this first set of words.

Do you understand?	*¿Entiende? (or ¿Comprende?)*
I understand.	*Entiendo (or Comprendo).*
How?	*¿Cómo?*
How much?	*¿Cuánto?*
Where (at)?	*¿Dónde?*
Where to?	*¿A dónde?*
Where from?	*¿De dónde?*

Stop for a moment to review these and set them firmly in memory. Then take time to do a bit of role-playing with these expressions. For each one, make up sentences like those above, adding English words as needed—or better, adding hand motions and facial expressions that will communicate what you need to say to meet an imagined situation. For example, you need a screwdriver. You communicate to your landlady what you need by pantomiming using a screwdriver and asking *¿Dónde?*. Do it as if you really meant it! Then do the same for the following: A telephone. A salt shaker. Scissors. A pen or pencil. A needle. A typewriter.

Ask the cost of the following by naming the item, pausing, then asking *¿Cuánto?* Do it as if you really meant it! Example: (*la blusa* "the blouse") *La blusa...¿cuánto?* (*La fruta...*"the fruit"; *el piano...*"the piano"; *el tren...*"the train"). Do a bit of playacting. Point to a friend's watch and ask, «*¿Cuánto costó?*»—"How much did it cost?" (Possible answers: «*Tres dolares*» "$3," «*Mucho*» "a lot," or «*No mucho*»—"not much.")

One use of *cómo* is in showing that you didn't understand what someone said. To say "How's that?" you would say, «*¿Cómo?*»

To say "How's that? I don't understand," you would say, «*¿Cómo? No entiendo.*»

Four Question Words

The next set of four question words will multiply the kinds of information you can get.

To ask "when," use *cuándo* (not c-*when*-do but *cuándo*). It begins like *cuánto* but has a *d* instead of a *t*. "*Cuándo* will I see you again?" "*Cuándo* will a bus get here?" "*Cuándo* did you leave?"

To ask "which," as in "Which is mine?" use *cuál* (like "squall" minus the *s*). "*Cuál* is mine?" "*Cuál* do you want, this one or that one?"

To ask "who," as in "Who came?" use *quién* (sounds like "key-EN"): "*Quién* came?" "*Quién* is that lady?"

13

Quién is used alone to mean "Who?" referring to the subject that *performs* something (*Quién* hit the ball?) or *is* something (*Quién* is your leader?). To ask "To whom?" put the sound *ah* before *quién*. "*A quién* shall I give this?" "*A quién* did you deliver the package?"

Review this second set of words.

When?	*¿Cuándo?*
Which one?	*¿Cuál?*
Who?	*¿Quién?*
To whom?	*¿A quién?*

Ask the identity of persons you can point to in an imaginary picture. Example:

Ese señor...¿quién es? That gentleman...who is [he]? *Esa señora...¿quién es?* That lady...who is [she]?

A very important application of cómo is in asking the question how something is said. The regular spelling of this phrase is *¿Cómo se dice?* It resembles COmo say THIS-eh? except that THIS is pronounced THEES. Say it rapidly two or three times: COmo say THEES-eh?

To ask how to say "house" you could say "COmo say THEES-eh 'house'?" (The answer can be: "Say THEES-eh 'casa.'" or "It is called 'casa.'") Now practice using *¿Cómo* say THEES eh? to ask the name of several animals: elephant, tiger, lion.

Two Question Words

Two more words will give you a full set of interrogative expressions. *Qué* sounds like K or Kay and means "what," as in "What do you want?" "*¿Qué* are you doing?" "*¿Qué pasa?*" ("What's happening?")

To ask "Why," use *¿por qué?* (literally "for what?"). "*¿Por qué* did you do it?" "*¿Por qué* are you laughing?"

Now review your entire set of expressions. Cover the Spanish except to confirm your response.

How?	*¿Cómo?*
How do you say __?	*¿Cómo se dice __?*
Where (at)?	*¿Dónde?*
Where to?	*¿A dónde?*
Where from?	*¿De dónde?*
How much?	*¿Cuánto?*
When?	*¿Cuándo?*
Which one?	*¿Cuál?*
Who?	*¿Quién?*
To whom?	*¿A quién?*
Do you understand?	*¿Entiende?*
I understand.	*Entiendo.*
What?	*¿Qué?*
Why? (for what?)	*¿Por qué?*

14

🔊 A SPANISH DITTY

Here's a little ditty you can memorize. It takes very little effort.

NO SAY k-JUAN-doe	*No sé cuándo,*	I don't know when,
NO SAY KEY-N	*No sé quién,*	I don't know who,
NO SAY NAH-thah	*No sé nada*	I don't know anything
MOO-ey B.N.	*muy bien.*	very well.
NO SAY th-OWN DAY	*No sé dónde,*	I don't know where,
NO SAY k-WALL	*No sé cuál,*	I don't know which,
SAY MOO-ey POCO	*Sé muy poco,*	I know very little,
E. S.O.C.S. mahl.	*Y eso sí es mal.*	And that is indeed bad.

🔊 What you have learned in this workshop is of considerable importance. Take time for periodic review to make it part of you. Find ways to use it "for real."

5

🎞 Self-Quiz

This quiz covers material from the beginning. Before taking it, review the expressions you feel you should know. Then respond either aloud or in writing to the conversational statements below. You can check your answers in the appendix.

1. You're a security guard at an airbase in Florida. Seeing a suspicious character sneaking around, you stop him. In just two words, ask where he's going: —
2. Surprised, he asks if you speak Spanish: —
3. You ask him if he speaks English: —
4. Thinking he can bribe you, he asks to know the amount needed: —
5. He shows you something you don't recognize. You ask what (it is): —
6. After handcuffing him, you give him a candy bar. He accepts it, saying: —
7. He offers you a lollipop. You politely refuse it, saying: —
8. In explaining something to him, you want to know if he understands. You ask: —
9. He answers in the affirmative: —
10. He says, "Watch me!" and does a double backflip. You compliment him: —
11. You wonder where he is from and ask: —
12. He tells you he is from Cuba. He says: —
13. He is curious where you are leading him and asks: —
14. Coming to the security office door, you bid him to go on in: —
15. He doesn't see the door and asks its location: —
16. He sees there are two doors side-by-side and asks which one: —
17. You indicate which door you want him to go in: —
18. He goes in, saying that he understands: —
19. Once inside, you politely ask him to be seated. You say: —
20. He doesn't obey. You ask him if he understands. You say: —
21. Now he indicates that he understands and sits down, thanking you: —
22. He asks you how to say, "Gimme a break!" in Spanish: —
23. You answer truthfully that you don't know: —
24. Leaving him handcuffed to the chair, you bid him farewell: —
25. He screams after you, "Why?": —
26. You answer that you don't know why: —
27. He screams after you, "Who?": —
28. You answer that you don't know who: —
29. Your answer recalls the ditty, so you recite it: —
30. He laughs and compliments you: —

6

🎞️ Getting Ready to Read Spanish

CD ROM

Tape off. Read carefully, *carefully*, then listen to the reading of the third column.

🎞️ You can guess the approximate pronunciation of most letters, but you might not guess that "h" is always silent ("hotel" is /otel/), that (in American Spanish) the letters *z* and *s* both make the same sound , and the letters "b" and "v" also make same sound.

THE CORRESPONDENCE OF LETTER TO SOUND

Here's a first approximation to the sound of letters you might not guess. Listen to the words in the third column.

Letter	English	🎞️ Spanish	Meaning
a	ah	*mamá*	mother
ai, ay	eye, sigh, guy	*caites*	sandals
ae	ah-EH	*maestro*	master
alle	AH-yey	*calle*	street
e	eh	*José*	Jose
ei, ey	eight, lay	*ley*	law
i, y	Mimi	*Mimi, y*	Mimi, and
ya, ia	yacht	*ya, fiasco*	already, fiasco
ye, ie	yes	*Yermo, bien*	(place name), well
yo, io	yo-yo	*yo, piojo*	I, louse
o	Lola	*Lola*	Lola
oy, oi	boy, voice	*hoy*	today
u	Lulu	*ruta*	route
uy, ui	phooey	*muy*	very
uo	quota	*cuota*	quota
ue	way (clipped)	*bueno*	good
uey	way	*buey*	ox
ua	squash	*guapo*	handsome
uay	"Y," Wye	*Guaymas*	(place name)
z	s as in Sony	*zona*	zone
j	ho (scraped H)	*ojo*	eye
g (before i, e)	(same as j)	*gente*	people
g (elsewhere)	g	*garganta*	throat

🎞️ Go back and read *very* carefully the information at the top of this page. Take note!

Points, Lines, and Figures

Puntos, Líneas, y Figuras

A. SCATTER CHART

1	2 dos	3	4 cuatro	5	6 seis
uno		tres		cinco	

4 5 2 3
6   1   •   _____   &
números   punto   línea   y

B. LOOK, READ, AND LISTEN

1. •   *Un punto.*

2. _____   *Una línea.*

3. 1   *Un número, el número uno.*

4. •• ____   *Dos puntos y una línea.*

5. ___ ___ ___ •• 3   *Tres líneas, dos puntos, y un número, el número tres.*

6. 3 2 1 ___ ___   *Tres números; los números tres, dos, y uno; y dos líneas.*

7. • • • • ___ ___ 2   *Cuatro puntos, dos líneas, y un número, el número dos.*

8. ___ ___ ___ 3 4   *Tres líneas y dos números, los números tres y cuatro.*

9. 1 2 3 4 5 • • • • •   *Cinco números; los números uno, dos, tres, cuatro, cinco; y cinco puntos.*

10. • • • • • ____ ____   *Cinco puntos y dos líneas.*

11. ____ • • • • • •   *Una línea y seis puntos.*

12. 1 2 3 4 5 6   *Seis números, los números uno, dos, tres, cuatro, cinco, y seis.*

C. LOOK AND LISTEN

1. •   2. ____   3. 1   4. •• ____

5. ____ ____ ____ •• 3   6. 3 2 1 ____ ____

7. • • • • ____ ____ 2   8. ____ ____ ____ 2 3 4

9. 1 2 3 4 5 • • • • •   10. • • • • • ___ ___

11. ___ • • • • •   12. 1 2 3 4 5 6

D. Multiple-Choice Frames

Tape off. Read the instructions.

Below, you will see a series of frames, each with four sections.

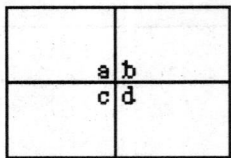

You'll hear the frame number and then a sentence referring to what is in one of the four sections. In the following pause, identify which section is referred to and listen for the answer. For each frame there will be at least three identification problems. Control the pace by stopping and starting the tape. The script is in the appendix.

(A) 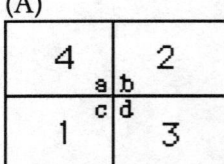   (B)   (C)   (D)   (E)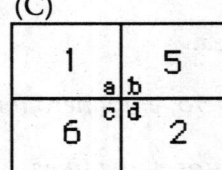

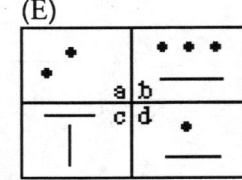

(F) 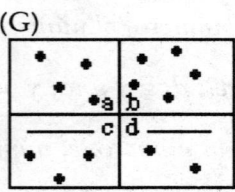   (G) 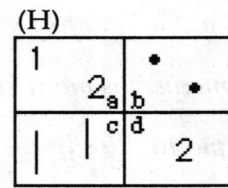   (H) 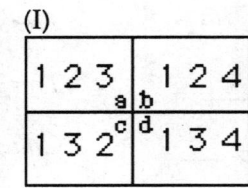   (I)   (J)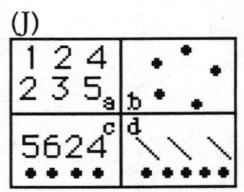

E. Listen and Draw

Listen and draw quickly what is called for. Stop the tape if the pace is too fast. The answers are in the appendix.

1.   2.   3.   4.   5.

F. Read for Meaning

Read the Spanish phrases for meaning. Can you translate them into English? Look in the appendix for an English translation of them.

1. *Una línea y el número uno.*
2. *Un punto y el número cinco.*
3. *Dos números, los números tres y cuatro.*
4. *Seis puntos, tres líneas, y dos números; los números tres y uno.*

8

 More on Numbers

Más acerca de los Números

CD ROM

TEN / *DIEZ*

Using four letters—D, S, C, and N—you have the makings of the numbers *ten* and *hundred*. The Spanish word for 10, *diez* or *dec-* comes from Latin *dec-* or *des-*, which we recognize in *dec*ade, *dec*imal, *dec*iliter, and other words having to do with the concept *ten*.

Listen to it: *diez*. One way to spell that would be the initials "D.S.," said rapidly.

Repeat "D.S." Associate the meaning with *ten*. Say it as one syllable, accenting the "S": *diez*.

HUNDRED / *CIEN*

The Spanish word for 100, *cien* or *cen-*, comes from the Latin *cent-*, which we recognize in *cen*tury, *cen*tennial, and other words having to do with the concept *hundred*.

Listen to it: *cien*. One way to spell that would be the initials "C.N."

Repeat "C.N." (standing for *cen-*), associating it with the meaning *hundred*.

So, with the four letters "D.S." and "C.N." (*diez* and *cien*), you have the pronunciation of *ten* and *hundred* in Spanish.

THOUSAND / *MIL*

Like *diez* and *cien*, the Spanish word for 1000 (*mil*) comes from Latin. We recognize it in words like *mill*-levy, *mill*imeter, and *mill*ennium, all having to do with the concept *thousand*.

Listen to it: *mil*. It sounds more like *meal* than *mill*. You can associate it with its English sound-alike, as in *cornmeal* (corn ground up into a *thousand* tiny grains). Repeat *mil*, associating it with its meaning *thousand*.

Listen and repeat: 10; 100; 1000; 10,000; 100,000.

Note: Some English numbers change slightly in different combinations, for example, we say *five* but *fif*teen.

The same happens with some Spanish numbers. In certain combinations the word for *hundred* is "C.N.-toe" (*ciento*). For example, 110 is not "C.N.D.S." (*cien-diez*), but "C.N.-toe D.S." (*cientodiez*), said rapidly in three syllables, not five.

Listen and repeat: 10;   1000;   110;   10,100;   10,010;   10,110

100,000;   100,010;   100,100;   100,110;   110,110.

A short pause will be left for you to say each number before it is said on the tape. Ready? Say it: 1000;   100;   10;   110;   10,000;   100,000;   10,100;   10,110.

Review for production; the numbers: *seis, cinco, cuatro, tres, dos,* and *uno*

You've already learned three of the seventeen elements of the Spanish numeric system: 10, 100, 1000. Stop the tape and say them.

📼 SIX /*SEIS*

The Spanish word for 6 (*seis*), like our English word *six*, is related to Latin *seks* (as in *sextet*). Spanish dropped the "k" sound. Listen to it: *seis*. This independent form rhymes with *ace*, doesn't it? Listen: *seis*. Say *seis* a couple of times with the meaning in mind.

FIVE/*CINCO*

The Spanish word for 5 (*cinco*) and its alternate (*quin-*) is from Latin *quin-* (as in *quin*tuplets). The first part of *cinco* reminds us of the English word *sink*. It will help you to see that a *sink* has *five* surfaces: four sides and a bottom! Listen: *cinco*. Say *cinco* a couple of times with the meaning in mind.

Now stop the tape and review in your mind these numbers: 📼 6, 10, 5, 100, 6, 5, 10, 1000, 6, 5, 10.

📼 FOUR / *CUATRO*

The Spanish word for 4 (*cuatro* or *cator-*, and also *cuar-*) is from Latin *quattuor*. English has it in *quart, quart*et, etc., all having to do with the concept *four*. The first part of *cuatro* rhymes with *squat*, as in "*squat* down on all *fours*." Listen: *cuatro*. Say *cuatro* a couple of times with the meaning in mind.

Stop the tape and review in your mind these numbers: 📼 4, 5, 6, 10, 100, 1000.

📼 Point to the number you hear: 6, 4, 5, 10, 100, 1000.

📼 TWO/ *DOS*

The Spanish word for 2 is *dos*. It comes from Latin *duo*. It sounds much like a *dose* of medicine. *Two* spoonfuls make a *dose*. Listen: *dos*. Say *dos* a couple of times with its meaning in mind.

📼 THREE / *TRES*

The Spanish word for 3 is *tres*. It sounds much like *trace*, but rhymes more with *dress*. Think of *tracing* a number 3 on a *dress*. Listen: *tres*. Say *tres* a couple of times with its meaning in mind.

Point to the number you hear in cluster A, then in cluster B. Repeat each number, thinking of its meaning.

		(A)					(B)		
		4					10		
2				1		2			5
		10						1	
6			5				4		6
		3					3		

21

Stop the tape and review these numbers: 📻 3, 6, 4, 2, 5, 1, 6, 3, 4, 10, 100, 1000.

THE ADVENTURE CONTINUES

📻 You move forward toward the goal. Now comes the application of your new knowledge. Here is the combination to the deposit boxes. Listen and write the numbers. Then turn off the tape and read the instructions.

The combination to box #47 is: _____ _____ _____ _____ _____ _____

The combination to box #93 is: _____ _____ _____ _____ _____ _____

Now turn off the tape and proceed.

🌐 You must simultaneously unlock the north door and the south door. They let you into an elevator that will take you down to a landing. On reaching that landing, you will face the challenge of getting through the gateway, and then you must follow the map given below. Before reaching the innermost chamber you will face twelve locked gateways, at each of which you will confront a new challenge in order to pass through to the landing.

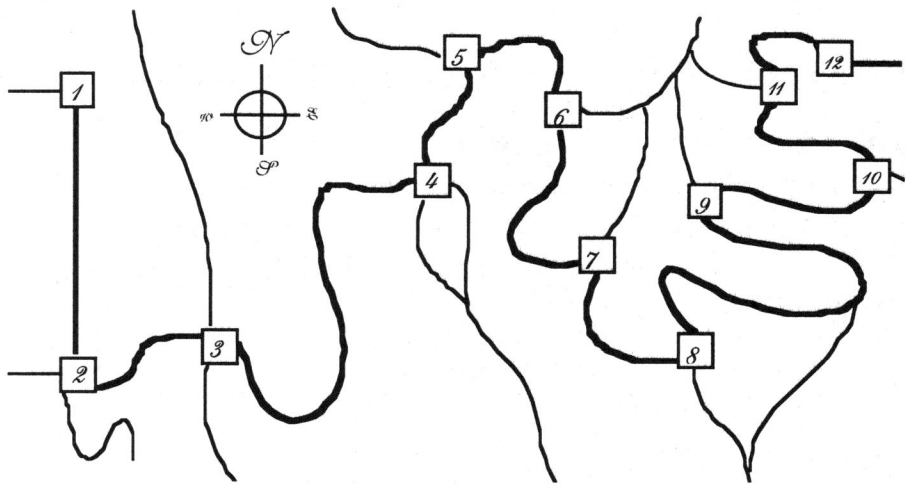

The challenges mostly depend on your receiving and producing communications in Spanish. You can move forward in your quest only by applying your skills in understanding, speaking, reading, and writing Spanish. You already have made significant progress toward reaching the inner chamber. Completion of your quest will require near fluency in Spanish. The doors are programmed to open up as you complete the tasks your notebook asks of you. You must discipline yourself to test your progress and see that you are improving before you enter each of the doors. Read in your notebook to find out what you need to do before you enter the elevator and descend to the gateway to the landing.

Listen to "Words and Patterns 1" in the following lesson, then test yourself to see how well you are doing. Once you feel confident and can answer fourteen out of seventeen correctly on the "Rapid Oral Translation Exercise," then you may enter the elevator and continue on your quest.

9

 Toward Fluency 1

CD ROM

WORDS AND PATTERNS 1

Who?	¿Quién? (key-enn)
Who is Pedro? And who is Julio?	¿Quién es Pedro? ¿Y quién es Julio?
So, then…	Entonces…(enTONE-sess)
So then who is José?	Entonces ¿quién es José?
Who is it?	¿Quién es?
Is it Roberto?	¿Es Roberto?
No, it is Carlos.	No, es Carlos.
It is not Carlos.	No es Carlos.
Right? (Isn't it so?)	¿No?
but	pero

Tape off. Work down the page on your own.

Rapid Oral Translation Exercise 1

Rapidly translate each of the following sentences. The answer key is in the appendix.

1. Who is Pedro?
2. And who is Julio?
3. So then, who is Alberto?
4. Alberto is Juan.
5. But who is Juan?
6. Who is it?
7. Is it Jorge?
8. No, it is not Jorge.
9. Is it Manuel?
10. It is not Manuel.
11. It is Amado, right?
12. No, it's not Amado.
13. Then who is it?
14. It's Jaime.
15. Jaime?
16. Yes, Jaime.
17. Oh, Jaime.

Review

1. Go through the oral translation exercises again, aiming for fluency. Speak with expression and confidence. Imagine you are telling a story to children.

2. Close your eyes, breathe deeply, and relax, letting your mind create sentences made up of material from this lesson module. See how many meaningful statements you can generate from this material in two minutes.

First two-minute trial: _____ statements   Second two-minute trial: _____ statements

WORDS AND PATTERNS 2

a prince	un príncipe	You are…	Usted es…
a princess	una princesa	an enemy (m)	un enemigo
a friend (m)	un amigo	an enemy (f)	una enemiga
a friend (f)	una amiga	formidable	formidable
a fool	un bobo	terrible	terrible
He is…	El es…	very	muy
She is…	Ella es…	also	también

either...or...	o...o...		the other (m)	*el otro*
			the other (f)	*la otra*

Sample Sentences

Who is it? It's a friend, Carlos.	*¿Quién es? Es un amigo, Carlos.*
You are not Carlos. You are not a friend.	*Usted no es Carlos. Usted no es amigo.*
Who is Alberto? A friend?	*¿Quién es Alberto? ¿Un amigo?*
Yes, Alberto is a prince.	*Sí, Alberto es un príncipe.*
Renaldo is a friend, right?	*Renaldo es un amigo, ¿no?*
No, he is an enemy.	*No, él es un enemigo.*
A terrible, formidable enemy.	*Un enemigo formidable, terrible.*
And the other prince is an enemy also.	*Y el otro príncipe es un enemigo también.*
Either an enemy or a fool.	*O un enemigo o un bobo.*
But the other princess is a friend.	*Pero la otra princesa es una amiga.*

⊚ Rapid Oral Translation Exercise 2

Rapidly translate each of the following sentences. You can check your answers in the appendix.

1. José is a friend.
2. He is a prince.
3. Josefina is a princess, right?
4. Yes, she is a princess and a friend also.
5. And Matilda?
6. She's an enemy.
7. But she's a princess, right?
8. Yes, she's a princess, but also an enemy.
9. A very formidable enemy.
10. Alfonzo is a prince, but he is an enemy also.
11. He is a terrible prince but a formidable enemy.
12. So then, who is a fool?
13. You are a fool.
14. He is not a prince, he's a fool.

Review

1. Go through the oral translation exercises again, aiming for fluency. Speak with expression and confidence. Imagine you are telling a story to children.

2. Close your eyes, breathe deeply, and relax, letting your mind create sentences made up of material from this lesson module. See how many meaningful statements you can generate from this material in two minutes. Par is fourteen statements in two minutes. Can you beat par?

⌚ First two-minute trial: _____ statements   ⌚ Second two-minute trial: _____ statements

THE ADVENTURE CONTINUES

As you and Stump approach the opening to the second door, Stump is tempted to barge right through. You restrain him, telling him to read your instructions in the notebook. He hesitates but then grudgingly opens the notebook and reads:

Study the lesson "Stringing Together Your Own Narratives." Once you feel ready, practice telling your own narratives until you feel you have improved your Spanish. Remember, the more fun you have, the more Spanish you will learn.

10

 Stringing Together Your Own Narratives

Instructions: (1) Study the words in the scatter chart below. (2) Read the practice sentences. (3) Translate the sentences of the sample story plot. (4) Refer to the chart and use only those words to make up your own stories.

SCATTER CHART

<table>
<tr><td>farmacia [farmasia]</td><td></td><td></td><td>señora</td><td></td></tr>
<tr><td>tienda [tyenda]</td><td></td><td></td><td>maestra [ma-eh-stra]</td><td></td></tr>
<tr><td>a</td><td>la</td><td></td><td>compra</td><td></td></tr>
<tr><td>en</td><td>una</td><td></td><td>vende</td><td></td></tr>
<tr><td></td><td></td><td>va</td><td></td><td></td></tr>
<tr><td>dice [dee-say]</td><td></td><td></td><td></td><td></td></tr>
<tr><td>botella de</td><td></td><td></td><td></td><td>y</td></tr>
<tr><td>pero</td><td></td><td>oquei</td><td></td><td></td></tr>
<tr><td></td><td>si</td><td></td><td></td><td></td></tr>
<tr><td>no</td><td></td><td></td><td>medicina</td><td></td></tr>
<tr><td>ella [eh-ya]</td><td></td><td></td><td>limonada</td><td></td></tr>
<tr><td>prueba [prweva]</td><td>trae [tra-eh]</td><td></td><td>naranjada</td><td></td></tr>
<tr><td>lleva [yeva]</td><td></td><td>es buena</td><td></td><td></td></tr>
<tr><td></td><td>no es buena</td><td></td><td></td><td></td></tr>
</table>

English Equivalent

<table>
<tr><td>pharmacy</td><td></td><td>lady</td></tr>
<tr><td>store (Tienda also means "tent." Anciently a store was a tent.)</td><td></td><td>teacher</td></tr>
<tr><td>to (a place or person)</td><td>the</td><td>buys (Relate compra to "compare.")</td></tr>
<tr><td>in</td><td>a</td><td>sells (Vende is related to "vend.")</td></tr>
<tr><td></td><td>goes</td><td></td></tr>
<tr><td>says (Dice is related to dictate.)</td><td></td><td></td></tr>
<tr><td>bottle of</td><td></td><td>and</td></tr>
<tr><td>but</td><td>okay</td><td></td></tr>
<tr><td></td><td>yes</td><td></td></tr>
<tr><td>no</td><td></td><td>medicine</td></tr>
<tr><td>she</td><td>brings (Relate trae to "tray"—as in "bring it on a tray.")</td><td>lemonade</td></tr>
<tr><td>tries, tastes (Prueba is related to "probe.")</td><td></td><td>orangeade</td></tr>
<tr><td>takes, carries</td><td>is good</td><td></td></tr>
<tr><td></td><td>is not good</td><td></td></tr>
</table>

Practice Sentences

A lady comes to the pharmacy.	*Una señora viene a la farmacia.*
She buys medicine.	*Ella compra medicina.*
She tastes the medicine.	*Ella prueba la medicina.*
She says, "The medicine is not good."	*Ella dice, «La medicina no es buena.»*
She sells the medicine.	*Ella vende la medicina.*

Sample Story Plot

Give the Spanish equivalent of the following sentences. You can check your answers in the appendix.

1. A lady goes to the store.
2. She buys a bottle of lemonade.
3. She takes the bottle to a teacher.
4. The teacher goes to the pharmacy.
5. She buys a bottle of medicine.
6. She brings the medicine to the lady.
7. The medicine is good.
8. The lemonade is not good.
9. The teacher takes the bottle of lemonade to the store and says, "The lemonade is not good."
10. The lady in the store says, "The bottle is good."
11. The teacher says, "No, the lemonade is not good. The bottle is good, but the lemonade in the bottle is not good."
12. The lady in the store says, "Okay, the lemonade in the bottle is not good."
13. The teacher says, "Okay," and takes a bottle of orangeade.
14. She says, "The orangeade is good."

SPEED LEARNING

This is a two-minute section. First, recall learning how to say foot, hand, head, mouth:

foot	*pie*	(sounds a bit like P.A.)
hand	*mano*	(<u>man</u>ual—<u>hand</u>book)
head	*cabeza*	(not ca<u>boose</u>-ah but ca<u>base</u>-ah)
mouth	*boca*	("Put a *coca* in your *boca!*")

Second, add six more body-part words.

arms	*brazos*	(em*brace* with arms of *brass*)
legs	*piernas*	(*Pierre* has a *pair* of *piernas*)
face	*cara*	(a *face* on a *car* is a *cara*)
nose	*nariz*	(pronounced a lot like *gnaw-reese*)
hair	*pelo*	(You *pay-low* for your *pelo*)
bald	*calvo*	(<u>Calv</u>in is *calvo*…without *pelo*)

At first, children learn to use language in very limited functions, needing time to get a number of things under control. Then, as need is felt to meet broader and more demanding functions, children gradually extend their repertoires and their skills. Adults are impatient to take on all the functions of language use at once. The result is that they become overburdened with the demands of full-blown language to meet social conditions they are not prepared to meet. The answer may be for adults to take satisfaction in their use of their new language at first for very elementary functions, such as giving monologues and hearing and telling stories. Once the skills involved in such less-demanding communication functions are mastered, they can then proceed to the more demanding functions of two-way conversation.

Challenge

Write or say aloud ten or more sentences using the words in the scatter chart and the body part words you have learned.

1.

2.

3.

4.

5.

6.

7.

8.

9.

10.

THE ADVENTURE CONTINUES

Once you and Stump have composed ten or more sentences, you enter the second passageway and move quickly down the winding corridor to the third entrance.

11

 The Broken Window

A Diglot-Weave Narrative

CD ROM

THE STORY OF DIGLOT-WEAVE NARRATIVES

The story of the diglot-weave reader is interesting. (*Diglot* means two languages. *Polyglot,* as in a *polyglot Bible*, means many languages.) Professor Rudy Lentulay of Bryn Mawr University was invited to teach a class in Russian for twenty minutes a day, two days a week, to kindergarten children. Lacking previous experience teaching small children, he hesitated to accept the invitation. For one thing, he doubted children could learn any significant amount of language under such a limited schedule.

By chance, he had just finished reading Anthony Burgess's novel *A Clockwork Orange,* in which teenagers use almost two hundred slang words—all of them Russian words in English spelling. The reader, as well as the teenagers in the story, must learn the meaning of these words from context. From this came the inspiration to make a game out of learning Russian, a word game that even small children could play. So he accepted the job.

From the first day he made telling stories the focus of the course. Each week he told a story with Russian words sprinkled here and there—at first sparsely, then gradually more and more abundantly, each story using as much as possible of the vocabulary employed in previous stories. Since the learners were children just beginning first grade, nothing was written for them in English or Russian. They had to understand the words and their meanings not through translation, but through visual and verbal context.

Through the use of pictures in a verbal and nonverbal context, Professor Lentulay engaged the young learners in playful but meaningful use of new expressions. The game was this: once an expression started in circulation, the children were expected to use it in place of its English equivalent thereafter. The "game" was to catch someone using an English word or phrase where the Russian equivalent was called for. The rules of the game of Musical Chairs were often used to eliminate from play those who slipped. Central to the activity was the story.

Before the end of the term, he was telling complete stories—even stories from Russian literature—entirely in Russian, and the six-year-old American children were understanding them.

THE BROKEN WINDOW—*LA VENTANA ROTA*

A *Cuento* about a Smashed *Ventana*

Would you like me to tell you *un cuento? Oquei,* let me tell you *un cuento* about some naughty *muchachos*—some *muchachos y* some *muchachas*—who were playing with a ball in *la calle* near *una casa.* In this *dibujo* you can see *la casa. Mi cuento* concerns *estos muchachos, la pelota* that they are playing with, *y una* glass *ventana* on *la segunda* story *de la casa.*

Besides being about some *muchachos* playing *pelota en la calle* near *una casa* with glass *ventanas*, this *cuento* is about *un hombre* who is *el* owner *de la casa*. This *hombre* is not out *en la calle* with *los muchachos*. No. He is *en* his *casa* when *el cuento* begins. I can tell you now, *el hombre en la casa* gets *muy enojado* at *los muchachos*. Maybe I had better describe *el hombre* to you. You see, *el hombre es muy alto*. He is *tres* meters *alto* and weighs four hundred pounds. *El es un gigante, un gigante* like Goliath *en la Biblia*.

Here is *un dibujo* of *el gigante* who is *el* owner *de la casa*. Look at his *manos* and his *pies*, how *grandes* they are. Look at his *brazos* and his *piernas*, how *largos* they are. *Su cabeza* is as *grande* as a Texas watermelon. Look at *el gigante: su cara, su boca, su nariz,* how *grandes* they are.

In the beginning of *el cuento*, some little *muchachos* and *muchachas* are playing *pelota en la calle* near *esta casa*. Probably they shouldn't be playing *pelota en la calle* near *la casa*, but not all *muchachos* are aware of what can happen. As you might guess, one *de los muchachos* hits *la pelota*, and *la pelota* sails up high *en el aire. En este dibujo* you can see *la pelota* up in *el aire*. I think you know what's going to happen. But before continuing *mi cuento*, let me describe some of the features *de la casa*. You can see them in *este dibujo. La casa tiene una puerta. Esta es la puerta.* Of course, almost every *casa tiene* at least *una puerta.* Have you ever seen *una casa* that didn't have *una puerta*? When you leave your *casa*, do you usually go out *la puerta,* or do you open *una ventana* and crawl out?

End Tape 1, Side A

Take Test 1 (located in Teachers' Guide/Test Book) now. There is one test for each side of a tape.

12

 The Story of the Broken Window Continues

Back to some of the features *de la casa. La casa tiene un* roof, *un techo. Natúralmente el techo* is on top *de la casa. Este es el techo de la casa.* You might have *visto una casa* without *una puerta,* and you might have *visto una casa* without *una ventana,* but you *probablemente* haven't *visto una casa* without *un techo.* What usually sticks up out of *un techo? Correcto, una chimenea.* Y, sure enough, sticking up out of *el techo de esta casa es una chimenea. Esta es la chimenea,* and you see black *humo* billowing out of it. That's what *chimeneas* are for—to let *el humo* out into *el aire.* You wouldn't want your *casa* to fill up with *humo,* would you? The *humo* would *probablemente* choke you and would surely blacken the inside of *la casa.* Does *una chimenea* serve any other purpose than to let *el humo* out *de la casa* into *el aire?* Does it make *una casa* look pretty? Can you enter *una casa* through *la chimenea?*

What other things does *la casa tiene* besides *puertas, un techo,* and *una chimenea* sticking out of *el techo?* Well of course, *la casa tiene ventanas.* From what you can see *en este dibujo, la casa tiene dos ventanas* on *la segunda etapa.*

To review then, *esta casa tiene una puerta, un techo con una chimenea,* billowing out of which is black *humo, y natúralmente la casa tiene ventanas—dos ventanas* that you can *ver, dos ventanas* on *la segunda etapa.*

If you could look through *esta ventana*, you could *ver* something inside. You could *ver* that there is *un hombre* sitting at *la ventana*. And he's holding something *en sus manos*. It's a *libro*. He is reading *un libro*. Who is *este hombre*? *El* is none other than the *dueño de la casa,* who plays a role *en el cuento*.

Other details we need to mention. Growing near *la casa* is *un árbol*. And hanging from a limb *del arbol* is an apple, *una manzana*. On the other side *de la calle* is a forest, *un bosque*. Now you know that danger lurks *en el bosque*, but sometimes *los muchachos* forget about danger.

Well now, what will happen? *¿Qué piensas tú? ¿Piensas que la pelota* breaks *la puerta?* No, *la pelota no rompe la puerta. ¿Piensas que la pelota* lands on *el techo?* No, *la pelota no aterriza en el techo. ¿Piensas que la pelota deciende* through *la chimenea?* No, *la pelota no deciende por la chimenea. ¿Piensas que la pelota* crashes through *la ventana? Exactamente eso es lo que pasa. La pelota* crashes *por la ventana y* hits the *gigante* right in his *nariz...ay ay*.

Now, *que piensas que va a pasar? Piensas que los muchachos* will run away? *Piensas que el hombre, el dueño de la casa,* will punish them? *Piensas que los muchachos* will have to *pagar* the cost of *la ventana?*

Escucha bien to the *continuación del cuento*.

When *la pelota* breaks *la ventana y* smacks the *gigante* on his *nariz, él* jumps up *y* looks out *la ventana. El ve a los muchachos. O él* is *enojado, muy enojado.* Why? *¿Por qué* is *el hombre enojado?* Well, wouldn't *tú* be *enojado* if *unos muchachos* threw *una pelota y* broke *la ventana de* your *casa? Y si la pelota* smacked you right on your *nariz?*

So *que pasa* after that? *Piensas que el gigante* jumps out *de la ventana y* pursues—*persigue*—the naughty *muchachos? Piensas que el gigante* climbs up *la chimenea* onto *el techo y* then jumps off? *Bueno,* what does *el hombre* really do?

El throws *la pelota* back out *de la ventana y* calls out gruffly, «*¡Muchachos!*» *¿Y qué piensas que los muchachos* do? *¿Piensas que* they pick up *la pelota y* go knock *a la puerta de la casa y* apologize *al dueño? ¿O piensas que ellos* leave *la pelota* behind *y* run away? *Exactamente eso es lo que hacen. Ellos* start to run up *la calle. ¿Por qué?* They are afraid. *Ellos tienen miedo* that *el gigante* will catch them. *Ellos tienen miedo que* they will be punished. *Ellos tienen miedo que* they'll have to *pagar el costo de la ventana rota. ¿No piensas tú que el hombre* has a right to punish the *muchachos? ¿No piensas tú que él tiene* the right to make them *pagar por la ventana rota?*

Bueno, to *continuar el cuento*. As *los muchachos corren* up *la calle* (the highway), *ellos* see a lady, *una mujer,* coming toward them. *La mujer ve a los muchachos* go *corriendo* up *la calle*. She calls out to them. «*¡Muchachos!* Wait. *¡Esperense!*» *Qué piensas que la mujer* wants to do?

Now look at the woods. A close look will reveal something sticking out from under *un árbol*. There's an arrow—*una flecha*—pointing to it. *Mira. He aquí la flecha*. What could *la flecha* be pointing to? Could it be a tail? Yes, it could be pointing to *una cola*. Could it be *la cola de un lobo?* A big bad *lobo? ¿Piensas tú que la flecha indica la cola de un lobo?* Perhaps a ferocious wolf, *un feroz lobo* is hiding under *un árbol* there *en el bosque*.

Are you afraid *que el feroz lobo* is going to eat *los niños? Escucha* closely as *mi cuento* unfolds, *y tú* will find out what *pasa*. After *el gigante* calls out, «*¡Muchachos!*» *los muchachos* don't stop. *Ellos* run off into *el bosque. Ellos* are more afraid *del hombre, del gigante,* than they are *del feroz lobo.*

Just as *ellos* enter *en el bosque, ellos* see something hiding behind *un árbol*. Could it be *el feroz lobo*? Or is it only *Bobi, un* big dog, *un gran perro* that loves to play *en el bosque con los muchachos*? It *no es Bobi*. It *es el feroz lobo. Y el lobo es muy* hungry. Just as *el lobo* charges, *los muchachos* catch sight of *el gran perro que* likes to play *en el bosque con los muchachos*. «*¡Bobi! ¡Bobi!*» cry *los muchachos. Bobi* comes running, chases *el feroz lobo, y* saves *los muchachos. Bobi es un heroe. Los muchachos* run out *del bosque. Ellos* go back to *la casa*, knock *a la puerta, y* offer to *pagar por la ventana rota*.

Now *el hombre no* is angry, *no está enojado. El dice a los muchachos*, "That's all right. *La ventana rota no importa*. I'm just happy *que el lobo* did not eat you."

⊞ REVIEW

How many of the Spanish words do you recognize? Put a check next to each one that you know.

____ aquí	____ árbol	____ continuación	____ bosque	____ calle
____ casa	____ chimenea	____ cola	____ con	____ costo
____ cuento	____ de	____ deciende	____ del	____ dibujo
____ dice	____ dos	____ dueño	____ enojado	____ feroz
____ flecha	____ gigante	____ gran	____ heroe	____ hombre
____ indica	____ libro	____ lobo	____ manos	____ manzanade
____ miedo	____ muchachos	____ mujer	____ muy	____ nariz
____ natúralmente	____ niños	____ pagar	____ pasa	____ pelota
____ perro	____ piensas	____ por	____ puerta	____ puertavisto
____ que	____ rompe	____ rota	____ segunda	____ si
____ sus	____ techo	____ tiene	____ tú	____ va
____ ve	____ ventana	____ ver	____ y	

13
Ditties

CD ROM

Read the "Magic of Ditties and Jingles" and then listen to some.

THE MAGIC OF DITTIES AND JINGLES

Unless you grew up on the moon, you likely know these (and countless other) ditties and jingles shared by speakers of American English.

(A)
> One potato, two potato, three potato, four,
> Five potato, six potato, seven potato more.

(B)
> One for the money, two for the show,
> Three to get ready, and four to go.

The wonderful thing about such pieces is that they are easily learned and retained without much effort. You don't remember when or how you learned these. You picked them up as a child, on first or second hearing, and even if you haven't heard or spoken them in decades, you still know them by heart.

What makes such ditties and jingles so easy to pick up and retain in memory over a lifetime? They are simple: they have rhyme and rhythm and they have catchy wording or some other feature that lends itself to learning.

You can use the magic of ditties and jingles to multiply your speed in learning Spanish. A small investment of time in learning a few of them can yield significant dividends.

One caution: being able to sing or say a ditty by heart is not the same as putting the words to real use. It is by using the phrases communicatively that they become functional. After learning each ditty, take its phrases and use them first to role-play in your imagination. Then apply them to real communication.

SOME DITTIES TO THE TUNE OF "GOOD NIGHT LADIES"

I'll demonstrate the first one completely, then only the first and last lines of the rest.

Hola, joven.	Hi, young man.	*Muy bien, gracias.*	Very well, thanks.
Hola, joven.	Hi, young man.	*Muy bien, gracias.*	Very well, thanks.
Hola, joven.	Hi, young man.	*Muy bien, gracias.*	Very well, thanks.
¿Qué tal está usted?	How are you?	*Estoy bastante bien.*	I'm quite well.
Buenos días.	Good morning.	*¿Cómo anda?*	How's it going?
Buenos días.	Good morning.	*¿Cómo anda?*	How's it going?
Buenos días.	Good morning.	*¿Cómo anda?*	How's it going?
Me alegro verles hoy.	I'm glad to see you today.	*Pues todo anda bien.*	Well, everything's going fine.

Buenas tardes.	Good afternoon.	*Buenas noches.*	Good night.
Buenas tardes.	Good afternoon.	*Buenas noches.*	Good night.
Buenas tardes.	Good afternoon.	*Buenas noches.*	Good night.
Más tarde volveré.	Later I'll return.	*¡Que duerma bien, bien, bien!*	May you sleep very well.
¿Qué tal, viejo?	How is it, old man?	*Hasta luego.*	Till later.
¿Qué tal, viejo?	How is it, old man?	*Hasta luego.*	Till later.
¿Qué tal, viejo?	How is it, old man?	*Hasta luego.*	Till later.
Me siento muy bien.	I feel very well.	*Y que le vaya bien.*	And may it go well with you.
Chau, pues, Carlos.	'Bye, then, Carlos.	*Ven conmigo,*	Come with me.
Chau, pues, Carlos.	'Bye, then, Carlos.	*Ven conmigo,*	Come with me.
Chau, pues, Carlos.	'Bye, then, Carlos.	*Ven conmigo,*	Come with me.
Mañana volveré.	Tomorrow I'll return.	*Oh gracias, sí, oquei.*	Oh thanks, yes, okay.

▣ THE ADVENTURE CONTINUES

You and Stump are having so much fun singing these little ditties that you hardly notice the door right in front of you. In fact, Stump runs right into it. Before you go through the door, you read in the notebook:

> In your best voice, sing three ditties to each other before going through this door.

After your best rendition of a few Spanish ditties, you hear the lock click open. Stump applauds and holds the door open for you. As the two of you walk into darkness, a creepy feeling seeps into your bones. You feel a sense of urgency, but you also feel a need to really concentrate on learning Spanish. You turn the tape back on and listen as you cautiously proceed down the path.

14

🔲 *Puntos, Líneas, y Figuras*
Points, Lines, and Figures

🔘
CD ROM

🔲 This activity will help your listening comprehension. It presents problem-solving tasks that invite you to learn skills in inferring (guessing) meaning.

A. SCATTER CHART

●	_____	—
punto grande	*línea larga*	*línea corta*
▬▬▬▬▬	____	●
línea gruesa	*línea delgada*	*punto pequeño*

🔲 B. LISTEN, LOOK, AND READ

1. ● ·   *Un punto grande y un punto pequeño.*

2. _____ __   *Una línea larga y una línea corta.*

3. ▬▬▬▬ 5   *Una línea gruesa y un número pequeño, el número cinco.*

4. ● _____   *Un punto grande y una línea delgada.*

5. ·· _ _   *Dos puntos pequeños y dos líneas cortas.*

6. ● ● ● ● ● 6 1   *Cinco puntos grandes y dos números pequeños, los números seis y uno.*

7. ·   *Este punto es pequeño. Es un punto pequeño.*

8. ●   *Este punto es grande. Es un punto grande.*

9. ▬▬▬▬▬   *Esta línea es gruesa. Es una línea gruesa.*

10. · · · · ·   *Estos puntos son pequeños. Son puntos pequeños.*

11. ____ ____   *Estas dos líneas son delgadas. Son líneas delgadas.*

12. · · · ● ● ●   *Estos tres puntos son pequeños y estos tres son grandes.*

C. LOOK AND LISTEN

1. ● ·   2. _____ —   3. ▬▬▬▬ 5

4. ● —   5. ·· — —   6. ● ● ● ● ● 6 1

7. ·   8. ●   9. ▬▬▬▬

10. · · · · ·   11. ____ ____   12 · · · ● ● ●

D. MULTIPLE-CHOICE FRAMES

Point to the sector whose contents are described, then listen for the answer.

(A) 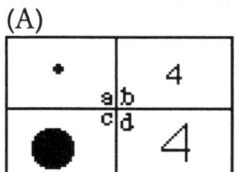   (B) 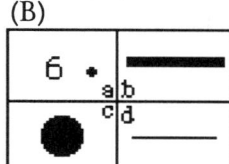   (C) 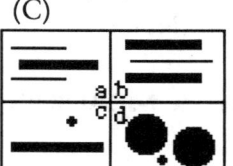   (D) 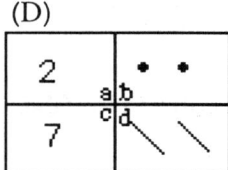   (E)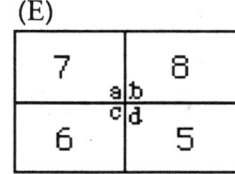

(F) 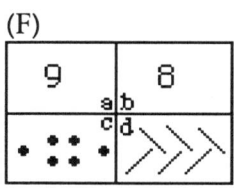   (G) 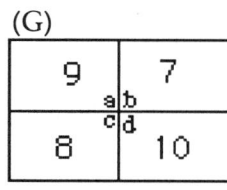   (H)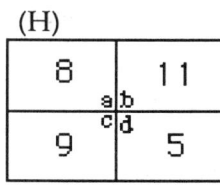

(I)

8 10	10 8
10 9	9 10

(J)

12 11	12 10
12 9	12 7

E. LISTEN AND DRAW

(Stop the tape if the pace is too fast. Check your answers in the appendix.)

1.   2.   3.   4.

F. READ FOR MEANING

Read the Spanish phrases for meaning. Can you translate them into English? Look in the appendix for an English translation of them.

1.   Dos líneas: una gruesa y una delgada.
2.   Dos más dos son cuatro (2+2=4). Dos puntos más dos puntos son cuatro puntos.
3.   Tres líneas más dos líneas son cinco líneas.
4.   Estas líneas son gruesas; estas dos líneas son delgadas.
5.   Estos son puntos grandes, y estos son puntos pequeños.
6.   Estos dos puntos son pequeños, y estos dos son grandes. Estos son puntos pequeños y puntos grandes.
7.   Estas dos líneas son largas, y estas dos son cortas.

15

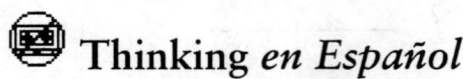 Thinking *en Español*

CD ROM

Give this your careful attention. Tape off.

In becoming bilingual, you learn to turn your thoughts and feelings directly into Spanish without translation. What follows is designed to lead you toward that goal. Using pictographs rather than words as stimuli, you will first create short, simple sentences, then longer, more elaborate sentences that make a story. You are to go through it on your own. Give it your best shot! You will make strides toward thinking *en español*. (Note: This is entirely a tape-off activity.)

PART 1: PICTOGRAPHS AND THEIR MEANING

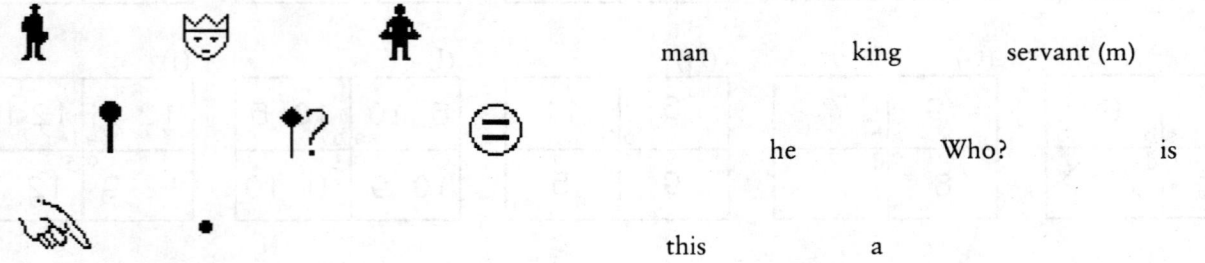

	man	king	servant (m)
	he	Who?	is
	this	a	

Chart 1—Sentence Building Blocks (Words)

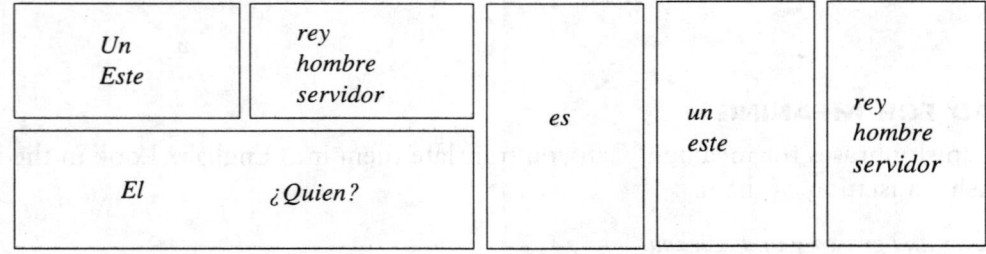

Chart 2—Sentence Building Blocks (Pictographs)

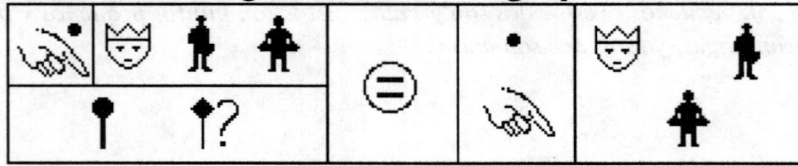

37

Sample Sentences

Un rey es un hombre.

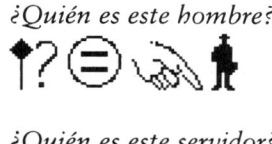

¿Quién es este hombre?

El es un rey.

Un rey es un servidor.

¿Quién es este servidor?

El es un rey.

Reading Activity

Read the nine pictographic sentences out loud. If you have any difficulty, you may check the appendix for the Spanish equivalent.

1. _____   2. _____   3. _____

4. _____   5. _____   6. _____

7. _____   8. _____   9. _____

PART 2: PICTOGRAPHS AND THEIR MEANING

woman	queen	servant (f)

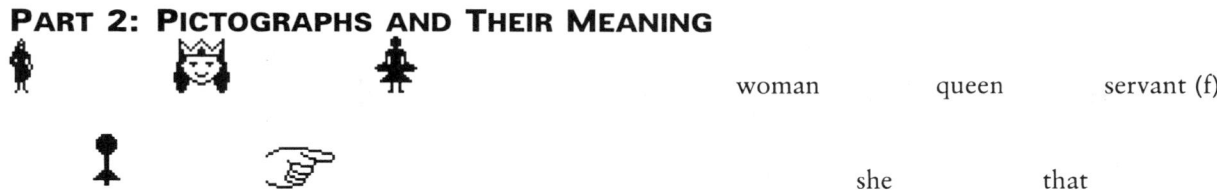

she   that

Chart 3—Sentence Building Blocks (Words)

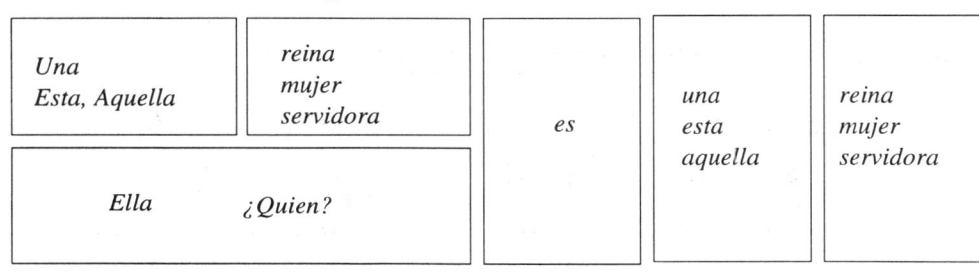

Una Esta, Aquella	reina mujer servidora	es	una esta aquella	reina mujer servidora
Ella ¿Quien?				

38

Chart 4—Sentence Building Blocks (Pictographs)

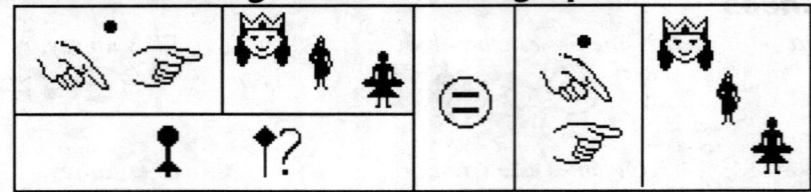

Sample Sentences

Una mujer es una reina.

Una servidora es una reina.

¿Quién es esta mujer?

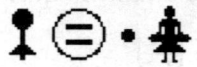

¿Quién es aquella mujer?

¿Quién es esta servidora?

Ella es una servidora.

Ella es una reina.

Ella es una mujer.

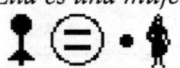

Reading Activity

Read the nine pictographic sentences out loud. If you have any difficulty, you may check the appendix for the Spanish equivalent.

1. _____

2. _____

3. _____

4. _____

5. _____

6. _____

7. _____

8. _____

9. _____

REVIEW PRACTICE

Instructions: Form sentences from these icons.

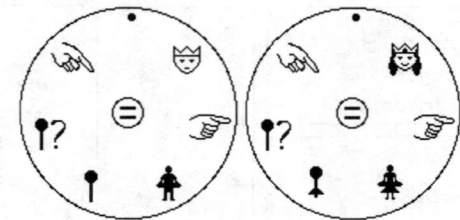

39

16

Toward Fluency 2

CD ROM

WORDS AND PATTERNS 1

Who is this (m)?	*¿Quién es éste?*
Who is this (f)?	*¿Quién es ésta?*
This is David, this is María.	*Éste es David, ésta es María.*
my father and my mother	*mi padre y mi madre*
your father or your mother	*su padre o su madre*
here	*aquí*

Sample Sentences

Who is this? It's a friend (f). It's my friend.	*¿Quién es ésta? Es una amiga. Es mi amiga.*
She is a princess.	*Ella es una princesa.*
Where is she from?	*¿De dónde es?*
She's from here. From Spain. From Madrid.	*Es de aquí. De España. De Madrid.*
And David? Where is he from?	*¿Y David? ¿De dónde es?*
David is from Malta.	*David es de Malta.*
From where? From Malta.	*¿De dónde? De Malta.*

Rapid Oral Translation Exercise 1

Translate the following sentences into Spanish. You can check your answers in the appendix.

1. Where is José from? From Mexico?
   (or From where is José?)
2. No, he is from Chile.
3. Maria is from Chile too.
4. And is Matilda also from Chile?
   (or And Matilda is also from Chile?)
5. No, she is from Spain, from Sevilla.
6. And who is this (f)?
7. This is my mother.
8. And this (m)?
9. It's my father.
10. Where is your father from?
11. From here.
12. My mother is from here too.
13. Your father is from here,
    and your mother is from here too.
14. Your father is your friend,
    and your mother is your friend too.

Review

1. Go through the three oral translation exercises again found in Toward Fluency 1 and 2, aiming for rapid, smooth delivery. Speak with expression and confidence.

2. Close your eyes, breathe deeply, and relax, letting your mind create sentences made up of material from this lesson module. See how many meaningful statements you can generate from this material in two minutes. Keep a tally. Par is fourteen statements in two minutes. Can you beat par?

First two-minute trial: _____ statements   Second two-minute trial: _____ statements

THE ADVENTURE CONTINUES

It seems that you have been walking forever. When you and Stump finally approach the fourth door, you are relieved to be able to sit down and rest. You complete the rest of the assignment, knowing that once you can meet the par requirement, you may enter the fourth door.

📼 WORDS AND PATTERNS 2

Is it certain that...?	*¿Es cierto que...?*	Of course, indeed.	*Claro.*
I know that...	*(Yo) sé que...*	Me too.	*Yo también.*
Do you know...?	*¿Sabe usted...?*	Me neither.	*Yo tampoco.*
If, whether	*Si*	I am...	*Soy...*
Who knows if...?	*¿Quién sabe si....?*	We are...	*Somos...*
I don't know if...	*(Yo) no sé si...*	Roberto's (= of Roberto)	*de Roberto*

Sample Sentences

Who are you? And who am I?	*¿Quién es usted? ¿Y quién soy yo?*
We are friends. We are not enemies.	*Somos amigos. No somos enemigos.*
I am a prince. You are a princess.	*Yo soy un príncipe. Usted es una princesa.*
Am I a princess? And are you a prince?	*¿Soy yo una princesa? ¿Y es usted un príncipe?*
Of course!	*¡Claro!*
Sr. Gomez, do you know if Pancho is a friend?	*Señor Gomez ¿sabe usted si Pancho es un amigo?*
Of course. Of course he's a friend.	*Claro. Claro que es un amigo.*
But is it certain that he is a friend?	*¿Pero es cierto que es un amigo?*
Who knows if he is a friend?	*¿Quién sabe si es un amigo?*
I am not a friend of Pancho.	*Yo no soy un amigo* de Pancho.*
I am not a friend of Pancho.	*Yo no soy amigo* de Pancho.*
Me neither.	*Yo tampoco.*

🔊 *These differ in meaning, but both are right. Compare "He is a friend of Anita" and "He is friends with Anita": *El es un amigo de Anita* and *El es amigo de Anita.*

Rapid Oral Translation Exercise

Translate the following sentences into Spanish. You can check your answers in the appendix.

1. Who is this (m)? I don't know who it is.

2. I don't know if he is a friend or an enemy.
3. Are you my friend (m)?
4. Of course. Aren't you my friend (f)?
5. I am a friend (f) of Alberto. Me too.
6. But I am not a friend (f) of Roberto. Me neither.
7. Do you know if Pancho is a friend of Anita?

8. It's certain that he is a friend of Maria, but I don't know if he is also a friend of Anita.
9. Who is Francisco? I don't know who he is.
10. Of course we are not princes.
11. But it is certain that we are friends.
12. I know that you are my friend, Carlos.
13. Do you know if Pancho is a friend of the prince?
14. No, I don't know.

Review

1. Go through the previous four oral translation exercises again, aiming for fluency.

2. Close your eyes, breathe deeply, and relax, letting your mind create sentences made up of material from this lesson module. See how many meaningful statements you can generate from this material in two minutes. Par is fifteen statements in two minutes. Can you beat par?

⏱ First two-minute trial: _____ statements   ⏱ Second two-minute trial: _____ statements

17

 Chatter at a Royal Ball

CD ROM

Read and prepare carefully, then go on to the next page.

PREPARATION FOR CONVERSATION

This module aims to help you map your thoughts into Spanish. This is a different approach to grammar, one so simple that a child can do it. If you don't know a verb from a noun, don't let that concern you. The goal here is not to make a grammarian out of you, but to help you discover meaning in Spanish. Be enthusiastic! Push yourself to create new phrases. You're trying to tell tales and weave of stories.

Materials needed: Paper, pencil, and several 3"x 5" cards (cut in half) or small slips of paper

Learning Pictographs

Task 1

Familiarize yourself with the words and pictographs.

the king *el rey*   sings *canta*   well *bien*   Who? *¿Quién?*

Which king? *¿Cuál rey?*   plays (on the drum) *toca (en el tambor)*   better than *mejor que*

funeral chants *cantos fúnebres*   the one (m) who... *el que*   always *siempre*

to play funeral chants on the drum *tocar cantos fúnebres en el tambor*   he *él*

Additional Signs
Which? *¿Cuál?*   yes *sí*   no *no*   no? *¿no?*   and *y*

Self-Test on Recognition of the Pictographs

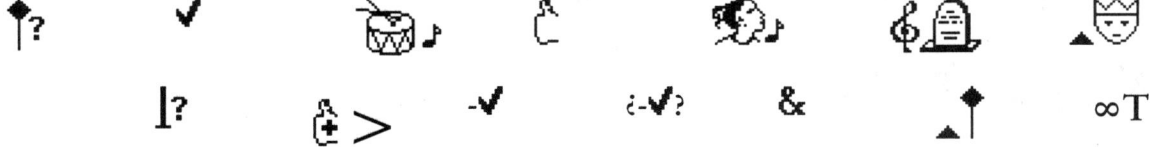

Checklist:

¿Quién?	sí	toca	bien	canta	cantos fúnebres	el rey
¿cuál?	mejor que	no	¿no?	y	el que	siempre

📼 CONVERSATION 1

📼 Task 2

With your eyes closed, listen several times to this dialogue until you fully understand the conversation.

The Setting:

A royal ball is in process in a royal palace. Two servants are observing and commenting about members of the royal families.

••:	Who is singing?	*¿Quién está cantando?*
•:	The king, the king is singing.	*El rey, el rey está cantando.*
••:	Which king?	*¿Cuál rey?*
•:	The one who always used to play funeral chants on the drum.	*El que siempre tocaba cantos fúnebres en el tambor.*
••:	Oh, it's the king who used to play funeral chants on the drum.	*Oh, es el rey que siempre tocaba cantos fúnebres en el tambor.*
•:	Yes, and (he) sings well, doesn't he?	*Sí, y canta bien, ¿no?*
••:	(He) sings better than (he) plays.	*Canta mejor que toca.*

📼 Task 3

Use your hands as puppets and dramatize the dialogue, looking only at the English. Visualize the situation and get into the spirit of the conversation. Ham it up. Aim for a flowing Spanish quality. Then go on to the next task.

Pictographic Representation of the Same Dialogue

Task 4

Do the same as in Task 3, but now look only at the pictographic representation of the dialogue below. Throw yourself into this performance. Bring thought down to Spanish *without thinking in English*. Aim for high-quality performance.

THE ADVENTURE CONTINUES

You pass through door number four and continue down a long, winding path. It is frightening to see Stump losing energy and dragging his feet—especially when you know you are probably being followed! Stump's relief is apparent when he hugs the door at the entrance to chamber number five. You quickly get out the notebook and read:

> Relate "Chatter at the Royal Ball" to each other. Do not enter until you feel confident that you can pass for an invited guest at the royal ball. Exaggerate your Spanish accent and try to sound regal.

Stump impresses you with his kingly manner. You are still speaking in majestic tones as you enter door number five and scurry down the corridor, rejuvenated. You feel anxious to go on learning Spanish.

18

 El Alfabeto Romano

The Roman Alphabet

This is an exercise in *inferring* meaning—making sense of spoken and written texts, even though you may not yet be able to understand all of it. Don't worry about understanding every detail; it's more important to understand the main idea.

Existen varios alfabetos: el alfabeto romano, el alfabeto ruso, el alfabeto griego, et cétera.

El alfabeto romano es la lista de letras de español, italiano, inglés, y otras lenguas de Europa, Norte América, y Sud América.

El alfabeto romano no es el alfabeto del árabe, ni del hebreo, ni del ruso, ni del griego.

El árabe, el hebreo, el ruso, y el griego tienen su proprio sistema de escribir y no usan el alfabeto romano.

Las letras de un alfabeto representan los sonidos de un idioma.

Las letras del alfabeto español representan los sonidos del español.

Las letras del alfabeto italiano representan los sonidos del italiano.

Las letras del alfabeto inglés representan los sonidos del inglés.

El alfabeto de inglés tiene veintiseis (26) letras.

El alfabeto de español tiene veintinueve (29) letras, tres letras más que el alfabeto inglés.

Las tres letras de español que no ocurren en inglés son ñ, rr, y ll.

(El doble-<r> y el doble-<v> son letras, así como la <r> y la <l>.)

El español tiene vienticuarto consonantes y cinco vocales. El inglés tiene vientuno consonantes y cinco vocales.

Entre todas las letras del alfabeto español, cinco son vocales y las otras veinticuatro son consonantes.

El punto (.) y la coma (,) no son letras sino signos de puntuación. El signo de interrogación (?) también es un signo de puntuación: el signo de interrogación.

En el español (como también en el inglés) hay, como ya dije, cinco vocales principales: A E I O U.

La vocal <O> ocurre una vez en NO y dos veces en MONO.

La vocal <A> ocurre una vez en LA, dos veces en CASA, y tres veces en PALABRA.

Estas cinco vocales también son las vocales del inglés: A E I O U, pero en español los nombres de estas letras se pronuncian A E I O U:

> *A como en MAMA*
> *E como en META*
> *I como en MIMI*
> *O como en MOLE*
> *U como en LULU*

Repita los nombres de las cinco vocales: A E I O U. Repita otra vez: A E I O U.

19

More on Numbers
Más acerca de los Números

You've already learned nine of the seventeen number elements. These are 10, 100, 1000, 1, 2, 3, 4, 5, 6. Look off into space and say them. Stop the tape.

Now four more numbers.

ZERO / *CERO*

The Spanish word for 0 (*cero*) sounds much like *say-doe*, not like *zee-row*. Listen and repeat: 01.0, 2.0, 3.0, 0.4, 0.5, 0.6, 1.05.

SEVEN / *SIETE*

The Spanish word for 7 (*siete* or *sete-* or *set-*) comes from Latin *sept-*. We have it in *Sept*ember (the seventh month of the Roman calendar), *sept*uplets, etc. Listen: *siete*. The main part of it sounds like *see-yet*. When you are *seven*, you can't *see-yet*—*siete*. Repeat *siete* a couple of times with the meaning in mind.

Listen and repeat: 7, 0, 6, 7-0-6, 6.7, 7.0, 2.07, 110, 107

EIGHT / *OCHO*

Latin *octo* (8), as in *octopus*, becomes *ocho* in Spanish. But an *octo*pus is not an *ocho*puss. Listen: *ocho*. Repeat *ocho* a couple of times with the meaning in mind.

Listen and repeat: 7, 8, 108, 10.5, 7.8, 8.6, 8-0-7, 1008, 108.

Review to yourself. 6, 8, 7, 10, 5, 4, 3, 100, 1000, 1, 2.

If any of these numbers does not come readily to mind, review the memory aids.

NINE / *NUEVE*

Nine (9) in both English and Spanish (*nueve* and *nove-*) begins with the letter *n*. In *nueve,* the *n* is followed by *wave a: n-wave a—nueve. Wave a* is a wave with nine peaks and troughs. *Nueve* comes from Latin *nove-,* as in *November* (the ninth month in the Roman calendar). Listen: *nueve*. Repeat *nueve* a couple of times with the meaning in mind.

Listen and repeat: 8, 9, 7, 10.9, 8.8, 7.9, 8-0-9, 109, 108.

Now point to the numbers you see in the clusters below as they are spoken in Spanish.

	(A)					(B)		
	10					5		
8		7			6		7	
0	1,000	100		8		2		3
	9				9		4	
						1		

Now stop the tape and say the numbers in cluster B, then follow with the tape off.

Count from 1 to 10. Then count backward from 10 to 0. Test yourself by closing your eyes and imagining one number at a time from 0 to 9. Give the Spanish name for each number.

Forming the "Teens" in Spanish with Dieci- and -ce

You have learned thirteen of the seventeen elements of the Spanish numeric system: 10, 100, 1000, 1, 2, 3, 4, 5, 6, 7, 8, 9, and 0. These are the independent forms. But you have also seen some dependent forms. To review:

Independent	Dependent
cuatro (4)	*cator-, cuar-*
cinco (5)	*quin-*

These dependent forms occur in compound numbers such as fifteen, forty-five, and so on, which you will learn now.

Compounds

From sixteen to nineteen, the numbers are formed like Roman numerals: 10 and 6 *(diez y seis)*, *10 y 7, 10 y 8, 10 y 9*. Note that only the spelling is slightly changed (from *y* to *i*). Listen: *dieciseis* (16), *diecisiete* (17), *dieciocho* (18), *diecinueve* (19).

Point to the number you hear:

	(A)				(B)	
	10			116	117	119
17	16	18			118	
	1000				100,000	

Stop the tape and proceed on your own for a bit.

Say each number in cluster A. Count from 16 to 19. Then count backward from 19 to 11.

Numbers eleven to fifteen are formed with a suffix *-ce*, which sounds like "say," and means "-teen." A teen has the *"say"*! With this, the forms you would expect would be *uno-ce, dos-ce, tres-ce, cuatro-ce, cinco-ce*. However, the "-teen" suffix *(-ce)* combines with the dependent form of a number. If you recognize the dependent forms *quin-* (five) and *cator-* (four), you can recognize the following numbers: 15, 14, 13, 12, 11.

Note that eleven is <u>once</u> (roughly OWN-SAY), not <u>unce</u>.

Below is an etymological spelling matched with standard spelling:

Etymological Spelling	Standard Spelling
quin-ce	*quince*
cator-ce	*catorce*
tres-ce	*trece*
dos-ce	*doce*
un-ce	*once*

🔊 Listen to the count from eleven to nineteen.

Listen and repeat: 18, 15, 11, 19, 14, 12, 16, 13, 13,000, 16,000, 14.05.

Point to the number you hear:

```
            11          14
   13    18     19     16
      17    12    15
```

Just to keep active some things learned a while back, say these one at a time before the voice on the tape does: 10,000; 11,000; 12,000; 13,000; 14,000; 16,000; 17,000; 18,000.

Self-Test

🔊 Close your eyes and imagine one number at a time from 11 to 19, giving the Spanish name for each number.

🔊 *ARITMÉTICA—ADICIÓN*/ARITHMETIC—ADDITION

10 mas 1 son 11	*10 mas 2 son 12*
10 mas 3 son ?	*10 mas 4 son ?*
10 mas 5 son ?	*10 mas 6 son ?*
10 mas 7 son ?	*10 mas 8 son ?*
10 mas 9 son ?	

Stop the tape and work ahead on your own.

🔊 You have now learned nearly all of the elements of the Spanish numeric system. You can say and understand the numbers 100, 1000, and 1–19. All that is lacking is the decades 20–90 and the hundreds 200–900. These are easy. Since they use dependent forms of numbers with a suffix, it will pay to go over the dependent forms once again quickly. To review:

Number	Independent	Dependent
4	*cuatro*	*cator-, cuar-*
5	*cinco*	*quin-*
6	*seis*	*ses-*
7	*siete*	*sete-*
9	*nueve*	*nove-*

THE ADVENTURE CONTINUES

As you approach door number six, you feel pleased to have made it halfway. You are also pleased to read in the notebook this simple instruction:

Review numbers until you feel confident enough to go on.

You do what the notebook says and calmly enter door number six.

20

📼 Demonstration Lecture 1

paper / pencil
This is a pencil.
It's a pencil.
Paper. This is a (piece of) paper.
Say it: pencil, paper (—,—)
Again: (—,—)
Very good.
white / yellow / also
This pencil is white.
It's a white pencil.
This paper is white also.
It's white paper.
This paper is yellow.
It's yellow paper.
This pencil is yellow also.
It's a yellow pencil.
white pencil and yellow pencil
white paper and yellow paper

papel / lápiz
Este es un lápiz.
Es un lápiz.
Papel. Este es un papel.
Dígalo: lápiz, papel (—,—)
Otra vez: (—,—)
Muy bien.
blanco / amarillo / también
Este lápiz es blanco.
Es un lápiz blanco.
Este papel es blanco también.
Es papel blanco.
Este papel es amarillo.
Es papel amarillo.
Este lápiz es amarillo también.
Es un lápiz amarillo.
lápiz blanco y lápiz amarillo
papel blanco y papel amarillo

Stringing Together Your Own Narratives

CD ROM

Instructions: (1) Study the words in the scatter chart below. (2) Read the sample story plot.
(3) Refer to the chart and use only those words to compose sentences and story plots. (This is a
tape-off module, but one of considerable importance for extending your story-telling ability.)

SCATTER CHART

```
              (el) mercado            come                    (los) dulces
                 (el) comedor          amigo              (un) dulce
    vendedor
              su                          prueba            vende
              a                    el            compra
    toma              da
                              va
    un                                          entonces
              no son (muy) buenos      son (muy) buenos
                 el                       otro
                       más
              viene              sí
    pregunta si...                    no         trae
          responde que...                              lleva
              un kilo de...              y
                 (muy) dulce!
```

English Equivalent

```
              (the) [open]market        eats                  (the) sweets, candy
                 (the) eating place, dining hall   friend (m)   (a) sweet, piece of candy
    vendor, salesman
              his                        tries, tastes        sells
              to (a place or person)     the          buys
    takes, picks up          gives
                              goes
    a                                          then
              are not (very) good      are (very) good
                 he                       other, another
                       more
              comes              yes
    asks if...                    no         brings
          answers that...                              takes, carries
              a kilogram of...              and
                 (very) sweet!
```

Sample Story Plot

Say aloud Spanish equivalents of the following sentences. Then try writing the Spanish below the English sentence. You can find the key to the story plot in the appendix.

1. A vendor sells sweets in the market.

2. His friend Manuel comes to the market.

3. Manuel asks if the sweets are good.

4. The vendor answers that the sweets are very good.

5. He gives a piece of candy to his friend.

6. The friend takes the piece of candy.

7. He tastes the candy and says, "Mmm, yes, the sweets are very good."

8. The vendor sells a kilo of candy to his friend.

9. Manuel takes the sweets to a dining hall.

10. A friend in the dining hall tastes the sweets.

11. He says, "Mmm, very sweet."

12. He tries another and says, "Mmm, very, very sweet!"

13. Manuel gives the sweets to his friend.

14. The friend eats more sweets.

15. He eats more and more.

16. He eats the kilo of candy.

17. Manuel asks, "Very sweet, no?"

18. His friend doesn't answer.

19. Manuel asks, "Very sweet, no?"

20. His friend answers, "No, the sweets are not good."

21. The friend goes to the market and buys a kilo of candies.

22. He brings the candies to Manuel.

23. He gives the candies to Manuel.

24. Manuel takes the candies.

25. He tastes the candies.

26. He eats the candies.

27. He says, "The candies are very good."

Challenge

Say aloud or write twelve or more sentences using the words in this scatter chart (and previous ones if you like). One way to do this is to look at the scatter chart and string together words that make meaningful and well-formed sentences.

THE ADVENTURE CONTINUES

You arrive at door number seven in short order. Handing the notebook to Stump, you ask him to read the instructions. Neither of you is surprised when Stump reads:

> After you have done twelve sentences, you may enter the door.

You keep working on this task for as long as it takes you—even though you feel that the people following you are in the same room. Once you have composed your twelve sentences, you rush through the door and sprint all the way to door number eight. Before you read your instructions, you take a few minutes to rest and concentrate on learning more Spanish.

22

 Chatter at a Royal Ball

PREPARATION FOR CONVERSATION

Task 1
Familiarize yourself with the words and pictographs.

the queen ▲ *la reina* (reign-ah)

the princess ▲ *la princesa*

she ♀ *ella*

the one (f.) who ▲ ♦ *la que*

in the tower ⊔ ▲ ⊓ *(en) la torre*

in the bathroom ⊔ ▲ ⌒ *(en) el baño*

the prince ▲ *el príncipe*

I believe, I think... ⌁ *Creo...*

It pleases him/her (= he/she likes it) ☺ *Le gusta*

It pleases them (= they like it) ☺☺ *Les gusta*

with ℣ *con*

but ⌐ *pero*

Who knows? ↑? ⌁ *¿Quién sabe?*
(⌁ represents the brain)

cry ☺ *llor-* (imp*lore*)

also ✝ *también*

For what (reason)? Why? **R?** *¿Por qué?*

because **R=** *porque*

more or less ± *más o menos*

Self-Test on Recognition of the Pictographs
Review previously introduced pictographs.

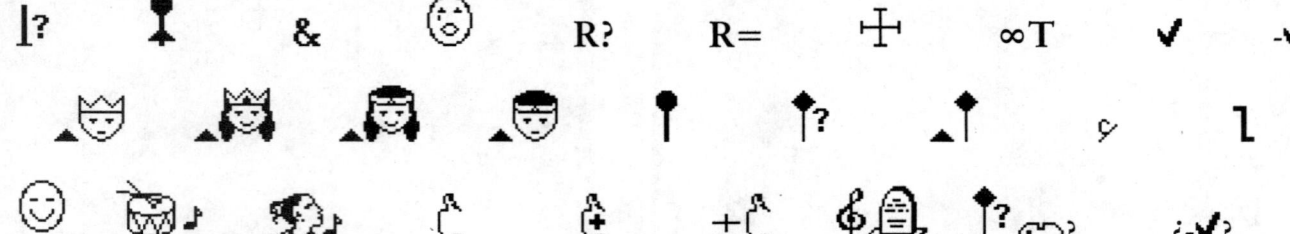

Checklist

¿cuál?   ella   y   llor-   ¿por qué?   porque   también

siempre	*sí*	*no*	*el rey*	*la reina*	*la princesa*	*el príncipe*	
él	*¿Quién?*	*el que*	*con*	*pero*	*le gusta*	*toc-*	
cant-	*bien*	*mejor*	*más o menos bien*	*cantos fúnebres*	*¿quién sabe?*	*¿no?*	

Task 2

Listen several times to the reading of this dialogue until you can understand the conversation comfortably with eyes closed.

🔊 CONVERSATION 2

••:	The queen also is singing.	*La reina también está cantando.*
•:	Which queen?	*¿Cuál reina?*
••:	The one who always cried in the bathroom with the princess, I believe.	*La que siempre lloraba en el baño con la princesa, creo.*
•:	Oh yes, it's the queen who used to cry in the bathroom with the princess.	*Oh sí, es la reina que siempre lloraba en el baño con la princesa.*
••:	She is singing in the tower with the king.	*Ella está cantando en la torre con el rey.*
•:	The king and the queen are singing funeral chants in the tower?	*¿El rey y la reina están cantando cantos fúnebres en la torre?*
••:	Yes. And don't they sing well?	*Sí. ¿Y no cantan bien?*
•:	Well yes, they sing more or less well. But why do they sing in the tower?	*Pues sí, cantan más o menos bien. ¿Pero por qué cantan en la torre?*
••:	They like to sing in the tower.	*Les gusta cantar en la torre.*
•:	And why do they sing funeral chants?	*¿Y por qué cantan cantos fúnebres?*
••:	Who knows?	*¿Quién sabe?*

🎞 THE ADVENTURE CONTINUES

Approaching door number eight, Stump reads in the notebook:

> Listen to Conversation 2 again. After you hear the English, translate it into Spanish. Then listen to the Spanish to see if you were right.

You and Stump do exactly what the notebook says. Just as you finish your last Spanish translation, the door swings open and you run through.

Task 3

Use your hands as puppets and dramatize the dialogue, looking only at the English. Drop all shyness and throw yourself into this performance. Aim for a flowing Spanish quality. Then go on to Task 4.

Task 4

Play the taped dialogue again, looking only at its pictographic representation below. Then do the same as Task 3 but without the tape. Throw yourself into this performance. Bring thought down to Spanish without thinking in English. Aim for high-quality performance.

Pictographic Representation of the Same Dialogue

••: [pictographs]

••: [pictographs]

••: [pictographs]

••: ✔ & -✔ [pictographs] (¡s) ℃ ?

••: [pictographs]

••: [pictographs]

•: ↓? [pictographs]

•: Oh ✔, [pictographs]

•: [pictographs] & [pictographs] ?

•: Pues ✔ ... (¡s) [pictographs] ± ℃

  ↳ R? (¡s) [pictographs] ?

•: & R?(¡s) [pictographs] ?

55

23

🔲 Observing Closely How Spanish Works

Take a while now to examine the phrases and sentences below. Make three passes through them as follows:

1st pass: Compare the Spanish forms and their meaning with the English. (Read the Spanish out loud, then look away and say it, thinking of its meaning and form.)

2nd pass: Cover the English and see if you can translate the Spanish into English.

3rd pass: Cover the Spanish and see if you can translate the English into Spanish.

GROUP A

king and queen	*rey y reina*
queen with king	*reina con rey*
the king and the queen	*el rey y la reina*
Which king and which queen?	*¿Cuál rey y cuál reina?*
Which king with which queen?	*¿Cuál rey con cuál reina?*
the queen with the princess	*la reina con la princesa*
The queen is with the princess.	*La reina está con la princesa.*
The king and the queen are with the princess.	*El rey y la reina están con la princesa.*

GROUP B

plays and sings and cries	*toca y canta y llora*
used to play and sing and cry	*tocaba y cantaba y lloraba*
playing and singing and crying	*tocando y cantando y llorando*
Who sings, who plays, and who cries?	*¿Quién canta, quién toca, y quién llora?*
The king sings; the queen plays; the princess cries.	*El rey canta; la reina toca; la princesa llora.*
(He) sings; (they) sing.	*Canta; cantan.*
(He) used to sing; (they) used to sing.	*Cantaba; cantaban.*
(He) is singing; (they) are singing.	*Está cantando; están cantando.*
The king and the queen are singing.	*El rey y la reina están cantando.*
The queen and the princess are crying.	*La reina y la princesa están llorando.*

GROUP C

The king and queen sing.	*El rey y la reina cantan.*
They are singing in the tower.	*Ellos están cantando en la torre.*
Which king is singing?	*¿Cuál rey está cantando?*
Does he sing well?	*¿Canta bien?*
Which king and which queen are singing?	*¿Cuál rey y cuál reina están cantando?*
Do they sing well?	*¿Cantan bien?*
(They) sing more or less well.	*Cantan más o menos bien.*
The king sings better than (he) plays.	*El rey canta mejor que toca.*
He plays worse than the queen.	*El toca peor que la reina.*
He sings better than the queen.	*El canta mejor que la reina.*

GROUP D

Who cries in the bathroom?	*¿Quién llora en el baño?*
The princess or the queen.	*La princesa o la reina.*
Who with? Who does she cry with?	*¿Con quién? ¿Con quién llora ella?*
Who is she crying with?	*¿Con quién está llorando ella?*
With which queen?	*¿Con cuál reina?*
With the one (f) who sings with the king.	*Con la que canta con el rey.*
Who is singing in the tower?	*¿Quién está cantando en la torre?*
Which king is with the queen in the tower?	*¿Cuál rey está con la reina en la torre?*
The one who used to play drums in the bathroom?	*¿El que tocaba el tambor en el baño?*

GROUP E

The queen pleases him. (= He likes the queen).	*Le gusta la reina.* (Note inverse order).
The queen pleases them. (= They like the queen).	*Les gusta la reina.*
The king pleases her. (= She likes the king).	*Le gusta el rey.*
The king pleases them. (= They like the king).	*Les gusta el rey.*
To sing pleases him. (= He likes to sing).	*Le gusta cantar.*
To sing used to please him. (= He liked to sing).	*Le gustaba cantar.*
To cry pleases her. (= She likes to cry).	*Le gusta llorar.*
To cry used to please them. (= They liked to cry).	*Les gustaba llorar.*
To sing pleases [to] <u>him</u>; to cry pleases [to] <u>her</u>.	*A <u>él</u> le gusta cantar; <u>a ella</u> le gusta llorar.*
To cry pleases [to] the queen. (= The queen likes to cry).	*A la reina le gusta llorar.*
To sing pleases [to] the king. (= The king likes to sing).	*Al rey le gusta cantar.*
To sing pleases [to] the dukes. (= The dukes like to sing).	*A los duques les gusta cantar.*
To sing pleases [to] the queens. (= The queens like to sing).	*A las reinas les gusta cantar.*

Review groups A–E above so that you can translate each sentence *without hesitation* from English to Spanish.

THE ADVENTURE CONTINUES

As you arrive at door number nine, you feel someone breathing down your back. You turn around to see who it is, but no one is there. "Strange," you think to yourself. You want to hurry through the door, but you feel it is important to check your notebook to see what you need to do. Handing the notebook to Stump, you ask him to read.

> Before you can enter Gateway Nine you must successfully complete the self-test below. Cover the Spanish sentences and put the English sentences into Spanish. After that, you are to take at least 40 minutes to quickly review stories, ditties, dialogues, narratives, etc. in preparation for giving a 20-minute sampling of what you can do.

"Stump," you say with great excitement, "we've made it to the ninth door, the gateway to the inner chamber. That's where we'll learn the secret of this place and the answer to why the invaders came. But hey, tomorrow is our tenth day. At midnight the submarine will be waiting for us. We're so close, but now our time is running out and we haven't achieved our goal. What can we do?"

"Skip the self-test and the 40 minute preparation," says Stump. "Let's force the door."

He takes a small card from his wallet and jams it into the gap of the door latch. "No, Stump," you say. "No. We'd better play it safe, we're almost there."

Ignoring your warning, he yanks on the knob and gasps as the airtight seal around the door breaks and the door shakes on its hinges. A deafening whistle like the sound of a jet engine fills the room. You feel yourself being blown back by a hurricane-force wind. You grab onto Stump's feet as he clings onto the door handle. At the top of your lungs you yell, "Hold on, Stump, hold on!"

Suddenly the wind dies down and you both slump to the floor, shaken but unhurt. As the noise fades away, Stump draws a deep breath. "Whew!" you say, "let that serve as a warning to us."

"Yeah, I guess we'd better do what we're told to do before we take on what's behind that door," Stump says.

You say firmly: "Right, from now on we're going by the book, Stump, okay?" "Right."

Forcing aside your nagging concern about making it to the north side of the island by midnight tomorrow for the rendezvous with the submarine, you set to work on the self-test, and then devote a full 40 minutes of rapid review of stories, ditties, dialogues, numbers and narratives to display a sampling of what you can do in Spanish.

SELF-TEST

Instructions: Cover the Spanish column with your hand. Translate the English into Spanish and then check your answer. Mark for later review those items with which you have difficulty.

1.	The king sings or plays.	*El rey canta o toca.*
2.	The king is singing or playing.	*El rey está cantando o tocando.*
3.	The king used to sing or play.	*El rey cantaba o tocaba.*
4.	The king and the queen sing.	*El rey y la reina cantan.*
5.	They are singing and playing.	*Están cantando y tocando.*
6.	Which princess cries?	*¿Cuál princesa llora?*
7.	The king used to sing worse…worse than the queen.	*El rey cantaba peor…peor que la reina.*
8.	The queen and the princess used to sing better.	*La reina y la princesa cantaban mejor.*
9.	Which princess used to cry?	*¿Cuál princesa lloraba?*
10.	She likes to sing in the tower.	*Le gusta cantar en la torre.*
11.	She used to like to sing in the bathroom.	*Le gustaba cantar en el baño.*
12.	The queen used to like to sing in the bathroom.	*A la reina le gustaba cantar en el baño.*
13.	The king likes to sing in the tower.	*Al rey le gusta cantar en la torre.*
14.	Why does he sing? Because he likes to sing.	*¿Por qué canta? Porque le gusta cantar.*

THE ADVENTURE CONTINUES

The next day you approach the ninth door again. Your heart is pounding. You turn the knob and the door opens. You find yourselves facing a dignified lady who smiles and says: "*Bienvenidos.*"

She comes over to the door and runs her hand over the damaged door seal, speaking in rapid Spanish that you can't understand. "She is the one who holds the key to the secret, whatever it is," Stump whispers without looking at you. You introduce yourselves and *la señora* says, "*Correcto,*" as if she already knew who you were.

She then proceeds to ask some probing questions. You understand what she is asking. When, after each of your truthful answers, she softly says: "*Eso es correcto*," you realize she somehow knew the answers already. She requests that you keep speaking, as if testing your language skills. You point nervously to your watch: "No time for that!" you say, but she simply looks at you, waiting. "We have no other choice, Stump," you say. "Let's put some things together for her." Taking from Chatter at a Royal Ball, Broken Window, ditties, points, lines and figures, numbers and other material you've worked on, you ham it up together in an impressive 20-minute performance. She laughs and claps with delight.

You look at your watch. It is now 18:00—six hours before midnight. Even if she could reveal the secret at that moment, you still would need four hours to make it to the rendezvous point. Stump points to a gold colored door behind *la señora*. "That has to be the door to the treasure."

You hold back feelings of urgency and beg her "*por favor*," to open the next door. She shakes her head and says: "You are not quite prepared to go through the ninth gateway, there are important things still missing in your Spanish. Please, put aside your worries and focus on learning a little more. When you pass the self-test I can open the real ninth door."

"No time!...*No hay tiempo*!" you insist, pointing to your watch.

"You have time," she says smiling as she calmly guides you through three unmarked doors. "Where was she earlier?" you and Stump think simultaneously as you raise your eyebrows at each other. Realizing your first map was intentionally inaccurate, you feel grateful to know this woman is on your side. You proceed to the assigned task.

24
 Focus on the Language 1–7

FOCUS 1

Masculine and feminine nouns with indefinite articles *un, una*.

a king and a queen	*un rey y una reina*
one king and one queen	*un rey y una reina*
a cat (m) and a cat (f)	*un gato y una gata*
a drum and a tower	*un tambor y una torre*

1. Every Spanish noun is either feminine or masculine gender. A noun such as *rey*, referring to a male, is masculine; one such as *reina*, referring to a female, is feminine. Such person nouns as king, queen, prince, princess are said to have "natural gender"—their gender matches their sex. Likewise with other animate nouns: there is a different form for males than for females. (The feminine counterpart of *gato* "cat" is *gata* and of *perro* "dog" is *perra*.) Feminine nouns require feminine-marked modifiers (*una reina, la princesa*) and masculine nouns require masculine-marked modifiers (*un rey, el príncipe*).

2. Nouns such as tower and drum do not have natural gender but do have assigned gender: *una torre* (not *un torre*), *un tambor* (not *una tambor*). Spanish has no neuter nouns; every noun is either masculine or feminine. Why tower is a "she" and drum is a "he" no one knows. There's no logic or reason for the gender of such nouns; it's just a fact of life.

Translate Orally from and into Spanish

a king and a queen	*un rey y una reina*
a drum and a tower	*un tambor y una torre*
a duke and a duchess	*un duque y una duquesa*
a male cat and a female cat	*un gato y una gata*
a male dog and a female dog	*un perro y una perra*

FOCUS 2

Four forms of the definite article: *el, la, los, las*.

| the king and the queen | *el rey y la reina* |
| the kings and the queens | *los reyes y las reinas* |

1. Whereas the English definite article *the* doesn't change, its Spanish counterpart has four forms: *el, la, los,* and *las*.

2. Always *el* goes with masculine and *la* goes with feminine. You'll never hear *la rey* or *el reina!*

3. Before a plural noun, *la* requires an *s*: *las reinas* (not *la reinas*). Before a plural noun, *el* changes to *los*: *los reyes* (not *el reyes*) "the kings."

Translate Orally from and into Spanish

the king and queen	*el rey y la reina*
the kings and queens	*los reyes y las reinas*
the duke and the duchess	*el duque y la duquesa*
the dukes and the duchesses	*los duques y las duquesas*
the drum and the towers	*el tambor y las torres*
the bathroom and the tower	*el baño y la torre*
the tower and the drums	*la torre y los tambores*

Focus 3

Linking singular with singular, plural with plural.

The king *is* in the tower.	*El rey está en la torre.*
The kings *are* in the tower.	*Los reyes están en la torre.*
NOT: The kings <u>is</u> in the tower.	NOT: *Los reyes <u>está</u> en la torre.*
NOR: The king <u>are</u> in the tower.	NOR: *El rey <u>están</u> en la torre.*
The king sings.	*El rey canta.*
The kings sing.	*Los reyes cantan.*
NOT: The king sing.	NOT: *El rey cantan.*
NOR: The kings sings.	NOR: *Los reyes canta.*

In Spanish (as in standard English) the verb takes different forms when tied to a singular subject and a plural one. This is called subject-verb link: singular with singular, plural with plural.

Translate Orally from and into Spanish

The king is in the tower.	*El rey está en la torre.*
The dukes are in the tower, too.	*Los duques están en la torre también.*
The king is singing.	*El rey está cantando.*
The dukes are singing, too.	*Los duques están cantando también.*
The king sings and the dukes sing, too.	*El rey canta y los duques cantan también.*

THE ADVENTURE CONTINUES

On successfully completing the self-test two hours later, you ask *la señora* if she would now open the door. *"Con mucho gusto,"* she answers. As the door opens, you see there is nothing there but a stone wall. Stump snorts: "Oh no!" *La señora* smiles, reaches up to a slot in the wall and pulls out what looks and feels like a stone, but on close examination is, in fact, a palm-sized computer disk.

You ask what it is and she explains: *"El disque simboliza el gran tesoro."* The words *gran tesoro* excite you. So, it <u>is</u> a great treasure you're after. She continues, *"El disque no es el tesoro, solamente es un símbolo del tesoro."* You know what she means: the disk itself is not the treasure, but only a symbol of the treasure. *La señora* continues and you understand her as though she were speaking in your native language. "You have proven yourselves trusting and truthful and have shown that even with limited Spanish you can communicate. Through your intelligence, bravery and diligence you have made it through the first part of your adventure. *El disque* I have given you symbolizes your remarkable achievements so far."

You recognize that what you have accomplished is amazing! But your goal is not yet achieved, and time has run out. Not knowing how to explain that it's already too late, you point to your watch

You recognize that what you have accomplished is amazing! But your goal is not yet achieved, and time has run out. Not knowing how to explain that it's already too late, you point to your watch and grimace helplessly. She nods knowingly and says, *"Sí, yo sé."* You find little comfort in that, but what's to be done? You put the "stone disk" in your pouch.

She then pulls out a small scroll, yellowed with age. "This is a schematic map of *el laberinto*, the labyrinth, which lies ahead of you, protecting the treasure. You cannot possibly find your way through it without this map. You must never let it out of your grasp! It is irreplaceable. But remember this: the map without *el disque* is useless. Like the map and *el disque*, the treasure you are after is inseparable from the language you are learning—which, as you are beginning to see, is a great treasure in itself." She hands you the map.

"Can you tell us what the treasure is that we are after?" you ask. "No," she replies, "but you will find out when you have made your way inside *el laberinto*." She then hands you the scroll, and what appear to be two ordinary pairs of glasses. You unroll the scroll and can't see anything. She instructs both of you to put the glasses on, and when you look at the map, you see a large rectangular grid with many cells, eight of which are shaded.

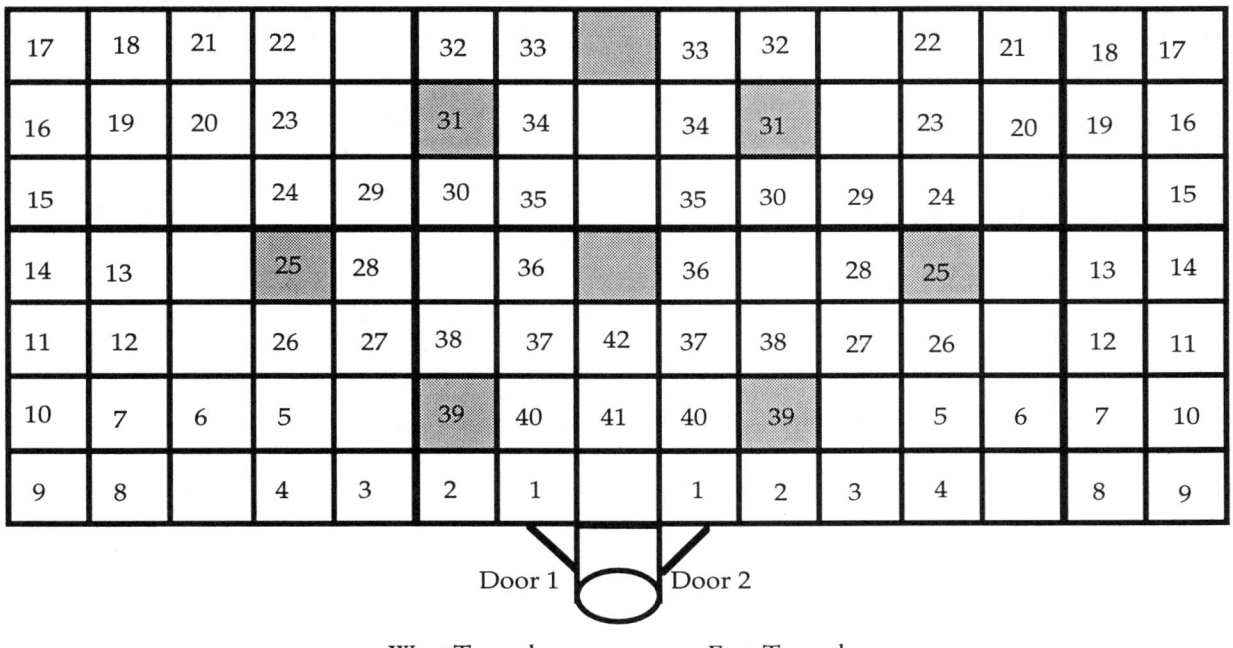

The woman explains, "These glasses are actually sophisticated nanocomputers. The lenses are actually liquid crystal display plates that are controlled through the chips in the frame. The glasses have been programmed to decode the map, so don't lose them! The map is useless without the glasses."

You look at the map again and on looking closely at the shaded cells, you make out faint images of what could be a king, a town, a park, a house, a room, a vase, a flower, all arranged around a key that lies at the center. "What do you suppose these mean?" Stump asks. "I haven't the slightest idea," you say. "Wait. Look here at the side of the scroll," you say, noticing a pattern of dots, lines and figures. You and Stump look at each other and in unison exclaim *"Puntos, líneas y figuras!"* La señora nods and smiles at you approvingly.

FOCUS 4

The infinitive form of the verb.

The king sings.	*El rey canta.*
The king and queen sing.	*El rey y la reina cantan.*
to sing	*cantar*

You have encountered verbs in different forms, for example *canta, cantan; cantaba, cantaban.* These are so-called "finite" forms of the verb *cantar* (finite forms are tied to a subject: "He sings," etc.). The form *cantar* is called the infinitive or the "list-form (the way you'd see it if written in a list of verbs)," not being tied to a subject. Actually the infinitive form can function as a noun: *Cantar es llorar.* "To sing is to cry" (or "Singing is crying"). *El cantar de la reina.* "The singing of the queen."

FOCUS 5

How to express "X pleases her"—or its synonym "She likes X":

(Literal) Him pleases the queen.	*Le gusta la reina.*
(Standard English) The queen pleases him.	
or *He likes the queen.*	*Le gusta la reina.*
(Literal) Him pleases to sing.	*Le gusta cantar.*
(Standard English) To sing (singing) pleases him.	
or *He likes to sing.*	*Le gusta cantar.*
(Literal) Me pleases the king.	*Me gusta el rey.*
(Standard English) The king pleases me.	
or *I like the king.*	*Me gusta el rey.*

Carefully compare each paired set. Don't look for an English way to express the idea "to like."

FOCUS 6

How to express "X pleases the king"—or its synonym "The king likes X":

(Literal) To the queen (to her) pleases to sing.	*A la reina *le gusta cantar.*
(Standard English) To sing (singing) pleases the queen.	
or The queen likes to sing.	*A la reina le gusta cantar.*
(Literal) To the king (to him) pleases to play.	*Al rey *le gusta tocar.*
(Standard English) To play (playing) pleases the king.	
or The king likes to play.	*Al rey le gusta tocar.*
(Literal) To me (me) pleases the queen.	*A mí *me gusta la reina.*
(Standard English) The queen pleases me.	
or I like the queen.	<u>*A mí*</u> *me gusta la reina.*

In the Spanish above, *le* and *me* cannot be translated into English and make sense. They refer to the preceding indirect object (to the queen/to me) and not to something or someone else.

Translate Orally from and into Spanish

Remember, you cannot model the Spanish on the English!

The princess likes the duke.	*A la princesa le gusta el duque.*
The duke likes the princess.	*Al duque le gusta la princesa.*
The princesses like the duke.	*A las princesas <u>les</u> gusta el duque.*
The dukes like the princess.	*A los duques <u>les</u> gusta la princesa.*
The duchesses like the king.	*A las duquesas <u>les</u> gusta el rey.*
The dukes don't like the king.	*A los duques <u>no les</u> gusta el rey.*
I don't like the king.	*A mí <u>no me</u> gusta el rey.*

Focus 7

How to turn statements into questions:

Look at the following sentences. Note how a statement can be made into a question by simply placing the verb at the beginning of the sentence.

El rey canta.	The king sings.
¿Canta el rey?	Does the king sing?
La princesa cantaba.	The princess used to sing.
¿Cantaba la princesa?	Did the princess use to sing?
La reina está tocando el tambor.	The queen is playing the drum.
¿Está tocando el tambor la reina?	Is the queen playing the drum?

Note that in the last sentence the phrase *"está tocando el tambor"* is kept and is followed by *"la reina"* — literally "Is playing the drum the queen?" That sounds strange, but putting the elements of the Spanish sentence in the English order *(¿Está la reina tocando el tambor?)* sounds strange to Spanish ears.

25

Questions in Spanish

SPANISH QUESTION FORM

Study the examples of question forms below. Note that the Spanish question pattern parallels the Old English question pattern.

Normal English Form	Old English Form	Spanish Equivalent
Does the king cry?	Cries the king?	*¿Llora el rey?*
Did the queen cry?	Cried the queen?	*¿Lloraba la reina?*
Do they sing?	Sing they?	*¿Cantan ellos?*
Do the king and queen sing songs?	Sing songs the king and queen?	*¿Cantan cantos el rey y la reina?*
Did the king and queen sing songs?	Sang songs the king and queen?	*¿Cantaban cantos el rey y la reina?*

Caution: Don't try to translate the English *do, does, did* in question sentences like those above—it just won't work. The temptation to do this is one of the most common pitfalls for the beginning student. Instead, rephrase normal English questions into the Old English form that parallels the Spanish question pattern.

Is the king singing?	Is singing the king?	*¿Está cantando el rey?*
Are the king and queen crying?	Are crying the king and queen?	*¿Están llorando el rey y la reina?*
Is the queen playing the drum?	Is playing the drum the queen?	*¿Está tocando el tambor la reina?*

Having looked at the above examples of question formation, note also that rising voice inflection (or intonation—how you emphasize a word to give it meaning) can also be used to indicate that a question is being asked.

Practice in Translation

Who likes to sing?	*¿A quién le gusta cantar?*
Does Robert like to sing?	*¿A Roberto le gusta cantar?*
Do Maria and Anita like to sing?	*¿A María y Anita les gusta cantar?*
Which king likes to sing?	*¿A cuál rey le gusta cantar?*
Doesn't the princess like to sing?	*¿A la princesa no le gusta cantar?*
Didn't the king used to like to sing?	*¿Al rey no le gustaba cantar?*

THE ADVENTURE CONTINUES

After a while, you decide to open the notebook and see the instructions. It does not surprise you to read:

> Take the following "Self-Test." Once you can pass it easily, you may enter the door and behold the treasure.

SELF-TEST

Instructions: Translate out loud. Cover the Spanish except to check your translation. Remember that the Spanish question form parallels the Old English form. Mark those items with which you have difficulty.

Does the king sing?	*¿Canta el rey?*
Does he like to sing?	*¿Le gusta cantar?*
Did the queen used to cry?	*¿Lloraba la reina?*
Did she like to cry?	*¿Le gustaba llorar?*
Do the king and the queen sing?	*¿Cantan el rey y la reina?*
Do they like to sing?	*¿Les gusta cantar?*
Did the prince and the king use to sing better?	*¿Cantaban el príncipe y el rey mejor?*
Is the princess singing or crying?	*¿Está cantando o llorando la princesa?*
Are the king and the princess singing?	*¿Están cantando el rey y la princesa?*
Does the dog sing well too?	*¿Canta el perro bien también?*
Do the dog and the cat sing worse?	*¿Cantan el perro y el gato peor?*
Were the princesses singing?	*¿Cantaban las princesas?*
Or were they crying in the bathroom?	*¿O lloraban en el baño?*
The princess likes to cry in the bathroom.	*A la princesa le gusta llorar en el baño.*
The king likes to sing in the tower.	*Al rey le gusta cantar en la torre.*
Does the princess like to sing?	*¿A la princesa le gusta cantar?*
Doesn't the duchess like to sing?	*¿A la duquesa no le gusta cantar?*
Who doesn't like to sing?	*¿A quién no le gusta cantar?*
Which duke likes to sing?	*¿A cuál duque le gusta cantar?*

THE ADVENTURE CONTINUES

Before leaving you to your own resources, the lady hands Stump a tiny jar labeled "horseradish" and you a tiny jar labeled "aloe vera oil," saying simply, "Keep these in your pouches."

Then she hands each of you a strange-looking wrist watch, and says, "These are Mitrons—nicknamed "Mighty Mights" or "Mites." They are actually very powerful computers that are electronically linked with the glasses I have given you. In the upper corner on the frames of your glasses are microcameras that will transmit video signals to the Mitron. Most importantly though, the Mitrons will allow you to communicate with the captain of the submarine. The submarine will constantly monitor video feedback from the cameras in the glasses and the audio feedback from the Mitron itself. You need to initiate contact with the submarine before the satellite link will be activated. This will be your only means of communication with the captain, so guard these Mitrons with your life. If the invaders ever got hold of them, it would be a catastrophe. Now I must leave you. Know that your mission is of monumental importance to mankind. If you succeed you will make the world a better place. If you fail—or worse, if the invaders beat you to it—well, just don't let that happen. I feel that you *will* succeed. Good luck to you and God bless you!"

26

 Puntos, Líneas, y Figuras

Points, Lines, and Figures

Tape off while you study the scatter chart, then go on.

A. SCATTER CHART

|	/	_____
línea vertical	*línea diagonal*	*línea horizontal*
•_____		_____•
un punto delante de una línea		*una línea delante de un punto*
el punto precede la línea		*el punto sigue la línea*

B. LISTEN, LOOK, AND READ

(Cover the Spanish and just listen to the tape if you like.)

1. \| *Esta es una línea vertical.*

2. _____ *Esta es una línea horizontal.*

3. \ *Y ésta es una línea diagonal.*

4. \\\ *Estas líneas son diagonales.*

5. /// *Estas líneas son diagonales también.*

6. _____ *¿Es vertical esta línea? Nó, es horizontal.*

7. _____ *¿Es horizontal esta línea también? Sí.*

8. // *¿Son horizontales estas líneas? Nó, son diagonales.*

9. \| \| \| *¿Son verticales estas líneas? Sí. (Son verticales.)*

10. \| *Esta no es una línea diagonal.*

11. •\| *Este es un punto delante de una línea vertical. (El punto precede la línea.)*

12. \| \| • *Estas son dos líneas verticales delante de un punto. (El punto sigue las líneas.)*

C. LISTEN AND LOOK

1. | 2. _____   3. \   4. \\\

5. ///   6. _____   7. _____   8. //

9. | | | 10. | 11. •| 12. | | •

D. MULTIPLE-CHOICE FRAMES

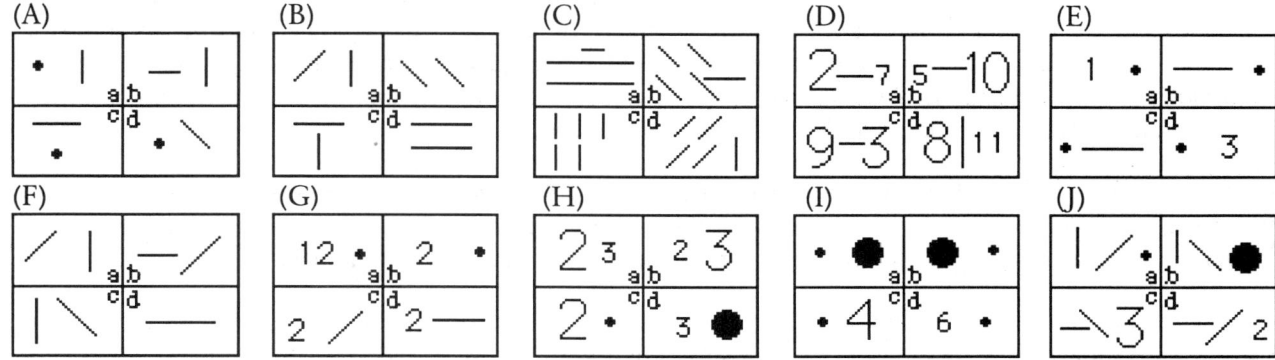

†The second sentence in frame G does not read the answer "d."

E. LISTEN AND DRAW

(Stop the tape if the pace is too fast. The answer key is in the appendix.)

1.   2.   3.   4.

⊡ F. READ FOR MEANING

Read the following sentences and see if you can understand them. The English translations are in the appendix.

1. *Esta no es una línea horizontal, es una línea diagonal.*
2. *Estas son dos líneas verticales y dos otras líneas horizontales.*
3. *Este es el número seis delante de una línea larga y gruesa.*
4. *Y ésta es el número siete delante de un punto grande.*
5. *Esta es una línea delgada delante de una línea gruesa y de un punto pequeño.*
6. *Esta es una línea vertical y una línea diagonal delante de una letra grande, la letra M.*
7. *Esta es un punto pequeño y un punto grande delante de una línea larga y delgada.*

THE ADVENTURE CONTINUES

After experimenting a bit with your Mitrons, you access the cryptic-mail function that you hope will allow you to send a coded message to your captain in the submarine. You request a five-day postponement of your rendezvous time, hoping that that will give you time to make your way through *el laberinto*, secure the treasure, and make your way back. There is no response. Your heart sinks. "They have got to be close now," you say. Again you transmit. Again there is no response. Stump has his teeth clenched with worry.

"Have they aborted the mission and left us here?" you ask in a shaky voice.

"Let's give it one more try," Stump urges.

Within a minute a coded message is received: Request Confirmed.

"Wow, it works!" Stump shouts.

"Nice to make contact," you add.

You next find the computer function that provides guidance for the continuation of your quest. You place your Mitron close to your ear and listen to the captain's voice: I'm glad we've finally made contact. I want you two to know that we are now in range and your Mitron is passively broadcasting information to the submarine where a team of experts is interpreting the data. We will contact you often now to guide you through the more difficult part of the journey.

I need to give you a warning: the invaders have somehow gained entrance to el laberinto. Exactly where they are is unknown, but they are lost without the map to guide them. You have the map, so the advantage is yours. They will go to any length to obtain what they believe you have.

Your captain, through the Mitron, further informs you that to obtain the key to the gateway of *el laberinto*, you are now to speed-learn five short dialogues—hopefully in fifteen minutes! You think, Wow! Is it possible? But, accepting the challenge, as always, you find a restful spot under a banana tree on the bank of a clear forest pool. There the two of you set about your assigned task. You will record your performance after just 15 minutes of preparation. You set the time-clock function and begin memorizing. The middle column enables you to memorize faster than you thought possible. DO THIS BEFORE GOING ON.

27

▨ Speed Learning
Five Minidialogues

⊙
CD ROM

▨ To achieve par, you must be able to perform all five dialogues, cueing only from the English. Try to do it after only 15 minutes. Use the memory and pronunciation aids in the middle column to help you.

▨ *Dialogue 1*

| • • : | How have you all been? | KAY TALL HONEST STAr THOUGH? | *¿Qué tal han estado?* |
| • : | More or less well. | MOSS oh MAY nose B.N. | *Más o menos bien.* |

Dialogue 2

• • :	Where are you going?	AH th-OWN DAY VOSS?	*¿A dónde vas?*
• :	I'm going to my house.	BOY A MI CASA	*Voy a mi casa.*
• • :	Till later.	AH-stall WAY-go	*Hasta luego.*
• :	G'bye.	CHOW	*Ciao.*

Dialogue 3

• • :	That's it. That's surely it!	S.O.S! S.O.C.K.S!	*Eso es. ¡Eso sí que es!*
• :	Maybe.	Key SAUCE *or* Key SAW	*Quizás/Quizá.*
• • :	I'm not lying.	No me -N.-toe (myento)	*No miento.*
• :	I know [it], but nevertheless…	Low-SAY, PAY-row scene-embargo…	*Lo sé, pero sin embargo. . .*

Dialogue 4

• • :	It's that way.	S. ah-C.	*Es así.*
• :	Perhaps.	Tall VASE	*Tal vez.*
• • :	That's how it is.	Ah-SEE S.	*Así es.*
• :	No, it's not that way.	No, no S. ah-C.	*No, no es así.*

Dialogue 5

| • • : | That's bad. | S. O. S. tamal. | *Eso está mal.* |
| • : | Yes, that's really bad. | C, S. O. C. S. tamal. | *Sí, eso sí está mal.* |

▨ ⏱ start _____   ⏱ finish _____

THE ADVENTURE CONTINUES

How long did it take you to complete the task? Stop your memorization and perform the five dialogues the best you can.

28

 A Mother Talks to Her Small Child

Una Madre Habla a Su Niñito

CD ROM

THE ADVENTURE CONTINUES

While still sitting under the banana tree doing time trials on the dialogues, you hear a lady nearby talking to her baby. Your Mitron buzzes softly and says: **The lady is one of our local informants and has no objection to your recording her voice. Use the record function of the Mitron.** You press the record button and sit there listening, marveling at how clear her talk is. It is a superb learning experience.

Hand. Foot.	*Mano. Pie.*
Hands. Feet.	*Manos. Pies.*
One hand. Two hands.	*Una mano. Dos manos.*
One foot. Two feet.	*Un pie. Dos pies.*
Two hands and two feet.	*Dos manos y dos pies.*
This is my hand.	*Esta es mi mano.*
This is my foot.	*Este es mi pie.*
These are my hands.	*Estas son mis manos.*
These are my feet.	*Estos son mis pies.*
These are my hands and my feet.	*Estos son mis manos y mis pies.*
Two hands and two feet.	*Dos manos y dos pies.*
Arm. Leg.	*Brazo. Pierna.*
This is my arm.	*Este es mi brazo.*
This is my leg.	*Esta es mi pierna.*
These are my arms.	*Estos son mis brazos.*
These are my legs.	*Estas son mis piernas.*
Two arms, two legs, two hands, and two feet.	*Dos brazos, dos piernas, dos manos, y dos pies.*
This is Maria.	*Esta es María.*
This is Juan.	*Este es Juan.*
These are Maria's arms.	*Estos son los brazos de María.*
These are her feet.	*Estos son sus pies.*
These are John's hands.	*Estas son las manos de Juan.*
These are his legs.	*Estas son sus piernas.*
This is Maria's head.	*Esta es la cabeza de María.*
And this is her face.	*Y ésta es su cara.*
Her face is pretty.	*Su cara es bonita.*
These are her eyes.	*Estos son sus ojos.*
She has pretty eyes, doesn't she?	*Ella tiene ojos bonitos, ¿no?*
Two pretty eyes. Very pretty.	*Dos ojos bonitos. Muy bonitos.*

Maria is beautiful.	*María es bonita.*

This is John's face.	*Esta es la cara de Juan.*
This is John's nose.	*Esta es la nariz de Juan.*
This is his mouth.	*Esta es su boca.*
And these are his ears.	*Y estas son sus orejas.*
His nose, his mouth, and his ears.	*Su nariz, su boca, y sus orejas.*
One nose, one mouth, and two ears.	*Una nariz, una boca, y dos orejas.*
John's face.	*La cara de Juan.*

Look at Maria's mouth.	*Mira la boca de María.*
She has a delicate mouth	*Ella tiene una boca delicada*
with pretty lips and teeth.	*con labios y dientes bonitos.*
Red lips and white teeth.	*Labios rojos y dientes blancos.*
Yes, she has a very pretty face	*Sí, ella tiene una cara muy bonita*
with red lips and white teeth.	*con labios rojos y dientes blancos.*

THE ADVENTURE CONTINUES

You hit the re-play button and listen again, taking in the whole scene, even writing down and reviewing new words.

You sense your comprehension of Spanish is improving hour by hour, but darkness is coming on and you have no place to spend the night. A message from your Mitron tells you to follow a trail northward through the thick jungle. Leaving the restful spot by the pond, you and Stump make your way down the narrow trail. Soon you come to a cottage with a sign on the door that says: WELCOME, R & S. PLEASE GO RIGHT IN. THERE'S FOOD FOR YOU IN THE FRIDGE. HELP YOURSELVES TO ANYTHING YOU FIND. WE'LL VISIT YOU LATER.

Incredible! You knock and wait. No one answers. You turn the knob and the door opens. You go in, feeling like Snow White entering the cottage of the seven dwarfs. It is nicely furnished. You notice a sign in the living room: *"Están en su casa"* literally "You're in your home"—a Spanish way of saying "Please feel at home."

In the fridge you find a pitcher of fresh-squeezed orange juice. You sit down and relax a bit with a refreshing drink, and then you consult your Mitron for advice on your next move. You listen to its soft voice: Our sensors tell us you are safe where you are. The invaders are no threat to you there. You have the evening and the morning before you, a large block of time to prepare for the great challenge you face at noon tomorrow. Right now you are to figure out for yourselves some details of Spanish grammar. Don't rush through it. Use these hours for this task and those that follow. Start with "From Word to Discourse." Invest yourselves and make it fun!

29

▦ From Word to Discourse

De la palabra al discurso

◉ Here is a scatter chart of words that you must learn to string together to make sentences. Sample strings are given below.

SCATTER CHART

> *he aquí*
>
> *es / son*
>
> *esta(s)*   *esa(s)*
>
> *la(s)*
>
> *una(s)*   *otra(s)*
>
> ## cosa(s)
>
> *y*
>
> *blanca(s)*   *negra(s)*
>
> *chica(s)*   *grande(s)*
>
> *sí*   *no*

Sample Strings of Words

Instructions: Carefully study these sentences, including the grammatically incorrect ones with the asterisk. Work out in your mind the rules for the correct formation of these kinds of word strings.

▦

1.	A thing. The thing.	*Una cosa. La cosa.*
2.	The things. Some things.	*Las cosas. Unas cosas.*
		*La cosas. *Una cosas.
3.	Here is a thing.	*He aquí una cosa.*
4.	Here is a white thing.	*He aquí una cosa blanca.*
		*He aquí una blanca cosa.
5.	And here is a black thing.	*Y he aquí una cosa negra.*
		*Y he aquí una negra cosa.
6.	Here are the things.	*He aquí las cosas.*
		*He aquí la cosas.
7.	Here are the other things, large things and small things.	*He aquí las otras cosas, cosas grandes y cosas chicas.*
		*He aquí las cosas otras.
8.	Here are some other things.	*He aquí unas otras cosas.*

9.	Some white things and some black things.	*Unas cosas blancas y unas cosas negras.*
10.	This thing is black.	*Esta cosa es negra.*
11.	The one is white; the other is black.	*La una es blanca; la otra es negra.*
12.	The black thing is large.	*La cosa negra es grande.*
		*La negra cosa es grande.
13.	The white thing is small.	*La cosa blanca es chica.*
		*La blanca cosa es chica.
14.	This thing is small, and that thing is large.	*Esta cosa es chica, y esa cosa es grande.*
15.	These things are small.	*Estas cosas son chicas.*
		*Estas cosas son chica.
16.	These small things are white.	*Estas cosas chicas son blancas.*
		*Estas chica cosas son blancas.
17.	Those large things are black.	*Esas cosas grandes son negras.*
		*Esas cosas grandes es negras.
18.	Is the black thing large? Yes, it's large.	*¿Es grande la cosa negra? Sí, es grande.*
		*¿Es la cosa negra grande?
19.	Is the white thing large? No, it's not large.	*¿Es grande la cosa blanca? No, no es grande.*
		*¿Es la cosa blanca grande? *No, es no grande.
20.	Are these things large and white?	*¿Son grandes y blancas estas cosas?*
		*¿Son estas cosas grandes y blancas?
21.	No, they aren't large and white.	*No, no son grandes y blancas.*
		*No, son no grandes y blancas.

🖦 *Preparing to Deal with Real Objects.*

Instructions: Look at the twenty-one sentences above again, but cover the Spanish with your hand or a piece of paper. Translate them into Spanish and check your version with the version next to it.

Instructions: For each sentence give the Spanish equivalent *and* a different sentence of parallel structure.

Example: A white thing. Here is a white thing.	*Una cosa blanca. He aquí una cosa blanca.*
Parallel Structure: A large thing. Here is a large thing.	*Una cosa grande. He aquí una cosa grande.*

1.	And here is a black thing.	5.	This thing is small.
2.	One white thing and one black thing.	6.	These things are large.
3.	Here are the white things.	7.	These large things are black.
4.	Some white things and some black things.	8.	The other things are white and small.

Dealing with Real Objects

Instructions: Set out on a table before you a number of *small white* things and *large black* things. They can be pieces of paper or whatever, as long as the smaller things are white and the larger ones are black. (You can even write "black" on larger pieces of white paper to represent black things.) Referring to these objects in front of you, see how many meaningful statements you can generate about them in two minutes. Keep a tally. Start with very short statements, then advance to more ambitious ones. Par for this is twelve statements in two minutes. Can you beat par?

🕐 Starting time: _____

After concentrating at **least** 40 minutes on this assignment, check this box ☐.

The Key of the King's Kingdom
La Llave del Reino del Rey

⊞ THE ADVENTURE CONTINUES

Mitron message: The Key of the King's Kingdom is a biggie—your first performance piece. Prepare to tell it both vocally and with hand signs to someone sitting in front of you. You can make up your own hand signs. When you're ready, go for it!

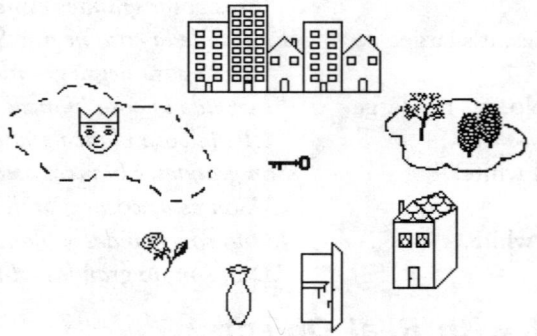

This is a key, a small key.

Here is a king.

And here is the king's kingdom.

In this kingdom, there is a town.

And in this town, there is a park.

And in this park, there is a house.

And in this house, there is a room.

And in this room, there is a vase.

And in this vase, there's a flower.

The flower in the vase,

the vase in the room,

the room in the house,

the house in the park,

the park in the town,

the town in the kingdom,

and this is the key of the king's kingdom.

Imagine!

Esta es una llave, una pequeña llave.

He aquí un rey.

Y he aquí el reino del rey.

En este reino hay un pueblo.

Y en este pueblo hay un parque.

Y en este parque hay una casa.

Y en esta casa hay un cuarto.

Y en este cuarto hay un florero.

Y en este florero hay una flor.

La flor en el florero,

el florero en el cuarto,

el cuarto en la casa,

la casa en el parque,

el parque en el pueblo,

el pueblo en el reino,

y he aquí la llave del reino del rey.

¡Imagínese!

Recognizing that the story contains the mysterious images seen on the scroll, you ask your Mitron, "Does this story have something to do with helping us negotiate the labyrinth?" The answer is: Definitely! You wonder what will occasion its performance, and what other performance pieces you will need, but you take the advice seriously and tell it several times with voice and signs.

A Lesson in Spanish
Una Lección de español

CD ROM

THE ADVENTURE CONTINUES

Your Mitron buzzes and you access a message: Next is a special lesson in Spanish. Listen at least three times. The second time, cover the English and see if you understand. The third time cover the Spanish and stop and start the recording as you try to say the Spanish phrase before it is spoken.

What is this?	*¿Qué es esto?*
A leaf. Another leaf. The other leaf.	*Una hoja. Otra hoja. La otra hoja.*
What's the difference?	*¿En qué está la diferencia?*
One is yellow. The other is white.	*Una es amarilla. La otra es blanca.*
What is this?	*¿Qué es esto?*
A sheet of paper.	*Una hoja de papel.*
And this?	*¿Y esto?*
Another sheet of paper.	*Otra hoja de papel.*
What's the difference?	*¿En qué está la diferencia?*
Correct. Exactly. Precisely.	*Correcto. Exactamente. Precisamente.*
Thing. The thing. This thing.	*Cosa. La cosa. Esta cosa.*
One thing yellow and one thing white.	*Una cosa amarilla y una cosa blanca.*
This yellow thing, what is it?	*Esta cosa amarilla ¿qué es?*
It's a pencil.	*Es un lápiz.*
This white thing, what is it?	*Esta cosa blanca ¿qué es?*
It's a sheet of paper.	*Es una hoja de papel.*
Yes, a white sheet of paper and a yellow pencil.	*Sí, una hoja de papel blanco y un lápiz amarillo.*
More. Two more things. So…	*Más. Dos cosas más. Entonces…*
Two more things: a yellow sheet of paper and a white pencil.	*Dos cosas más: una hoja de papel amarillo y un lápiz blanco.*
Two yellow things and two white things.	*Dos cosas amarillas y dos cosas blancas.*
So, a total of four things: two sheets of paper and two pencils.	*Entonces, un total de cuatro cosas: dos hojas de papel y dos lápices.*
These two things are white.	*Estas dos cosas son blancas.*
These two things are yellow.	*Estas dos cosas son amarillas.*

THE ADVENTURE CONTINUES

You receive a new message: At noon tomorrow, after final preparations, you will enter el laberinto. Its entrance is hidden behind a small park with trees on the south side of the castle that is due north of your present position. Stand close to the biggest tree there and repeat aloud the words "He aquí la llave del reino del rey." On that signal, an opening will appear giving you access to the antechamber. Your immediate task now is to take on 32 (Chatter at a Royal Ball) and 33 (Focus on Language) and wait for more instructions to direct you on entering el laberinto.

32

📼 Chatter at a Royal Ball

🔳 PREPARATION FOR CONVERSATION

dog 🐕 *perro* ("Perot")

cat 🐈 *gato* (cat-oh)

worse than 🜊> *peor que*

it appears, seems 👓 *parece*

It seems so. 👓✔ *Parece que sí.*

doesn't please her -✔😊 *no le gusta*
(= she doesn't like...)

Of course! **Cl!** *¡Claro!*

Imagine! ¡💡! *¡Imagínese!*

Oh gee! (or other exclamation) *i—!* *¡Ay-ay!*

together ⚌ *juntos*

• 🐕 & • 🐈 *un perro y un gato*

Why? Because. **R? R=** *¿Por qué? Porque.*

Self-Test on Recognition of the Pictographs

Review previously introduced pictographs.

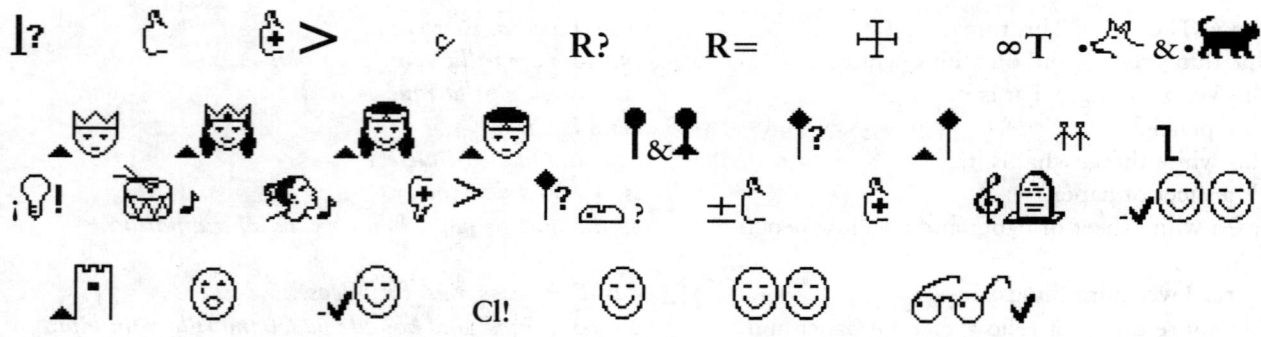

Checklist

¿cuál?	*bien*	*mejor que*	*con*	*¿por qué?*	*porque*	*también*
siempre	*un perro y un gato*	*el rey*	*la reina*	*la princesa*	*el príncipe*	*él y ella*
quien	*el que*	*juntos*	*pero*	*¡imagínese!*	*toca*	*canta-*
peor que	*¿quién sabe?*	*más o menos bien*	*mejor*	*cantos fúnebres*	*no les gusta*	*la torre*
llora	*no le gusta*	*¡claro!*	*le gusta*	*les gusta*	*parece que sí*	

🔲 CONVERSATION 3

•: Polo and Misti are singing, too. They are singing with the king and queen in the tower.	*Polo y Misti están cantando también. Están cantando con el rey y la reina en la torre.*
••: Polo and Misti?	*¿Polo y Misti?*
•: The cat and the dog.	*El perro y el gato.*
••: A king and a queen with a dog and a cat. And they're singing together?	*Un rey y una reina con un perro y un gato. ¿Y están cantando juntos?*
•: It appears so.	*Parece que sí.*
••: And the princess?	*¿Y la princesa?*
•: The princess is not singing.	*La princesa no está cantando.*
••: Why not?	*¿Por qué no?*
•: Because she doesn't like to sing. She doesn't sing well. She sings worse than the dog.	*Porque a ella no le gusta cantar. No canta bien. ¡Canta peor que el perro!*
••: But better than the cat!	*¡Pero mejor que el gato!*
•: Of course. Imagine!	*Claro. ¡Imagínese!*
••: Oh gee!	*¡Ay ay!*

🔲 Go back and listen several times to this conversation until you can understand it with eyes closed.

Task 1

Use your hands as puppets and dramatize the dialogue, looking only at the English. Drop all shyness and inhibitions and throw yourself into this performance.

Task 2

Do the same as in the previous task, but look only at the pictographic representation of the dialogue and express your thought in Spanish without thinking in English.

Pictographic Representation of the Same Dialogue

•: Polo & Misti

••: Polo & Misti?

•:

••:

•:

••:

•:

••: R?

•: R=

••:

•: Cl!

••: ¡—!

78

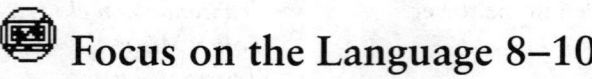

Focus on the Language 8–10

FOCUS 8

Gustar to please (Spanish for "he likes X" is formed like "He is pleased by X").

The queens please him/her. (= He/she likes the queens.)	*Le gust<u>an</u> la<u>s</u> reinas.*
To sing pleases them. (= They like to sing.)	*Les gust<u>a</u> cantar.*
To write doesn't please me. (= I don't like to write.)	*No me gust<u>a</u> escribir.*

Note: To say, "I like (something or someone)," one says, "Me pleases (something or someone)." Don't try to form a more direct translation equivalent! It may seem awkward or backward to express the idea of liking in this way, but that's how it is expressed in Spanish.

FOCUS 9

Gustar (with personal noun).

The queen likes to sing.	*<u>A</u> la reina <u>le</u> gusta cantar.*
The king likes to sing, too.	*<u>Al</u> rey <u>le</u> gusta cantar también.*
Who likes to sing with the cat?	*¿<u>A</u> quién <u>le</u> gusta cantar con el gato?*

The noun must have *a* before it when using *gustar: a la reina,* for example. *Le* in the three examples above must also be used before *gustar*. This is nearly untranslatable in English, but it is required in Spanish.

FOCUS 10

Gustar (with object pronoun after an infinitive).

(Literal) To him/her it pleases to sing it.	*Le gusta cantar<u>lo</u>.*
or *He/she likes to sing it.*	NOT **le gusta lo cantar.*
(Literal) To him/her it pleases to drink it.	*Le gusta tomar<u>lo</u>.*
or *He/she likes to drink it.*	NOT: **le gusta <u>lo</u> tomar.*

Translate Orally from and into Spanish

The queen pleases me.	*Me gusta la reina.*
I like the queen.	*Me gusta la reina.*
I like the dogs.	*Me gustan los perros.*
I don't like the queen.	*No me gusta la reina.*
To smoke doesn't please me.	*No me gusta fumar.*

I don't like to drink.	*No me gusta tomar.*
He (or she) likes to sing.	*Le gusta cantar.*
But he doesn't like to sing with the cat.	*Pero no le gusta cantar con el gato.*
Who likes the dog?	*¿A quién le gusta el perro?*
Who likes the cat and the dog?	*¿A quién le gustan el gato y el perro?*
Pablo likes María and Ana.	*A Pablo le gustan María y Ana.*
The dukes eat this.	*Los duques comen esto.*
They like to eat this.	*Les gusta comer esto.*
They don't like to eat it in the tower.	*Pero no les gusta comerlo en la torre.*
Who likes to sing and who likes to dance?	*¿A quién le gusta cantar y a quién le gusta bailar?*
I don't like to drink it.	*No me gusta tomarlo.*
The king pleases the queen.	*A la reina le gusta el rey.*

Note that the word *quiere* ("want") is used differently from *gustar: El rey quiere cantar.* The king wants to sing. *Quiere* follows regular usage for verbs, unlike *gustar.*

THE ADVENTURE CONTINUES

Another message comes over your mitron: We can now give you the rest of the information you will need to enter the labyrinth. When you enter the antechamber, you will see a heavy door. That is the main entrance to el laberinto. To open the door, you must locate the slot in the wall that your disk will fit into. The points, lines and figures on the side of your stone match those in the slot. Place the Disk correctly in the slot and repeat the words "La princesa no está cantando." After you remove your Disk, say the words "Por favor" and the door will open. After you enter, say: "Puntos, líneas y figuras," and the entryway behind you will close and lights will go on. Further instructions will be given you once you reach that point. It would pay for you now to take 30 minutes to look back and review previous material. Make a quick mental list of what you are now able to do in Spanish. Can you count? Ask questions? Tell stories (with a half-hour advanced notice)?, etc. DO THIS NEXT.

Just as you finish your review and are beginning to yawn, the owner of the cottage comes with her son to bring fresh sheets and food, which includes mangos, pineapples, and other tropical fruits full of vitamins and minerals. She prepares a juice blend that you find incredibly delicious. Her son tells you that the ancients on the island claimed that this blend, which they called *jugo de fuerza*— 'juice of strength,' aided the memory. You wink at Stump and say, "Hey, we could sure use that." They continue talking about various things. Whether from the juice or your increased exposure to spoken Spanish, it does seem that you understand more of what they are saying.

After their departure you make your beds and retire for the night with Spanish phrases dancing in your heads, along with visions of a wacky royal ball. Just before falling asleep, you review the formula for entering the cave: (1) *"He aquí la llave del reino del rey;"* then (2) the disk in the proper slot, matching the dots, lines and figures, and the words *"La princesa no está cantando;"* and *"por favor;"* then (3) the words *"Puntos, líneas y figuras."*

You wake up at 4 a.m. ready and eager to take on the mighty challenge of task 34, the final task preparatory to your entering *el laberinto* in pursuit of your quest. You have almost eight hours ahead of you to accomplish these two major tasks. They are truly major and deserve major effort. You'll not claim they are completed until you've given them your best effort.

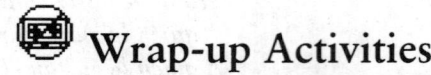 **Wrap-up Activities**

Speak Spanish before You Know It!

READING AND RESPONDING TO QUESTIONS

Instructions: Set yourself to give major effort to these wrap-up activities. Don't rush through them; enjoy them. The payoff will be equal to the effort you invest in them. In preparation, we suggest you take the following steps: (1) Have ready at hand the set of cards or slips of paper on which you have drawn pictographs, (2) Draw each of the question-word pictographs (see below) on a separate card and add these to your earlier set, (3) Any word for which you do not have a convenient representation, you may write on a card or slip of paper and add to the pile.

Question Words and Their Icons

Who? - *¿Quién?* (key-N.)   ↑◆?   (Person)

(To) whom? - *¿A quién?*   ⇒↑◆?   (⇒ arrow to…)

From whom? - *¿De quién?*   ⇐↑◆?   (⇐ arrow from…)

Which? - *¿Cuál?*   ↑?   (stick or torso)

Why? - *¿Por qué?* (for what?)   R?   (R for "reason")

How? - *¿Cómo?*   M?   (M for "manner")

Where? - *¿Dónde?*   @?   (@ for "at")

(To) where? - *¿A dónde?*   ⇒@?   (⇒ arrow to…)

From where? - *¿De dónde?*   ⇐@?   (⇐ arrow from…)

What? - *¿Qué?* ("K")   ▒?   (thing)

When? - *¿Cuándo?*   🗔?

How much? - *¿Cuánto?* $?

What is she doing?   *¿Qué está haciendo ella?*   ▒? ₛ↑?   (s = activity, doing)

With whom is she singing?   *¿Con quién está cantando?*   ♀↑? <k (↑)?

Instructions: Read the story just below, preparing to respond to the questions that follow it.

En esta historia hay (= there is) *un rey y una reina. Este es el rey* 👑 *y ésta es la reina* 👑 .

⬛? *están haciendo ellos? Están cantando. ¿L? están cantando? En la torre. Esta es la torre* 🏰

dónde están cantando ▲👑 *y* ▲👑? *¿*⬛? *clase (= type, kind) de cantos están cantando*

⌣▲🏰? *Cantos fúnebres. ¿Con* ◆? *están cantando? Con Polo y Misti. ¿M? cantan ellos?*

Más o menos bien. ▲👑 *canta mejor que* ▲👑, ▲👑 *canta mejor que el perro, y el perro canta*

mejor que el gato.

Hay una princesa también. Esta es la princesa 👸. *¿Está cantando* 👸? *No, ella no está*

cantando. ¿R? no? Pues ella no canta bien. Canta peor que el perro. ¿Peor que el perro? Sí, peor que

el perro… pero mejor que el gato. ¿⬛? *s* 👸? *¿No está llorando en el baño? ¿*◆? *sabe? ¿R?*

llora 👸 *en el baño? ¿*◆? *sabe? ¿Llora* ▲👑 *con* 👸 *en el baño? Sí, las dos lloran en el*

baño.

Questions

Put the following questions into pictographs. Answer them according to the pictograph answers given. A review of the previous pictographs may be helpful.

Example

Question

¿Qué está haciendo el gato? 😊

Answer

⬛? *s* ▲🐱? *El gato llora.*

1. *¿Qué está haciendo el rey?* 🐑♪

2. *¿Cómo canta el rey?* 🦢

3. *¿Qué está haciendo la reina?* 🐑♪ ✝

4. *¿Cuál canta mejor, el perro o el gato?* 🐕

5. *¿Qué clase de cantos tocaba el rey en el tambor?* ♪🪦

6. *¿Dónde está cantando el rey?* 🏰

7. *¿Con quién está cantando el rey?* 👑

8. *¿Canta él mejor que el perro?* ✔

9. *¿Está cantando la princesa con el rey?* ✔

82

10. *¿Cuál canta peor, el gato o la princesa?*

GENERATING YOUR OWN SENTENCES

Suppose you knew only four nouns, *butcher, baker, dog, cat,* and five possible interactions between them: *hates, loves, catches, ignores, hugs.* Suppose also that you had this simple rule for combining these elements into meaningful statements: Place a noun before an interaction word (a verb), and place a noun after the verb. Here is a combination chart of those elements. (Pick any item in column 1, then any in column 2, then any in column 3, and say them in that order 1-2-3.)

Sentence-Generation Chart

1 Agent (noun)	2 Impact (verb)	3 Patient (noun)
The butcher	hates	the dog.
The baker	loves	the cat.
The dog	catches	the butcher.
The cat	ignores	the baker.
	hugs	

Here are some sample sentences from this sentence "machine": The butcher ignores the baker. The cat loves the butcher. The dog catches the butcher.

To string into a story line several sentence combinations from this chart, you need give attention only to the logic or the story possibilities of the sequence. Here, for example, is a story line: The baker loves the cat. The baker loves the dog. The dog hates the cat. The cat hates the dog. The dog catches the cat. The dog ignores the cat. The baker hates the dog.

A language learner gains much by practicing telling such stories (and longer ones) fluently and expressively.

Here is some help in organizing your own sentence machine, one that will be much more powerful than the chart shown above. And from the statements you can form various combinations. From the various combinations of words, you can create stories.

Sentence and Discourse Functions You Know How to Express

ACTOR/PATIENT NOUNS: *rey, reina, princesa, gato (reyes, reinas, princesas, gatos)*

MODIFIERS: *el, la, un, una, este, esta (los, las, estes, estas)*

PRONOUNS: *ella, él (ellos, ellas)*

LOCATION NOUNS: *baño, torre*

LOCATION OR ACCOMPANIMENT: *en, con*

ACTION-VERB STEMS: *cant-, llor-, toc-*

ACTION-VERB ENDINGS: *-a(n), -aba(n), -ando*

AUXILIARY VERB: *está(n)*

MANNER: *mejor / peor (que); (muy) bien, mal*

INFORMATION QUESTION WORDS: *¿Qué? ¿Quién? ¿Dónde? ¿Cómo? ¿Cuál? ¿Por qué?*

ANSWERS OR REJOINDERS: *Sí. No. ¡Imagínese!*
OTHER WORDS: *y, pero, también*

Arrange your cards in separate piles according to the categories listed above.

Instructions. Using the words listed above (represented by your pictographs on cards), do the following:

1. Take three actor nouns and three action-verb stems, like {*rey*} and {*llor-*}. By adding the proper grammatical details, make up three quick sentences on the model of *El rey llora.*

2. Make your three sentences plural, on the model *Los reyes lloran.* (Be sure to put the plural-marker *-n* on the action word.)

3. Turn these sentences into yes-no questions by reversing the noun and the verb on the model of *¿Llora el rey?* (the reverse of *El rey llora*).

4. Turn the sentences into who-questions or where-questions as in *¿Quién llora? ¿Dónde llora la reina?*

5. Change the sentences to what-action questions as in *¿Qué hace el rey?* or *¿Qué hacen las princesas?*

6. Make three new sentences by joining two actors as sentence subject, on the model *El rey y la reina lloran.* (Be sure to put the plural marker *-n* on the action word.)

7. Expand your last three sentences by adding a location phrase *(en...)* and a "with" phrase *(con...)* on the model *El rey y la reina lloran en la torre con el gato.*

8. Choosing from this material, make up equally complex or even more complex sentences of your own.

CREATING YOUR OWN MINISTORY PLOTS

You're now urged to create your own ministory plots, to plan them out — perhaps even write them — then give them orally, aiming for a smooth flow of speech without hesitation. It will be wise to limit yourself to words you know, supplemented by a selection of a few additional words given below. Give this your best effort. The creating and telling of stories (or ministory plots) will play a major role in your learning to speak Spanish.

Instructions: (1) Write each of the new words below on a separate card and put the cards in their appropriate piles, (2) select certain cards that together can form meaningful statements and arrange them in the order you want, (3) aim at performing your story plots orally without reading. Aim at smooth-flowing diction. Caution: limit yourself to the words you know, supplemented by a selection of the additional words and phrases given here. (An example of a ministory plot is given at the end of this vocabulary.)

New Vocabulary

Subjects or Agents of Action

preacher	*predicador, predicadora*	helper	*(el/la) ayudante*
dancer	*bailador, bailadora*	actress	*(la) actriz*
director	*director, directora*	actor	*(el) actor*
trombone player	*(el/la) trombonista*	doctor	*(el) médico*
violinist	*(el/la) violinista*	chief, boss	*(el/la) jefe*
drummer	*(el/la) tambor*	commander	*(el/la) comandante*
secretary	*(el/la) secretaria*	teacher	*profesor, profesora*
student	*(el/la) estudiante*	person	*persona*

Action without Impact on Anyone Else (Intransitive Verbs)

enters	*entra*	relaxes	*relaja*
exits	*sale*	dances	*baila*
dies	*muere*	sleeps	*duerme*

Action with Impact on Persons or Things (Transitive Verbs)

attacks	*ataca*	observes	*observe*
defends	*defiende*	prepares	*prepara*
detests	*detesta*	studies	*estudia*
loves	*ama*	cures	*cura*
accepts	*acepta*	helps	*ayuda*
receives	*recibe*	insults	*insulta*
fabricates	*fabrica*	practices	*practica*
preaches	*predica*	commands/sends	*manda*

Settings

Place:	school/*escuela*	theater/*teator*	church/*iglesia*
Time:	one day/*un día*	one night/*una noche*	

CONCRETE OBJECTS AND ASSOCIATED VERBS

a document
The secretary <u>prepares</u> a document.

un documento
La secretaria <u>prepara</u> un documento.

a sermon
The preacher <u>preaches</u> a sermon at church.

un sermón
El predicador <u>predica</u> un sermón en la iglesia.

a package
The trombonist <u>receives</u> a package from the violinist.

un paquete
El trombonista <u>recibe</u> un paquete de la violinista.

a letter
The chief <u>sends</u> a letter to the actress.

una carta
El jefe <u>manda</u> una carta a la actriz.

the lesson
The student <u>studies</u> the lesson in school.

la lección
La estudiante <u>estudia</u> la lección en la escuela.

the cause
The helper <u>helps</u> the cause.

la causa ("cow-sa")
El ayudante <u>ayuda</u> la causa.

Sample Beginning of a Mini-story Plot

Below is the beginning of a story based on some of the vocabulary that was presented above. A translation is found in the appendix.

1. *Hay tres personas: un trombonista, una violinista, y un tambor.* 2. *El trombonista ama a la violinista.* 3. *Pero la violinista no ama al trombonista.* 4. *Ella odia...detesta al trombonista.* 5. *La violinista ama al tambor.* 6. *Pero el tambor no ama a la violinista.* 7. *El ama a una actriz.* 8. *El tambor canta y baila con la actriz.* 9. *El manda cartas a la actriz, y la actriz manda cartas al tambor.* 10. *Un día el trombonista manda una carta a la violinista.* 11. *La violinista recibe la carte del trombonista.* 12. *La violinista ataca al trombonista.*

Now create plots of your own — several each day. It may help to begin by selecting some of your pictographs and laying them out in front of you, subjects in one group, action verbs in another, etc. You don't need to create great pieces of fiction, just string statements together in some meaningful order. The more statements you can weave into each story, the better. Write two or more stories on paper, but then tell them without reading. Or better yet, sit back and relax, letting your mind spin off meaningful strings of statements that form a story line. In telling your stories out loud, aim for fluency of delivery, imitating a Spanish accent as well as you can.

THE ADVENTURE CONTINUES

Fifteen minutes before noon you head out to the park near the castle, taking with you a canteen full of *jugo de fuerza*. Standing near the biggest tree a few feet from the castle at exactly twelve noon, you repeat the words *"He aquí la llave del reino del rey."* You watch as an opening forms in the wall of the castle. You enter the antechamber and find several niches in the stone that look like they could be the slot for your disk, but on examination, only one has markings that match the dots, lines and figures embossed on the edge. You insert the disk and repeat the words: *"La princesa está cantando,"* and then remove your disk, say *"Por favor,"* and wait. Nothing happens!

Stump says: "Try it again, only this time with the negative word, the way she told you."

"Thanks, Stump, you're right. Where would we be without you!?" You insert the Disk again and this time say, *"La princesa no está cantando."* Then, when you remove the disk and say, *"Por favor,"* the huge door grinds its way open. You and Stump push the door the rest of the way open and, then turn around and say, *"Puntos, líneas y figuras,"* at which signal lights go on and the door slams shut with a jarring thump that reverberates through the tunnel. Controlling your fears, you wonder what you are to do next.

A message comes through on Mitron: You are now in the staging room, ready to enter the labyrinth itself. Be warned that the invaders have entered the labyrinth and are after the treasure. Without the map, their efforts are not a threat. The slam of the door can be heard throughout the labyrinth. They are no doubt aware that you just entered, and we must assume they know you must have the map. Given this unsettling situation, we have decided on a strategy. You are to cut the map in two. Each of you is to take half—Rump the west half and Stump the east. Before you can cut the map in half, though, you must complete task 35.

🔲 Toward Fluency 3

WORDS AND PATTERNS 1

a gentleman	*un señor*	You were	*Usted era*
the gentleman	*el señor*	I was	*Yo era*
a young lady	*una señorita*	It was me.	*Era yo.*
the young lady	*la señorita*	of the princess	*de la princesa*
lady	*señora*	of the prince	*del príncipe*
a friend <u>who</u>...	*un amigo <u>que</u>...*	I believe so.	*Creo que sí.*
he/she was	*él/ella era*	I believe not.	*Creo que no.*

Sample Sentences

You know who Albert was, don't you?	*Usted sabe quien era Alberto, ¿no?*
I know that he was a prince.	*Sé que él era un príncipe.*
He was the prince who was the friend of Anita.	*El era el príncipe que era amigo de Anita.*
And do you know who Richard was?	*¿Y sabe quien era Ricardo?*
I believe he was a friend of the princess.	*Creo que él era amigo de la princesa.*
Was he a friend of the prince too?	*¿Era amigo del príncipe también?*
No, he wasn't. For certain he wasn't.	*No, no era. Es cierto que no era.*
Who is it that was the prince's friend?	*¿Quién es que era amigo del príncipe?*
Wasn't it the gentleman from Verona?	*¿No era el señor de Verona?*
Who was it? Was it you? Yes, it was me.	*¿Quién era? ¿Era usted? Sí, era yo.*
Wasn't it him? No, sir, it was her.	*¿No era él? No, señor, era ella.*
Who is it? It's me/I am I, Don Quixote.	*¿Quién es? Soy yo, Don Quijote.*

🔲 Rapid Oral Translation Exercise 1

Translate the following sentences into Spanish. Check your answers in the appendix.

1. Rolando <u>was</u> a prince and <u>is</u> a prince.
2. Richard <u>was</u> not a prince and <u>is</u> not a prince.
3. José is a friend of Juanita, who is a princess.
4. Josephina's friend isn't a princess.
5. Pedro's friend was a prince, yes.
6. He was from Spain, and he was a friend of your mother. Maria too, right?
7. Who is Juanita? She's the princess who was Jose's friend.
8. You were a friend of José, right? Yes, I was a friend of the prince and the princess, but I was not Josephine's friend.
9. Was she an enemy? Yes, she was.
10. Yes, we're enemies. She <u>was</u> my enemy and she still <u>is</u> my enemy.

Review

1. Go through the previous oral translation exercises in the "Toward Fluency" chapters, aiming for rapid, smooth delivery. Speak with expression and confidence. Imagine you are telling a story to children.

2. Close your eyes, breathe deeply, and relax, letting your mind create sentences made up of material from this lesson module. See how many meaningful statements you can generate from this material in two minutes. Keep a tally. Par is fifteen statements in two minutes. Can you beat par?

⌚ First two-minute trial: _____ statements   ⌚ Second two-minute trial: _____ statements

⌚ Third two-minute trial: _____ statements   ⌚ Fourth two-minute trial: _____ statements

📼 WORDS AND PATTERNS 2

Where is...?	*¿Dónde está...?*	in the hospital	*en el hospital*
Where is the house?	*¿Dónde está la casa?*	in the garden	*en el jardín*
He, she, or it is here.	*Está aquí.*	in the house	*en la casa*
Where was...?	*¿Dónde estaba...?*	at home	*en casa*
Where was the house?	*¿Dónde estaba la casa?*	now	*ahora*
He, she, or it was here.	*Estaba aquí.*	Not now.	*Ahora no.*

Sample Sentences

Where is she? She's in the house.	*¿Dónde está ella? Está en la casa.*
But the prince is not at home.	*Pero el príncipe no está en casa.*
Is it certain he is not [there]?	*¿Es cierto que él no está?*
Where is he?	*¿Dónde está él?*
Is he here now?	*¿Está aquí ahora?*
Not now. He's not here; he's there.	*Ahora no. El no está aquí; está allá.*
Was she there?	*¿Estaba ella allá?*
No, she was not there; she was here.	*No, no estaba allá; estaba aquí.*

📼 Contrast the use of the verb:

El <u>es</u> de España. El <u>es</u> un amigo.   BUT NOT: *El <u>está</u> de España. El <u>está</u> un amigo.*
El <u>está</u> aquí.   BUT NOT: *El <u>es</u> aquí.*

"To be (located somewhere)" takes the "to be" verb *estar*.
"To be (originated from somewhere)" and "to be (a friend)" take the verb *ser*.

Rapid Oral Translation Exercise 2

Translate the following sentences into Spanish. Check your answers in the appendix.

1. Where is the prince? Where is he from?
2. Do you know if he is from Spain?
3. Do you know if he is at home now?
4. Is the gentleman in the house?
5. Was the gentleman in the house?
6. Is the gentleman at home?
7. Was the gentleman home?
8. Where is the lady? Is she in the garden?
9. Where was the lady? Was she in the hospital?
10. The young lady who was here is not my friend.
11. Roberto is my friend, but he was not here.
12. Who was here and who was there?
13. Who was your friend (m) and who was your enemy (m)?

Review

1. Go through the oral translation exercises again, aiming for fluency. Speak with expression and confidence. Imagine you are telling a story to children.

2. Close your eyes, breathe deeply, and relax, letting your mind create sentences made up of material from this lesson module. See how many meaningful statements you can generate from this material in two minutes. Par is sixteen statements in two minutes. Can you beat par?

⌚ First two-minute trial: _____ statements   ⌚ Second two-minute trial: _____ statements

⌚ Third two-minute trial: _____ statements   ⌚ Fourth two-minute trial: _____ statements

THE ADVENTURE CONTINUES

"Done," you report, and continue listening:

There are two routes through the labyrinth to the inner chamber where the treasure is located. Each route has 42 chambers to challenge you—42 to reach the threshold of the innermost chamber—and to get back out —well, we'll give you more information on that once you gain entry to that key chamber.

"Got it. Forty-two steps to get there...and then do what we were sent here to do, then get back out, right?"

Right. Stump, you will take the east route, Rump will take the west. The portion of the map you each carry refers only to the route your partner must take. Let me put that in other words: your portion of the map will only help you guide your partner by communication with each other via your Mitron. Each of you, then, is dependent on the other. You cannot make it through alone. We felt it necessary to do this as a protection against the invaders, who, if they find you, will be determined to wrest the map from you.

"Can you give us any idea of what the treasure is?" you ask.

Yes, it is time for you to know what we suspect. The ancient inhabitants of the island, it seems, possessed some kind of health formula. It was a drink they called "juice of strength." One legend has it that those who drank the juice became immune to many sicknesses that afflicted others. Finding the drink is important to us because of the possibility that this drink will contain the missing properties needed to cure diseases such as cancer and MS.

Your heart jumps. You and Stump look at each other with amazement. You respond immediately, "Hold on a second! We might know something about that. They have a juice drink here by that name, and we were told it was an ancient concoction, believed to strengthen one's memory power...or something like that. Tell us more. We're all ears!"

On February 14th of this year, researchers discovered that some 300 years ago enemies of the inhabitants invaded the island in search of the formula, but, according to the legend, the king of the island managed to hide it deep inside a labyrinthine cave and it has never been found. An imitation blend by the same name is still on the island, but it lacks the ingredients and the properties claimed for the ancient drink.

"Yes, go on."

It appears that a certain powerful coalition of "interests" have suddenly taken the legend very seriously and are in pursuit of the formula. We are convinced that they will pay any price to obtain it. It is their agents who are the invaders!

You interrupt the transmission. "Why in the world are these companies in particular after this formula? "

They are convinced that the ancient formula, if it can be found, could help people overcome addiction to nicotine and other substances and make it so no one would ever have any desire to use them. The companies, in turn, would no longer make money.

"Wait a minute, are you thinking the formula *we* are after can really do that?"

It's possible. Our scientists have made computer projections of combinations of chemical compounds discovered in the juice of certain tropical fruits, including some we don't even have a name for that are—or used to be—found on that island. In combination with elements found only in horseradish and aloe vera oil, a certain blend of the juice of these fruits might do exactly what these companies fear—put them out of business!

"So, do I understand that the "treasure" we were sent here to obtain is the formula for this juice blend?"

That is correct. But there may be more. There is a missing piece to the puzzle. We suspect that there is—or was—a plant, perhaps unique to the island, that provides a critical element of the formula. Botanists have searched for it, but have found nothing that fits exactly. Three-hundred years ago it was a vanishing species, and now it is most likely extinct. It was a kind of cactus with a rose-like flower very similar to the cactus found on the Mexican flag. It is hoped that you will find out if it exists, and if it does, that you will obtain at least one of its seeds.

Now it is time to move ahead. You have your map pieces and the glasses. From now on, the requirements for each step forward will be found on your map, but visible only when you are wearing the glasses. One of you has the disk, and between you, you have the tiny jars of horseradish and aloe vera oil. And every bit as important as any of these, you have the Spanish you have acquired, plus a readiness for acquiring more. Really, the key to your progress is present in the Spanish you already know or will be learning. Also, the key to protection against the invaders will be found in the Spanish you know or will be learning.

Your companion's success in reaching the goal is in your hands—and vice versa. It won't help for just one of you to reach it, you must both reach it. Now say a prayer. Stump, you enter the tunnel now on the east end of the chamber where you are. Rump, you enter the tunnel on the west end, headed west. Report back here to your base when you have reached the threshold of the first chamber. Good luck.

You've each made your way through your tunnels into *el laberinto* and are standing at the threshold of your first chamber. At that point you make contact with home base, report that you have reached the threshold of chamber 1. You are both told to complete task 36 (More on the Alphabet) and report to base.

36

📼 More on the Alphabet

Más acerca del Alfabeto

LOS NOMBRES DE LAS CONSONANTES EN ESPAÑOL

La pronunciación de los nombres de las consonantes es así:

B	C	D	F	G	H	J	K
be-grande	ce	de	efe	ge	hache	jota	ka

L	LL	M	N	Ñ	P	Q	R
ele	elle	eme	ene	eñe	pe	qu	ere

RR	S	T	V	W	X	Y	Z
erre	ese	te	be-corta	doble-ve	equis	i-griega	zeta

La primera letra del alfabeto no es una consonante sino una vocal—la vocal <A>. <A> no es una consonante, ni en inglés ni en español. <A> siempre es una vocal.

La última letra del alfabeto no es una vocal sino una consonante—la consonante <Z>. <Z> no es una vocal, ni en inglés ni en español. <Z> siempre es una consonante.

En otras palabras, <A> es la primera letra del alfabeto romano y es una vocal, y <Z> es la última letra del alfabeto romano y es una consonante.

Despues de la letra <A> viene la letra <B>, y despues de la <B> viene la <C>. Antes de la letra <N> viene la letra <M>, y antes de la <M> viene la <L>. ¿Cuál letra viene antes de la <L>? La <K>. ¿Cuál letra viene entre la <A> y la <C>? La letra <B> viene entre la <A> y la <C>. Y la <C> viene entre la <B> y la <D>, ¿no?

En el alfabeto español, la letra <M> viene antes de la <N> y la <N> antes de la <Ñ>. Estos sonidos nasales son los únicos en el alfabeto. ¿Cuántas consonantes nasales hay en el alfabeto? Tres. ¿Y cuáles son? La <M>, la <N>, y la <Ñ>. ¿Cuál viene primero en el alfabeto? La letra <M> viene primero. La <O> viene después de la <Ñ> y no después de la <N>, como en el alfabeto del inglés. De estas cuatro letras, la <M>, la < N>, la < Ñ> y la <O>, ¿cuál es una vocal?

¿Es la <Y> siempre una consonante? No, no siempre. Ordinariamente la <Y> sirve como una consonante.

En las palabras ya, yeso, yo, yuca, por ejemplo, la <Y> sirve como una consonante. Pero en la palabra Y que significa "and," la <Y> es una vocal. Y en las palabras soy y doy, la <Y> es una semivocal—como en inglés.

Las letras <K> y <W> no son letras ordinarias del español. Estas letras—la <K> y la <W>—no ocurren en palabras de origen español. El alfabeto del inglés tiene dos letras nasales: la <M> y la <N>. El alfabeto del español tiene tres letras nasales: Las dos que hay en inglés más la letra <Ñ>.

La <D> más la <O> más la <S> construye la palabra dos. *La primera letra de* dos *es la <D>; la <O> es la segunda, y la <S> es la tercera y última letra.*

En el alfabeto, ningúna letra viene antes de la letra <A> y ningúna letra viene después de la <Z>. Es decir, la <A> es la primera letra y la <Z> es la última letra del alfabeto. Aquí se ve el alfabeto.

Aa, Bb, Cc, Dd, Ee, Ff, Gg, Hh, Ii, Jj, Kk, Ll, LLll, Mm, Nn, Ññ, Oo, Pp, Qq, Rr, RRrr, Ss, Tt, Uu, Vv, Xx, Yy, Zz

Nótese que cada letra tiene dos formas, la forma mayúscula y la forma minúscula. Las letras mayúsculas son más grandes que las letras minúsculas. Las letras mayúsculas se usan con nombres de personas en la posición inicial. Por ejemplo, mi nombre es Carlos. *Así se escribe mi nombre:* Carlos. *Nótese que la <C> inicial se escribe con mayúscula, pero las otras letras se escriben con minúscula.*

Todas las letras, sean mayúsculas o minúsculas, se pueden escribir en letra de bloque o en letra cursiva. Por ejemplo, aquí está mi nombre escrito en letra de bloque: Carlos. *Aquí en letra cursiva:*

Carlos

THE ADVENTURE CONTINUES

Having completed your tasks, you can advance.

You report, "Both now in Chamber 2. Forty steps from Target."

Instructions on your maps indicate that your partner can negotiate chambers 3 and 4 by carefully working through tasks 39 (Much Communication with Limited Means) and 40 (Speed Learning). The instructions call for an investment of **at least** 45 minutes. You transmit that message to Stump. In turn you receive the message that you can gain entry to chambers 3 and 4 by working carefully through tasks 37 (A Geography Lesson) and 38 (*De la palabra al discurso.*) You are to concentrate on it for **at least** 45 minutes and learn all you can from it. Estimated time = 45–55 minutes. You both set about your tasks.

37

A Geography Lesson
Una Lección de Geografía

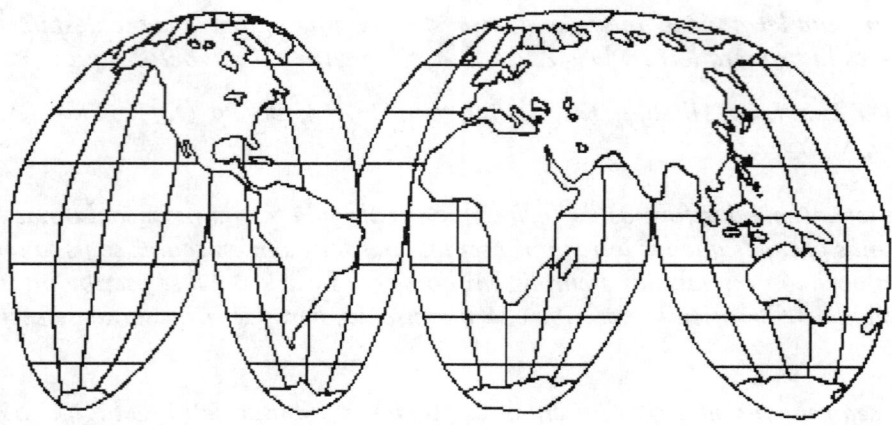

Here is a map of the world.	*He aquí un mapa del mundo.*
The earth is our spaceship.	*La tierra es nuestra nave espacial.*
It is one of nine planets that revolve around the sun.	*Es uno de los nueve planetas que giran alrededor del sol.*
Most of the surface of the earth is covered with water.	*La mayoría de la superficie de la tierra está cubierta de agua.*
There are three great oceans:	*Hay tres océanos grandes:*
the Pacific Ocean, the Atlantic Ocean, and the Indian Ocean.	*el océano Pacífico, el océano Atlántico, y el océano Indico.*
Here is the Pacific Ocean.	*Aquí está el océano Pacífico.*
It is the largest ocean.	*Es el océano más grande.*
Also the deepest.	*También el más profundo.*
Here is the Atlantic Ocean.	*Aquí está el océano Atlántico.*
It is situated between Europe and North America, also between Africa and South America.	*Está situado entre Europa y Norte America, también entre Africa y Sud America.*
Here is the Indian Ocean, which extends from Africa to Australia and touches Arabia and India.	*Aquí está el océano Indico, que se extiende de Africa hasta Australia y toca Arabia e India.*
The largest continent in the world extends from Europe to China.	*El continente más grande del mundo se extiende de Europa hasta la China.*
It is called Eurasia.	*Se llama Eurasia.*
This continent here is Africa.	*Este continente (aquí) es Africa.*
Africa is large, but it's not so large as Eurasia.	*Africa es grande, pero no es tan grande como Eurasia.*
Here on the other side of the Atlantic is situated another great continent, the one called South America.	*Aquí al otro lado del Atlántico está situado otro continente, el que se llama Sud América.*
And here is found the largest river in the world.	*Y aquí se halla el rio más grande del mundo.*
It is called the Amazon River.	*Se llama el rio Amazonas.*

38

 *De la Palabra al Discurso*

From Word to Discourse

This activity is entirely tape-off. From this scatter chart you can string together innumerable series of sentences. Sample strings are given below.

Instructions: Review previous scatter charts and sample sentences. Then carefully examine the following scatter chart and sample sentences.

SCATTER CHART

¿*verdad?*

es / son   *hay* (pronounced "eye")

ésta(s)[1]   *ésa(s)*[2]

(*no*) *está(n) parada(s)*
(*no*) *está(n) acostada(s)*

(*no*) *está(n) aquí*
(*no*) *está(n) allí* [pronounced *ayi* or "all *ye*"]

una(s)   *toda(s)*   *otra(s)*

cosa(s)   varilla(s)

pero   *y*

blanca(s)   *negra(s)*   *colorada(s)*

la(s)
chica(s)   *grande(s)*
        corta(s)   *larga(s)*

también   *sí*   *no*   *sobre*

[1] In Spanish, you'll encounter *esta*, *ésta*, and *está*. The first, *esta*, means "this" and is used before a noun: *esta cosa* ("this thing"). The second, *ésta*, means "this one" and is used by itself: *Sí, ésta es blanca* ("Yes , this one is white"). The third, *está*, is a form of the "be" verb: *La cosa blanca está sobre la cosa negra* ("The white thing is on the black thing"). Remember, accents are typically dropped when the letter is capitalized: *ésta*, *Esta*.

[2] Like *esta* and *ésta*, *esa* and *ésa* follow the same usage: *esa cosa* ("that thing") and *Sí, ésa es blanca* ("Yes, that one is white").

English Equivalent

is that so?

        is/are   there is/are (pronounced "eye")

this one   that one

                                  is/isn't standing (compare *parada* to "parade")

                                    is/isn't lying down

        is/isn't here

    is/isn't there

          a   all   others

             things   rod(s) or stick(s)

                pero   y

white   black   red

        the

small, little   big

        short   large

also   yes   no   on, on top of

Sample Sentences

The sentences with asterisks are incorrect.

1.   There is a rod, a white rod.
     Hay una varilla, una varilla blanca.

2.   There is another rod, a black rod.
     Hay otra varilla, una varilla negra.

3.   This rod is black; that one is white.
     Esta varilla es negra; ésa es blanca.

4.   And this one is long, but that one is short.
     Y ésta es larga, pero ésa es corta.
      *Y esta una es larga, pero esa una es corta.

5.   These ones are long, but those ones are short.
     Estas son largas, pero ésas son cortas.

6.   Is this black rod short?
     ¿Es corta esta varilla negra?
      *¿Es esta negra varilla corta?

7.   No, this one is long.
     No, ésta es larga.

8.   Is that one also long? Yes, that one is long too.
     It's long.
     ¿Es larga ésa también? Sí, ésa es larga también. Es larga.

9.   A black rod on a white rod.
     Una varilla negra sobre una varilla blanca.

10. The black rod is on the white rod.
     La varilla negra está sobre la varilla blanca.

11. It is a short rod.
     Es una varilla corta.

12. This black rod and this white one are short.
     Esta varilla negra y esta blanca son cortas.
      *Esta varilla negra y esta blanca son corta.

13. That black rod and that white one are long.
     Esa varilla negra y esa blanca son largas.
      *Esa varilla negra y esa blanca <u>una</u> son largas.

14. This short rod is standing on the black rod.
     Esta varilla corta está parada sobre la varilla negra.

15. This other rod is also here, standing on the black rod.
     Esta otra varilla tambien está aquí, parada sobre la varilla negra.

16. Some white rods are standing on the black rod.	*Unas varillas blancas están paradas sobre la varilla negra.* **Varillas blancas están parad...*
17. The black rod is long, but...	*La varilla negra es larga, pero...*
18. The white rods are short.	*Las varillas blancas son cortas.* **Las varillas blanca son corta.*
19. All the white rods are standing.	*Todas las varillas blancas están paradas.* **Toda la varillas blancas están parada.*
20. The black rod is lying there.	*La varilla negra está acostada allí.*
21. These two white rods are standing, but these two are lying.	*Estas dos varillas están paradas, pero estas dos están acostadas.* **... pero estas dos están acostada.*
22. These black rods are long, but these white rods are short, right?	*Estas varillas negras son largas, pero estas varillas blancas son cortas, ¿verdad?*
23. One is short, and the others are long.	*(La) una es corta y las otras son largas.*
24. Are all the black rods long? No, there are long ones and short ones.	*¿Son largas todas las varillas negras? No, hay unas largas y unas cortas.*
25. Are the white rods black? No, the white rods are white, and the black rods are black.	*¿Son negras las varillas blancas? No, las varillas blancas son blancas, y las varillas negras son negras.*
26. The white ones are here; the black ones are there.	*Las blancas están aquí, las negras están allí.*
27. Two white ones lying on one black one.	*Dos blancas acostadas sobre una negra.*

Practice Translation

Instructions: Look at the twenty-seven sentences above again, but cover the Spanish with your hand or a piece of paper. Translate them into Spanish and check your version with the version next to it.

Challenge

Compose fifteen sentences using the words in this scatter chart. One way to do this is to look at the chart and string together words that make meaningful and well-formed sentences. Work toward fluency.

THE ADVENTURE CONTINUES

Having completed your tasks you report, "Both now in Chamber 4. Thirty-eight steps from Target."

Instructions on your maps for negotiating chambers 5 and 6 require that you and Stump trade tasks. He does 37 and 38, while you do 39 and 40. Then you are to both do 41 (Chatter at a Royal Ball).

Note: If any task is, at the time, too steep for you to carry out, you may substitute a task within your reach: an extra hour of review, or better, a performance of something you have worked up, or can work up on your own.

Estimated time = 45-55 minutes.

 **Much Communication with Limited Means**

Give this thirty minutes of quiet (tape-off) concentration. It presents simple ways of saying useful things. First, look over the following words and then try understanding the Spanish sentences.

para	for, for the purpose of	*pero*	but
allá	there	*sin*	without
trabajar	to work, working	*vivir*	to live, living (compare "vivid," "vivify")
comer	to eat, eating	*poder*	to be able, being able (compare "power")
estar contento	to be happy	*dormir*	to sleep, sleeping (compare "dorm")
estar malcontento	to be unhappy	*reposar*	to rest, resting (compare "repose")
bien	well	*mucho*	much, a lot

Hay que	One must (you have to, it's necessary to)
Es estupido	(It) is stupid
Es (im)posible	It is (im)possible

USEFUL SPANISH SENTENCES

Get the meaning of the following sentences.

1. *Hay que trabajar allá.*
2. *Hay que trabajar mucho allá.*
3. *Hay que trabajar sin reposar y sin comer.*
4. *Hay que trabajar para comer.*
5. *Hay que trabajar bien para vivir bien.*

6. *Hay que trabajar bien para estar contento.*
7. *Hay que comer mucho para poder trabajar mucho.*

8. *Hay que dormir bien para poder trabajar bien.*
9. *Hay que trabajar para poder estar contento.*
10. *Trabajar es vivir.*
11. *Vivir es comer.*
12. *Trabajar sin poder dormir es vivir sin poder estar contento.*
13. *Es imposible trabajar sin reposar y sin comer.*
14. *Reposar sin dormir es posible.*

Equivalents of Spanish Sentences

In case you have doubts, here are the same sentences in English. Translate these back into Spanish.

1. One has to work there.
2. You have to work a lot there.

3. It's necessary to work without resting and without eating.
4. You have to work in order to eat.
5. One has to work well in order to live well.

6. It's necessary to work well in order to be happy.
7. You have to eat a lot in order to be able to work a lot.

8. You have to sleep well in order to work well.
9. One has to work in order to be able to be happy.
10. To work is to live (or, working is living).
11. To live is to eat (or, living is eating).
12. To work without being able to sleep is to live without being able to be happy.
13. It is impossible to work without resting and without eating.
14. It's possible to rest without sleeping (or, resting without sleeping is possible).

Translation Exercise

Create the Spanish equivalents of the following sentences. The answers are in the appendix.

1. Eating is living.
2. Sleeping is impossible there (or, it is impossible to sleep there).
3. Working without being happy is impossible there (or, it is impossible to work there without being happy).
4. It is stupid to eat a lot in order to sleep well (or, eating a lot in order to sleep well is stupid).
5. It is impossible to sleep without resting, but it is possible to rest without sleeping.
6. It is possible to work without resting, but it is stupid.

BONUS—SPELLING RULES OF COGNATE WORDS

In many cognate words—words that are very similar in different languages—double letters in English correspond to single letters in Spanish:

bb > b	*a*b*reviación, sa*b*ado* (compare "Sabbath")
cc > c	*o*c*upación, a*c*omodación, a*c*eptar, a*c*umulación*
dd > d	*a*d*ición*
ff > f	*e*f*ecto, a*f*licción*
gg > g	*a*g*resor, a*g*ravación*
ll > l	*i*l*usión, co*l*ección*
mm > m	*co*m*entario, aco*m*odación*
nn > n	*co*n*ección, a*n*ual*
pp > p	*o*p*resión*
ss > s	*mi*s*ión impo*s*ible, a*s*ociación, nece*s*ario*
tt > t	*a*t*ención, a*t*ractiva*

In many cognate words, consonant clusters are reduced to a single consonant:

ct > t	*respe*t*able*
ph > f	*f*oto, ele*f*ante, geogra*f*ía, pro*f*eta*
ks > j	*comple*j*o* (complex)

40

◉ Speed Learning
A Fifteen-Minute Workshop

◉ Give this lesson fifteen minutes of quiet concentration. It will help you expand your ability to ask questions. First review the question words you learned previously. Also review the iconic symbols used to represent these meanings.

¿Quién?	*¿A quién?*		*¿Cuál?* *¿Por qué?*		*¿Cómo?*		*¿Dónde?*	
¿Qué? *¿De dónde?*		*¿De quién?*	*¿Cuándo?*		*¿Cuánto?*		*¿A dónde?*	
▦?	R?	P?	⇒P?	M?	↑?	¡?	•?	⇒↑? x? L? T? ⇐↑?
⇐@?	⇒@?	Qm?	⇐P?	⇒L?	$?	T?	@? ⇐L?

Here are some additional question words and phrases you can tie to the ones you already know.

How many?	**Q**s**?**	*¿Cuantos?/¿Cuántas?*
How often? (with what frequency)	**F**r**?**	*¿Con qué frecuéncia?* [freh<u>kwen</u>sya]
For what (purpose)?	**P**ur**?**	*¿Para qué?*
Since when?	**T**⇒**?**	*¿Desde cuándo?* [dezz-day]
At what hour?	**H?**	*¿A qué hora?* [a kay <u>ora</u>]
What kind/what class of...?	**CL?**	*¿Qué clase de...?*

Stop for a moment to set these in memory. Then take time to role-play. Use hand motions and facial expressions that will communicate the ideas for which you lack vocabulary. For example, someone asks you to get some gentlemen and ladies to help them. Using your fingers as counters, you ask, *¿Cuantos señores? ¿Cuantas señoras?* Do this now. Then imagine situations where the other new questions would be appropriate.

SELF-QUIZ

1. Match the symbols with the Spanish words below. Remember that there are two icons for some of the question words.

H?	▦?	Pur?	R?	T?	$?	Fr?
T⇒?	L?	⇐@?	Qs?	Qm?	•?	CL?

¿A qué hora?   *¿Para qué?*   *¿Por qué?*   *¿Cuándo?*   *¿Con qué frecuéncia?*
¿Desde cuándo?   *¿Dónde?*   *¿De dónde?*   *¿Cuántas?*   *¿Cuánto?*   *¿Qué?*   *¿Qué clase de?*

2. Look only at the symbols and see if you can give their equivalents in Spanish.

3. Create several questions of your own, using these high-utility words.

41

📼 Chatter at a Royal Ball

🔲 PREPARATION FOR CONVERSATION

nor, not either	—┼	*tampoco*		never	—T	*nunca*
Really! / Indeed!	✔!	*De veras*		or	~	*o*
How strange!	¡—!	*¡Qué extraño!*		both	2	*los dos / las dos*
nothing more, only	Ø	*no más*		now	↓T	*ahora*
(he/she) goes	b	*va*		right away	T↓	*ahorita*
(he/she's) going to	b	*va a*		soon	T..↓	*pronto*
but	⌐	*sino* (correcting a negative)		no longer	—•T	*ya no*
still, yet	>T>	*todavía* (toda vía "all [the] way")				
already	•T	*ya* ("a point before present time")				

Sample Sentences

He's going to sing soon.	*El pronto va a cantar.*
Carlos no longer sings.	*Carlos ya no canta.*
Jose doesn't sing. Juan doesn't either. Me neither.	*José no canta. Juan tampoco. Yo tampoco.*
<u>Not</u> a king <u>but</u> a duke.	<u>No</u> un rey. <u>sino</u> un duque.
The duke sings. The duchess too.	*El duque canta. La duquesa también.*

🔲 CONVERSATION 4

•:	Now the king isn't playing but singing.	*Ahora el rey no está tocando sino cantando.*
••:	Yes, the king is only singing.	*Sí. El rey está cantando no más.*
	It's the queen that is playing.	*Es la reina que está tocando.*
•:	Doesn't the king play anymore?	*¿Ya no toca el rey?*
••:	Yes, he still plays, but now he's not playing.	*Sí, todavía toca, pero ahora no está tocando.*
•:	Is he going to play soon?	*¿Va a tocar pronto?*
••:	Yes, right away.	*Sí, ahorita.*
•:	The dog and cat, what are they doing?	*El perro y el gato, ¿qué están haciendo?*
••:	Both are singing with the king and the queen.	*Los dos están cantando con el rey y la reina.*
•:	How strange!	*¡Qué extraño!*
••:	Truly.	*De veras.*

🔲 *Pictographic Representation of the Same Dialogue*

Task 1

Use your hands as puppets and dramatize the dialogue, looking only at the English. Visualize the situation and get into the spirit of the dialogue. Aim for a flowing Spanish quality. Then go on to the next task.

Task 2

Do the same as in Task 1, but now look only at the pictographic representation below. Review pictographs from previous chapters as necessary. Throw yourself into this performance. Bring thought down in Spanish without thinking in English.

•: ↓T 🐱 -✔ 🥁♪ ..1 🌍♪.   ...: ✔ 🐱 🌍 ø. ⊜ 👸↑ 🥁♪.

•: — •T 🥁♪ 🐱 ?   ...: ✔, (♩) >T> 🥁♪, 1↓T (♩) ✔ 🥁♪.

•: b 🥁♪T.. ↓ ?   ...: ✔, T↓.

•: 🐕 & 🐈, Q? s?   ...: 2 🌍♪ᵧ 👸 & 👸.

•: i — !   ...: ✔!

THE ADVENTURE CONTINUES

Having completed your tasks, you report, "Both now in Chamber 6. Thirty-six steps from Target."

Instructions for negotiating chambers 7 through 10 call for a *major* investment of effort: #42 (Observing Closely How Spanish Works) will make you formulate your own ideas about how Spanish grammar works. Spend enough time that you feel confident with a basic understanding of how English sentence structures are expressed in Spanish. You set about your tasks with relish.

42

🖼 Observing Closely How Spanish Works

Instructions: Make three passes through the sentences in A, B, and C.

1st pass: Compare the Spanish forms and their meaning with the English. (Read the Spanish out loud, then look away and say it, thinking of its meaning and form. Also without looking at the Spanish, see if you can repeat the line just above.)

2nd pass: Cover the English and see if you can translate the Spanish into English.

3rd pass: Cover the Spanish and see if you can translate the English into Spanish.

GROUP A

He is playing the piano and singing.	*El está tocando el piano y cantando.*
He and she are playing the piano.	*El y ella están tocando el piano.*
Who (all) play the piano and who (all) sing?	*¿Quienes tocan piano y quiénes cantan?*
Who plays the piano and who sings?	*¿Quién toca piano y quién canta?*
She plays the piano and he sings.	*Ella toca piano y él canta.*
That princess doesn't play the piano.	*Aquella princesa no toca piano.*
That prince is not singing.	*Aquel príncipe no está cantando.*
He is talking.	*Está hablando.*

GROUP B

Do the prince and princess sing?	*¿Cantan el príncipe y la princesa?*
Yes, both sing.	*Sí, los dos cantan.*
Now they are both singing.	*Ahora los dos están cantando.*
The princess already sings.	*La princesa ya canta.*
The king no longer sings.	*El rey ya no canta.*
The prince sings a lot.	*El príncipe canta mucho.*
He used to speak Spanish a lot.	*El hablaba español mucho.*
He still speaks Spanish a little.	*Todavía habla español un poco.*
The princess doesn't speak Spanish yet.	*La princesa todavía no habla español.*

GROUP C

They don't drink milk.	*Ellos no toman leche.*
(They) don't eat either.	*Tampoco comen.*
They're not playing but singing.	*No están tocando sino cantando.*
Now the queen is singing a little. Not much.	*Ahora la reina está cantando un poco. No mucho.*
The king used to play the drum.	*El rey tocaba el tambor.*
They both play a little.	*Los dos tocan un poco.*
Neither the king nor the queen plays very well.	*Ni el rey ni la reina toca muy bien.*

SELF-TEST

Part 1

Match the numbered English with the lettered Spanish (answers in the appendix).

___1. how many	A. *más que*	H. *aquel*
___2. who?	B. *¿quién?*	I. *menos que*
___3. how?	C. *aquella*	J. *peor que*
___4. which one?	D. *mejor que*	K. *¿verdad?*
___5. fewer than	E. *¿cuántos?*	L. *¿por qué?*
___6. that one (f)	F. *¿cuál?*	M. *¿qué?*
___7. better than	G. *¿dónde?*	N. *¿cómo?*
___8. worse than		
___9. more than		
___10. right?		
___11. what?		
___12. why?		

___13. not anymore	A. *un poco*	H. *antes*
___14. not either	B. *también*	I. *nunca*
___15. a lot	C. *ni...ni*	J. *y...y*
___16. neither...nor	D. *todavía no*	K. *ahora*
___17. but rather	E. *sino*	L. *o...o*
___18. a little	F. *tampoco*	M. *hay*
___19. and...and	G. *pero*	N. *mucho*
___20. also		O. *ya no*
___21. either...or		
___22. not yet		
___23. there is		

Part 2

Translate the following phrases and sentences. Do not look at the Spanish except to check your answers. Mark those items you have difficulty with, and then come back and try those items again.

GROUP A

This king doesn't play the piano.	*Este rey no toca piano.*
He also doesn't sing.	*Tampoco canta.*
This queen isn't crying.	*Esta reina no está llorando.*
The princess isn't either.	*La princesa tampoco.*
The prince and princess drink water.	*El príncipe y la princesa toman agua.*
The prince also drinks milk.	*El príncipe toma leche también.*
This king doesn't drink milk.	*Este rey no toma leche.*
This queen doesn't either.	*La reina tampoco.*

GROUP B

That king does not play the piano yet.	*Ese rey todavía no toca piano.*
This prince still sings a lot.	*Este príncipe todavía canta mucho.*
The king still sings and plays.	*El rey todavía canta y toca.*
The king and the queen don't play the piano yet.	*El rey y la reina todavía no tocan piano.*

GROUP C

The prince already sings.	*El príncipe ya canta.*
He no longer plays.	*El ya no toca.*
They already sing.	*Ellos ya canta.*
Does the king no longer play?	*¿Ya no toca el rey?*
They no longer cry.	*Ellas ya no lloran.*

GROUP D

Who already plays the piano?	*¿Quién ya toca piano?*
That princess already plays the piano.	*Aquella princesa ya toca piano.*
That prince and this princess already play the piano.	*Aquel príncipe y esta princesa ya tocan piano.*
This queen doesn't play the piano; this king doesn't either.	*Esta reina no toca piano; este rey tampoco.*

GROUP E

The king that used to play now sings.	*El rey que tocaba ahora canta.*
The king that used to sing is now playing the drum.	*El rey que cantaba ahora está tocando el tambor.*

GROUP F

Neither he nor she sings.	*Ni él ni ella canta.*
Both the dog and the cat sing.	*Y el perro y el gato cantan.*
Both cry too.	*Los dos lloran también.*

Review: Take some time now for review. Go back to any words or sentences you had difficulty with and see if you can iron things out now. Then go on.

THE ADVENTURE CONTINUES

Having completed your tasks, you report, "Both are now in Chamber 10. Thirty-two steps from Target."

The instructions for negotiating chambers 11 and 12 again call for an investment of effort: #43 (*Mi primera visita a Méjico*), and #44 (*Continuation*). Each communicates this and you both set about the task, seeing you are making great progress in understanding the language.

Feeling a bit tired and hungry, you take a rest break at the end of #43. The rest refreshes you, and, amazingly, one swallow of the delicious "*jugo de fuerza*" from your canteens satisfies your hunger and thirst.

This task has a different evaluation procedure. At the end of #44 there is a list of over 120 words. You are told that you will likely recognize most of these words after listening two times to the two-part sequence, **with your focus on understanding it, not memorizing words!** After the second time listening through the narrative, you are each to go down the list and put a check (√) by every word you know well enough to use yourself, and a plus sign (+) by every word you recognize, even if you aren't ready to use it. If there are fewer than 30 words that are not marked with either sign, you can pass through four chambers of the labyrinth, and make your way into chamber 14.

43

🖭 *Mi Primera Visita a Méjico*
A Diglot-Weave Story

CD ROM

🖭 Instructions: As you listen and read through this story, you must guess at the meaning of the Spanish from the context inferencing—the natural method children employ so successfully in picking up a language, and one that adults must cultivate to succeed in mastering a language. Don't expect to get it all the first time. Don't even be concerned with learning a lot of Spanish from it. Just enjoy the story to the extent you can follow it, and notice how in repeated go-throughs, you understand more and more.

🖭 PARTE UNO

As I passed *la frontera,* I was excited by the prospect of *mi primera visita a Méjico,* but I felt shaky, *un poco* unsure of myself in this new *ambiente.*

Having lived in *California* for the greater *parte* of *mi vida, y* having long had *un interés* in «*nuestros vecinos*» to the south, I had absorbed *(por osmosis) un poco de español* through the years *pero* had never had *suficiente tiempo para realmente estudiar el idioma.*

I wanted to kick myself, *pero* now it was rather late—*sí, era un poco tarde* for that. I was comforted *muy poco* by my purchase of a *diccionario español-inglés en Tijuana.* But I determined to *practicar mi español* to the *límite.* I even made the *decisión* to write (I mean *escribir*) *mi diario en español* as much as *posible.*

I had no *misión oficial en Méjico.* I was going there *estrictamente* as *un turista,* mostly out of *curiosidad y un deseo* to enjoy *una experiencia diferente de lo usual.*

Having been a soccer player *toda mi vida*—that is, *un jugador de fútbol* since I was a small *muchacho,* I looked forward to *la oportunidad* to attend *un partido de fútbol* on *domingo.* An *amigo* had given me *una lista de palabras de alta frecuéncia* as a going-away *regalo* only a few *días* before. I appreciated his *regalo, y* I had *diligentemente* tried to *memorizar* some of *los terminos más comunes y útiles.*

After *unas horas de viaje,* I came to a small *pueblo y* made a *decisión* to stop and look around *un poco.* There was a lot of heat, *sí, mucho calor,* just as I had expected *en Méjico, y también,* as expected, *el pueblo* was *absolutamente tranquilo.* The ancient *proverbio* came to mind: «*EL SILENCIO ES ORO.*» It was *la hora de la siesta.*

(To be continued)

End Tape 2, Side A

44

📼 Continuing the Story
Mi primera visita a Méjico

As I walked around *la plaza*, I almost expected to see *un Mejicano* propped up against *las* prickly *espinas de un cacto*, his *sombrero* pulled down over his *cara*. I even conjured up *la aparición de un bandido*, his *machete, pistolas, y bandolero* under his *poncho* ready for *uso inmediato*.

Actually I saw *ni una persona, sólo un* mangy old *perro*, taking a *siesta en la* cool *sombra de un árbol, y una vaca tranquilamente masticando su* cud. Then suddenly a *radio* came on. *La locutora* opened *el programa con* these *palabras*:

«*Saludos, amigos, y muy buenas tardes. Este es radio Méjico, uno-dos-tres-cuatro. Amigo, amiga, tome Coca-Cola, el refresco más popular del mundo. Sí, amigos, ¡tomen Coca-Cola! ¡La Coca-Cola mejicana es excelente...magnífica...fantástica...indispensable! ¡Viva la Coca-Cola! ¡Viva Méjico!*»

She paused *por un momento*, then *continuó*:

«*Y ahora «La Hora de Meditación,» un programa de meditación con música y lectura de las Sagradas Escrituras del Nuevo Testamento de nuestro señor Jesucristo. Este programa es bajo la dirección del evangelista David Gomez, pastor de la iglesia bautista de Sonora, Méjico. Aquí con ustedes está el hermano Gomez:*»

«*Buenas tardes, hermanos y hermanas, amigos y amigas. El título de mi sermón para hoy es: El Señor es mi Pastor. En la Biblia (en el Antiguo Testamento), en el libro de Salmos, capítulo 23, versículo 1, se encuentra el famoso pasaje: «El Señor es mi Pastor, nada me faltará.» ¿Qué significa David, el salmista, con estas palabras?*»

From here *el evangelista* made *un comentario on el simbolismo poético de Salmo 23.* Yo was *muy impresionado* by the fact *que yo* was able to *comprender la mayor parte del sermón. El* short *sermón* was followed by *una selección de himnos* sung by *un coro. Generalmente no me gusta* to hear *himnos o música religiosa por radio* even *en inglés, pero en esta ocasión, ¡Ay, qué bonita! Me gustó mucho. Me impresionó muchísimo.*

After enjoying *la música por unos minutos,* yo walked through *la plaza,* crossed—*crucé—la calle central y entré en un restaurante* next to *El Hotel Casa Blanca.* I sat down at *una mesa y* was *admirando* the vase *de flores en medio de la mesa* when I heard *una voz* behind me which asked, «*¿Un menú, señor?*»

It was *realmente la voz de un ángel!* Yo looked *y* saw *una señorita muy bonita, una princesa encantadora.* «*No, gracias,*» I responded. «*Chile con carne, por favor, y papas fritas.*»

—*¿Una botella de vino, quizás? ¿O un vaso de leche pasteurizada?*

—*No, muchas gracias, señorita. Sólo agua purificada.*

—*Perdón, señor, no tenemos agua purificada. Tenemos agua filtrada. ¿Está bien?*

—*Sí, está bien. Un vaso de agua filtrada, por favor.*

—*Bueno, chile con carne, papas fritas, y un vaso de agua. ¿Sólo eso?*

—*Sólo eso, gracias.*

La señorita was *muy simpática.* She must've been eighteen *años* of age. Then I noticed that on the walls of *el restaurante* there were dozens—*docenas—de fotos de personas famosas, por ejemplo, presidentes de la república de Méjico (Benito Juarez y otros), líderes del gobierno (senadores, ministros, y otros), futbolistas (como Pelé) y otros atletas, revolucionarios (como Pancho Villa), personajes del cine y del teatro (como Cantinflas) y otros. Muy interesante,* I thought, *y muy raro* that *tantas personas famosas* had *visitado aquí.* Just then *la señorita* came *con mi orden, y otra vez* I heard *la voz de un angel,* «*Señor, su chile con carne, papas fritas, y un vaso de agua filtrada.*»

—*Gracias, señorita. Mmm, deliciosa. Comida deliciosa, rica.*

—*¿Música, señor?*

—*¿Cómo?*

—*¿Quiere usted música?*

—*¿Por qué no?*

—*¿Qué clase de música prefiere usted?*

—*Me gusta muchísimo la música clásica. Especialmente Chopin.*

I expected her to tell me they *sólo* had *música mejicana, pero* instead she smiled *y* sat down at *el piano.* Yo listened *como en un trance* as *la princesa encantadora* played *la famosa impromptu de Chopin, mi pieza favorita. Y nunca* had I heard it played *tan expresivamente y expertamente.*

Who could she be? *¿Quién será esta princesa encantadora?* I wanted to know more about her, but *mi español era extremadamente limitado.* When she finished playing *el impromptu,* I asked, hopefully, «*¿Habla usted inglés, señorita?*»

—*No, señor, lamentablemente. Sólo español.*

—*¡Que lástima! ¿Su nombre?*

—*María Martinez, para servirle.*

—*¿Es usted de aquí?*

—*De aquí, no. Soy de la capital, de la Ciudad de Méjico. Estoy aquí sólo durante el mes de agosto con mi tía que es la dueña del hotel. En septiembre regreso a mi casa en la capital. Y usted, señor, ¿está usted en Méjico por primera vez?*

—*Sí, por primera vez.*

—*Usted comprende muy bien. Usted sabe mucho español.*

—*No, no mucho. En realidad muy poco. El español es difícil para mí. ¡Soy muy tonto!*

—*No, no, señor. Usted no es tonto. Yo no hablo inglés, pero no soy tonta.*

¡Qué lástima! I thought. Yes, what a pity! *Aquí estoy en mi primera visita a Méjico con mi primera oportunidad de hablar con una señorita—una princesa—mejicana, y yo* was at a loss for *palabras para expresarme.*

Not wanting her to go away, I asked her *una pregunta estúpida, «¿Que piensa usted de los gringos que visitan Méjico?»* Her response—*respuesta*—took me by *sorpresa. Una breve digresión* here will help you *comprender mi* amazement at her *respuesta.*

Here's a partial *lista de palabras* you've met in the story so far. Go through each column and see how many *palabras* you remember from the story. Place a check mark by each one you are unsure of, and before you listen to the tape a second time, note which words are checked.

la frontera	*ambiente*	*los vecinos*	*suficiente*	*tarde*
la decisión	*misión oficial*	*mi deseo*	*una oportunidad*	*Sagradas Escrituras*
evangelista	*recomendar*	*modo de aprender*	*absolutamente*	*la siesta*
sombrero	*bandido*	*sombra*	*el programa*	*una breve digresión*
la voz de un angel	*simpática*	*los líderes*	*deliciosa (rica)*	*¿Por qué?*
silencio	*oro*	*machete*	*posible*	*curiosidad*
para expresar	*primera*	*parte*	*español*	*tiempo*
diccionario	*escribir*	*estrictamente*	*experiencia*	*servicios*
diligentemente	*Biblia*	*familiarizado*	*unas horas*	*tranquilo*
la plaza	*vista*	*uso inmediato*	*un poncho*	*saludos*
una sorpresa	*muy bonita*	*agua purificada*	*especialmente*	*estúpida*
¿Por qué no?	*iglesia*	*usted*	*versión*	*también*
mucho calor	*una botella de vino*	*visita*	*vida*	*pueblo*
realmente	*inglés*	*diario*	*turista*	*diferente*
domingo	*día*	*favorita*	*primera visita*	*cacto*
espinas	*una vaca*	*masticando*	*un perro*	*buenas tardes*
unos minutos	*muy raro*	*agua filtrada*	*por ejemplo*	*personas*
un vaso de leche	*muy poco*	*interés*	*pero*	*estudiar*
practicar	*comprender*	*yo*	*mi*	*nuestro*
idioma	*sí*	*límite*	*amigo*	*un regalo*
memorizar	*actividad*	*en mi opinión*	*no mucho*	*himno*
pistola	*locutor(a)*	*teatro*	*restaurante*	*encantadora*
¿Qué clase?	*la república*	*personajes*	*docenas de fotos*	*sólo*
alta frecuéncia	*inglés*	*proverbio*	*¿cómo?*	*me gusta*
Méjico, mejicano	*famoso*	*la respuesta*	*una lista de palabras*	

(To be continued)

THE ADVENTURE CONTINUES

Having completed your tasks so that your partner can advance, you report, "Both are now in Chamber 12. Thirty steps from Target."

The instructions are that to negotiate chambers 13 through 15 your partner must successfully complete tasks 45 (Focus on the Language), 46 (Self-test), and 47 (*Puntos, líneas y figuras*). You notice that as you get closer to the target, the requirements become more challenging. You are advised by Stump that your task is the same. You tackle this challenge with enthusiasm, feeling good about your phenomenal progress in the language but wondering what occasions lie ahead that will require use of what you have learned. You both throw yourselves into these challenging tasks.

Focus on the Language 11–12

FOCUS 11

Lo, la, los, las.

She speaks Chinese.	*Ella habla chino.*
She speaks it.	*Ella lo habla* (NOT **Ella habla lo*).
He doesn't speak it.	*El no lo habla* (NOT **El lo no habla*).
She speaks Chinese and Spanish.	*Ella habla chino y español.*
She speaks them.	*Ella los habla* (NOT **Ella habla los*).

Translate Orally from and into Spanish

They sing a funeral song.	*Ellos cantan un canto fúnebre.*
They sing it more or less well.	*Lo cantan más or menos bien.*
They sing hymns too.	*Cantan himnos también.*
They sing them very well.	*Los cantan muy bien.*
She drinks milk.	*Ella toma leche.*
She drinks it a lot.	*Lo toma mucho.*
He doesn't speak Chinese.	*El no habla chino.*
No, he doesn't speak it.	*No, no lo habla.*

FOCUS 12

Lo, la, los, las with a verb in the infinitive.

To drink the juice.	*Tomar el jugo.*
To drink it.	*Tomarlo* (NOT **Lo tomar*).
To drink the milk.	*Tomar la leche.*
To drink it.	*Tomarla* (NOT **La tomar*).
To speak Spanish and Chinese.	*Hablar español y chino.*
To speak them.	*Hablarlos* (NOT **Los hablar*).

Translate Orally from and into Spanish

What is it that he drinks?	*¿Qué es lo que él toma?*
He drinks milk. He drinks it a lot.	*El toma leche. La toma mucho.*
He likes to drink it.	*Le gusta tomarla.*
It's prohibited to drink it here.	*Está prohibido tomarla aquí.*
She doesn't eat the meat.	*Ella no come la carne.*
She doesn't like to eat it.	*No le gusta comerla.*
She speaks French.	*Ella habla francés.*
It's prohibited to speak it in the palace.	*Está prohibido hablarlo en el palacio.*
She likes to speak it with the prince.	*Le gusta hablarlo con el príncipe.*

Self-Test

MATCHING

Match the lettered Spanish with the numbered English. (Answers below the fence.)

___1. how many?   A. *más que*   H. *aquel*
___2. who?   B. *¿quién?*   I. *menos que*
___3. how?   C. *aquella*   J. *peor que*
___4. which one?   D. *mejor que*   K. *¿verdad?*
___5. fewer than   E. *¿cuántos?*   L. *¿por qué?*
___6. that one (f)   F. *¿cuál?*   M. *¿qué?*
___7. better than   G. *¿dónde?*   N. *¿cómo?*
___8. worse than
___9. more than
___10. right?
___11. what?
___12. why?

___13. not anymore   A. *un poco*   H. *solamente*
___14. not also   B. *también*   I. *nunca*
___15. a lot   C. *ni...ni*   J. *y...y*
___16. neither...nor   D. *todavía no*   K. *ahora*
___17. but rather   E. *sino*   L. *o...o*
___18. a little   F. *tampoco*   M. *hay*
___19. and...and   G. *pero*   N. *mucho*
___20. also   O. *ya no*
___21. either...or
___22. not yet
___23. there is
___24. never

Answer Key

(1) E. (2) B. (3) N. (4) F. (5) I. (6) C. (7) D. (8) J. (9) A (10) K. (11) M. (12) L. (13) O. (14) F. (15) N. (16) C. (17) E. (18) A. (19) J. (20) B. (21) L. (22) D. (23) M. (24) I.

Your score: _____ (try for a minimum 18 of 24 or better)

ERROR DETECTION

Of the following sentences, nineteen contain errors in translation. Identify them.

___	25. The one (m) who used to play cries.	*Aquel que tocaba llora.*
___	26. He used to either sing or play.	*El o cantaba o toca.*
___	27. The king that used to play now sings.	*El rey que tocaba ahora canta.*
___	28. The king that used to sing is playing the drum.	*El rey que canta está tocando el tambor.*
___	29. He is drinking milk.	*El está toma leche.*
___	30. He and she are drinking juice.	*El y ella está tomando jugo.*
___	31. She sings and he plays the piano.	*El canta y ella toca el piano.*
___	32. That queen doesn't sing.	*Aquella reina no está cantando.*
___	33. The prince and princess play piano.	*La príncipe y el princesa tocan piano.*
___	34. Now both are singing.	*Ahora los dos está cantando.*
___	35. The princesses already sing.	*Las princesas ya cantan.*
___	36. The princess already sings.	*La princesa todavía canta.*
___	37. The king no longer sings.	*El rey ya no canta.*
___	38. They don't drink, and they don't eat either.	*Ellos no toman, y tampoco comen.*
___	39. They're not playing but singing.	*No están tocando pero cantando.*
___	40. Neither the king nor the queen plays well.	*Ni el rey ni la reina toca bien.*
___	41. Who does the queen sing with?	*¿Con quién llora la reina?*
___	42. Who sings better, the princess or the duchess?	*¿Quién canta mejor, la princesa o la duquesa?*
___	43. They are singing and playing.	*Están cantando y tocando.*
___	44. Which princess used to cry?	*¿Cuál princesa lloraba?*
___	45. Does the cat sing in the tower?	*¿Canta el perro en el baño?*
___	46. Is she crying or singing?	*¿Están llorando o cantando ella?*
___	47. Do the king and the queen cry?	*¿Lloran el rey y la reina?*
___	48. Did the prince and the king used to sing better?	*¿Cantaba mejor el príncipe y el rey?*
___	49. Does the dog sing well too?	*¿Cantaba bien el perro también?*
___	50. Do the dog and cat sing worse?	*¿Cantaban peor el perro y el gato?*
___	51. Where does the queen cry?	*¿Cómo canta la reina?*
___	52. The one (f) who cries sings.	*Aquella que llora canta.*
___	53. This queen isn't crying.	*La reina no está llorando.*
___	54. The king doesn't drink; the duke doesn't either.	*El rey no toma; el duque también.*

Answer Key

Incorrect: 26, 28, 29, 30, 31, 32, 33, 34, 36, 39, 41, 45, 46, 48, 49, 50, 51, 53, 54

Your score: ____

Correct Versions of Incorrect Sentences

Check the following against the incorrect sentences above and note the differences.

26. *El cantaba o <u>tocaba</u>.*

28. *El rey que <u>cantaba</u> está tocando el tambor.*

29. *El está <u>tomando</u> leche.*

30. *El y ella <u>están</u> tomando jugo.*

31. *<u>Ella</u> canta y <u>él</u> toca el piano.*

32. *Aquella reina no <u>canta</u>.*

33. *<u>El</u> príncipe y <u>la</u> princesa tocan el piano.*

34. *Ahora los dos <u>están</u> cantando.*

36. *La princesa <u>ya</u> canta.*

39. *No están tocando, <u>sino</u> cantando.*

41. *¿Con quién <u>canta</u> la reina?*

45. *¿Canta el <u>gato</u> en <u>la torre</u>?*

46. *¿<u>Está</u> llorando o cantando ella?*

48. *¿<u>Cantaban</u> mejor el príncipe y el rey?*

49. *¿<u>Canta</u> bien el perro también?*

50. *¿<u>Cantan</u> peor el perro y el gato?*

51. *¿<u>Dónde</u> <u>llora</u> la reina?*

53. *<u>Esta</u> reina no está llorando.*

54. *El rey no toma; el duque <u>tampoco</u>.*

READING COMPREHENSION

Read the text and answer the questions.

En esta historia hay cuatro animales: un perro, un gato, un lobo, un cochinito (oink!). El perro toca himnos en la guitarra. Pero ahora no está tocando la guitarra. Ahora está cantando. Está cantando con el gato. Está cantando himnos con el gato en la iglesia. No. Eso no es correcto. El gato está tocando la guitarra y el perro está cantando solo. El perro canta mejor que el gato, pero el gato toca la guitarra mejor que el perro.

El lobo y el cochinito también cantan. Ellos cantan con el perro y el gato. Y ahora los cuatro están cantando himnos en la iglesia. Oh no, el gato está tocando la guitarra y los otros tres están cantando. Ellos no cantan muy bien, pero cantan. El cochinito canta peor que el gato. El lobo peor que el cochinito. El lobo toma mucho pero no fuma. El toma cuando está cantando (o canta cuando está tomando). El cochinito fuma, pero fuma sólamente cuando el lobo está tomando.

Questions

1. *¿Dónde está cantando el perro?*

En (a) *la iglesia*   (b) *la cantina*   (c) *ni <u>a</u> ni <u>b</u>*   (d) *no se sabe* (= not known)

2. *¿Cantan el lobo y el cochinito?*

(a) *sí*   (b) *no*   (c) *no se sabe*

3. ¿Canta el cochinito peor que el lobo?

(a) *sí*   (b) *no*   (c) *no se sabe*

4. ¿Cuál canta mejor?

(a) *el cochinito*   (b) *el perro*   (c) *no se sabe*

5. ¿Qué está haciendo el gato ahora?

(a) *está tocando la guitarra*   (b) *está cantando y tocando la guitarra*

6. El lobo toma, ¿no?

(a) *sí*   (b) *no*   (c) *no se sabe*

7. ¿Cuándo toma el lobo?

(a) *sólo cuando el cochinito toma*   (b) *sólo cuando está cantando*   (c) *no se sabe*

8. ¿Cuál de los animales fuma?

(a) *el lobo*   (b) *el cochinito*

9. ¿Toca la guitarra el perro?

(a) *sí*   (b) *no*   (c) *no se sabe*

10. ¿Toca el gato mejor que el perro?

(a) *sí*   (b) *no*   (c) *no se sabe*

11. ¿Qué clase de cantos están cantando los animales?

(a) *cantos fúnebres*   (b) *himnos*   (c) *no se sabe*

12. ¿Cuántos animales hay en esta historia?

(a) *dos*   (b) *tres*   (c) *cuatro*

Answer Key
(1) a. (2) a. (3) b. (4) c. (5) a. (6) a. (7) b. (8) b. (9) a. (10) a. (11) b. (12) c.

Your score: _____ (try for a minimum of 9 out of 12)

📼 *Puntos, Líneas, y Figuras*
Points, Lines and Figures

📼 A. SCATTER CHART

=	⇒	➡
	flecha blanca	*flecha negra*

|•| /•\	•	—	•|
entre las líneas	*arriba de la línea*	*debajo de la línea*	*al lado de la línea (al lado izquierdo)*

➡
indicando hacia la derecha
(hacia = toward)

⬅
indicando hacia la izquierda

⬆
indicando hacia arriba

⬇
indicando hacia abajo

📼 B. LOOK AND LISTEN

1. ⇒ ➡   *Aquí hay una flecha blanca y una flecha negra.*

2. ➡
   ⇒   *La flecha negra está arriba de la flecha blanca.*

3. ⇒
   ➡   *La flecha negra está debajo de la flecha blanca.*

4. •
   ⇒   *La flecha blanca está debajo del punto pequeño.*

5. ➡ ➡
   • ——   *Una flecha negra está arriba de un punto; la otra está arriba de una línea.*

6. ⇒ ——   *Una flecha blanca está arriba de una línea corta; la otra flecha blanca está debajo*
   —— ⇒   *de una línea larga.*

7. ⬆ —— ⬆   *Una línea horizontal está entre dos flechas negras.*

8. ➡ \| ➡   *Una línea corta vertical está entre dos flechas negras.*

9. ⬆ ⬇   *Una flecha indicando hacia arriba; la otra indicando hacia abajo.*

10. ⇒ ⬅   *La flecha blanca a la izquierda indica hacia la derecha; la flecha negra a la derecha*
                  indica hacia la izquierda.

11. ⬅ ⬅   *Esta flecha indica hacia la izquierda. La otra indica también hacia la izquierda.*

12. ⬅⬅⬅⬅⬇⬇⬇⬇   *Estas cuatro flechas no indican hacia arriba. Estas cuatro tampoco.*

C. Listen and Look

1. ⇒ ←   2. ⇒ ⇒ ⬇ ⬇   3. ➡ ←   4. • | •

5. ➡ • / ● ⇒   6. ➡ ——— / —— ⇒   7. ⇒ ⇒ ———   8. ⇒ | ←

D. MULTIPLE-CHOICE FRAMES

(A)	(B)	(C)	(D)	(E)

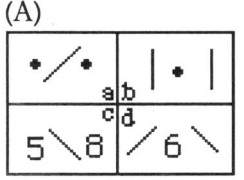 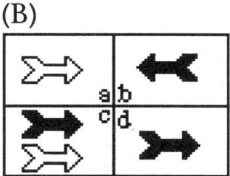 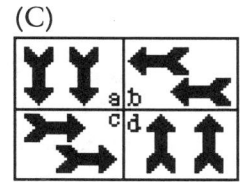 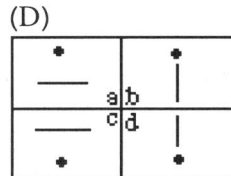 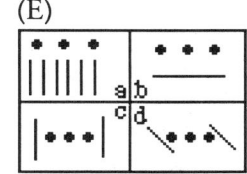

---

† The tape says the wrong answers for frame D. The answers should be: "a," "a," and "c."

E. Listen and Draw

Stop the tape if the pace is too fast. You can check your answers in the appendix.

1.   2.   3.   4.   5.

🔊 F. Read for Meaning

Read the following sentences aiming to understand the meaning. Check your comprehension by reading the English in the appendix.

1. *Dos flechas: una indicando hacia arriba y la otra hacia abajo.*
2. *Una flecha blanca indicando hacia un punto pequeño y una flecha negra indicando hacia un punto grande.*
3. *Una línea larga horizontal al lado de una línea corta vertical.*
4. *Dos líneas: una línea larga, gruesa, y horizontal; y una línea corta, delgada, y vertical.*
5. *La línea horizontal està al lado de la línea vertical.*
6. *Un número y un punto pequeño entre dos líneas diagonales.*
7. *El número cinco y dos puntos grandes entre dos líneas verticales.*
8. *Una flecha blanca indicando hacia la derecha y una flecha negra indicando hacia la izquierda.*
9. *El punto está al lado derecho de la línea vertical.*
10. *Dos puntos están al lado izquierdo de la línea diagonal.*

THE ADVENTURE CONTINUES

Having completed your tasks so that your partner can advance, you report, "Both now in Chamber 15. Twenty-seven steps from Target."

Instructed by the hidden writing in cells 16 and 17 on your map, you advise Stump that entry into those two chambers depends on successful completion of four tasks: Tasks 48 (*Las Llaves de Roma*) to 51 (*Una Lección de Español*). Stump gives you the same instructions. It dawns on both of you that the requirements are being raised, but the foundation of Spanish you have built makes the climb seem not too steep. You enjoy the challenge.

48

 The Keys of Rome

Las Llaves de Roma

CD ROM

Here are the keys of Rome.	*Estas son las llaves de Roma.*
Take them!	*¡Tómalas!*
In Rome there is a plaza.	*En Roma hay una plaza.*
In the plaza there is a street.	*En la plaza hay una calle.*
In the street there is a house.	*En la calle hay una casa.*
In the house there is a bed.	*En la casa hay una cama.*
In the bed there is a lady.	*En la cama hay una dama.*
At the lady's feet there is a parrot.	*A los pies de la dama hay un perico.*
And the parrot says,	*Y el perico dice,*
"DON'T TELL LIES!"	*«¡NO DIGAS MENTIRAS!»*
The lady isn't in the bed.	*La dama no está en la cama.*
The bed isn't in the house.	*La cama no está en la casa.*
The house isn't in the street.	*La casa no está en la calle.*
The street isn't in the plaza.	*La calle no está en la plaza.*
The plaza isn't in Rome.	*La plaza no está en Roma.*
And these keys are not the keys of Rome.	*Y estas llaves no son las llaves de Roma.*

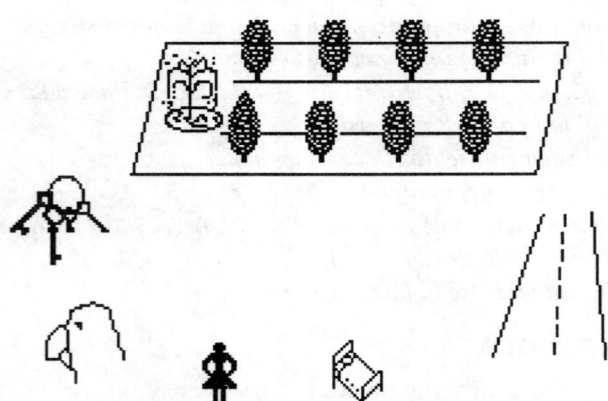

Listen again, following the illustration above. Then invest some time in learning to tell this story as if to a child sitting on your lap.

117

49

 Una Lección de Geografía
Spanish Only
A Geography Lesson

Listen to the Spanish, following the text in the left column. Then compare the Spanish and English. Finally, listen to the Spanish again.

Entre Sudamérica y Norteamérica, se encuentra Centroamérica.

Between South America and North America lies Central America.

Panamá está aquí.

Panama is here.

En Panamá encontramos un canal que une los océanos Atlántico y Pacífico.

In Panama there is a canal that links the Atlantic and Pacific Oceans.

El canal es un puente entre el este y el oeste.

The canal is a bridge between east and west.

Más hacia el norte está Méjico.

Farther north lies Mexico.

Su capital es la Ciudad de Méjico.

Its capital is Mexico City.

Está destinada a ser la ciudad más grande del mundo.

It is destined to become the world's largest city.

Al norte de Méjico están los Estados Unidos.

North of Mexico is the United States.

Los Estados Unidos están entre los océanos Pacífico y Atlántico.

The United States lies between the Pacific and Atlantic oceans.

La costa este toca el Atlántico.

The east coast touches the Atlantic.

La costa oeste toca el Pacífico.

The west coast touches the Pacific.

La costa sur toca el Golfo de Méjico.

The south coast touches the Gulf of Mexico.

Su capital, Washington, está en la costa este.

The capital, Washington, is on the east coast.

La ciudad más grande, Nueva York, está ahí también.

The largest city, New York, is there, too.

En la coste oeste está California.

On the west coast is California.

San Francisco está aquí en California.

San Francisco is here, in California.

Los Angeles está aquí.

Los Angeles is here.

En San Francisco y Los Angeles hay muchas personas que hablan español.

In San Francisco and Los Angeles there are many people who speak Spanish.

El estado de Utah es uno de los cincuenta estados de los Estados Unidos (E.U.).

The state of Utah is one of fifty states in the United States (U.S.).

No es ni el más grande ni el más pequeño de los estados.

It is neither the biggest nor the smallest state.

Está en la parte oeste, pero está lejos de la costa oeste.

It is located in the western part, but it is far from the west coast.

Utah es famoso por el lago salado y también por sus bellos parques.

Utah is famous for its salt lake and also for its beautiful parks.

118

50

🔊 Spanish Ditties

🔊 Now relax and enjoy a couple of silly ditties in Spanish.

«HOY ES SABADO»

Hoy es sabado
Hoy es sabado,
«Saturday» en inglés,
«Saturday» en inglés,
Y todo el tiempo estoy en mi casa,
Y todo el tiempo estoy en mi casa,
Y canto otra vez:
Hoy es sabado,
Hoy es sabado,
Y canto otra vez.

«MANZANA PARA EVA»

Manzana para Eva,	Apple for Eva,
Naranja para ti,	An orange for thee,
Piña para la niña,	Pineapple for the little girl,
Y uva para mí.	And grape for me.
Una para Eva,	One for Eva,
Una para ti,	One for thee,
Una para la niña,	One for the little girl,
Y una para mí.	And one for me.

«NO TENEMOS DINERO»

No tenemos dinero.	We don't have money.
No tenemos con que	We don't have whereby
compraríamos comida,	We would buy food,
No sabemos por que.	And we do not know why.
No tenemos frijoles.	We don't have beans.
No tenemos ni sal.	We don't even have salt.
Hace falta dinero,	Money is lacking,
Pero no está tan mal.	But it's not our fault.
Somos pobres, nos dicen,	We are poor folks, they tell us;
Somos pobres, pues sí.	We are poor folks, oh yes.
Pero poco sufrimos	But little we suffer
pues tenemos a ti.	For we always have thee.

51

📼 *Una Lección de Español*

Spanish Only
A Spanish Lesson

📼 Listen to the Spanish, following the text in the left column. Then compare the Spanish and English. Finally, listen to the Spanish again.

📼

En la mesa hay un lápiz negro, y en la silla hay uno rojo.

On the table there's a black pencil, and on the chair there's a red one.

Ambos son tuyos.

They are both yours.

Aquí tengo otros dos lápices, uno negro y uno rojo. Ambos son míos.

I have here two other pencils, one black and one red. Both are mine.

Tomaré uno de los míos, el rojo, y lo pararé en la mesa.

I will take one of mine, the red one, and stand it on the table.

Lo voy a parar cerca del tuyo, cerca del negro tuyo.

I will stand it near yours, near that black one of yours.

Ahora voy a tomar el otro, el negro mío, y lo voy a acostar en esta silla.

Now I will take the other, my black one, and lay it on this chair.

Lo voy a poner al lado del tuyo.

I will lay it at the side of yours.

Mira, primero tomé mi lápiz rojo y lo paré en la mesa cerca del negro tuyo.

Look, I first took my red pencil and stood it on the table near your black one.

Después tomé el negro mío y lo acosté en la silla al lado del tuyo.

Then I took my black one and laid it on this chair next to (at the side of) yours.

Ahora, haz lo que yo te diga.

Now, do as I tell you.

Selecciona uno de tus dos lápices, o el negro que está en la mesa o el rojo que está en la silla.

Select one of your two pencils, either the black one that's on the table or the red one that's on the chair.

Acuéstalo encima de este libro.

Lay it on top of this book.

Ahora toma tu otro lápiz y páralo en la mesa.

Now take the other pencil of yours and stand it on the table.

Ahora, dime qué es lo que hiciste con tus dos lápices.

Now, tell me what you did with your two pencils.

¿Cuál fue la primera cosa que hiciste?

What was the first thing you did?

Primero tomaste uno de los dos, el negro, y lo acostaste encima de este libro aquí.

First you took one of the two, that black one, and laid it on this book here.

Después tomaste otro lápiz, el rojo, y lo paraste en la mesa.

Then you took another pencil, the red one, and stood it on the table.

Ahora, ¿cuál es la situación de los cuatro lápices, los míos y los tuyos?

Now what is the situation of the four pencils, mine and yours?

Hay dos parados en la mesa, un rojo tuyo y un rojo mío.

There are two standing on the table, one red one of yours and one red one of mine.

Los otros dos, los negros, están acostados, sobre un libro y uno en la silla.

The other two, the black ones, are lying down, one on the book and one on the chair.

Mira, uno de los míos está parado, específicamente el rojo; y el otro, el negro, está acostado.

Look, one of mine is standing, specifically the red one; and the other one, the black one, is lying down.

Uno de los tuyos también está parado, y otro acostado.

One of yours is also standing, and another one lying down.

¿Cómo está el rojo tuyo?

How is the red one of yours?

¿Parado o acostado?

Standing or lying down?

¿De quién es el lápiz que está acostado en el libro?

Whose pencil is it that is lying on the book?

¿Tuyo o mío? Tuyo, ¿No?

Yours or mine? Yours, right?

¿Quién lo puso ahí?, ¿Tú o yo?

Who put it there, you or me?

¿Quién te dijo que lo pusieras ahí?

Who told you to put it there?

Yo te dije que lo pusieras ahí, ¿No?

I told you to put it there, right?

¿Quién paró mi lápiz rojo en la mesa?

Who stood my red pencil on the table?

Yo lo hice, ¿No?

I did it, right?

¿Quién me dijo que lo parara en la mesa?

Who told me to stand it on the table?

Nadie.

No one.

THE ADVENTURE CONTINUES

Having completed your tasks so that your partner can advance, you report, "Both now in Chamber 17. Twenty-five steps from target."

Instructed by the hidden writing in cells 18 and 19 on your map, you advise Stump that entry into the two next chambers will require successful completion of three tasks: 52 (*A Continuación: mi primera visita a Méjico*), 53 (More about Numbers), and 54 (A Joke in Spanish). The instructions you receive from Stump are the same. You eagerly dive into the challenge.

52

🖭 *A Continuación—Mi Primera Visita a Méjico*

🎞 PREPARATION

La «princesa encantadora» continua giving *su opinión de los gringos en Méjico.*

A week before I left, a friend had given me *una lista de palabras de alta frecuéncia.* "You'll be amazed at what *estas palabras* can do for you *en Méjico,*" he said. "Learn them by heart." I took his suggestion and kept *la lista* in my shirt pocket, taking it out to review *las palabras* at intervals. Here is that *lista de palabras:*

Spanish Infinitive	Spanish Verb Base Form	English Infinitive	English Verb Base Form	Memory Aids
leer	*lee*	to read	reads	as in "<u>le</u>gible"
aprender	*aprende*	to learn	learns	compare "<u>apprehend</u>"
suponer	*supone*	to suppose	supposes	
creer	*cree*	to believe	believes	as in "<u>cre</u>do"
saber	*sabe*	to know	knows	as in "<u>sa</u>vvy"
comer	*come*	to eat	eats	"<u>come</u> 'er" to eat
viajar	*viaja*	to travel	travels	related to "<u>v</u>o<u>ya</u>ge," "<u>via</u>"
trabajar	*trabaja*	to work	works	compare "<u>trav</u>a<u>il</u>"
gastar	*gasta*	to spend	spends	compare "waste"
andar	*anda*	to walk	walks	compare "<u>and</u>ante" in music
estar	*está*	to be	is	
tomar	*toma*	to take	takes	or drinks
hablar	*habla*	to speak	speaks	
esperar	*espera*	to hope	hopes	<u>despair</u> is absence of hope
pensar	*piensa*	to think	thinks	as in "<u>pens</u>ive"
vivir	*vive*	to live	lives	as in "re<u>vive</u>"
escribir	*escribe*	to write	writes	as in "scribe"
decir	*dice*	to say	says	"<u>dice</u> will <u>decide</u> what to <u>say</u>"
tener	*tiene*	to have	has	"<u>ten</u>acious," "<u>ten</u>able"
soler	*suele*	to do at times	does at times	
entender	*entiende*	to understand	understands	<u>intend</u> to…
querer	*quiere*	to want	wants	
poder	*puede*	to be able	s/he's able	

Spanish	English Equivalent	Memory Aids
veneno	poison	<u>venom</u>
comida	food	a form of <u>comer</u> "to eat"
dinero	money	money for "<u>dinner</u>o"
feo	ugly	"Oh, Faye is <u>feo</u>"
perezoso	lazy	"Mr. Perez is oh so <u>perezoso</u>!"
miedo	fear	
extraño	strange	"ex-<u>strange</u>-o"

As I was saying, *la respuesta* of *la «princesa encantadora»* took me by *sorpresa*. If you will spend just *cinco minutos* with the *lista de palabras de alta frecuéncia,* you'll get the same *sorpresa* I got as she spoke forcefully. (I'll help you with a *palabra* here or there, but mostly you can guess the meanings.) Here is what she said:

PARTE TRES

🔲 *El gringo típico, el turista norteamericano, es un tipo muy interesante cuando[1] viaja en Méjico. Por ejemplo, comunmente no sabe hablar ni leer español—y no quiere aprender, y espera que todo el mundo hable en inglés. Este tipo no toma agua porque tiene miedo a los microbios. No come tomate porque, créalo o no,[2] supone que es veneno. No le gusta la comida mejicana. Dice que es muy picante.[3] El gringo típico es rico. Vive en un hotel y gasta mucho dinero. No tiene respeto para con[4] los mejicanos, no aprecia nuestras costumbres.*

El gringo típico piensa que todos los mejicanos son bandidos[5] o tontos.[6] Piensa que Méjico es una colonia Norte-Americana. Imagínese! Nosotros tomamos a este tipo por un idiota vulgar. Pero no todos[7] son tontos. Por ejemplo, los voluntarios del cuerpo de paz no son tontos. Son diferentes, distintos. Hablan y entienden el español, y saben leer y escribir nuestra lengua. Y están acostumbrados[8] a la comida picante. Les gustan[9] los tacos, las enchiladas, los chiles rellenos. Los voluntarios del cuerpo de paz respetan a la gente mejicana y a las costumbres mejicanas. Ellos viven, comen y andan con el pueblo. Claro que no todos los voluntarios son iguales.[10] Algunos son inteligentes, otros no. Algunos son disciplinados y diligentes, otros no. Algunos trabajan diligentemente, otros no...

[1] when
[2] believe it or not
[3] spicy-hot
[4] toward
[5] bandits

[6] fools
[7] not all
[8] accustomed
[9] They like
[10] equal, same

Suddenly she stopped. A look of concern crossed her *cara*. *«Perdóneme, señor.»*

—*¿Por qué?*

—*Usted, señor, ¿de dónde es?*

—*Ahora de Boston.*

—*Oh, Boston es una ciudad muy grande, ¿verdad?*

—*Sí. Pero yo soy de una ciudad suburbana.*

—*Sí? ¿Conoce usted a la familia Kennedy?*

—(Do I know the Kennedy family?) *Creo que no. ¿Es una familia en Bostón?*

—*Sí*. John Kennedy.

—*¿El es amigo de usted?*

—*No exactamente. El nombre* John Kennedy *es famoso.*

—*¿Famoso?*

—*Sí. El era presidente.*

—*¿Presidente?* (I was leading her on.)

—*Sí, un presidente, como George Washington o Abrán Lincoln, pero John Kennedy era un presidente moderno, un presidente de nuestro tiempo.*

Esto es increíble, I thought. *Esta princesa mejicana tan bonita y tan encantadora y con tantos talentos sabe del presidente Kennedy.* «*¿Cómo sabe usted del presidente Kennedy?*» I asked.

—*Yo trabajo con los voluntarios del cuerpo de paz. Fue el presidente Kennedy quien hizo el cuerpo de paz.*

Her *voz* was *dulce y sincera. Yo inmediatamente* told her *que* I'd like to *saber más.* Then she told me about some of the *proyectos* they were working on. *Yo* listened *muy atentamente.* It was like *ella* herself *era un ángel de paz.*

Just then *entró otra persona—un mejicano, obviamente,* but *un hombre impresionante. El me habló en español,* «*Buenas tardes, señor. ¿Cómo está usted?*»

—*Muy bien, gracias. ¿Y usted?*

—*Bien, gracias.*

«*¿Habla usted inglés?*» I asked.

—*Un poco. Con varios compañeros norte-americanos.*

—*¿Compañeros norte-americanos?*

He smiled, *y la encantadora* laughed. Her laugh *era como una* fresh *brisa* from the seashore. «*El está hablando de su proyecto.*»

—She says I talk about my project.

«*El está hablando de los compañeros que tenía en su proyecto,*» she *continuó.*

«*Yo trabajaba con el cuerpo de paz,*» he explained.

—Oh, *¿Ustedes son hermano y hermana?*

She asked him something then *que yo* didn't catch. I was afraid *que ella* was going to leave, so I thought of inviting them to have *una copa de café.* «*Permítanme comprarles algo para tomar. ¿Qué toman ustedes?*»

—*Agua, leche, jugos…*

—*¿Jugos? ¿Qué es eso?*

—*Jugo de tomate, jugo de piña, jugo de naranja…jugo de frutas.*

—*Ah, ahora entiendo*: juices. *Permítanme ofrecerles un vaso de leche o de jugo de fruta.*

—*Gracias, usted es muy simpático.*

While we were drinking our *jugos, la puerta* opened, and in came *dos jovenes norte-americanos en* blue jeans. *La encantadora dijo, «Estos son nuestros amigos. Pero perdónennos. Nosotros vamos al Ballet Folklórico. Tenemos que ir ahora.»*

—Oh, you're going to *el Ballet Folklórico.*

«*Sí, pero nuestros amigos aquí pueden explicar todo,*» she said, gesturing to the two *jóvenes en camisas para trabajar y* blue jeans.

And with that, *mi ángel desapareció* with her *amigo.* I turned to *los dos jóvenes* when *uno de ellos dijo, «¿Qué sabe Ud. de fútbol?»*

🖳 BONUS: FAMILIAR WORDS

English words of Latin derivation share many endings with Spanish words. The following words are spelled the same in English and Spanish

-AL

vertical	horizontal	minimal	total	moral	continental
final	normal	fundamental	formal	plural	mental
local	habitual	personal	postal	social	criminal
cultural	tropical	diagonal	eternal	celestial	principal
capital	universal	internal	actual	terminal	accidental

-OR

honor	tenor	labor	rumor	favor	clamor
actor	labor	motor	superior	editor	error
inspector	posterior	horror	color	mentor	pastor
interior	tremor	reflector	exterior	anterior	rigor
humor	tractor	favor	director	tutor	

-AR

regular	insular	particular	seminar	vulgar
peninsular	circular	peculiar	triangular	popular
similar	vernacular	lunar	perpendicular	solar
familiar	molecular	nuclear		

53

▣ More about Numbers

THE "CENTURY" NUMBERS: 100–900

You have learned virtually all of the elements of the Spanish numeric system, including the word *cien* for 100 with its alternate *ciento*. To say "hundreds and hundreds" you would say "*cientos y cientos*," using the plural form of *ciento*.

The one element you will now add is the plural form *cientos*, which is used in forming 200 to 900.

Listen and repeat: 200, 300, 400, *500, 600, *700, 800, *900.

The starred items above require the dependent form before the *-cientos*.

      Not *nueve-cientos*, but *nove-cientos*.

      Not *siete-cientos*, but *sete-cientos*.

      Not *cinco-cientos* and not *quin-cientos*, but *quin-ientos*.

● (This last one would be *quincientos*, but the *initial* of *cientos* is deleted.)

Say the hundreds from 900 downward: *nove-_____, ocho-_____, sete-_____,   seis-_____, quin-_____, cuatro-_____, tres-_____, dos-_____.*

▣ Listen and repeat: *500, 800, 400, *900, *700, 300, 600, 200, *500, *900.

● Look off into space, turn off the tape, and let these numbers drift through your mind.

▣ Listen and point to the number pronounced on the tape:

200

700   500

400   600   800

100   900

300

Listen to the tape and point to the number pronounced:

	(A)			(B)	
2200	1100		1033	1992	
7700	1050	55000	1776	1918	1820
9900	6600		33	1643	
4400	8800	3300	1984	1492	1945

126

⊡ *Review*

1. Read the following numbers and give the English equivalent.

cien	*doscientos*	*ochocientos*
seiscientos	*trescientos*	*cuatrocientos*
setecientos	*quinientos*	*novecientos*

2. Say these numbers in Spanish (across columns then down rows).

800	8000
900	9000
600	6000
770	7770
400	4000
500	5500
300	3300
200	2220

Close your eyes and imagine one number at a time from 100 to 900, giving the Spanish name for each number.

54

📼 A Joke in Spanish
Spanish Only

We'll end Tape 2 with a note of humor.

¡Toc, Toc! ¿Quien Es?	**Knock, Knock! Who's There?**
¿Me recordarás en un día?	Will you remember me in a day?
Sí, claro que te recordaré en un día.	Yes, of course I'll remember you in a day.
¿Me recordarás en una semana?	Will you remember me in a week?
Pues sí. Seguro que te recordaré en una semana.	Why yes. For sure I'll remember you in a week.
¿Y me recordarás en un mes?	And will you remember me in a month?
Sí, por supuesto te recordaré en un mes. No te olvidaré.	Yes, of course I'll remember you in a month. I won't forget you.
¿Me recordarás en un año?	Will you remember me in a year?
Sí, sí. Nunca te olvidaré.	Yes, yes. I'll never forget you.
¡Toc, toc!	Knock, knock!
¿Quién es?	Who's there?
¡Pues ya me olvidaste!	Why, you forgot me already!

End Tape 2, Side B

THE ADVENTURE CONTINUES

Having completed your tasks so that your partner can advance, you report, "Both now in Chamber 19. Twenty-three steps from Target."

Instructions given you for negotiating chambers 20 and 21 require the successful completion of three tasks: 55 (Chatter at a Royal Ball), 56 (Focus on the Language), and 57 (Wrap-up Activities). You relay the same message to each other and tackle the challenge.

55

📼 Chatter at a Royal Ball

📼

| There is/there are | *hay* | This (f)/this (m) | *esta/éste* |
| There was/there were | *había* | These(f)/these (m) | *estas/éstos* |

📼

There's a king. This is the king 👑 .

Hay un rey. Este es el rey 👑 .

There was a king. This was the king 👑 .

Había un rey. Este era el rey 👑 .

There's a queen. This is the queen 👸 .

Hay una reina. Esta es la reina 👸 .

There was a queen. This was the queen 👸 .

Había una reina. Esta era la reina 👸 .

There's a princess. This is the princess 👧 .

Hay una princesa. Esta es la princesa 👧 .

There's a prince. This is the prince 🤴 .

Hay un príncipe. Este es el príncipe 🤴 .

There are animals. These 🐕 🐈 are animals.

Hay animales. Estos 🐕 🐈 son animales.

There's this dog 🐕 and this cat 🐈 .

Hay este perro 🐕 y este gato 🐈 .

Which ones sing?

¿Cuáles cantan?

These (m) sing. These (f) don't.

Estos cantan. Estas no.

📼 Tape-off next several pages. Dig in!

56

 **Focus on the Language 13–14**

Enfoque sobre le Lengua

FOCUS 13

es: era, son: eran

He is king. He was king.	*El es rey. El era rey.*
They are dukes. They were dukes.	*Ellos son duques. Ellos eran duques.*

Translate Orally from and into Spanish

She is queen. She was queen.	*Ella es reina. Ella era reina.*
They are princesses. They were princesses.	*Ellas son princesas. Ellas eran princesas.*

FOCUS 14

hay 'there **is**, there **are**' and *había* 'there **was**, there **were**'

Note that in formal, written Spanish there is no plural form of *hay* and *habia*; however, many Spanish speakers use *habian* when speaking. So, if you are writing or taking a test, don't use *habian*. On the other hand, if you're talking to someone, you can use it all you want.

There is a king. There was a king.	*Hay un rey. Había un rey.*
There are dukes. There were dukes.	*Hay duques. Habían duques.*

Translate Orally from and into Spanish

There is a queen. There was a queen.	*Hay una reina. Había una reina.*
There are princesses. There were princesses.	*Hay princesas. Había princesas.*

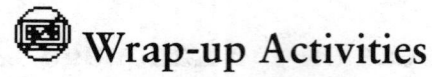 Wrap-up Activities

Speak Spanish before You Know It!

RESUMEN

En esta historia hay un rey, un rey que no toma y no fuma. Es el rey que tocaba el tambor. Tocaba cantos fúnebres. Pero ahora no está tocando el tambor. Ahora está cantando. Está cantando con la reina, ¿verdad? Está cantando cantos fúnebres con la reina en la torre. El rey canta mejor. Sí, él canta mejor que ella...mejor que la reina. Ella canta más o menos bien...no muy bien. Pero ella toca bien el tambor.

En la historia hay un perro también y un gato que cantan con el rey y la reina. Sí, y ahora el perro y el gato están cantando. Están cantando con el rey y la reina en la torre. Imagínese. Un perro y un gato que cantan...que cantan cantos fúnebres. No cantan bien, pero cantan. El perro toma leche, pero no toma agua; el gato toma agua pero no toma leche. El perro tambien toma jugo, pero sólo toma cuando está cantando...o sólo canta cuando está tomando. ¡Muy extraño! ¡Increible! ¡Absolutamente increible!

La reina está en la torre ahora con el rey. Ambos están cantando, pero sólo la reina está tocando el tambor. Ella no toma. El rey tampoco. Interesante, ¿no?

READING COMPREHENSION QUESTIONS

After reading the above story, read the questions below out loud and respond orally to them.

1. *¿Cantan el perro y el gato?*
2. *¿Con quiénes cantan?*
3. *¿Dónde cantan?*
4. *¿Cantan bien el rey y la reina?*
5. *¿Cantan bien el perro y el gato?*
6. *¿Cuál canta mejor, el perro o el gato?*
7. *¿Qué clase de canto están cantando?*
8. *El perro toma agua, ¿no?*
9. *¿Cuándo toma?*
10. *¿Cuál canta, el perro o el gato?*
11. *¿Cuándo canta el gato?*

Some Explanations

Why does the king sing?
¿Por qué canta el rey?

The king sings because he loves the queen.
El rey canta porque él ama a la reina.

Why does the queen sing?
¿Por qué canta la reina?

The queen sings because she loves the king.
La reina canta porque ella ama al rey.

Why do they love each other?
¿Por qué se aman?

Who knows?
¿Quién sabe?

Why do kings and queens love each other?
¿Por qué se aman los reyes y las reinas?

When does the king sing?
¿Cuándo canta el rey?

The king sings when the queen is content.
El rey canta cuando la reina está contenta.

When does the queen sing?
¿Cuándo canta la reina?

The queen sings when the king is content.
La reina canta cuando el rey está contento.

They sing together when they both are content.
Ellos cantan cuando ambos están contentos.

And when are they content?
¿Y cuándo están contentos ellos?

They are content when they're singing.
Están contentos cuando están cantando.

GENERATING SENTENCES FOR ORAL PRACTICE

(Functions you know how to express)

ACTOR-NOUNS: *príncipe, reina, princesa, duque, duquesa, perro, gato*

MODIFIERS: *el, la, un, una, este, esta (los, las, estes, estas)*

PRONOUNS: *él, ella (ellos, ellas), los dos*

LOCATION: *el bar/la cantina, la torre, el baño, la sala de bailar, aqui, allí, allá*

ACTION-VERB STEMS: *cant-, llor-, toc-, fum-, tom-, habl-*

ACTION-VERB ENDINGS: *-a(n), -aba(n), -ando*

AUXILIARY VERB: *está(n)*

COMPLEMENTS: *(habl-) español, chino*

MANNER: *mejor / peor (que); (muy) bien, mal*

INFORMATION-QUESTION WORDS: *¿Qué? ¿Cuál? ¿Dónde? ¿Cómo? ¿Cuánto? ¿Cuál? ¿Por qué?*

ATTESTATION PREFACE: *el sabe que, el piensa que, el dice que, el lee que, el observa que*

QUANTITY INFORMATION: *mucho, un poco*

CONJUNCTIONS AND OTHER WORDS: *pero, ni...ni, y...y, también, todavía*

REJOINDERS/ANSWERS: *Sí, no, imagínese, finalmente, es todo, por supuesto, de veras, es verdad, formidable, terrible, de acuerdo, creo que si, cuan extraño, exactamente, probablemente, que lastima, imagínate*

Instructions: Using mainly the above list of forms, do the following:

1. Take three actor-nouns and three action-words, e.g. {*perro*} and {*cant-*}. By adding the proper grammatical details, make up three quick sentences on the model of *El perro canta*.

2. Make your three sentences plural, on the model *Los perros cantan*. (Be sure to put the plural-marker -n on the action verb.)

3. Turn these sentences into yes-no questions by reversing the noun and the verb, on the model of *¿Canta el perro?* (the reverse of *El perro canta*).

4. Turn the sentences into which-questions or where-questions as in: *¿Cual canta? ¿Donde canta la princesa?*

5. Change the sentences to what-action questions as in: *¿Que esta haciendo el perro?* or *¿Que estan haciendo las princesas?*

6. Make three new sentences by joining two actors as sentence subject, on the model *El perro y la princesa cantan*. Be sure to put the plural-marker -n on the action verb.)

7. Expand your last three sentences by adding modifiers such as *todavia, solo, también*, on the model *El perro todavia canta mucho*.

8. Compose sentences with a "preface" construction: *El sabe que el perro canta* (He knows that the dog sings), *El cree que el gato habla* (He believes that the cat talks), *El observa que el rey toca* (He observes that the king plays), *El jura que el perro toma jugo* (He swears the dog drinks juice).

9. Make up equally or even more complex sentences of your own choosing from this material.

THE ADVENTURE CONTINUES

Having completed your tasks so that your partner can advance, you report, "Both now in Chamber 21. Twenty-one steps from Target. We're halfway there!"

Instructions given you for negotiating chambers 22 and 23 require the successful completion of two tasks: 58 (Creating Your Own Mini-Story Plots) and 59 (Focus on Action). You so advise Stump, and he advises you the same. You both take particular delight in creating your own zany plots and feel you could go on for a long, long time.

58

🖻 Creating Your Own Mini-Story Plots

You are now urged to create more mini-story plots, to write them out and give them orally. Limit yourself to words you know, supplemented by a selection of a few additional words given below. Examples of mini-story plots are given at the end of this lesson.

The court poet...
    composes a poem.
    reads his poem to the queen.
The member of the cabinet...
    considers the situation.
    observes the action.
The attractive secretary...
    listens with much interest.
    works with enthusiasm.
    copies the document.
    has the key.
The humble gardener...
    has an idea.
    hides the flowers in the garden.
    hides *himself* among the flowers.
The malicious thief...
    hides himself in the garden.
    enters the treasury.
    steals the jewels.
The inspector...
    investigates the crime.
    finds the jewels in the bathroom.
    encounters the thief.
The impartial judge...
    denounces the crime.
    pardons the gardener.
    condemns the thief.
The court magician...
    invents a formula.
    still insists the formula is good.
The vice-president...
    proposes a plan.
    contests the decision of the judge.
    accuses the president.
The innocent child...
    responds to the question.
    declares the truth.
The young engineer...
    identifies the problem.

El poeta de la corte...
    compone un poema.
    lee su poema a la reina.
El miembro del gabinete...
    considera la situación.
    observa la acción.
La secretaria atractiva...
    escucha con mucho interés.
    trabaja con entusiasmo.
    copia el documento.
    tiene la llave.
El humilde jardinero...
    tiene una idéa.
    esconde las flores en el jardín.
    <u>se</u> esconde entre las flores.
El ladrón malicioso...
    se esconde en el jardín.
    entra en el tesorería .
    roba las joyas.
El inspector...
    investiga el crimen.
    halla las joyas en el baño.
    encuentra al ladrón.
El juez imparcial (juez rhymes with "ace")
    denuncia el crimen.
    perdona al jardinero.
    condena al ladrón.
El mago de la corte...
    inventa una fórmula.
    todavía insiste que la fórmula es buena.
El vice-presidente...
    propone un plan.
    conteste la décision del juez.
    acusa al presidente.
Un niño inocente...
    responde a la pregunta.
    declara la verdad.
El ingeniero joven...
    identifica el problema.

explains the problem.	*explica el problema.*
solves the problem.	*soluciona el problema.*
The intrepid driver...	*El chofer intrépido...*
divulges the secret.	*divulga la secreta.*
adopts the duchess' plan.	*adopta el plan de la duquesa.*
provokes an argument.	*provoca una disputa.*
The suspicious policeman...	*El policía sospechoso...*
suspects the poet is culpable.	*sospecha que el poeta es culpable.*
argues with the judge.	*disputa con el juez.*
insults the secretary.	*insulta a la secretaria.*
The leader of the society...	*El líder de la sociedad...*
refutes the argument.	*refuta el argumento.*
admits her mistake.	*admite su error.*
pardons the secretary.	*perdona a la secretaria.*
The leader of the union of matadors...	*El líder de la unión de matadores...*
provokes an argument.	*provoca una disputa.*
denies (negates) the accusation.	*niega la acusación.*
disobeys the order.	*desobedece el orden.*
The lawyer (advocate)...	*El abogado...*
contests the decision.	*contesta la decisión.*
presents incontestable evidence.	*presenta evidencia incontestable.*
The minister of finances...	*El ministro de finanzas...*
believes the poet is guilty.	*cree que el poeta es culpable.*
speaks with the chief by phone.	*habla con el jefe por teléfono.*
The vice-president...	*El vice-presidente...*
makes the soup.	*hace la sopa.*
insists that the soup is good.	*insiste que la sopa es buena.*

PERCEPTION

Some of the sentences of your mini-story plots may involve expressions such as "The policeman insults the lady." Many learners of Spanish overlook a certain detail in sentences where a PERSON is "acted upon." If you haven't noticed it before, a quick look at the following should help you see how native speakers handle this.

Observe these three paired Spanish sentences and note how 1a, 2a, and 3a parallel their English equivalents word for word, but 1b, 2b, and 3b contain an extra piece in Spanish.

1a.	*El busca su libro.*	He (looks for) his book.
1b.	*El busca <u>a</u> la reina.*	He (looks for) _ the queen.
2a.	*El recibe paquetes.*	He receives packages.
2b.	*El recibe <u>a</u> las princesas.*	He receives _ the princesses.
3a.	*El perdona el crimen.*	He pardons the crime.
3b.	*El perdona <u>al</u> criminal.*	He pardons _ the criminal.

Each pair of sentences shows the same contrast. In 1a, 2a, and 3a something is done to some THING. In 1b, 2b, and 3b something is done to some PERSON. The * in these three English sentences marks the place where the Spanish equivalent has an extra piece. If English had the same structure, when we spoke of something being done to a person, we would have to say: "He looks for TO the queen," "He pardons TO the criminal," "He receives TO the princesses."

ABOUT THE STRUCTURE OF STORIES

Stories generally follow a more or less predictable story line that consists of several parts:

1. Introduction. Setting the story and its character(s) in time and place: *"Once there was a king who lived in a tower..."*

2. Further characterization: *"This king was wicked, but he had a wife who was kind..."*

3. Rise in suspense or anticipation of conflict: *"She liked to sing, but he didn't like to hear her sing..."*

4. Conflict: *"He said to her: 'Don't sing or I'll get angry.'"*

5. Climax: *"But she sang anyway, and he got so angry he had a heart attack."*

6. Conclusion or resolution of conflict: *"Everyone felt relieved that the wicked king was dead."*

Observe this structure in the following story plots. You can find an English translation of the plots in the appendix.

SAMPLE PLOT ONE

1. En esta historia hay un palacio. 2. El rey está en el palacio. 3. El rey tiene un tesoro. 4. El tiene joyas. 5. El adora sus joyas. 6. Es un secreto donde el tiene las joyas. 7. Pero la secretaria sabe el secreto. 8. Y el duque tambien sabe donde el rey tiene las joyas. 9. En esta historia hay un ladrón. 10. El ladrón está también en el palacio. 11. El no sabe donde están las joyas. 12. Pero el piensa que están en el baño. 13. El entra en el baño. 14. El busca y busca, pero no halla nada. No halla las joyas. 15. El piensa que las joyas están en la torre. 16. El sube la torre 17. El busca y busca, pero no halla las joyas. No halla nada. 18. El piensa que las joyas estan en el cuarto de la reina. 19. El entra en el cuarto de la reina. 20. El busca y busca y finalmente halla las joyas.

Here is a sentence-generation chart you can use to practice generating some typical story beginnings.

Había	*un*	*principe*	*que*	*era*	*pobre.*
There was	a	prince	who	was	poor.

Había	*dos*	*duques*	*que*	*eran*	*ricos.*
There were	two	dukes	who	were	rich.

Practice generating some story beginnings from the chart. Most important is to understand what your sentences mean, but of course you should give attention to certain details of grammatical correctness: matching singular noun with singular verb form and plural noun with plural verb-form; and keeping the tense consistent: present with present, past with past (There <u>is</u> a king who <u>is</u> vs. There <u>was</u> a king who <u>was</u>).

Now create your own mini-story plots. Plan them out, using words you have used before plus new expressions taken from the material in this lesson. Write some stories out and practice presenting them orally (without reading). Do not start by writing out a story in English and then trying to find words and structures to translate it. Do not try to go beyond the words supplied. Practice telling them until you can tell them fluently from only an outline or from a sequence of the pictographs you have drawn on cards. Fluency is your aim, hesitation your enemy.

59

📼 Focus on Action
Enfoque sobre la Acción

Study the scatter chart, take the self-quiz, then go to the multiple–choice frames at (C).

📼 In the *"Enfoque sobre la Acción"* module, pictographs represent various actions. In the scatter chart (A) you are given the pictographs' English equivalent, then you are quizzed in (B) to make sure you know the pictographs' meanings. Then follow the now familiar multiple-choice frames (C) where you are presented with fifteen listening-comprehension tasks.

A. SCATTER CHART

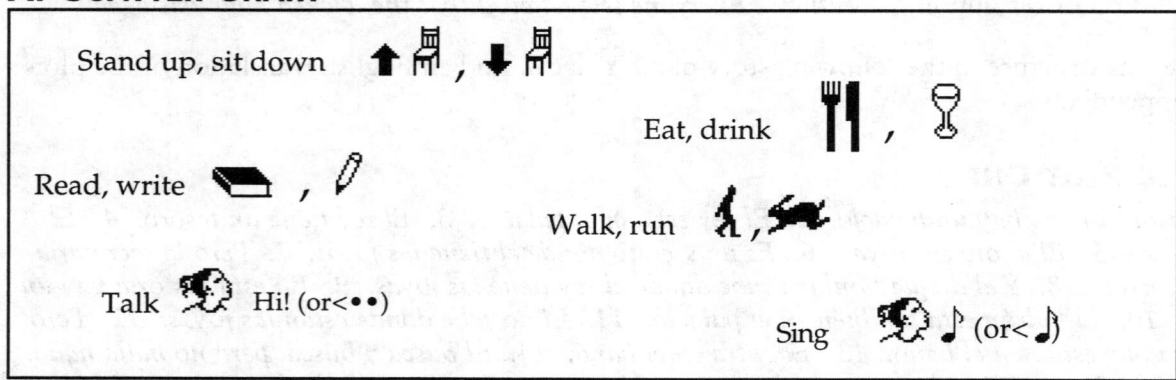

B. SELF-QUIZ
Can you "read" these pictographs in English?

📼 FOCUS ON SPELLING
The pictographs are matched with the written Spanish.

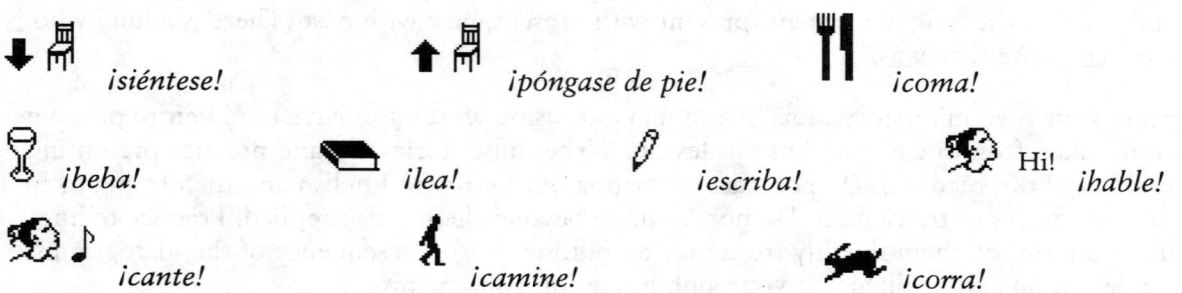

Listen and identify which part of the frame contains the *acción* or series of *accións* described on the tape. Then listen for the correct response.

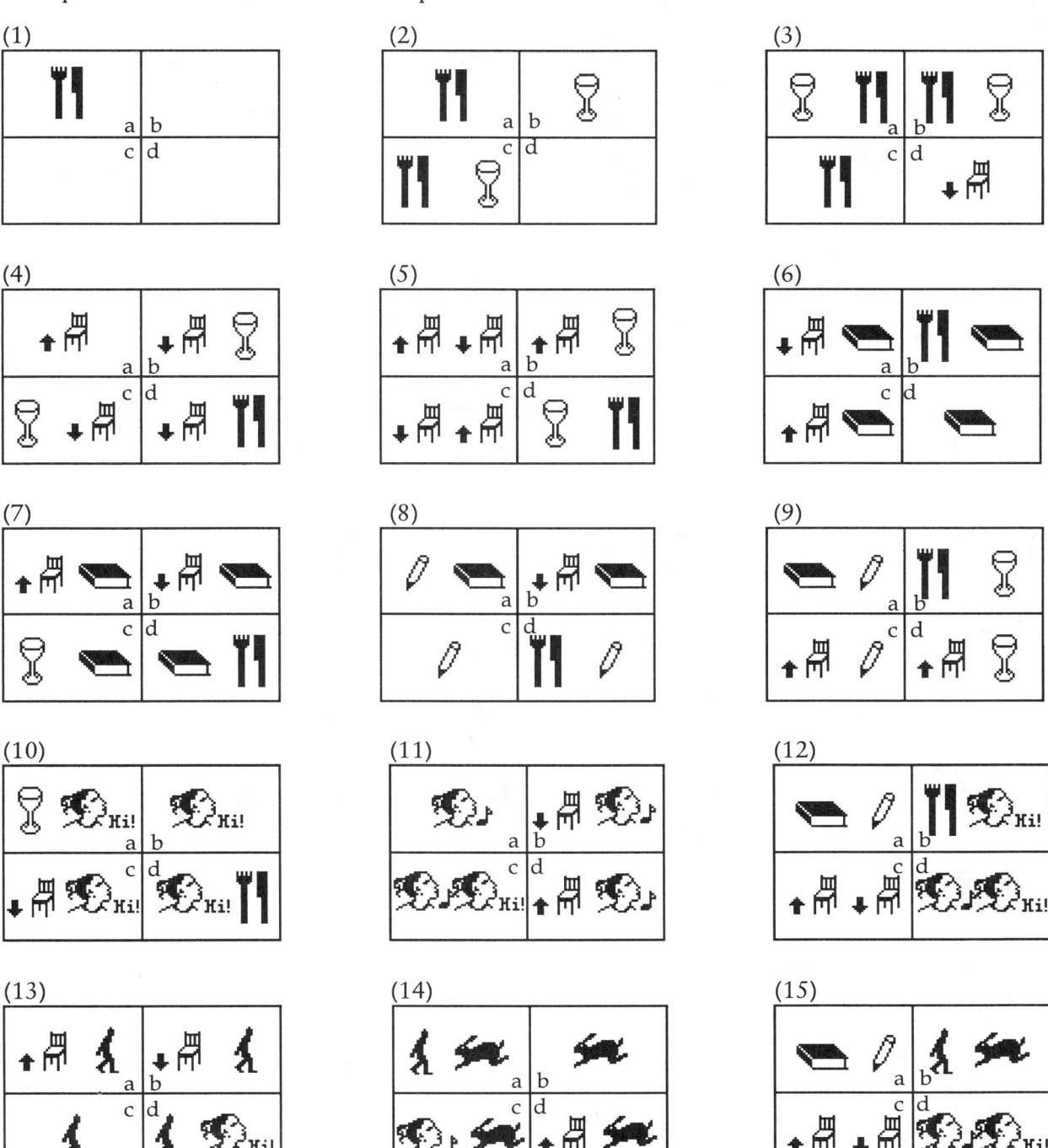

Script of Multiple-choice Frames

1. ¡Coma! (a)
2. ¡Beba! (b)   ¡Coma! (a)   ¡Coma y beba! (c)
3. ¡Beba y coma! (a)   ¡Coma y beba! (b)   ¡Siéntese! (d)
4. ¡Siéntese y coma! (d)   ¡Siéntese y beba! (b)   ¡Pongase de pie! (a)
5. ¡Pongase de pie y beba! (b)   ¡Pongase de pie y siéntese! (a)   ¡Siéntese y pongase de pie! (c)
6. ¡Lea! (d)   ¡Siéntese y lea! (a)   ¡Pongase de pie y lea! (c)
7. ¡Beba y lea! (c)   ¡Siéntese y lea! (b)   ¡Pongase de pie y lea! (a)
8. ¡Escriba! (c)   ¡Escriba y lea! (a)   ¡Coma y escriba! (d)
9. ¡Lea y escriba! (a)   ¡Coma y beba! (b)   ¡Pongase de pie y escriba! (c)
10. ¡Hable! (b)   ¡Siéntese y hable! (c)   ¡Beba y hable!(a)
11. ¡Cante! (a)   ¡Cante y hable! (c)   ¡Pongase de pie y cante! (d)
12. ¡Coma y hable! (b)   ¡Cante y hable! (d)   ¡Lea y escriba! (a)
13. ¡Camine! (c)   ¡Pongase de pie y camine! (a)   ¡Camine y hable! (d)
14. ¡Corra! (b)   ¡Camine y corra! (a)   ¡Pongase de pie y corra! (d)
15. ¡Lea y escriba! (a)   ¡Camine y corra! (b)   ¡Cante y hable! (d)

D. LISTEN AND ANTICIPATE THE RESPONSE

You'll hear, for example, (1) "What is this man doing?" "¿Qué hace este hombre?" followed by a short pause while you anticipate the response: "He eats." "El come."

1.
2.
3.
4.
5.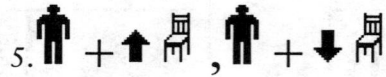
6.
7.
8.
9.
10.

Key to Listen and Anticipate the Response

1. ¿Qué hace este hombre?   El come.
2. ¿Qué hace esta mujer?   Ella bebe.
3. ¿Qué hacen estas personas?   Ellos cantan.
4. ¿Qué hacen estas personas?   Ellos hablan. Los tres hablan.
5. ¿Qué hacen estas personas?   Uno se pone de pie, el otro se sienta.
6. ¿Qué hacen estas personas?   Una corre, y el otro camina.
7. ¿Qué hacen estas personas?   Dos escriben y dos leen.
8. ¿Qué hace esta mujer?   Ella come, bebe y canta.
9. ¿Qué hacen estas personas?   Una se pone de pie y corre, la otra se sienta y lee.
10. ¿Qué hacen estas personas?   Ellos comen, los dos comen.

🔊 E. ACT OUT OR PANTOMIME WHAT YOU HEAR

Script

¡Póngase de pie!
¡Lea y escriba!
¡Siéntese y escriba!
¡Siéntese!

¡Beba!
¡Póngase de pie y camine!
¡Lea y hable!

¡Siéntese y coma!
¡Cante y hable!
¡Póngase de pie, camine, y corra!

🔊 F. READ AND PERFORM THE ACCIÓN

Póngase de pie. Siéntese. Coma. Beba. Lea. Escriba. Camine. Corra. Hable. Cante. Siéntese y lea. Póngase de pie y cante. Siéntese y coma. Póngase de pie y hable. Siéntese, beba, coma, y hable. Póngase de pie, escriba, lea , cante, hable, y siéntese.

G. LOOK AND REVIEW

Look back at the set of pictographs in (B) and see how many of them you can say in Spanish.

THE ADVENTURE CONTINUES

Having completed your tasks so that your partner can advance, you report, "Both now in Chamber 23. Nineteen steps from Target."

Curious about cell 25, one of the shaded cells on the map, you look at it closely through the glasses. Slowly a faint outline emerges of what appears to be a rose, but it is growing on a cactus, of all things! You haven't forgotten what was told you about a rose growing on a cactus. Stump, in turn, sees the outline figure of a house in your cell 25. Anxious to learn what you will actually find in that chamber, you read the written instructions for Stump to negotiate chambers 24 and 25. And Stump again gives you identical instructions. You are each to complete four tasks: 60 (A Mother Talks with her Baby) to 62 (About Verb Conjugation), and 30 (Key of the King's Kingdom). You are further informed that a guard stands at the entrance of chamber 25. To enter, you must give the correct password—which is a satisfactory performance of 61 (Questions of a Child) and 30 (Key of the King's Kingdom). You send a message to Stump: "Maybe the shaded cells are special test points, chambers with a guard who requires a performance of something. What do you think?" Stump responds: "Let's assume you're right." You take on the tasks.

60

🔊 A Mother Talks with Her Baby

Una Madre Habla a Su Niñito

Here is your little girl dolly.	*Esta es tu muñequita.*
Her name is Anita.	*Ella se llama Anita.*
Anita has hands and feet.	*Anita tiene manos y piés.*
Her hands and feet are like yours.	*Sus manos y sus piés son como los tuyos.*
But they are very little. Look.	*Pero son chiquitos. Mira.*
Look how little they are.	*Mira cuán chiquitos que son.*
Two tiny little hands.	*Dos manos chiquititas.*
Two tiny feet.	*Dos piés chiquititos.*
Here is Pinocchio.	*Esta es Pinocchio.*
He is Anita's big brother.	*El es el hermano mayor de Anita.*
Does Pinocchio have hands and feet?	*¿Tiene Pinocchio manos y pies?*
He has hands and feet like Anita's.	*El tiene manos y piés como los de Anita.*
He has hands and feet just like yours.	*El tiene manos y piés exactamente como los tuyos.*
Look, his hands and feet are like yours.	*Mira, sus manos y sus piés son como los tuyos.*
Does Pinocchio have a nose?	*¿Tiene Pinocchio una nariz?*
Yes, look at his nose.	*Sí, mira su nariz.*
He has a large nose.	*El tiene una nariz larga.*
Is his nose like Anita's nose?	*¿Es su nariz como la de Anita?*
No, Pinocchio's nose is long.	*Nó, la nariz de Pinocchio es larga.*
Look how large his nose is.	*Mira que larga que es su nariz.*
Where is your nose?	*¿Donde está tu nariz?*
Here it is. Here is your nose.	*Aquí está. Aquí está tu nariz.*
Is it large like Pinocchio's?	*¿Es ella larga, como la de Pinocchio?*
No, it's not a large nose.	*Nó esta no es una nariz larga.*
You don't have a large nose like Pinocchio.	*Tu no tienes una nariz larga como Pinocchio.*
You have a little nose.	*Tu tienes una nariz pequeña.*
Look at Anita's face.	*Mira la cara de Anita.*
She has a pretty face, doesn't she?	*Ella tiene una cara bonita, ¿no es cierto?*
Where are Anita's eyes?	*¿Dónde están los ojos de Anita?*
Here are her eyes.	*Estas son sus ojos.*
Her eyes are pretty, aren't they?	*Sus ojos son bonitos ¿no?*
Two pretty eyes.	*Dos ojos bonitos.*
Anita is a pretty dolly.	*Anita es una muñeca bonita.*
Where are Pinocchio's ears?	*¿Donde están las orejas de Pinocchio?*
Here they are. Here are his ears.	*Aquí están. Aquí están sus orejas.*
He has two ears and two eyes.	*El tiene dos ojos y dos orejas.*
How many eyes do you have?	*¿Cuantos ojos tienes tu?*
You have two eyes, of course.	*Tienes dos ojos, por supuesto.*
And how many ears? Two.	*¿Y cuántas orejas? Dos.*
You have two ears and two eyes.	*Tú tienes dos orejas y dos ojos.*
Two ears to hear with.	*Dos orejas para oír.*
Two eyes to see with.	*Dos ojos para ver.*

141

61

🔲 Questions of a Child
Preguntas de un Niño

Daddy, where do giraffes live?
Giraffes live in Africa.
Do I live in Africa?
No, you don't live in Africa.
You and mama, do you live in Africa?
No, we don't live in Africa.
Why?
Because we're not giraffes.

¿Papa dondé viven las jirafas?
Las jirafas viven en Africa.
¿Vivo yo en Africa?
No, tú no vives en Africa.
Tu y mamá ¿viven ustedes en Africa?
No, no vivimos en Africa.
¿Por qué?
Porque no somos jirafas.

🔲About Verb Conjugation

A few centuries back, the English verb system was more complex than it is today. Compare the conjugation pattern of the present tense of the verb "to bind" in the English of today and of then.

	Today's English	Early English
1st person:	I bind	I bind-<u>e</u>
2nd person:	you bind	thou bind-<u>est</u>
3rd person:	he bind-<u>s</u>	he bind-<u>eth</u>

The verb endings -*e*, -*est*, and -*eth* (1st, 2nd, and 3rd person, respectively) have given way to a simpler contrast: bind-*s* (3rd person) vs. bind (1st or 2nd person). In Spanish, the corresponding pattern of endings is like that of early English, a different ending *tied to* (i.e. conjugated with) each "person."

	Spanish	Early English
1st person:	*yo tom-<u>o</u>*	I take
2nd person:	*tú tom-<u>as</u>*	Thou takest
3rd person:	*él tom-<u>a</u>*	He taketh

There are two verb classes, called (because of their "thematic" vowels) -*ar* verbs (Class 1) and -*er* or -*ir* verbs (Class 2). The -*er* and -*ir* verbs are so much alike they are each viewed as submembers of Class 2.

1. Verbs with thematic vowel A are called "-ar verbs" (*tom<u>ar</u>, cant<u>ar</u>*)

2a. Verbs with thematic vowel E are called "-er verbs" (*com<u>er</u>, comprend<u>er</u>*)

2b. Verbs with thematic vowel I are called "-ir verbs" (*recib<u>ir</u>, viv<u>ir</u>*)

PRESENT TENSE -AR VERBS

Singular	Plural	Singular	Plural	The endings isolated	
I take	we take	*tom-o*	*tom-<u>a</u>mos*	-o	-amos
you take	you take	*tom-<u>a</u>s*	*tom-<u>a</u>n*	-as	-an
he takes	they take	*tom-<u>a</u>*	*tom-<u>a</u>n*	-a	-an

PRESENT TENSE -ER VERBS

Singular	Plural	Singular	Plural	The endings isolated	
I receive	we receive	*comprend-o*	*comprend-<u>e</u>mos*	-o	-emos
you receive	you receive	*comprend-<u>e</u>s*	*comprend-<u>e</u>n*	-es	-en
he takes	they receive	*comprend-<u>e</u>*	*comprend-<u>e</u>n*	-e	-en

PRESENT TENSE -IR VERBS

Singular	Plural	Singular	Plural	The endings isolated	
I live	we live	yo viv-o	nosotros viv-imos	-o	-imos
you live	you live	tú viv-es	ustedes viv-en	-es	-en
he lives	they live	el/ella viv-e	ellos/ellas viv-en	-e	-en

THE VERB SER 'TO BE' IS IRREGULAR

Singular	Plural	Singular	Plural
I am	we are	yo soy	nosotros somos
you are	you are	tú eres	ustedes son
s/he is	they are	él/ella es	ellos son

THE ADVENTURE CONTINUES

Having completed your tasks so that your partner can advance, you report, "Both now in cell 25, which Stump dubs 'the place of the cactus rose' and I dub 'the place of the gingerbread house.' Both passed the password test with flying colors and had great fun doing it. Seventeen steps from Target."

The next instructions mark another steep climb in the effort-&-time-cost of your progress, but also an increase in the enjoyment of accomplishment. Now, in order to negotiate the next three chambers, each of you must complete the next **eight** modules: 63 (*Puntos, líneas y figuras*) through 70 (*Una lección de geografía*). You wonder, are you ready for this challenge? You relax a bit, think noble thoughts, then take a deep breath and a swallow of the delicious *jugo de fuerza*, and plow ahead, determined to do your best.

▦ Dots, Lines, and Figures

Puntos, Líneas y Figuras

▦ A. SCATTER CHART

△ *triángulo*	△ ○ □ ☆ *figuras*	□ *cuadrado*
☆ *estrella*	✚ *cruz*	○ *círculo*

▦ B. LOOK, LISTEN AND READ

1. ✚
   ¿Qué es esto? Es una cruz.

2. ✚ ✚ ☆ ☆ ☆
   ¿Qué son estas? Estas son cruces y estrellas.

3. ☆ ☆ □ □ □
   ¿Y qué son estas? Son figuras: estrellas y cuadrados.

4. ○ ○ △ △
   Aquí están otras figuras: círculos y triángulos.

5. ○ △ □ ☆
   Los círculos, los triángulos, los cuadrados y las estrellas, todas éstas son figuras.

6. ○
   ¿Qué tipo de figura es éste? Es un círculo. Y también es la letra o.

7. ▬▬▬
   ¿Cuál tipo de línea es este? Es una línea horizontal, larga, y gruesa.

8. —
   ¿Cuál tipo de línea es este? Es una línea horizontal, corta, y delgada.

9. ▫▫
   ¿Estas figuras son triángulos o cuadrados? Son cuadrados.

10. △ ▽ △ ▽
    Todas estas figuras son triángulos, dos indicando hacia arriba y dos indicando hacia abajo.

11. ▫□△ □▽ ▫▫
    Varios cuadrados y triángulos. Los cuadrados son grandes y pequeños, pero todos los triángulos son grandes.

12. ___||||\\//
    Todas éstas son líneas rectas: líneas horizontales, líneas verticales y líneas diagonales.

C. Look and listen

1. ✚

2. ✚ ✚ ☆ ☆ ☆

3. ☆ ☆ □ □ □

4. ○ ○ △ △

5. ○ △ □ ☆

6. ○

7. ▬▬▬

8. —

9. □ □

10. △ ▽ △ ▽

11. □ □ △ ▽ □ □

12. ___ | | | | \\\/

D. Multiple-Choice Frames

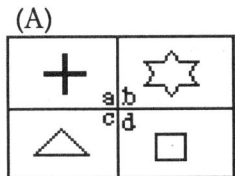
(A)

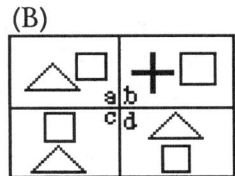
(B)

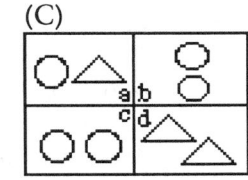
(C)

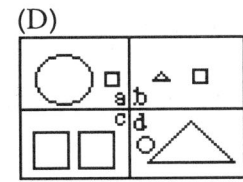
(D)

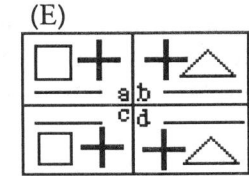
(E)

E. Listen and Draw

(Stop the tape if the pace is too fast. Check your answers in the appendix.)

1.　　　2.　　　3.　　　4.　　　5.

F. Read for Meaning

See if you can understand the following sentences. You don't need to know every word to understand the general meaning of the sentence! An English translation is in the appendix.

1. *¿Cuál letra es ésta? ¿Es la letra D o la letra O? Es una D.*
2. *¿Qué tipo de figura es esta? ¿Es un círculo o un cuadrado?*
3. *Todos estos triángulos indican hacia arriba y todas estas flechas indican hacia abajo.*
4. *Estas dos figuras están entre dos líneas verticales.*
5. *¿Qué tipo de figura precede la letra F?*
6. *¿Qué tipo de figura sigue la letra F?*
7. *¿Cuál letra sigue el triángulo grande, y cuál precede el círculo grande?*
8. *¿No sigue el triángulo grande la letra B?*

64

A Spanish Lesson
Una Lección de Español

Write your name on this paper.	*Escriba su nombre en este papel.*
(You're writing your name.)	*(Ud. está escribiendo su nombre.)*
Very well. You wrote your name.	*Muy bien. Ud. escribió su nombre.*
Now cross it out.	*Ahora táchelo.*
(You're crossing out your name.)	*(Ud. está tachando su nombre.)*
Very well. You wrote your name, and then you crossed it out.	*Muy bien. Ud. escribió su nombre, y luego lo tachó.*
Write the name of your father or mother.	*Escriba el nombre de su padre o madre.*
(You're writing your father's name.)	*(Ud. está escribiendo el nombre de su padre.)*
Very well. You wrote your father's name, right?	*Muy bien. Ud. escribió el nombre de su padre, ¿verdad?*
Now write your mother's name.	*Ahora escriba el nombre de su madre.*
Now cross out your father's name.	*Ahora tache el nombre de su padre.*
Very well. You wrote your own name and then crossed it out.	*Muy bien. Ud. escribió su propio nombre y luego lo tachó.*
Then you wrote your father's name and crossed it out.	*Luego escribió Ud. el nombre de su padre y lo tachó.*
And then you wrote your mother's name and crossed it out.	*Y luego escribió el nombre de su madre y lo tachó.*
Now write my name and then cross it out.	*Ahora escriba el nombre mío y luego táchelo.*
Take your pencil. Take it.	*Tome su lápiz. Tómelo.*
Put your pencil here. Put it here.	*Ponga su lápiz aquí. Póngalo aquí.*
Take your white paper. Take it.	*Tome su papel blanco. Tómelo.*
Put your paper here. Put it here.	*Ponga su papel aquí. Póngalo aquí.*
Take my red pencil. Take it.	*Tome mi lápiz rojo. Tómelo.*
Put my pencil here. Put it here.	*Ponga mi lápiz aquí. Póngalo aquí.*
Take my red paper. Take it.	*Tome mi papel rojo. Tómelo.*
Put my paper here. Put it here.	*Ponga mi papel aquí. Póngalo aquí.*
Excellent!	*¡Magnífico!*
Sack. Box. There is or there are.	*Bolsa. Caja. Hay.*
Here there's a pencil.	*Aquí hay un lápiz.*
Here there are two pencils.	*Aquí hay dos lápices.*
How many pencils? Two.	*¿Cuántos lápices? Dos.*
Put this one in the box.	*Meta éste en la caja.*
Put it in.	*Métalo.*
Put these in the box too.	*Meta estos en la caja también.*
Put them in.	*Métalos.*
Take a paper and put it in this box.	*Tome un papel y métalo en esta caja.*
Take another paper and put it in the same box.	*Tome otro papel y métalo en la misma caja.*
Take two pencils and put them in this sack.	*Tome dos lápices y métalos en esta bolsa.*
Take another pencil and put it in the same sack.	*Tome otro lápiz y métalo en la misma bolsa.*

65

An Overview of Broad Features of Spanish Verb Structure

PART 1

Suppose that a Spanish-speaker recognized the basic meaning of the English verb "speak," but was ignorant of the forms it takes in its various grammatical functions (speaking, speaks, spoke, spoken). For him it would make perfect sense to fit English words into Spanish patterns, producing such forms as the following. We'll call this hybrid language "Spanglish."

Spanglish Form	Parallel to Normal English	Technical Name
él SPEAK-a	he speaks	simple present
él SPEAK-ará	he will speak[1]	future
él SPEAK-aría	he would speak[1]	conditional
él SPEAK-aba	he spoke (at times)[2]	imperfective (unbounded/not closed)
él SPEAK-ó	he spoke (on a given occasion)[2]	preterite or perfective (bounded/closed)
SPEAK-a!	speak! (address to a familiar)[3]	familiar singular imperative
SPEAK-e!	speak! (formal address)[3]	formal singular imperative
SPEAK-en!	speak! (formal address)	plural imperative
SPEAK-ar	to speak	infinitive form
SPEAK-ando	speak-ing	present participle form
SPEAK-ado	spok-en	past participle form
él ha SPEAK-ado	he has spok-en	present perfect
él había SPEAK-ado	he had spok-en	past perfect
él habrá SPEAK-ado	he will have spok-en	future perfect
él habría SPEAK-ado	he would have spok-en	conditional perfect

[1]Note that Spanish uses suffixes to express future and condition whereas English uses modals such as *will* and *would*.

[2]Spanish is different than English because it distinguishes between past actions viewed as unbound/not completed vs. bound/completed. An example of this difference would be the English sentences "When I was at college, I called home and <u>spoke</u> to my parents every week" vs. "Last week I called home and <u>spoke</u> to my parents for over an hour."

[3]Note the distinction between familiar and formal address.

PART 2

Furthermore, as you can see from what you already know of Spanish verbs, this Spanish speaker would feel that the following ways of linking verb with pronoun makes perfect sense. In fact, because of the distinctive verb endings, he would feel comfortable speaking without the subject pronoun, if the context were clear.

	Singular				Plural			
	English		Spanglish		English		Spanglish	
First Person	I	speak	*yo*	*SPEAK-o*	we	speak	*nosotros*	*SPEAK-amos*
Second Person	you	speak	*tu*	*SPEAK-as*	you	speak	*ustedes*	*SPEAK-an*
Third Person	he she it	speaks	*él* *ella*	*SPEAK-a*	they	speak	*ellos*	*SPEAK-an*

PART 3

The auxiliary word of paramount importance for forming the "I <u>have</u> spoken" form of the verb is *haber*. Its conjugation is: *he, has, ha, hemos, han, han.*

yo *he* SPEAK-*ado* ... I have spoken
tú *has* SPEAK-*ado* ... you (sg) have spoken
él/ella *ha* SPEAK-*ado* ... he has spoken
nosotros *hemos* SPEAK-*ado* ... we have spoken
ustedes *han* SPEAK-*ado* ... you (pl) have spoken
ellos/ellas *han* SPEAK-*ado* ... they have spoken

66

Familiar Words

Here are some Spanish cognates that you should recognize.

-ABLE/-IBLE

(im)posible   *venerable*   *invincible*   *(in)tolerable*
(in)visible   *(in)variable*   *(in)corruptible* *(in)disputable*
perceptible   *(in)separable* *(ir)redimible*   *(in)perdonable*
(in)corrigible   *(in)curable*   *(in)tangible*   *(ir)refutable*
(im)permeable   *(in)variable*   *(in)formidable*

-CION (COMPARE TO ENGLISH -TION, -SION)

participación *invención*   *inspección* *visión*   *misión*
inflección   *formación*   *dirección*   *refutación*   *operación*
obligación   *variación*   *corrupción* *preparación* *opreción*
federación   *percepción* *disputación* *insulación*   *omisión*
nación   *corrección* *veneración* *elaboración* *reflección*

67

📼 Chatter at a Royal Ball

🔊 GETTING READY FOR *CONVERSACIÓN*

To dance	*Bailar*	I know	*(Yo) sé*
To know, know how	*Saber*	Listen!	*¡Escucha!*
Knows how to dance	*Sabe bailar*	Listen to me!	*¡Escúchame!*
(S/he) has	*Tiene*	Can you beat that?!	*¡Fíjese!*
To joke	*Bromear*	In fact	*De hecho*
I'm not joking	*No estoy bromeando*	Don't tell me!	*¡No me digas!*

📼 CONVERSATION

• : The king of France has a horse. — *El rey de Francia tiene un caballo.*

•• : Of course he has a horse. What king doesn't have a horse? — *Por supuesto tiene un caballo. ¿Qué rey no tiene caballo?*

• : And you know, his horse is white. — *Y, ¿sabes? su caballo es blanco.*

•• : Of course I know. What king doesn't have a white horse? — *Claro que lo sé. ¿Qué rey no tiene un caballo blanco?*

• : Listen to me! His horse knows how to dance. — *¡Escúchame! Su caballo sabe bailar.*

•• : Whose horse knows how to dance? — *¿El caballo de quién sabe bailar?*

• : The horse of the king of France. — *El caballo del rey de Francia.*

•• : You are joking. — *Estás bromeando.*

• : I'm not joking. It's true. His horse knows how to do the cha-cha-cha. — *No estoy bromeando. Es la verdad. Su caballo sabe bailar el cha-cha-cha.*

•• : Can you beat that?! — *¡Fíjese!*

• : In fact, the horse and the dog and the cat dance together. — *De hecho, el caballo, el perro, y el gato bailan juntos.*

•• : Don't tell me! The white horse of the king of France dances with the dog and cat? — *¡No me digas! ¿El caballo blanco del rey de Francia baila con el perro y el gato?*

• : Precisely. — *Precisamente.*

68

An Incident in a Park in Central America 1

Un Incidente en un Parque en Centro América

Let me *contar* you *una historia*. Do you see this picture? It's a *dibujo* of a *parque* where people come to enjoy themselves. And it is *en este parque* that my *historia* takes place. *El incidente* that I'm going to *contar* about involved some soldiers, some *soldados* in this small *pueblo en centro america*. Some of *los soldados* were *de Cuba, los otros* were *de Norteamerica, de los Estados Unidos de America*. Picture that: *soldados norte-americanos y soldados cubanos en* a nice little *parque...un parquecito...en* a nice little *pueblo...un pueblito...*somewhere *en centro america*. Can you anticipate *que pasa?* I don't think so.

Look at *el dibujo*. In it you can see *el pueblito, y aqui en el pueblito* you can *ver el parquecito*. What do you suppose *que los soldados norteamericanos* were doing *en el parque?* Do you suppose *que* they *estaban* working...*trabajando?* No, *ellos* weren't *trabajando...no estaban trabajando*. If *los soldados norteamericanos no estaban trabajando en el parque, ¿que estaban haciendo?* They were playing *beisbol...jugando beisbol*, that's what. *Ellos estaban jugando beisbol*.

(To be continued)

69

📼 Chatter at a Royal Ball

📼 GETTING READY FOR *CONVERSACIÓN*—WORDS

To assure	*Asegurar*	Owner	*Proprietario*
To lie	*Mentir*	Frankly	*Francamente*
To prove	*Probar*	I can do it.	*Yo puedo hacerlo.*
To be able, can	*Poder*	When	*Cuando*
To eat	*Comer*	Once in a while	*De vez en cuando*
To say	*Decir*	To swallow	*Tragar*
To cook	*Cocinar*	To have <u>oneself</u> a swig	*Tomar<u>se</u> un trago*
To work	*Trabajar*	While	*Mientras*
To dance	*Bailar*		

Phrases

You're lying.	*Estás mintiendo.*	I can prove it.	*Puedo probarlo.*
I don't lie.	*No miento.*	That's fantastic!	*¡Eso es fantástico!*
You're pulling my leg!	*¡Me estás tomando el pelo!*	It's no big thing.	*No es gran cosa.*
I assure you it is so.	*Te aseguro que es así.*	Don't tell me!	*¡No me digas!*
I don't believe you.	*No te creo.*	Who can believe it?	*¿Quién puede creerlo?*
I don't believe it.	*No lo creo.*	How can I believe that?	*¿Cómo puedo creer eso?*
I can't believe it.	*No puedo creerlo.*		

His (her/your/their) restaurant	*Su restaurante*
The cook is in the kitchen cooking.	*El cocinero está en la cocina cocinando.*
You're not telling the truth.	*No dices la verdad.*
I'm telling the truth.	*Digo la verdad.*

📼 CONVERSATION

•: Where do the duchess's dog and cat eat now? — *¿Dónde comen el perro y el gato de la duquesa ahora?*

••: They always eat together in their restaurant. — *Siempre comen juntos en su restaurante.*

•: Do the dog and the cat have a restaurant now? — *¿El perro y el gato ahora tienen un restaurante?*

••: Yeah, the dog is the owner and the cat is the cook…he works in the kitchen. — *Sí pues, el perro es el proprietario y el gato es el cocinero…trabaja en la cocina.*

•: Ha! That's fantastic! — *¡Ja! ¡Eso es fantástico!*

••: That is fantastic. And they say the cat dances while he cooks. — *Eso sí es fantástico. Y dicen que el gato baila mientras cocina.*

•: Don't tell me! I can't believe it! — *¡No me digas! ¡No puedo creerlo!*

••: I'm telling the truth. — *Digo la verdad.*

•: I don't believe you. You're lying. You're pulling my leg. — *No te creo. Estás mintiendo. Me estás tomando el pelo.*

••: I assure you it is so. I'm not lying. I can prove it. — *Te aseguro que es así. No miento. Puedo probarlo.*

70

🔲 A Geography Lesson
Spanish Only
Una Lección de Geografía

Last time, we discussed the general situation of our planet, the earth, in the solar system.	*La última vez hablamos sobre la situación general de nuestro planeta, la tierra, en el sistema solar.*
We identified its geography and briefly discussed the United States.	*Identificamos su geografía y hablamos brevemente de los Estados Unidos.*
Today I would like to take you on a little trip around a beautiful part of our world; I would like us to visit Europe.	*Hoy quisiera llevarlos a un pequeño viaje a una parte muy bella de nuestro mundo; me gustaría que visitáramos Europa.*
Here is a map of Europe. If you remember, Europe is situated in the northern hemisphere.	*Aquí tenemos un mapa de Europa. Si se acuerdan, Europa está situada en el hemisferio norte.*
Let's start with these islands here.	*Comencemos con estas islas aquí.*
These are what we call the British Isles.	*Estas son las que llamamos Las Islas Británicas.*
Here is an easy question for you:	*Aquí hay una pregunta fácil para ustedes:*
What language is spoken in England?	*¿Qué idioma se habla en Inglaterra?*
English, just like in the United States and many other countries.	*Inglés, tal como en los Estados Unidos y en muchos otros países.*
Just across the English Channel is France.	*Justo al otro lado del Canal de la Mancha está Francia.*
What is the capital of France?	*¿Cuál es la capital de Francia?*
Paris, of course! Everyone knows.	*¡Paris, por supuesto! Todos lo saben.*
And what do you know about Paris?	*¿Y qué saben ustedes de Paris?*
Right, that's where the Eiffel Tower is!	*Bien, ¡Ahí es donde está la Torre Eifel!*
Look here, this is a peninsula.	*Miren aquí, esto es una península.*
On this peninsula, we find Spain and Portugal, homelands of the beautiful Spanish and Portuguese languages.	*En esta península encontramos España y Portugal, hogar de los bellos idiomas español y portugues.*
Do you know anyone who speaks Spanish or Portuguese?	*¿Conocen a alguien que hable español o portugues?*
This country in the shape of a boot is Italy.	*Este país con forma de bota es Italia.*
And this one that looks like a hand is Greece.	*Y esta que parece mano es Grecia.*
Wouldn't you like to live there and swim in the Mediterranean sea? I would!	*¿No les gustaría vivir ahí y nadar en el Mar Mediterráneo? ¡A mí sí!*
Right here in the middle is the tiny country of Switzerland.	*Justo aquí en el centro está el pequeño país de Suiza.*
An interesting characteristic of Switzerland is that in spite of its small size, it has three national languages: Italian, French, and German.	*Una característica interesante de Suiza es que a pesar de su pequeño tamaño tiene tres idiomas nacionales italiano, francés, y alemán.*
In what other country is German spoken?	*¿En qué otro país se habla alemán?*
In Germany, of course, but also here in Austria.	*En Alemania, por supuesto, pero también aquí en Austria.*
There is another language that is closely related to German.	*Hay otro idioma que está muy relacionado con el alemán.*

It is called Dutch.	*Se llama holandés.*
Do you know where Dutch is spoken?	*¿Sabes dónde se habla holandés?*
Yes, here in Holland.	*Sí, en Holanda.*
Next to Holland are Belgium and Luxemburg.	*Al lado de Holanda están Bélgica y Luxemburgo.*
These two countries are also French-speaking.	*En estos dos países también se habla francés.*
To the North here, we have what we call Scandinavia.	*Hacia el norte, aquí, tenemos lo que llamamos Escandinavia.*
Five countries are included in Scandinavia:	*Escandinavia incluye cinco países:*
Denmark, Finland, Sweden, Norway and way out here we have Iceland.	*Dinamarca, Finlandia, Suecia, Noruega y lejos, por allá, tenemos Islándia.*
All the countries we have talked about so far form Western Europe.	*Todos los países de los que hemos hablado hasta ahora forman la Europa Oxidental.*
In Eastern Europe are found Poland, Czechoslovakia, Hungary, Bulgaria, Romania, and other countries.	*En la Europa Oriental se encuentran Polonia, Checoslovaquia, Hungría, Bulgaria, Rumania, y otros países.*
There's another important country in Eastern Europe.	*Hay otro país importante en Europa Oriental.*
Can you guess? It's Russia, of course.	*¿Puedes adivinarlo? Es Rusia, por supuesto.*
Part of Russia is included in Eastern Europe and the rest in Asia.	*Parte de Rusia está incluída en Europa Oriental y el resto en Asia.*
It is a very large country.	*Es un país muy grande.*
It stretches from Finland to Japan.	*Se extiende desde Finlandia hasta Japón.*
It is the largest country in the world.	*Es el país más grande del mundo.*
Well, we're out of time.	*Bueno, se nos acabó el tiempo.*
How did you like our little trip?	*¿Les gustó nuestro viaje?*
So many countries, so many languages, so many cultures.	*Tantos países, tantos idiomas, tantas culturas.*
Now go back and review, review, review!	

End Tape 3, Side A.

THE ADVENTURE CONTINUES

Having completed your tasks so that your partner can advance, you report, "Both now in chamber 28. Fourteen steps from Target."

Instructions on your maps for negotiating chamber 29 require that you and Stump review your most challenging tasks. Practice telling some of the stories you have learned. You can expect to be called on later to give performances of your selections.

Having completed that task, you report, "Both now in chamber 29. Thirteen steps from Target."

Cell 31 on your schematic map is another shaded cell. Examining it through your glasses, you make out the faint image of a king's castle high on a hill overlooking a kingdom. On his map Stump makes out the faint image of a park. Your written instructions tell you that to negotiate chambers 30 and 31 you're each to complete six tasks: 71 (An Incident in a Park) through 76 (A Mother Talks with her Child). You are to memorize several of the poems and ditties (tasks 72 and 73) and perform them in front of the guard who stands at the end of the chamber. He will also require a performance of some of the stories that you have prepared.

Tape 3, Side B

Continuing now with:

71

An Incident in a Park in Central America 2

Un Incidente en un Parque en Centro América

¿Y que estaban haciendo los soldados cubanos? ¿Supone usted que estaban trabajando ellos? No, ellos no estaban trabajando. ¿Estaban jugando beisbol? No, no estaban jugando beisbol tampoco. Si los soldados cubanos no estaban trabajando y no estaban jugando beisbol, ¿que era que estaban haciendo? Ellos estaban eating their lunch *y* listening to *musica en la radio.* That's right, *ellos estaban* seated at *una mesa comiendo* their *almuerzo y escuchando musica.* That is to say, *ellos estaban* relaxing...*relajandose.* Do you like to *relajarse en un parque* sometimes *y* eat your *almuerzo y escuchar musica?*

Look at *el dibujo* again. *El parque* is beautiful, *¿verdad? Hermoso. En el parque* there are *arboles...algunos arboles, no muchos. Aqui en el centro del dibujo* is *un arbol muy alto. Es una* palm tree, *una palmera. Este arbol es el arbol mas alto en el parque. Tambien en el parque* there are *muchas* fragrant *flores de varios colores: rojas, amarillas, azules, blancas...las flores son bonitas, ¿no?*

Tambien en el parque hay mesas to eat on *y bancos* to sit on. *Aqui, sentado en este banco, hay un* dog, *un perro. ¿Ve usted el perro? Y aqui* on *el* same *banco* where *el perro esta sentado, hay una radio. ¿Ve usted la radio? Usted puede ver la radio, pero no puede* hear *la radio...no puede oir la musica en la radio. ¿Por que no puede oir la musica? Eso no es posible* because *este es un dibujo nada mas ¿verdad?*

En la mesa hay tasty-looking *comida: frutas y sandwiches. ¿Puede usted* smell *la comida? No, no puede oler la comida...y no puede oler las flores tampoco. ¿Por que no puede? Porque este es un dibujo nada mas. Pero* surely *el perro y los soldados cubanos pueden oir la musica y pueden oler la comida y las flores.*

The scene…*la escena*…is peaceful, *tranquila. Pero* something is about to happen. Will there be *conflicto entre los cubanos y los norteamericanos…un encuentro violento*, perhaps? Will *los cubanos* shout: "Go home, *yanquis*!" Or will *los cubanos y los yanquis* perhaps become *amigos?* Well, *esto es lo que paso: uno de los norteamericanos* hit *la pelota* high *en el aire. Y donde supone usted que la pelota* landed? *Supone que ella aterrizo en la mesa donde los soldados cubanos estaban sentados comiendo su almuerzo? No, la pelota no aterrizo en la mesa. ¿Supone usted que la pelota* got caught *en las* branches *del arbol, la palmera alta? Exactamente, eso es lo que paso. La pelota* got caught *en las ramas de la palmera alta. Y uno de los soldados cubanos vio lo que paso. El vio que la pelota* was caught *en las ramas del arbol. Este soldado* climbed up *el arbol, recojio la pelota y* threw it back to *los soldados norteamericanos.*

Then *¿que hicieron los norteamericanos? Ellos* cheered. And when the *soldado cubano descendio del arbol, ellos* went over to him *y le dijeron: "Muchas gracias." Y el cubano dijo: "No hay porque."* Then *los cubanos ofrecieron comida a los yanquis: sandwiches y frutas. Uno de los norteamericanos* went *y* brought *un cassette** de musica americana y* gave it to *el soldado que* retrieved *la pelota. Este dijo: "Gracias, muchas gracias."* Then *los yanquis invitaron a los cubanos* to play *beisbol* and they had a good time together. Even *el perro* played *con ellos.* So, as *el incidente* turned out, *los yanquis y los cubanos se hicieron amigos.*

⬛ PREPARATION FOR RETELLING IN YOUR OWN WORDS

Preparing to retell the story in your own words (weaving Spanish with English to the extent you need), review new words and phrases you will want to use. After review, see how well you can recall the Spanish equivalents for:

the picture	an incident	town	nice-little-town
nice-little-park	park	soldier	North American
the United States	Cuban	working	playing baseball.
What were they doing?	music on the radio	listening [to] the music	lunch
eating lunch	flowers of various colors	a tall tree	dog
palm tree	you can	the tallest tree	benches and tables
nothing more	you can't	that is not possible	

Pronunciation and Key-Link Memory Aids

English	Spanish	Memory Aids
to hear	*oir*	Oh -EAR
listening	*escuchando*	"Skootch" could be English slang for "listen"
relaxing	*relajandose*	Ree-La-Hand-Oh-See
eating	*comiendo*	Co-Myen-Dough
lunch	*almuerzo*	All-muWEAR-so
they became	*se hicieron*	SAY EASY ARROWn --> SAY EA<u>SS</u>Y ARROWn

Review and see how well you can recall the Spanish for:

A tranquil scene	conflict between the Cubans and the Yankees
the branches of a palm tree	he saw the ball
he came down from the tree	he said "thanks"
he said "you're welcome"	they became friends
they offer food	it's not possible

---

* some say *una cassette*, others say *un cassette.*

Reading Activity

Read the following sentences. Try to understand the main ideas. A translation of the sentences is in the appendix.

1. *En este dibujo Ud. puede ver un parque.*
2. *Y en el parque puede ver algunas mesas y algunos bancos.*
3. *También en el parque hay soldados de dos países.*
4. *Este es un soldado norteamericano.*
5. *Los otros son de Cuba.*
6. *Estos son los soldados cubanos.*
7. *El parque está situado en un pueblo en un país de Centro America.*
8. *¿Qué estaban haciendo los cubanos en el parque, trabajando o relajándose?*
9. *Y los yanquis, ¿qué estaban haciendo ellos?*
10. *¿Trabajando o jugando?*
11. *¿Quiénes están escuchando música en la radio, los yanquis o los cubanos?*

Comprehension Questions

Answer the following questions. First, see if you can answer the questions in English. Then, try to answer the questions in Spanish. Check your answers in the appendix.

1. *¿Dónde* took place *este incidente? ¿En los Estados Unidos de America o en Centro America?*
2. *¿En qué país de Centro America? ¿En Nicaragua?*
3. *En el parque había dos grupos: un grupo era de norteamericanos. ¿Y el otro grupo?*
4. *¿Qué estaban jugando los norteamericanos? ¿Poker?*
5. *¿Qué estaban haciendo los cubanos?*
6. *¿Qué estaban comiendo? ¿Pizza?*
7. *¿Qué clase de música prefieren los cubanos generalmente, la música norteamericana o la música cubana?*
8. *¿Escuchan la música cubana generalmente los norteamericanos?*
9. *¿Quién subió el árbol y recogió la pelota? Uno de los cubanos o uno de los norteamericanos?*
10. *¿Quién dijo «No hay porque»?*
11. *¿A quién se lo dijo esto? ¿A uno de los norteamericanos o a uno de los cubanos?*

Preparing to Retell the Story in Your Own Words

In preparation for telling this story in your own bilingual weave, you may wish to review some of the key words and add a few more.

historia	*bancos y mesas*	*las ramas del árbol*	*tampoco*
incidente	*flores...colores*	*también*	*hermoso*
dibujo	*comida*	*nada más*	*¿Dónde supone Ud. que...?*
pueblo/pueblito	*palmera*	*un árbol alto*	*¿Qué supone Ud. que...?*
parque/parquecito	*soldado*	*los otros*	*¿Por qué?*

Now retell the story using as much Spanish as you can.

Now here are some poems for you to enjoy:

72

 **Poems**

Only One Mouth

Two eyes to see with,
Two ears to hear with,
Two hands to work and pray
Two feet to walk with,
But only one mouth to eat and speak with.

Birds and Me

At night birds sleep like this.
They hide their eyes and don't see me.

They pay no attention to the dark,
They just fall asleep with tranquillity.

By day birds fly like this.
They stretch their wings and fly about me.

Sólo una Boca

Dos ojos con que ver,
Dos orejas con que oír,
Dos manos con que trabajar y orar
Dos pies con que caminar,
Pero solo una boca con que comer y hablar.

Los pájaros y Yo

De noche los pájaros duermen así.
Esconden sus ojos y no ven a mi.

No se dan cuenta de l'oscuridad,
Se duermen, se duermen con tranquilidad.

De dia los pájaros vuelan así,
Estiran sus alas y vuelan sobre mí.

Now here are some ditties for you to enjoy. (Spanish only)

73

🔲 Ditties

Good evening,	*Buenas tardes,*
You, how're you?	*¿Tú qué tal?*
More or less good,	*Más o menos bien,*
And more or less bad.	*Y más o menos mal.*
G'morning	*Buenos días,*
Mrs. Tren,	*Señora Tren,*
How have you been?	*¿Qué tal ha estado?*
Fine, fine, fine.	*Bien, bien, bien.*
Little boy,	*Muchachito,*
Well then,	*Bueno pues,*
How many years are you?	*¿Cuántos años tienes?*
Two or three.	*Dos o tres.*
Now I go,	*Ya me voy,*
He-he-he! Ho-ho-ho!	*Ji-ji-ji, jo-jo-jo.*
Do you wanna go with me?	*¿Quieres ir conmigo?*
Oh, you bet!	*¡Cómo no!*
When're you coming?	*¿Cuándo vienes?*
I don't know,	*Yo no sé,*
Tell me it tomorrow?	*¿Mañana me lo dices?*
Yes, O.K.	*Sí, oquei.*
See you later,	*Ya nos vemos,*
Eleanor, my sweetheart.	*Eleanor, mi amor.*
Wanna come with me?	*¿Quieres ir con migo?*
No, señor. Please.	*No, señor. Por favor.*
We're going now,	*Ya nos vamos,*
So good-bye,	*Adios,*
Come along with us,	*Vengan con nosotros,*
Two by two.	*Dos en dos.*

 Focus on Action

Enfoque sobre la Acción

A. SCATTER CHART

Eleven new action pictographs.

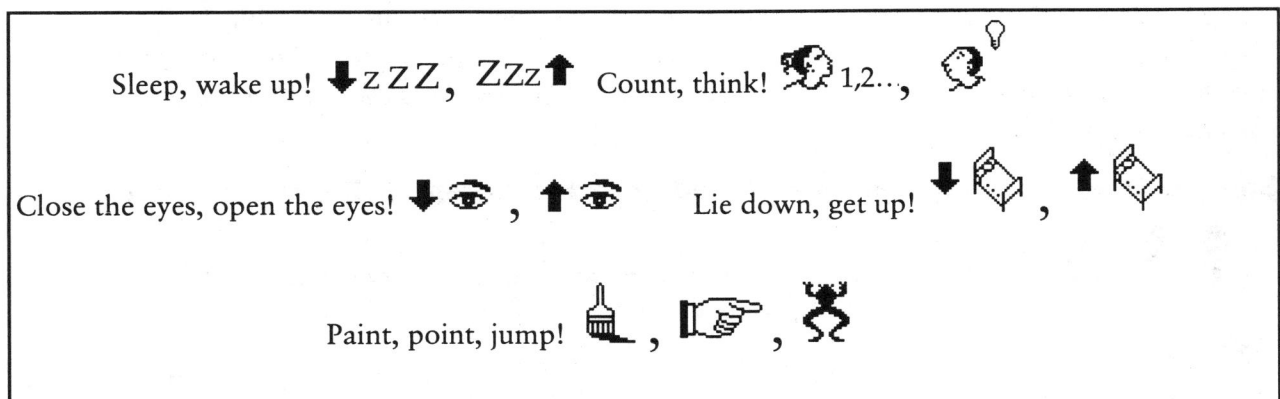

B. SELF-QUIZ

Without looking at the scatter chart, can you interpret the new action-pictographs in English?

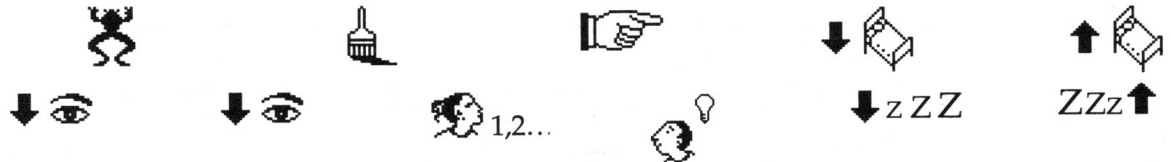

Review of Previously Presented Pictographs

¡Póngase de pie!   *¡Siéntese!*   *¡Coma!*   *¡Beba!*   *¡Lea!*
¡Escriba   *¡Hable!*   *¡Cante!*   *¡Camine!*   *¡Corra!*

The Eleven Action Pictographs with Written Spanish

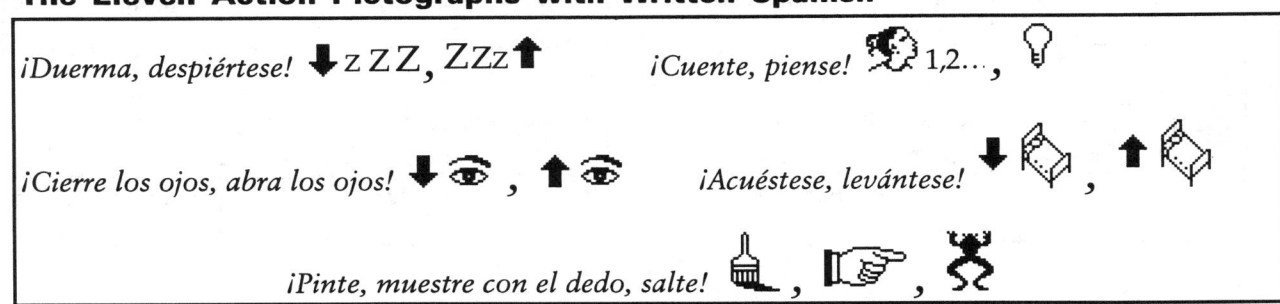

Read and Act out the Called-for Action

¡Pinte y cante!	*¡Muestre con el dedo y hable!*
¡Siéntese y coma!	*¡Muestre con el dedo y pinte!*
¡Acuéstese y hable!	*¡Cierre los ojos y abra los ojos!*
¡Cuente y cante!	*¡Siéntese, cierre los ojos y hable!*
¡Duerma y pinte!	*¡Abra los ojos y cante!*
¡Piense y escriba!	*¡Siéntese, cierre los ojos, y duerma!*
¡Acuéstese y lea!	*¡Acuéstese, cierre los ojos, piense, y hable!*
¡Póngase de pie y salte!	*¡Acuéstese, cierre los ojos, y cuente!*
¡Abre los ojos y lea!	*¡Despiértese y muestre con el dedo y piense!*
¡Levántese y siéntese!	*¡Despiértese, abra los ojos, y levántese!*
¡Levántese y ande!	

Sample Question and Responses Tied to a Pictographic Representation

¿Qué están haciendo estas personas? What are these persons doing?	*Ellos están saltando.* They are jumping.	Present
¿Qué va a hacer estas personas? What are these persons going to do?	*Ellos van a saltar.* They are going to jump.	Imminent Future

Now on your own. The first time, read the Spanish; the second time compose the sentences on your own, looking only at the pictographs.

1.		*¿Qué está haciendo este hombre?*	*El está pintando.*	Present
		¿Qué va a hacer este hombre?	*El va a pintar.*	Imminent Future
2.		*¿Qué está haciendo esta mujer?*	*Ella está mostrando con el dedo.*	Present
		¿Qué va a hacer esta mujer?	*Ella va a mostrar con el dedo.*	Imminent Future
3.		*¿Qué están haciendo estas personas?*	*Ellos están durmiendo.*	Present
		¿Qué van a hacer estas personas?	*Ellos van a dormir.*	Imminent Future
4.		*¿Qué están haciendo estas personas?*	*Todos están contando.*	Present
		¿Qué van a hacer estas personas?	*Todos van a contar.*	Imminent Future

5.		¿Qué están haciendo estas personas?	Uno se está acostando y el otro se está levantando.	Present
		¿Qué van a hacer estas personas?	Uno va a acostarse y el otro va a levantarse.	Imminent Future
6.		¿Qué están haciendo estas personas?	Una está saltando y el otro está contando.	Present
	1,2...	¿Qué van a hacer estas personas?	Uno va a saltar y el otro va a contar.	Imminent Future
7.		¿Qué está haciendo esta mujer?	Ella se está acostando, cerrando los ojos y pensando.	Present
		¿Qué va a hacer esta mujer?	Ella va a acostarse, cerrar los ojos y pensar.	Imminent Future

75

A Spanish Lesson

Spanish Only
Una Lección de Español

Look at these two objects I have.	*Mire estos dos objetos que tengo.*
Compare them.	*Compárelos.*
In what way are they the same?	*¿En que forma son similares?*
Yes, both are blocks.	*Sí, ambos son bloques.*
Are they the same size?	*¿Son del mismo tamaño?*
Yes, they are both the same length.	*Sí, ambos son del mismo largo.*
Are they the same color?	*¿Son del mismo color?*
No, they are different colors.	*No, son de diferentes colores.*
One is black, the other is yellow.	*Uno es negro, el otro es amarillo.*
And in what other way are they different?	*¿En qué formes son diferentes?*
Are they the same weight?	*¿Pesan lo mismo?*
Pick them up (and wave them).	*Tómalos y pésalos.*
This one is heavier than that one.	*Este es más pesado que ése.*
That one is lighter than this one.	*Ese es más liviano que éste.*
Now close your eyes.	*Ahora cierra los ojos.*
I'll take the two blocks.	*Yo tomaré los dos bloques.*
Now open your eyes.	*Ahora abre los ojos y mira.*
Can you tell which is which?	*¿Puedes distinguir cual es cuál?*
Which is relatively heavy, this one or that one?	*¿Cuál es relativamente pesado, éste o ése?*

76

A Mother Talks with Her Child
Una Madre Habla con Su Niño

This man's name is Peter.	*El nombre de este hombre es Pedro.*
Peter has a long, black beard.	*Pedro tiene una barba larga y negra.*
But he doesn't have hair on top of his head.	*Pero no tiene pelo encima de la cabeza.*
You have hair on the top of your head, don't you?	*Tu tienes pelo encima de la cabeza, ¿no?*
Mama has hair on top of her head too.	*Mamá tiene pelo encima de la cabesa también.*
This is a baby, a little baby boy.	*Este es un niño, un niñito.*
He has a mouth, but he doesn't have teeth yet.	*El tiene la boca, pero todavía no tiene dientes.*
He doesn't have hair on his head yet.	*Y no tiene pelo encima de la cabesa.*
Does this little baby have a beard?	*¿Lleva este niñito barba?*
No, babies don't have beards.	*No, los niñitos no llevan barbas.*
Your mama doesn't have a beard either.	*Tu mamá no lleva barba tampoco.*
No, mamas don't have beards.	*No, las mamás no llevan barbas.*
This man is called Smee.	*Este hombre se llama Smi.*
Smee is a pirate.	*Smi es un pirata.*
Poor Smee!	*¡Pobre Smi!*
He has only one eye.	*El tiene solamente un ojo.*
And only one ear.	*Y solamente una oreja.*
And only one leg.	*Y solamente una pierna.*
He doesn't have a pretty face.	*No tiene cara bonita.*
But worse yet, he doesn't have friends.	*Pero todavía peor, él no tiene amigos.*
Here is another pirate, a well-known pirate.	*He aquí otro pirata, un pirata bien conocido.*
Do you recognize him?	*¿Lo reconoces?*
It's Captain Hook.	*Es el capitán Gancho.*
He has only one arm: his right arm.	*El tiene solamente un brazo: su brazo derecho.*
Do you know why he has only one arm?	*¿Sabes por qué tiene solamente un brazo?*
Do you know why he is missing his left arm?	*¿Sabes por qué le falta el brazo izquierdo?*
It's because a crocodile ate his other arm. Ah!	*¡Ay! Es porque un cocodrilo se lo comió. ¡Ay!*
Does Captain Hook have friends?	*¿Tiene amigos el capitán Gancho?*
No, he doesn't have even one friend.	*No, él no tiene ni un amigo.*
Imagine!	*¡Fíjate!*
But he still has his eyes and his ears.	*Pero todavía tiene sus ojos y sus orejas.*
He can see with his eyes.	*Con sus ojos él puede ver*
He can hear with his ears.	*Con sus orejas él puede oir.*
He listens constantly to hear the tic-toc of a clock.	*El escucha constantemente para oír el tic-toc de un reloj.*
You know why, don't you?	*Tú sabes por qué, ¿no?*
Here is a person without eyes.	*He aquí una persona sin ojos.*
He is blind, poor fellow.	*Es ciego, pobrecito.*
He can't see. He can't see anything.	*No puede ver. No puede ver nada.*
Without eyes you can't see anything.	*Sin ojos uno no puede ver nada.*
Do you know a blind man?	*¿Conoces a un hombre ciego?*
Do you know a person with only one eye?	*¿Conoces a una persona con solamente un ojo?*

Here is a giant, a monster.	*He aquí un gigante, un monstruo.*
He was born with only one eye in the middle of his forehead.	*El nació con un solo ojo en medio de la frente.*
He can see. He is not blind.	*El puede ver. No es ciego.*
But he doesn't have friends.	*Pero él no tiene amigos.*
Why doesn't he have any friends?	*¿Por qué no tiene amigos?*
Because everybody is afraid of him.	*Porque todo el mundo le tiene miedo.*

The Adventure Continues

Having completed your tasks so that your partner can advance, you report, "Stump has encountered kings and queens, princes and princesses, dukes and duchesses, and a dog and a cat—all on their way to a royal ball. He dubs it 'the place of the king's kingdom.' I am in a park—not an ordinary park, but one where giraffes walk freely about, eating leaves in the tree tops. I call it 'Giraffic Park.'"

Both of you passed the "password" test with flying colors and were complimented on your performances. "Both now in chamber 31. Eleven steps from Target."

To make it through chambers 32 and 33 you're each to complete six more tasks: 77 (Irregular Verbs) through 82 (Wrap-up Activities).

> Note again: If any task is too steep for you to carry out, you may substitute a task within your reach—an extra hour of review, or better, a performance of something you have worked up, or can work up on your own.

77

🈺 Irregular Verbs

There are quite a few verbs whose roots have alternate forms. For example, look at the forms of the verb *ten-Er* "to have."

Present realis		Present irrealis	
teng-o	ten-Emos	teng-A	teng-Amos
tien-Es	tien-En	teng-As	teng-An
tien-E	tien-En	teng-A	teng-An

Notice the peculiarity: In the infinitive *tener* the root is *ten-*, as it is also in *ten-Emos*. The root has the form *tien-* whenever it is stressed and when it precedes a front vowel (E or I). The root has the form *teng-* whenever it precedes a back vowel (O or A). So we have three roots: *ten-*, *tien-* and *teng-*. Look at an -Ir verb (*ven-Ir*, "come") that follows this same pattern. Identify the three root forms and account for their variation as in the explanation above.

Present realis		Present irrealis	
veng-o	ven-Imos	veng-A	veng-Amos
vien-Es	ven-Is	veng-As	veng-An
vien-E	vien-En	veng-A	veng-An

Here is an -Ir verb (*sal-Ir*, "leave") with two root forms.

Present realis		Present irrealis	
salg-o	sal-Imos	salg-A	salg-Amos
sal-Es	sal-Is	salg-As	salg-An
sal-E	sal-En	salg-A	salg-An

Compare the following verbs:

poner, "to put" (*pongo, pones...*)
valer, "to value" (*valgo, vales...*)
caer, "to fall" (*caigo, caes...*)
decir, "to say" (*digo, dices...*)
traer, "to bring" (*traigo, traes...*)

Here is an -Er verb (*volv-Er* "return") with two root forms.

vuelv-o	volv-Emos	vuelv-A	volv-Amos
vuelv-Es	volv-Eis	vuelv-As	volv-Ais
vuelv-E	vuelv-En	vuelv-A	vuelv-An

Notice that the root has the form *vuelv-* whenever it is stressed, otherwise it is *volv-*.

166

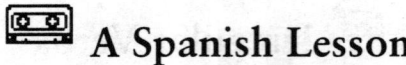 **A Spanish Lesson**
Spanish Only
Una Lección de Español

Compare these two lines.	*Compara estas dos líneas.*
In what way are they similar?	*¿De qué forma son similares?*
Both are long, thin lines, aren't they?	*Ambas son líneas largas y finas, ¿no?*
Now contrast these similar lines.	*Ahora contrasta estas líneas similares.*
What kind of line is this?	*¿Qué tipo de línea es ésta?*
Straight or curved?	*¿Derecha o curva?*
It's straight. It's a straight line.	*Es derecha. Es una línea derecha.*
With your finger, draw a straight line.	*Con tu dedo dibuja una línea derecha.*
Below it, draw a curved line.	*Debajo de esta dibuja una línea curva.*
On top, draw another curved line.	*Encima dibuja otra línea curva.*
What kind of lines are these?	*¿Qué tipo de líneas son éstas?*
All are curved.	*Todas son curvas.*
Among them there is no straight line.	*Entre ellas no hay ninguna línea derecha.*
Now add a straight line.	*Ahora añade una línea derecha.*
All the lines except this one are curved.	*Todas las líneas excepto ésta son curvas.*
Only this line is straight.	*Sólo esta línea es derecha.*
Count from ten to twenty in Spanish.	*Cuenta de diez a veinte en español.*
Count from one to ten in English and again in Spanish.	*Cuenta de uno a diez en inglés y de nuevo en español.*
Make a dot. Draw a cluster of dots.	*Haz un punto. Haz un grupo de puntos.*
A moment ago you drew a straight line with your finger.	*Hace un momento dibujaste una línea derecha con el dedo.*
After drawing that line, what line did you draw?	*Despues de dibujar esa línea, ¿que línea dibujaste?*
Was it a straight line or a curved line?	*¿Fue una línea derecha o una línea curva?*
Was it the straight line or the curved that was on top? Do you remember?	*¿Era la línea derecha or la curva la que estaba encima? ¿Te acuerdas?*
The curved line was on top, wasn't it?	*La línea curva estaba encima, ¿no?*
Another curved one was below.	*Había una línea curva abajo.*
Draw another line and put a dot at the midpoint.	*Dibuja otra línea y ponle un punto en medio.*
Label the midpoint X.	*Nombra el punto de en medio X.*
Label the end C and the beginning D.	*Nombra el final C y el principio D.*
Under that line draw a broken line.	*Debajo de esta línea dibuja una línea quebrada.*
What's the difference between the two lines?	*¿Cuál es la diferencia entre las dos líneas?*
One is a solid line; the other is a broken line.	*Una es una línea sólida, y la otra es una línea quebrada.*
What's the difference between these two?	*¿Cuál es la diferencia entre estas dos?*
One is a straight line; the other is a curved line.	*Una es una línea derecha, y la otra es una línea curva.*

What's the difference between these two?	¿Cuál es la diferencia entre estas dos?
One is a curved line; the other is a wavy line.	Una es una línea curva, y la otra es una línea ondeada.
This crooked line looks like steps.	Esta línea chueca parece unas escaleras.
Here is another crooked line.	Aquí hay otra línea chueca.
Draw a line like this one.	Dibuja una línea como ésta.
Draw a broken line above it.	Dibuja una línea quebrada sobre ella.
At the side of this line draw a tall vertical line.	Al lado de esta línea dibuje una línea vertical larga.
Draw a short, thick horizontal line on top of the tall vertical line.	Dibuja una línea horizontal corta y gruesa sobre la línea vertical larga.
These lines intersect at point A.	Estas líneas se intersectan en el punta A.
These two lines touch, but don't intersect.	Estas dos líneas se tocan, pero no se intersectan.
These two lines are perpendicular.	Estas líneas son perpendiculares.
This is a right angle, therefore this is a right triangle.	Este es un ángulo recto; por lo tanto éste es un triángulo recto.

Questions of a Child

Preguntas de un Niño

Mama, how much does a horse weigh?	*Mamá, ¿cuánto pesa un caballo?*
500 kilos more or less, I imagine.	*Quinientos kilos, más o menos, me imagino.*
Do I weigh 500 kilos?	*¿Peso yo quinientos kilos?*
No, son, you don't weigh that much.	*No, hijito, tú no pesas tanto.*
Do you weigh 500 kilos?	*¿Pesas tú quinientos kilos?*
No, I don't weigh that much.	*No, yo no peso tanto.*
Does Papa weigh 500 kilos?	*¿Pesa papá quinientos kilos?*
No, not even half (of that).	*No, ni la mitad.*
Why don't we weigh so much?	*¿Por qué nosotros no pesamos tanto?*
Well…because we're not horses, son.	*Bueno…porque no somos caballos, hijito.*

Conjugation of the verb *pesar*, "to weigh":

yo	*peso*	*nosotros*	*pesamos*
tu	*pesas*	*ustedes*	*pesan*
el/ella	*pesa*	*ellos/ellas*	*pesan*

80

🔊 Chatter at a Royal Ball

🔊 GETTING READY FOR *CONVERSACIÓN*

Wrote poetry	*Escribía poesías*	To write	*Escribir*
Knew the lady	*Conocía a la señora*	To know (someone)	*Conocer*
Knew so many languages	*Sabía tantas lenguas*	To learn	*Aprender*
So that, so...	*Así que...*	To think	*Pensar*
Sends gifts	*Manda regalos*	To send	*Mandar*
Has begun to write	*Ha comenzado a escribir*	To begin	*Comenzar*
Lovely, beautiful	*Bella*	To live	*Vivir*
Long ago	*Hace mucho tiempo*	To remember	*Acordarse*
Young	*Joven*	To suffer	*Sufrir*
Even more	*Aún más*	To fall in love	*Enamorarse*

Has suffered a lot	*Ha sufrido mucho*
Would suffer <u>even</u> more	*Sufriría <u>aún</u> más*
(He) fell in love with her.	*Se enamoró de ella.*
How did you know?	*¿Cómo sabía Ud.?*
How did you come to know?	*¿Cómo supo Ud.?*
How did you come to know?	*¿Cómo supiste tú?*
He knew Tarzan.	*El conocía a Tarzan.*
He met Tarzan.	*El conoció a Tarzan.*
He was learning Albanian.	*El aprendía albanés.*
He learned Albanian.	*El aprendió albanés.*
A famous love poem	*Un famoso poema de amor*
She's thinking of living there.	*Ella piensa vivir allá.*
No (room for) doubt.	*No cabe duda.*
What's to become of her?	*¿Qué será de ella?*

•:	And the lovely princess who knew so many languages and wrote poetry…you remember her, don't you?		Y la bella princesa que sabía tantas lenguas y escribía poesías…te acuerdas de ella, ¿no?
••:	The one who knew Tarzan and wrote the famous love poem?		¿La que conocía a Tarzan y escribió el famoso poema de amor?
•:	That one. What's become of her, do you know?		Esa misma. ¿Qué le ha pasado a ella, sabes?
••:	Oh, not long ago she met a young Albanian prince…		Oh, no hace mucho tiempo ella conoció a un joven príncipe Albanés…
•:	…and fell in love with him, right?		…y se enamoró de él, ¿verdad?
••:	Right. So now she's learning Albanian and…		Correcto. Así que ahora está aprendiendo albanés y…
•:	…and has already begun to write crazy things in Albanian to that prince, right?		…y ya ha comenzado a escribirle tonterías en albanés a ese príncipe, ¿verdad?
••:	Right. How did you know?		Correcto. ¿Cómo sabías?
•:	And he sends gifts <u>to her</u>.		Y él <u>le</u> manda regalos <u>a ella</u>.
••:	Exactly. Oh, you know about everything.		Exactamente. Oh, tú sabes de todo.
•:	So now what is the princess going to do?		Así que ahora, ¿qué va a hacer la princesa?
••:	She's thinking of living in Albania.		Ella piensa vivir en Albania.
•:	Oh, poor thing! She's suffered a lot, and there she'd suffer even more.		¡Ay, pobrecita! Ha sufrido mucho, y allá sufriría aún más.
••:	Indeed. There's no doubt.		Sí pues. No cabe duda.
•:	Ay, What is to become of her?		¡Ay! ¿Qué será de ella?

81

Verbs: *Saber* vs. *Conocer*

Although both *saber* and *conocer* may be translated "know," *saber* means "know" in a different sense than *conocer*. *Saber* has reference to knowing things like facts. *Conocer* means "being acquainted with, being familiar with." One can "*conocer*" not only people, but also places (*El conoce Méjico bien*) and works of art (*Ella conoce la Biblia, la música de Bach, las obras de Milton*).

He knows things.	*El sabe cosas.*
She knew a lot about politics.	*Ella sabía mucho de la política.*
He knows that 2 + 2 = 4.	*El sabe que 2 + 2 = 4.*
But not:	**Ella conoce que 2 + 2 = 4*

He knew Saint Francis.	*El conocía a San Francisco.*
She knew San Francisco (the city)	*Ella conocía San Francisco.*
But not:	**El sabía a San Francisco* or
	El sabía San Francisco.

PRACTICE A

Determine which verb is appropriate, *saber* or *conocer*. Write S for *saber* and C for *conocer*. The answer key is in the appendix.

1. The prince knew the answer.   (   )
2. The prince knew everyone.   (   )
3. The king knew what happened.   (   )

4. The queen knows the answer.   (   )
5. Who knows the city best?   (   )
6. Who knows who?   (   )

7. Who knows who is singing?   (   )
8. Who knows if John came?   (   )
9. He knows Shakespeare's plays.   (   )
10. He knows the judge is right.   (   )

PRACTICE B

Cover the English column and try to understand the Spanish. Then cover the Spanish column and translate the English into Spanish.

1.	Ana knows many things.	*Ana sabe muchas cosas.*
2.	Ana knows many queens.	*Ana conoce a muchas reinas.*
3.	Ana knows that the princess drinks milk.	*Ana sabe, que la princesa toma leche.*
4.	She knows the princess well.	*Ella conoce bien a la princesa.*
5.	Yes, she knows her very well.	*Sí, la conoce muy bien.*
6.	She knows a lot about her.	*Ella sabe mucho de ella.*

172

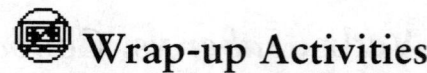 Wrap-up Activities

Speak Spanish Before You Know It!

Preparation for creating your own mini-story plots:

NEW VOCABULARY

Persons and Samples of Associated Verbs

The fat-one...	*El gordo...*
eats the whole watermelon.	*come la sandía entera.*
The cook...	*La cocinera...*
prepares the food.	*prepara la comida.*
The parrot...	*El perico...*
tells the truth.	*dice la verdad.*
The doctor...	*El doctor...*
cures the ill-one (f).	*cura a la enferma.*
The baker...	*El panadero...*
eats the bread.	*come el pan.*
The sailor...	*El marinero...*
guards the ship.	*guarda el nave.*
The athlete...	*El atleta...*
jumps over the table.	*salta sobre la mesa.*
The fisherman...	*El pescador...*
eats the fish.	*come el pescado.*
The shepherd...	*El pastor de ovejas...*
counts the sheep.	*cuenta las ovejas.*
The fireman...	*El bombero...*
puts out the fire.	*apaga el fuego.*
The cowboy...	*El vaquero...*
loves the cows.	*ama las vacas.*

Places and Associated Verbs

the kitchen	*la cocina*
works in the kitchen	*trabaja en la cocina*
the bridge	*el puente*
crosses the bridge	*cruce el puente*

Concrete Objects and Associated Verbs

watermelon	*sandía*
eats the whole watermelon	*come la sandía entera*
water	*agua*
pours water in the soup	*echa agua en la sopa*
juice	*jugo*
drinks the juice	*bebe el jugo*
hammer	*martillo*
uses his pistol	*usa su martillo*

Adverbs

in fact	*de hecho*
In fact, he always speaks truth.	*De hecho, el siempre dice la verdad.*

Verbs and associated nouns

goes out of	*sale de* sallies-forth from.
She leaves the kitchen.	*Ella sale de la cocina.*
contains	*contiene*
The soup contains poison.	*La sopa contiene veneno.*
crosses	*cruce* (compare *la cruz*, "the cross")
He crosses the bridge.	*El cruce el puente.*
listens	*escucha*
He listens but hears not.	*El escucha pero no oye.*
hears	*oye*
He hears something.	*El oye algo.*
dies	*muere*
The parrot dies.	*El perico muere.*
uses	*usa*
He uses his hammer.	*El usa su martillo.*
buys	*compra*
The baker buys the juice.	*El panadero compra el jugo.*

SAMPLE MINI-STORY PLOT

Hay un perico. Es el perico de la princesa. El perico siempre dice la verdad. La princesa nunca dice la verdad. El perico dice que el rey viene. La princesa dice que el rey no viene. De hecho, el rey viene. El viene con la reina. La princesa detesta el perico porque el perico siempre dice la verdad. La princesa está en la cocina con la cocinera. La cocinera está preparando sopa de tomate para dar al perico. El agente secreto número cero cero siete ve que la princesa echa algo en la sopa. ¿Piensa Ud. que el perico bebe la sopa? ¿Piensa Ud. que el agente secreto número cero cero siete viene?

You can find the English equivalent of the story in the appendix. Now create more of your own mini-story plots. Write them out or, better, just plan them and give them orally.

THE ADVENTURE CONTINUES

Having completed your tasks so that your partner can advance, you report, "Both now in chamber 33. Nine steps from Target."

To make it through the next 2 chambers, cells 34 and 35, you're each to complete three more tasks: 83 (A Surprising Discovery), 84 (What a Beautiful Sight), and 85 (Questions and Answers). Task 83 or 84 is to be prepared for later performance.

🔲 A Surprising Discovery
Un Revelación Asombrosa

One night when I was small,
I looked through a keyhole,
and this is what I saw:
  I saw a table,
  I saw a chair,
  I saw a cushion,
  and I saw a candle.

The table was on the floor,
the chair was on the table,
the cushion was on the chair,
and the candle lit up the room.

I blinked my eyes and looked again,
and this is what I saw:
  I saw a candle,
  I saw a cushion,
  I saw a chair,
  and I saw a table.

The cushion was under the candle,
the chair was under the cushion,
the table was under the chair,
the floor was under the table,
and you know, the same candle
  lit up the room.

Una noche, cuando yo era chica,
miré por la cerradura de una puerta,
y esto es lo que ví:
  ví una mesa,
  ví una silla,
  ví un cojín,
  y ví una vela.

La mesa estaba sobre el piso,
la silla estaba sobre la mesa,
el cojín estaba sobre la silla,
y la vela iluminaba el cuarto.

Parpadeé mis ojos y miré de nuevo,
y esto es lo que ví:
  ví una vela,
  ví un cojín,
  ví una silla,
  y ví una mesa.

El cojín estaba debajo de la vela,
la silla estaba debajo del cojín,
la mesa estaba debajo de la silla,
el piso estaba debajo de la mesa,
y ¿sabes?, la misma vela iluminaba
  el cuarto.

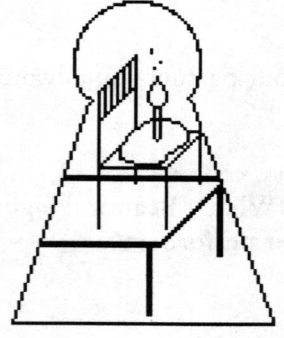

84

📼 What a Beautiful Sight!
¡Que Hermosa Vista!

One day when I was small,
I looked out the window
and this is what I saw:
    I saw a bird,
    I saw a tree,
    I saw a kite,
    I saw an airplane,
    I saw a cloud,
    and I saw the sun.
And the sun lit up the sky.
The sun was behind the cloud,
the cloud was behind the plane,
the plane was behind the kite,
the kite was behind the tree,
and the tree was behind the bird,
and I thought: what a beautiful sight!
I blinked my eyes and looked again,
and this is what I saw:
    I saw the same bird,
    I saw the same tree,
    I saw the same kite,
    I saw the same plane,
    I saw the same cloud,
    and I saw the same sun.
But now...
the bird was in front of the tree,
the tree was in front of the kite,
the kite was in front of the plane,
the plane was in front of the cloud,
the cloud was in front of the sun,
and the sun lit up the sky.
And I thought again:
What a beautiful sight!

Un día, cuando yo era pequeño,
miré por la ventana hacia afuera
y esto es lo que ví:
    ví un pájaro,
    ví un árbol,
    ví un cometa,
    ví un avión,
    ví una nube,
    y ví al sol.
Y el sol iluminaba el cielo.
El sol estaba detrás de la nube,
la nube estaba detrás del avión,
el avión estaba detrás del cometa,
el cometa estaba detrás del árbol,
el árbol estaba detrás del pájaro,
y yo pensé: ¡qué hermosa vista!
Parpadeé mis ojos y miré otra vez,
y esto es lo que ví:
    ví el mismo pájaro,
    ví el mismo árbol,
    ví el mismo cometa,
    ví el mismo avión,
    ví la misma nube,
    y ví el mismo sol.
Pero ahora...
el pájaro estaba enfrente del árbol,
el árbol estaba enfrente del cometa,
el cometa estaba enfrente del avión,
el avión estaba enfrente de la nube,
la nube estaba enfrente del sol,
y el sol iluminaba el cielo.
Y yo pensé de nuevo:
¡Qué hermosa vista!

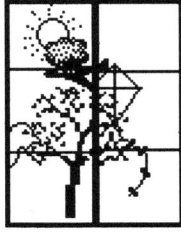

We'll end tape 3 with some helpful questions and answers.

85

📼 Questions and Answers
Preguntas y Respuestas

May I?	*¿Puedo?*
Yes, you may.	*Sí, puede.*
May I come in?	*¿Puedo entrar?*
Come in, please.	*Adelante, por favor.*
Understood?	*¿Entendido?*
Yes, understood.	*Entendido.*
What happened?	*¿Qué pasó?*
Nothing of importance.	*Nada de importancia.*
What's happening here?	*¿Qué pasa aquí?*
Nothing is happening.	*No pasa nada.*
What's new?	*¿Qué hay de nuevo?*
Nothing much.	*No mucho.*
What's new?	*¿Qué hay de nuevo?*
Nothing.	*Nada especial.*
Don't you believe it?	*¿No lo crees?*
No, I can't believe it.	*No, no puedo creerlo.*
May I come in?	*¿Puedo entrar?*
Surely. Please come in.	*Sí, claro. Pase adelante.*
Shall we go on?	*¿Seguimos?*
Of course. Go right ahead.	*¿Cómo no? Siga, nomás.*
Can it be done?	*¿Se puede?*
It certainly can. Of course.	*Sí se puede. Claro que sí.*
How are you?	*¿Cómo le va?*
Very well, thanks, and you?	*Muy bien, gracias, ¿y ud.?*
Who is going to win?	*¿Quién va a ganar?*
Who knows?	*¿Quién sabe?*
What's happening?	*¿Qué pasa?*
Nothing is happening.	*No pasa nada.*
Where do you live?	*¿Dónde vive usted?*
Not far from here.	*No lejos de aquí.*
What is this?	*¿Qué es esto?*
I think it's a computer.	*Creo que es una computadora.*

By the way, have you any change?	*A propósito, ¿tiene usted cambio?*
Not a penny.	*Ni un centavo.*
Where is the entrance?	*¿Dónde está la entrada?*
Over there, next to the telephone.	*Allá, al lado del teléfono.*
Where is the exit?	*¿Dónde está la salida?*
Over there on the other side, do you see?	*Allá al otro lado, ¿ve ud.?*
Mom, are we having fun now?	*Mamá, ¿ya estamos divirtiéndonos?*
I suppose so, son.	*Supongo que sí, hijito.*
Are there cherubim in the world now?	*¿Hay querubines en el mundo ahora?*
Not that I know of.	*Que yo sepa, no.*
Don't you believe me?	*¿No me cree ud.?*
No way.	*De ninguna manera.*
Do you understand?	*¿Entiende ud.?*
Please speak louder. I don't hear well.	*Por favor, hable más alto. No oigo bien.*
Do you have any change?	*¿Tienes cambio?*
How much do you need?	*¿Cuánto necesitas?*
Do you want to come?	*¿Quiere venir ud.?*
You bet!	*¡Ya lo creo!*
Can it be done?	*¿Se puede hacer?*
Sure it can.	*Sí, se puede.*
Did you understand?	*¿Entendió ud.?*
No, I didn't understand. Please say it again.	*No, no entendí. Por favor, dígalo otra vez.*
What happened to you, man?	*¿Qué te pasó, hombre?*
Nothing. Nothing happened to me.	*Nada. No me pasó nada.*
Today or tomorrow?	*¿Hoy o mañana?*
Tomorrow. Tomorrow night will be best.	*Mañana. Mañana [la noche] será mejor.*

End Tape 3, Side B

THE ADVENTURE CONTINUES

Having completed your tasks so that your partner can advance, you report, "Both now in chamber 35. Seven steps from Target."

Examining cells 36, 37 and 38 on your map, you advise Stump to take on six more tasks: 86 (In the Aquarium) through 91 (The Farmer and the Turnip). You receive the same directions from Stump. Completion of these six tasks will bring you to cell 38. You are told that in chamber 36 you should not be surprised to hear a distant rumbling noise. You haven't worried about invaders, but now begin to wonder if they might be the ones causing the noise. It is an issue you will soon face. You realize you are rapidly closing in on your Target.

86

In the Aquarium
En el Acuario

Look at that big fish.
It's a shark.
Sharks live in the ocean.
They have very large mouths.
And they have a lot of sharp teeth.

Sharks are dangerous, they say.
Some sharks attack people.
A big shark can take off your leg in one bite.

Are you afraid of sharks?

Are all sharks big?
No, some are small, like those fish there,

but others are as big as a bus.
Would you like to play with a shark?
It's dangerous to play with a shark.

Mira ese pez tan grande.
Es un tiburón.
Los tiburones viven en el océano.
Tienen una bocas muy grande.
Y tienen muchos dientes agudos.

Los tiburones son peligrosos, dicen.
Algunos tiburones atacan a la gente.
*Un tiburón grande puede quitarte la pierna de
    una mordida.*
¿Tienes miedo de los tiburones?

¿Son grandes todos los tiburones?
*No, algunos son pequeños, como los peces
    esos,*
pero otros son grandes como un autobus.
¿Te gustaría jugar con un tiburón?
Jugar con un tiburón es peligroso.

87

📼 A Small Child Answers the Phone

Spanish Only

📼 A small child's voice answers the telephone in a muffled whisper, as if in a closet.

📼

Whisper:	Hellooo.	*Allooo.*
Caller:	Hello. Is your mother there?	*Allo. ¿Está tu mamá?*
Whisper:	Yeees.	*Síí.*
Caller:	May I talk with her?	*¿Puedo hablar con ella?*
Whisper:	Nooo.	*Nooo.*
Caller:	Why not?	*¿Por qué no?*
Whisper:	She's busssyy.	*Está ocupadaaa.*
Caller:	Is your father there?	*¿Está tu papá?*
Whisper:	Yeees.	*Síí.*
Caller:	May I talk with him?	*¿Puedo hablar con él?*
Whisper:	Nooo.	*Nooo.*
Caller:	Why not?	*¿Por qué no?*
Whisper:	He's buzzzyy.	*Está ocupadooo.*
Caller:	Well, is anyone else there?	*Bueno, ¿esta alguien más?*
Whisper:	Yeees.	*Síí.*
Caller:	Who?	*¿Quién?*
Whisper:	Mmm.	*Mmm.*
Caller:	Who? Tell me.	*¿Quién? Digame.*
Whisper:	Some neighbors and some police.	*Algunos vecinos y la policía.*
Caller:	Oh, is there something wrong?	*Oh, ¿hay algo malo alli?*
Whisper:	Nooo.	*Nooo.*
Caller:	Well could I talk with one of them?	*Bueno, ¿puedo hablar con uno de ellos?*
Whisper:	Nooo.	*Nooo.*
Caller:	Why not?	*¿Por qué no?*
Whisper:	They're all buzzzyy.	*Todos están ocupadoos.*
Caller:	Well what are they doing?	*Bueno, ¿Qué están haciendo?*
Whisper:	They're looking for me.	*Me están buscando.*

88

💾 Encounter at the University
Un Encuentro en la Universidad

•:	Hi!	•:	*¡Hola señorita!*
••:	Sir?	••:	*¿Señor?*
•:	Hey, I have a question.	•:	*Oye, tengo una pregunta.*
••:	Yes.	••:	*¡Sí!*
•:	Where are you going?	•:	*¿A dónde vas?*
••:	Over there.	••:	*Allá.*
•:	Oh, me too.	•:	*Oh, yo también.*
••:	What a coincidence!	••:	*¡Qué coincidéncia!*
•:	Listen, I have an idea.	•:	*Oye, tengo una idea.*
••:	Tell me.	••:	*Dígame.*
•:	Let's go together, okay?	•:	*Vamos juntos, ¿está bien?*
••:	Okay. Why not? With pleasure.	••:	*Está bien. ¿Por qué no? Con mucho gusto.*
•:	I'm Vincent. You're Rosa, right?	•:	*Me llamo Vicente. Tú te llamas Rosa, ¿verdad?*
••:	No. I'm [called] Nancy.	••:	*No, me llamo Nancy.*
V:	Nancy, delighted to make your acquaintance.	V:	*Nancy, encantado de conocerte.*
N:	It's a pleasure for me.	N:	*Es un placer para mí.*
V:	What're you studying here?	V:	*¿Qué estudias?*
N:	Music. I'm a pianist.	N:	*Música. Soy pianista.*
V:	Very interesting. I am too.	V:	*Muy interesante, yo también.*
N:	My husband is also a pianist, you know?	N:	*Mi esposo también es pianista ¿sabes?*
V:	Truly?!	V:	*¿De veras?*
N:	Yes, it's true.	N:	*Sí, es cierto.*
V:	What is his name?	V:	*¿Cómo se llama él?*
N:	Don Quijote. Do you know him?	N:	*Don Quijote. ¿Lo conoces?*
V:	You're making a joke!	V:	*¡Estás bromeando!*
N:	No. It's the truth.	N:	*No, es verdad.*
V:	Oh, I forgot!	V:	*¡Oh, se me olvidó!*
N:	What did you forget?	N:	*¿Qué?*
V:	Excuse me. I have to go home.	V:	*Perdóneme. Tengo que ir a casa.*
N:	So soon?	N:	*¿Tán pronto?*
V:	Yes. Excuse me.	V:	*Sí. Disculpe.*
N:	But of course.	N:	*¿Cómo no?*
V:	Good-bye. Till later! My compliments to your husband.	V:	*Adiós. ¡Hasta la próxima! Mis felicitaciones a su esposo.*
N:	Thanks. Thanks much. Good-bye.	N:	*Gracias. Muchas gracias. Adiós.*
V:	Good luck!	V:	*¡Buena suerte!*

89

📼 Chatter at a Royal Ball

🔘 GETTING READY FOR CONVERSACIÓN

To understand	*Entender*	In fact	*De hecho*
To attend	*Assistir* (not "assist"!)	Church	*Iglesia*
Including the queen	*Incluso la reina*	There	*Allá*
Almost	*Casi*	In fact	*De hecho*
They <u>do</u> speak it.	*Sí lo hablan.*	Not everyone	*No todos*
How is [it] that...?	*¿Cómo es que...?*		
(He) only speaks it there	*Lo habla solamente allá*		
Almost without an accent.	*Casi sin acento.*		

📼 *CONVERSACIÓN*

•: The prince speaks Chinese, right?

Sólo el príncipe habla chino, ¿verdad?

••: No. He doesn't speak it. He understands it a bit, but he doesn't speak it.

No, él no lo habla. Lo entiende un poco, pero no lo habla.

•: Then it's the princess that speaks it.

Entonces es la princesa que lo habla.

••: Only her. She doesn't speak it much.
In fact, she only speaks it at church.
But she speaks it almost without an accent.

Sólo ella. No lo habla mucho.
De hecho, lo habla solamente en la iglesia.
Pero lo habla casi sin acento.

•: How is it that she speaks it at church?

¿Cómo es que lo habla en la iglesia?

••: Apparently she likes to talk it there. She doesn't like to talk it in the palace, it seems.

Aparentemente le gusta hablarlo allá. No le gusta hablarlo en el palacio, parece.

•: And who does she talk Chinese with at church?

¿Y con quién habla chino en la iglesia?

••: Well, she knows many Chinese who attend church, including the queen of Canton.

Pues ella conoce a muchos chinos que asisten a la iglesia, incluso la reina de Cantón.

•: Oh, does the princess know the queen of Canton?

¿Conoce la princesa a la reina de Cantón?

••: Yes, she knows her well.

Sí, la conoce bien.

•: And she knows the king of Canton too and all the royal family.

Y conoce al rey de Cantón también y a toda la familia royal.

••: How interesting!

¡Que interesante!

•: Really.

De veras.

182

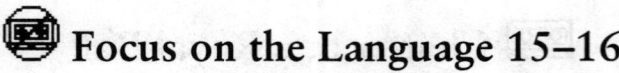 Focus on the Language 15–16

FOCUS 15

Object pronouns with finite verbs. Note how the object pronoun comes *before* the finite verb.

He sees the duchess.	*El ve a <u>la</u> duquesa.*
Yes, he sees her.	*Sí, él <u>la</u> ve. (Not *El ve <u>la</u>.)*
He sees the duke.	*El ve <u>al</u> duque.*
Yes, he sees him.	*Sí, él <u>lo</u> ve. (Not *El ve <u>lo</u>.)*

Observe Closely

Does Juan know the duchess?	*¿Conoce Juan a la duquesa?*
Yes, he knows her.	*Sí, <u>la</u> conoce.*
And does he know the duke too?	*¿Y conoce al duque también?*
Yes, he knows him.	*Sí <u>lo</u> conoce.*
He knows the plan, doesn't he?	*El sabe el plan, ¿no?*
Yes, he knows it well.	*Sí, <u>lo</u> sabe bien.*

Translate Orally from and into Spanish

Roberta knows Roberto.	*Roberta conoce a Roberto.*
Roberto knows Ana.	*Roberto conoce a Ana.*
He knows the princess.	*El conoce a la princesa.*
Roberto knows her.	*Roberto la conoce.*
Alberta knows him.	*Alberta lo conoce.*
She knows the prince.	*Ella conoce al príncipe.*
Who knows Maria?	*¿Quién conoce a María?*
Who does Maria know?	*¿A quién conoce María?*
Who knows whom?	*¿Quién conoce a quién?*
Who knows him?	*¿Quién conoce a él? (or ¿Quién lo conoce?)*
He doesn't know her.	*El no la conoce.*
Do they know Roberto and Alberto?	*¿Conocen a Roberto y Alberto?*
Yes, (they) know them.	*Sí, los (las) conocen.*

FOCUS 16

Object pronouns with infinitive verbs. Note how the object pronoun comes *after* an infinitive verb.

He hopes to see the duchess.	*El espera ver a la duquesa.*
Yes, he hopes to see her.	*Sí, él espera ver<u>la</u>. (Not *El espera la ver.)*
He desires to see the duke.	*El desea ver al duque.*
Yes, he desires to see him.	*Sí, él desea ver<u>lo</u>. (Not *El desea lo ver.)*

Observe Closely

Does Juan expect to know the plan?	*¿Es que Juan espera saber el plan?*

Yes, he expects to know it.	*Sí, él espera saberlo.*
Does he want to sing the song?	*¿Quiere él cantar la canción?*
Yes, he wants to sing it.	*Sí, él quiere cantarla.*

Further Observation

She speaks Chinese.	*Ella habla chino.*
She speaks it.	*Ella lo habla.*
She wants to speak it.	*Ella quiere hablarlo.*
She speaks Chinese and Spanish.	*Ella habla chino y español.*
She speaks them.	*Ella los habla.*
She wants to speak them.	*Ella quiere hablarlos.*
He doesn't speak Chinese.	*El no habla chino.*
He doesn't speak it.	*El no lo habla.*

Translate Orally from and into Spanish

What is it that he drinks?	*¿Qué es lo que él toma?*
He drinks juice.	*El toma jugo.*
Drinks it a lot.	*Lo toma mucho.*
Likes to drink it.	*Le gusta tomarlo.*
They sing a funeral song.	*Ellos cantan un canto fúnebre.*
Sing it more or less well.	*Lo cantan más or menos bien.*
What is it that he drinks?	*¿Qué es lo que él toma?*

PERFORMANCE TEST

Instructions: Translate orally from and into Spanish. Work with care, but don't be concerned about your pronunciation. Mark for later review those items you have difficulty with.

Which-one (of them) speaks Chinese?	*¿Cuál habla chino?*
Only the princess speaks it.	*Sólo la princesa lo habla.*
Speaks it in the church.	*Lo habla en la iglesia.*
She knows many Chinese.	*Ella conoce a muchos chinos.*
Knows them well.	*Los conoce bien.*
Talks with them there.	*Habla con ellos allá.*
Who knows?	*¿Quién sabe?*
Who knows it?	*¿Quién lo sabe?*
Who knows Tarzan?	*¿Quién conoce a Tarzan?*
Who knows the king?	*¿Quién conoce al rey?*
Who knows them? (Ana and Maria)	*¿Quién las conoce?*
Who knows them? (Juan and Jose)	*¿Quién los conoce?*
Who knew many things?	*¿Quién sabía muchas cosas?*
Who used to speak with her?	*¿Quién hablaba con ella?*
The princess used to cry a lot.	*La princesa lloraba mucho.*
Did the prince used to cry with her?	*¿Lloraba el príncipe con ella?*
(They) used to drink and sing and cry.	*Tomaban y cantaban y lloraban.*
(They) didn't used to attend church.	*No asistían a la iglesia.*
(They) didn't know the prince.	*No conocían al príncipe.*
Nor (did they know) the king.	*Tampoco al rey.*
Robert likes the princess.	*A Roberto le gusta la princesa.*
And she doesn't like him.	*Y a ella no le gusta él.*

184

91

🖭 The Farmer and the Turnip
El Campesino y el Nabo

A Folktale from Russia

Once upon a time there was a farmer,
  and the farmer planted some seeds,
  and he watered them,
  and the sun shone.
And after a time, a tiny plant grew out.
And he watered it,
  and the sun shone,
  and the little plant grew.
And he watered it,
  and the sun shone,
  and the little plant grew even more.
And he watered it,
  and the sun shone,
  and the little plant grew and grew.
And finally, one day the farmer said:
  The plant is ripe.
So the farmer took hold of the plant,
  and tugged and tugged and tugged,
  but the plant didn't come out.
So the farmer called his wife:
  "Wife, come here, wife."
And so the wife came and took hold of the farmer,
  and the farmer grabbed the plant,
  and they tugged, and they tugged, and they tugged,
  but the plant didn't come out.
So the farmer called his daughter:
  "Daughter, come here, daughter."
And so the daughter came and took hold of the wife.
  And the wife grabbed on to the farmer,
  and the farmer grabbed the plant,
  and they tugged and tugged and tugged,
  but the plant didn't come out.
So they called the dog: "Dog, come here, dog."

So the dog came,
  and the dog grabbed on to the daughter,
  and the daughter grabbed on to the wife,
  and the wife grabbed on to the farmer,
  and the farmer grabbed the plant,
  and they tugged, and they tugged, and they tugged,
  but the plant didn't come out.

Un Cuento Folklorico de Rusia

Había una vez un campesino,
  y el campesino plantó unas semillas,
  y les echó agua,
  y brilló el sol.
Y después de un tiempo, creció una plantita.
Y le echó agua,
  y brilló el sol,
  y la plantita creció.
Y le echó agua,
  y brilló el sol,
  y la plantita creció aún más.
Y le echó agua,
  y brilló el sol,
  y la plantita creció y creció.
Y por fin, un día el campesino dijo:
  La planta está madura.
Entonces el campesino tomó la planta,
  y estiró y estiró y estiró,
  pero la planta no salió.
Entonces el campesino llamó a su esposa:
  "Esposa, ven aquí, esposa."
Y entonces la esposa vino y tomó al campesino,
  y el campesino agarró la planta,
  y estiraron, y estiraron, y estiraron,
  pero la planta no salió.
Entonces el campesino llamó a su hija:
  "Hija, ven aquí, hija."
Y entonces vino la hija y tomó a la esposa.
  Y la esposa agarró al campesino,
  y el campesino agarró la planta,
  y estiraron, y estiraron, y estiraron,
  pero la planta no salió.
Entonces llamaron al perro: "Perro, ven aquí,
  perro."
Entonces vino el perro,
  y el perro agarró a la hija,
  y la hija agarró a la esposa,
  y la esposa agarró al campesino,
  y el campesino agarró la planta,
  y estiraron, y estiraron, y estiraron,
  pero la planta no salió.

So the farmer called the cat: "Cat, kitty-kitty, come here, cat."

So the cat came, and the cat grabbed on to the dog,
and the dog grabbed on to the daughter,
and the daughter grabbed on to wife,
and the wife grabbed on to the farmer,
and the farmer grabbed the plant,
and they tugged, and they tugged, and they tugged,
but the plant didn't come out.

Then, at that moment, a little mouse came by.
And the mouse said: "What goes on here?"

And the farmer explained that they
were not able to get the plant out.

Then the mouse said: "I can help."

And they all laughed at him: "Ha-ha-ha-ha.
You, so small, how are you going to help?"

But the mouse convinced them.

And so the mouse grabbed on to the cat,
and the cat grabbed on to the dog,
and the dog grabbed on to the daughter,
and the daughter grabbed on to the wife,
and the wife grabbed on to the farmer,
and the farmer grabbed the plant
and they tugged and tugged and tugged,
and the plant came out.

Entonces el campesino llamó al gato: "Gato, miau-miau-miau, ven aquí, gato."

Entonces vino el gato, y el gato agarró al perro,
y el perro agarró a la hija,
y la hija agarró a la esposa,
y la esposa agarró al campesino
y el campesino agarró la planta,
y estiraron, y estiraron, y estiraron,
pero la planta no salió.

Entonces, en ese momento, pasó un ratoncito.
Y el ratóncito dijo: ¿Qué pasa aquí?

Y el campesino explicó que no podían
sacar la planta.

Entonces el ratóncito dijo: "Yo puedo ayudar."

Y todos se rieron de él: "Ja-ja-ja-ja.
Tú, tan pequeño, ¿cómo vas a ayudar?"

Pero el ratoncito les convenció.

Y entonces el ratoncito agarró al gato,
y el gato agarró al perro,
y el perro agarró a la hija,
y la hija agarró a la esposa,
y la esposa agarró al campesino,
y el campesino agarró la planta,
y estiraron, y estiraron, y estiraron,
y la planta salió.

THE ADVENTURE CONTINUES

Having completed your tasks so that your partner can advance, you report, "Enjoying the challenges. Learning much. Now in chamber 38. Four steps from Target."

In chamber 36 you hear the rumbling sound, but figure it is only a distant waterfall in a chamber east of where Stump is and west of where you are. You can no longer hear it in chamber 37. You suppose it has no meaning for you or your mission.

You read the instructions for the next two chambers, cells 39 and 40 on your maps. Cell 39 is a shaded cell on both map pieces. On close examination, Stump makes out the vague outline of a room on your side, and you make out the vague outline of a vase on Stump's side. The circle of pictographs that represent the children's poem "The Key of the King's Kingdom" is emerging. You wonder what it means.

Instructions state that you are to complete **ten** tasks: 92 (A Spanish Lesson) through 101 (Review). You know it will be very challenging but also very rewarding. You look back at all you have learned. Amazing! You both plunge into these tasks with aroused energy, sensing the proximity of the Target Chamber.

92

A Spanish Lesson
Una Lección en Español

How do you say "bag" in Spanish?	*¿Cómo se dice "bag" en español?*
Is it "*caja*" or "*bolsa*"?	*¿Es "caja" o "bolsa"?*
It's "*bolsa*."	*Es "bolsa."*
How do you say "*caja*" in English?	*¿Cómo se dice "caja" en inglés?*
In English it's "box."	*En inglés se dice "box."*
How do you say "pencil" in Spanish?	*¿Cómo se dice "pencil" en español?*
Is it "*lapicero*" or "*lápiz*"?	*¿Es "lapicero" o "lápiz"?*
"*Lápiz*."	*"Lápiz."*
What does "*lapicero*" mean?	*¿Qué quiere decir "lapicero"?*
"*Lapicero*" means "pen" (ballpoint pen).	*"Lapicero" quiere decir "pen."*
A block of wood. Another block.	*Un trozo de madera. Otro trozo.*
On the table there are various blocks of wood.	*En la mesa hay varios trozos de madera.*
Here, for example, is one block.	*Aquí, por ejemplo, hay un trozo.*
It is standing on the table.	*Está parado sobre la mesa.*
Here is another block of wood.	*Aquí hay otro trozo de madera.*
Now, please pay attention.	*Ahora, ponga atención, por favor.*
Watch. Observe what I do.	*Mire. Observe lo que hago.*
I take this block and lay it down.	*Tomo este trozo y lo acuesto.*
I lay it on the table.	*Lo acuesto sobre la mesa.*
What did I do?	*¿Qué hice?*
I took the block and laid it down.	*Tomé el trozo y lo acosté.*
I laid it on the table.	*Lo acosté sobre la mesa.*
Here it is, laid out on the table.	*Aquí está, acostado sobre la mesa.*
The two blocks are on the table.	*Los dos trozos están en la mesa.*
The one is standing and the other is lying.	*El uno está parado y el otro está acostado.*
Put down. Insert (place inside).	*Poner. Meter.*
Pick up. Extract (remove from inside).	*Tomar. Sacar.*
Here we have a book, a bag, and a box.	*Aquí tenemos un libro, una bolsa, y una caja.*
Again, please pay attention.	*Otra vez, ponga atención, por favor.*
Observe what I do.	*Observe lo que hago.*
I take one piece of wood, a red one, and I place it on the book.	*Tomo un trozo de madera, un rojo, y lo pongo sobre el libro.*
I again take another piece of wood, a black piece.	*Otra vez tomo un trozo de madera, un trozo negro.*
I put it in this box.	*Lo pongo en está caja.*
Better said, I stand it in the box.	*Mejor dicho, lo paro en la caja.*
Lastly, I take a white piece and put it inside this bag.	*Al fin, tomo un trozo blanco y lo meto en la bolsa, en esta bolsa.*
You should remember the position of each of the pieces.	*Se debe recordar la posición de cada uno de los trozos.*

Remember, the red one is lying on the book,
    the black one is standing in the box,
    and the white one is in the bag.
	Recuerda, el rojo está acostado sobre el libro,
	    el negro está parado en la caja,
	    y el blanco está en la bolsa.

Do you have a book?	*¿Tiene Ud. un libro?*
Show me. Fine.	*Enséñeme. Bien.*
Now take the book and stand it up.	*Ahora, tome el libro y párelo.*
Stand it up on the table.	*Párelo sobre la mesa.*
Yes, stand it there.	*Sí, párelo allí.*
Right.	*Correcto.*
What did you do?	*¿Qué hizo?*
You took your book and stood it on the table.	*Usted tomó su libro y lo paró en la mesa.*

Now take your book again
    and lay it on the chair.
	Ahora tome el libro otra vez
	    y acuéstelo sobre la silla.

Right, take it and lay it there.	*Correcto, tómelo y acuéstelo allí.*
Exactly. Very good.	*Exactamente. Muy bien.*
What did you do?	*¿Qué hizo?*
You first took the book and stood it on the table.	*Primero Usted tomó el libro y lo paró en la mesa.*
Then you laid it on the chair.	*Después lo acostó sobre la silla.*

93

▣ Focus on Scene
Enfoque Sobre la Escena

DESCRIPCIÓN

En este diseño hay varias cosas. En el centro del diseño hay una maleta. Y a un lado de la maleta vemos a dos adultos, un hombre, y una mujer. Al otro lado hay dos infantes. A la izquierda en uno de los extremos del diseño, hay dos casas. A la derecha en el otro extremo, hay cuatro edificios grandes. Talvés es un centro de una ciudad. Arriba hay un reloj. El reloj indica 9:05. Abajo hay una calle, y ensima de la calle hay un carro y un chofer. Delante del carro hay un semáforo.

Translation in Appendix

94

 Storytime: The Story of the Three Bears
El Cuento de los Tres Osos

A family of bears.	*Una familia de osos.*
A big bear. The daddy.	*Un oso grande. El papá.*
A middle-sized bear. The mama.	*Un oso mediano. La mamá.*
A tiny bear. The little son.	*Un oso chiquito. El hijito.*
The morning.	*La mañana.*
The mama prepares breakfast.	*La mamá prepara el desayuno.*
Puts it on the table.	*Lo pone en la mesa.*
Calls: Daddy Bear, Little Bear.	*Llama: Papá Oso, Osito.*
Come and eat.	*Vengan a comer.*
The food is very hot.	*La comida está muy caliente.*
Too hot.	*Demasiado caliente.*
The Bear family goes out.	*La familia de osos sale de la casa.*
They walk in the woods.	*Caminan en el bosque.*
A little girl walks through the woods.	*Una niñita anda por el bosque.*
She sees a house.	*Ve una casita.*
It's the house of the bears.	*Es la casa de los osos.*
She knocks at the door.	*Golpea la puerta.*
There is no one home.	*No hay nadie en la casa.*
So she enters.	*Entonces entra.*
She sees three plates of food.	*Ve tres platos de comida.*
She is hungry.	*Tiene hambre.*
She tries papa bear's plate.	*Prueba el plato del papá oso.*
It's a big plate, right?	*Es un plato grande, ¿verdad?*
Ahh! The food is too hot.	*¡Ay! La comida está demasiado caliente.*
She tries mama bear's plate.	*Prueba el plato de la mamá osa.*
It's a middle-sized plate, right?	*Es un plato mediano, ¿verdad?*
Ahh! It's too cold.	*¡Ay! Está demasiado fría.*
She tries baby bear's plate.	*Prueba el plato del osito chiquito.*
It's a little plate, right?	*Es un plato chiquito, ¿verdad?*
Hmm. Perfect.	*Mmm. Perfecto.*
She eats all the food.	*Se come toda la comida.*
She sees three chairs.	*Ve tres sillas.*
She sits in papa's chair.	*Se sienta en la silla del papá.*
It's big, right?	*Es grande, ¿verdad?*
Ahh! It's too hard.	*¡Ay! Es demasiado dura.*
She sits in mama's chair.	*Se sienta en la silla de la mamá.*
It's too soft.	*Es demasiado suave.*
She sits in baby's chair.	*Se sienta en la silla del osito chiquito.*
It's a tiny chair, right?	*Es una silla chiquita, ¿verdad?*

Hmm. Perfect.	*Mmm. Perfecto.*
But the chair breaks.	*Pero la silla se rompe.*
She goes to the bedroom.	*Ella va al dormitorio.*
She sees three beds.	*Ve tres camas.*
She lies down on papa's bed.	*Se acuesta en la cama del papá.*
It's too hard.	*Es demasiado dura.*
She lies down on mama's bed.	*Se acuesta en la cama de la mamá.*
Too soft.	*Demasiado suave.*
She lies on baby's bed.	*Se acuesta en la cama del nene.*
Hmm. Perfect.	*Mmm. Perfecto.*
And she falls asleep.	*Y se duerme.*
Now the bears return home.	*Los osos ya vuelven a su casa.*
The daddy looks at his plate.	*El papá mira su plato.*
He says: Someone has tasted my [food.]	*Dice: Alguien ha probado mi comida.*
The mama looks at her plate and says:	*La mamá mira el plato suyo y dice:*
Someone has tasted my food too.	*Alguien ha probado mi comida también.*
The baby looks at his plate:	*El osito mira el plato suyo:*
Someone has tasted my food too.	*Alguien ha probado mi comida también.*
And ate it all.	*Y se la comió toda.*
The little bear cries.	*El osito llora.*
The bears see the chairs.	*Los osos ven las sillas.*
Papa looks at his chair and says:	*El papá mira su silla y dice:*
Someone has sat in my chair.	*Alguien se ha sentado en mi silla.*
Mama looks at her chair and says:	*La mamá mira la silla suya y dice:*
Someone has sat in my chair too.	*Alguien se ha sentado en mi silla también.*
The baby looks at his chair and says:	*El osito mira la silla suya y dice:*
And someone has sat in my chair too and has broken it.	*Y alguien se ha sentado en mi silla también, y la ha roto.*
The little bear cries.	*El osito llora.*
The bears go to the bedroom.	*Los osos van al dormitorio.*
The daddy looks at his bed and says:	*El papá mira su cama y dice:*
Someone has lain on my bed.	*Alguien se ha acostado en mi cama.*
The mama looks at her bed and says:	*La mamá mira su cama y dice:*
Someone has lain on my bed too.	*Alguien se ha acostado en mi cama también.*
The baby looks at his bed and says:	*El osito mira su cama y dice:*
And someone lay on my bed too.	*Y alguien se ha acostado en mi cama también.*
And is still there.	*Y todavía está allí.*
The little girl wakes up.	*La niñita se despierta.*
She sees the bears.	*Ve a los osos.*
She is extremely frightened, and she screams.	*Está sumamente asustada y grita.*
She jumps from the bed and runs out.	*Brinca de la cama y sale corriendo.*
And she never returns to the woods.	*Y nunca vuelve al bosque.*

95

📼 Chatter at a Royal Ball

📼 RESUMEN

In the royal family not everyone speaks Chinese.
In fact, only the princess speaks it.
And she speaks it only at church.

(The prince doesn't speak it, but he understands it a bit.)

Of course the Chinese speak Chinese, including those that attend church, but they're not of the royal family.

In reality, not all Chinese speak Chinese.

Those that attend church with the princess do speak it, but they speak it with a Castilian accent.

In the castle where they live, they always speak in Spanish.
They don't like to speak Chinese there.

It's that the king doesn't like Chinese.
Nor does the queen.
He doesn't understand it.
Nor does the queen.

En la familia real no todos hablan chino.
De hecho, sólo la princesa lo habla.
Y ella lo habla solamente en la iglesia.

(El príncipe no lo habla, pero lo entiende un poco.)

Claro que los chinos hablan chino, incluso los que asisten a la iglesia, pero ellos no son de la familia real.

En realidad, no todos los Chinos hablan chino.

Los que asisten a la iglesia con la princesa sí lo hablan, pero lo hablan con el acento castellano.

En el castillo donde viven, siempre hablan en español.

No les gusta hablar en chino allá.

Es que al rey no le gusta el chino.
A la reina tampoco.
El no lo entiende.
La reina tampoco.

96

📼 Chatter at a Royal Ball

📼 GETTING READY FOR *CONVERSACIÓN*

To eat	*Comer*	Of course	*Desde luego*
To drink	*beber* (im<u>bibe</u>, wine-<u>bib</u>ber)	To be mistaken	*Equivocarse*
To cover	*Cubrir*	Butter	*Mantequilla*
Fat, stout	*Gordo/(a)*	Everyone	*Todo el mundo*
To get fat	*Engordarse*	Each day	*Cada día*
Unfortunately	*Desgraciadamente*	At least	*Por lo menos*
Principally	*Principalmente*	Very often.	*Muy a menudo*

How disgusting!	*¡Que disgusto!*
Butter covered with chocolate	*Mantequilla cuvierta de chocolate*
If I'm not mistaken.	*Si no me equivoco.*
I don't want to get fat.	*No quiero engordarme.*
I don't want to be a fat person.	*No quiero ser gorda.*

📼 CONVERSACIÓN

•:	Who's that fat little lady there talking with?	*¿Con quién está hablando la gordita esa?*
••:	With her cats…and with her son, the fat duke.	*Con sus gatos…y con su hijo, el duque gordo.*
•:	What are they drinking?	*¿Qué están bebiendo?*
••:	What they're drinking is cream, if I'm not mistaken.	*Lo que están bebiendo es crema, si no me equivoco.*
•:	Cream? Cream from milk?	*¿Crema? ¿Crema de leche?*
••:	They don't drink alcoholic beverages, but they very often drink cream.	*Ellos no toman bebidas alcohólicas, pero muy a menudo beben crema.*
•:	Well then, of course they're fat.	*Pues desde luego que son gordos.*
••:	What is the duke eating?	*¿Qué es lo que está comiendo el duque?*
•:	Butter…covered with chocolate.	*Mantequilla…cubierta de chocolate.*
••:	How disgusting!	*¡Que disgusto!*
•:	He eats at least a kilogram of butter and chocolate every day.	*Come por lo menos un kilo de mantequilla y chocolate cada día.*
••:	Really?	*¿Sí?*
•:	Unfortunately, it's the truth. Everybody knows it.	*Desgraciadamente, es la verdad. Todo el mundo lo sabe.*
••:	My goodness!	*¡Ay caray!*

📼 REVIEW—A SERVANT ANSWERS HER SMALL CHILD'S QUESTIONS

Mama, why is the duke so fat?	*Mamá, ¿por qué es tan gordo el duque?*
It's because he eats and drinks so much.	*Porque él come y bebe tanto.*
What is it he eats?	*¿Qué es lo que come?*
Butter and chocolate, principally.	*Mantequilla y chocolate, principalmente.*
And what is it he drinks?	*¿Y qué es lo que bebe él?*

Cream. Nothing but cream.
Do you eat butter, mama?
Not much. I eat very little butter. Almost never.

Do you drink cream?
No, I don't drink cream. Never.
Why don't you eat butter and drink cream?
Because I don't want to get fat.
Why don't you want to get fat?
Because I don't want to be fat like the duke is.

Crema. Pura crema.
¿Comes tú matequilla, mamá?
No mucho. Como muy poco de mantequilla. Casi nunca.

¿Bebes crema?
No, no bebo crema. Nunca.
¿Por qué no comes mantequilla y no bebes crema?
Porque no quiero engordarme.
¿Por qué no quieres engordarte?
Porque no quiero ser gorda como es el duque.

A Geography Lesson
Spanish Only
Una Lección de Geografía

This continent here is Africa.	*Este continente de aquí es Africa.*
Africa is very large, but it doesn't measure even half as large as Eurasia.	*Africa es muy grande, pero no mide ni la mitad de Eurasia.*
In the northern part of Africa is Egypt.	*En la parte norte de Africa se encuentra Egipto.*
Through Egypt flows a great river called the Nile.	*Por Egipto pasa un gran río llamado el Nilo.*
The great Egyptian civilization developed here over 6,000 years ago.	*La gran civilización egipcia se desarrolló aquí hace más de 6.000 años.*
Here you see another great continent.	*Aquí puede verse otro continente.*
This is South America.	*Este es Sudamérica.*
Here is found another great river.	*Aquí se encuentra otro gran río.*
It is the largest river in the world.	*Es el río más grande del mundo.*
It is called the Amazon River.	*Se llama el Río Amazonas.*
It flows east through Brazil	*Corre hacia el este a través de Brasil.*
Brazil is a very large country.	*Brasil es un país muy grande.*
It's the largest nation in South America.	*Es el país más grande de Sudamérica.*
It is as large as the continental U. S.	*Es tan grande como Los Estados Unidos.*
It is almost as large as China.	*Es casi tan grande como China.*
But its population is relatively small.	*Pero su población es relativamente pequeña.*
Most of Brazil is covered with forest, and in the forest live a great variety of animals.	*La mayor parte de Brasil está cubierta por selva, y en la selva vive una gran variedad de animales.*
There are many snakes and reptiles.	*Hay muchas culebras y reptiles.*
Not many people live in the forest.	*No mucha gente vive en la selva.*
The large cities of Brazil are on the coast.	*Las ciudades más grandes de Brasil están en la costa.*
This is Sao Paulo, Brazil's largest city and one of the largest cities in the world.	*Este es San Pablo, la ciudad más grande del Brasil y una de las más grandes del mundo.*
And here is Rio de Janeiro, one of the most beautiful cities in the world.	*Y aquí está Río de Janeiro, una de las ciudades más bellas del mundo.*
In the western part of South America is found a great mountain chain.	*En la parte oeste de Sudamérica encontramos una gran cadena de montañas.*
There are many peaks above 5,000 meters.	*Tienen muchos picos sobre los 5.000 metros.*
In those mountains there is much gold and silver.	*En esas montañas hay mucho oro y plata.*
There is also much tin and iron.	*También hay mucho estaño y hierro.*
In ancient times a civilization developed in this area: the Inca Civilization.	*En la antiguedad se desarrolló una civilización en esta área: la civilización incaica.*

98

A Geometry Lesson
Una Lección de Geometría

Answer this question.	*Contesta esta pregunta.*
How many corners does a square have?	*¿Cuántas esquinas tiene un cuadrado?*
Four. A square has four corners.	*Cuatro. Un cuadrado tiene cuatro esquinas.*
It has four sides and four corners.	*Tiene cuatro lados y cuatro esquinas.*
Look! Four sides and four corners or angles.	*Mira, cuatro lados y cuatro esquinas o ángulos.*
Answer these questions.	*Contesta estas preguntas.*
Does a circle have corners?	*¿Tiene esquinas un círculo?*
No, a circle doesn't have corners.	*No, un círculo no tiene esquinas.*
Does a circle have straight lines?	*¿Tiene líneas rectas un círculo?*
No. It doesn't have straight lines.	*No, no tiene líneas rectas.*
Crooked lines?	*¿Líneas chuecas?*
No, it doesn't have crooked lines either.	*No, tampoco tiene líneas chuecas.*
It has only one curved line.	*Tiene solo una línea curva.*
Does a square have any curved lines?	*¿Tiene líneas curvas un cuadrado?*
No it doesn't.	*No, no tiene líneas curvas.*
It has only straight lines,	*Sólo tiene líneas rectas,*
perpendicular lines.	*líneas perpendiculares.*
It has four straight lines and four right angles.	*Tiene cuatro líneas rectas y cuatro ángulos rectos.*
In which box are there two squares?	*¿En qué caja hay dos cuadrados?*
In the first or in the second?	*¿En la primera o la segunda?*
Does the first box contain circles or squares?	*¿La primera caja contiene círculos o cuadrados?*
It contains two squares.	*Contiene dos cuadrados.*
The second contains two circles.	*La segunda contiene dos círculos.*
Touch the box that contains a triangle in which	*Toca la caja que contiene un triángulo en el que hay*
there is a star.	*una estrella.*
Point to the box that contains a star.	*Apunta a la caja que contiene una estrella.*
Point to the box that contains nothing.	*Apunta a la caja que no contiene nada.*
There is nothing in it. It is empty.	*No hay nada en ella. Está vacía.*

🖭 Questions from a Child

Preguntas de un Niñito

Mama, why is it that birds eat insects?	*Mamá, ¿por qué es que los pájaros comen insectos?*
Because they like to eat them.	*Porque a ellos les gustan comerlos.*
Do I eat insects?	*¿Como yo insectos?*
No, you don't eat insects.	*No, tu no comes insectos.*
You and Daddy, do you eat insects?	*¿Tú y papá, comen ustedes insectos?*
No, we don't eat insects.	*No, nosotros no comemos insectos.*
Why?	*¿Por qué?*
Because we are not birds.	*Porque no somos pájaros.*

🖭 Conjugation of the verb *comer*, "to eat":

Yo	*como*	*Nosotros*	*comemos*
Tú	*comes*	*Ustedes*	*comen*
El/ella	*come*	*Ellos/ellas*	*comen*

100

🖭 Focus on Scene

Enfoque sobre la Escena

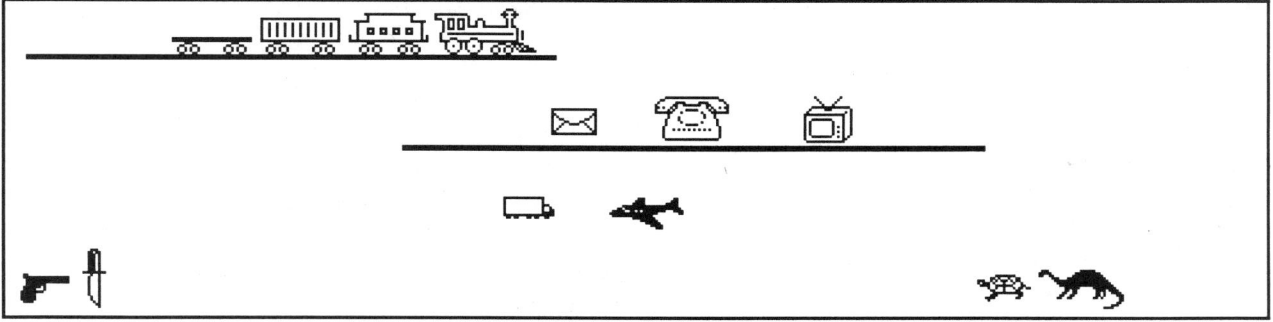

DESCRIPCIÓN

En este diseño hay varios objectos. Encima del diseño hay un tren que va de la izquierda hacia la derecha. Debajo del tren y al centro del dibujo hay tres instrumentos para comunicación a larga distancia. El instrumento de la izquierda de los tres es una carta. El instrumento a la derecha es un televisor. Y el instrumento de en medio es un teléfono. De bajo de la línea horizontal, vemos dos modos de transporte. Uno es mas rapido que el otro. Estos son un avión y un camión. El avión esta a la izquierda del camión y se dirija hacia la izquierda. El camión se dirige hacia la derecha. En la base a la izquierda vemos dos generos de armas: una pistola y un cuchillo. La pistola esta a la izquierda del cuchillo. Al lado opuesto de las armas vemos dos generos de animales: una tortuga y un dinosauronte. El ultimo esta a la derecha.

Translation in Appendix

101

 **Review**

Tape 4, Side A will shortly come to an end. But in the tape-off bonus activities that follow, there is a challenge for you. Plunge into this material; see how much you can learn. Then, before you take on side B, go back and review previous material that you feel warrants review.

Look at the following sentences and review what you've learned.

GROUP A

Anna doesn't know the queen.	*Anna no conoce a la reina.*
I know it. I know that she doesn't know her.	*Lo sé. Sé que ella no le conoce.*
She doesn't know the king either.	*No conoce al rey tampoco.*
I know it. I know she doesn't know him.	*Lo sé. Sé que no le conoce.*
I know she doesn't know them.	*Sé que no les conoce a ellos.*

GROUP B

The princess is not eating.	*La princesa no está comiendo.*
She is not drinking either.	*No está tomando tampoco.*
The prince drinks all the time.	*El príncipe toma todo el tiempo.*
The princess never drinks.	*La princesa nunca toma.*
The fat duke does nothing but eat.	*El duke gordo no hace nada menos comer.*
They do nothing but eat.	*Ellos no hacen nada menos comer.*

GROUP C

Does the prince speak Chinese?	*¿Habla la princesa chino?*
No, only the princess speaks it.	*Nó, solamente lo habla la princesa.*
She doesn't speak it often.	*No lo habla amenudo.*
She speaks it only in church.	*Lo habla solamente en la iglesia.*
She knows the Chinese people.	*Conoce a la gente china.*
She knows some Chinese people.	*Conoce a algunos chinos.*
She knows the truth.	*Ella sabe la verdad.*
She knows a lot of things.	*Sabe muchas cosas.*

GROUP D

The Chinese attend church.	*Los chinos asisten a la iglesia.*
Some Chinese attend church.	*Algunos chinos asisten a la iglesia.*
The Chinese used to live in China.	*Los chinos vivian en la china.*
Now some Chinese live in the castle.	*Ahora, algunos chinos viven en el castillo.*
Some princes lived here.	*Algunos príncipes vivian aquí.*
Where do the princes of Cali live?	*¿Donde viven los príncipes de Cali?*
One of them lives here in the bar.	*Uno de ellos vive aquí en el bar.*

GROUP E

What is it she likes?	*¿Qué es lo que a ella le gusta?*
She likes butter and cream.	*A ella le gusta mantequilla y crema.*
No, what is it she likes to do?	*¿Nó, que es lo que le gusta hacer?*
Oh, she likes to sing.	*Oh, a ella le gusta cantar.*
What is it she prefers to do, eat butter or drink cream?	*¿Qué es lo que prefiere hacer, comer mantequilla o tomar crema?*
She prefers to eat.	*Prefiere comer.*
What is it she doesn't like?	*¿Qué es lo que no le gusta?*
She doesn't like water.	*No le gusta agua.*
What is it she doesn't like to do?	*¿Que es lo que no le gusta hacer?*
She doesn't like to sleep.	*No le gusta dormir.*

GROUP F

The cat drinks juice when the dog sings.	*El gato toma jugo cuando el perro canta.*
The dog drinks juice when the cat sings.	*El perro toma jugo cuando el gato canta.*
The cat drinks only when the dog sings.	*El gato toma solamente cuando el perro canta.*
The dog drinks only when the cat sings.	*El perro toma solamente cuando el gato canta.*
That's shocking!	*¡Qué chocante!*
In reality, it's no big thing.	*En realidad, no es gran cosa.*
I agree.	*Estoy de acuerdo.*

THE ADVENTURE CONTINUES

Having completed your tasks so that your partner can advance, you report, "Now in chamber 40. Two steps from Target."

You radio Stump: "Hey, look where we are. Just two chambers more and we're at the very threshold of the Target Chamber."

"Let's go for it," comes Stump's reply.

You read the next instructions: to reach chamber 41, you are each to complete **two** tasks: 102 (Focus on Action) and 103 (The Story of the Pig at the Stile). After a rest and a review of some of the things learned so far, you tackle the tasks with aroused energy.

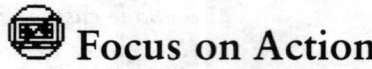 **Focus on Action**

Enfoque sobre la Acción

A. SCATTER CHART

Twelve new action-pictographs:

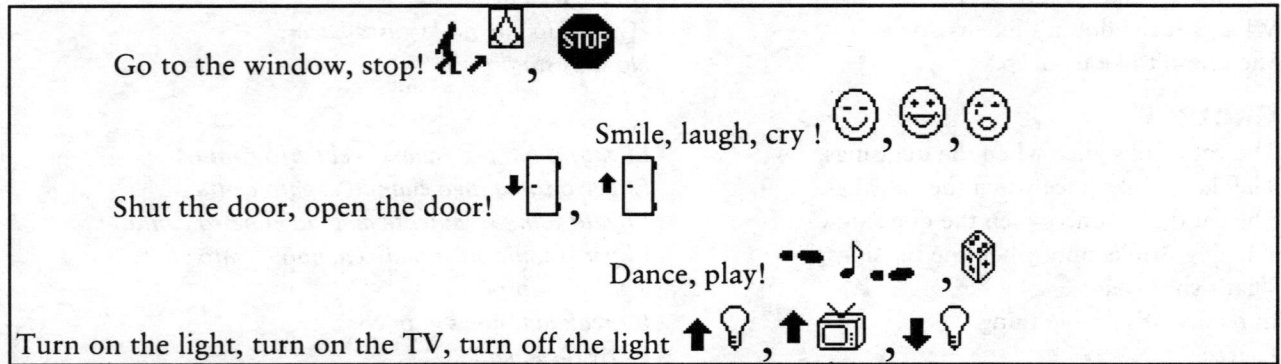

Go to the window, stop! ,

Smile, laugh, cry ! , ,

Shut the door, open the door! ,

Dance, play! ,

Turn on the light, turn on the TV, turn off the light , ,

B. SELF-QUIZ

Without looking at the scatter chart, can you say what the new action-pictographs are in English?

Review of pictographs (see the word equivalents below)

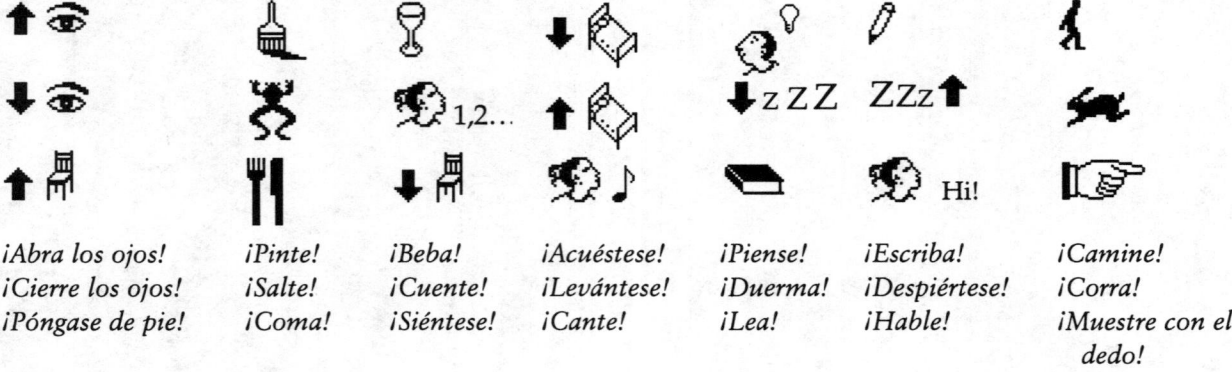

¡Abra los ojos!	¡Pinte!	¡Beba!	¡Acuéstese!	¡Piense!	¡Escriba!	¡Camine!
¡Cierre los ojos!	¡Salte!	¡Cuente!	¡Levántese!	¡Duerma!	¡Despiértese!	¡Corra!
¡Póngase de pie!	¡Coma!	¡Siéntese!	¡Cante!	¡Lea!	¡Hable!	¡Muestre con el dedo!

THE 13 ACTION-PICTOGRAPHS WITH WRITTEN SPANISH

Read and act out the called-for action

¡Póngase de pie!
¡Cante y baile!
¡Cierre la puerta!
¡Lea y conte!
¡Ríase y llore!
¡Párese y salte!
¡Coma y beba!
¡Ríase y llore!
¡Lea y escriba!
¡Juegue y trabaje!
¡Siéntese y sonría!
¡Lea, cuente y escriba!
¡Ande y abre la puerta!
¡Cierre los ojos y hable!

¡Encienda la luz y cante!
¡Vaya a la ventana y párese!
¡Póngase de pie y ande!
¡Siéntese, pinte y escriba!
¡Acuéstese y cierre los ojos!
¡Apague la televisor y siéntese!
¡Abre los ojos, levántese y corra!
¡Despiértese, levántese y trabaje!
¡Vaya a la puerta, párese y sonría!
¡Acuéstese, cierre los ojos y duerma!
¡Apague la luz y ponga la televisión!
¡Cierre la puerta y abra la puerta!
¡Encienda la luz, ponga la televisor y baile!
¡Apague la luz, acuéstese y duerma!

How many of these commands can you say in Spanish?

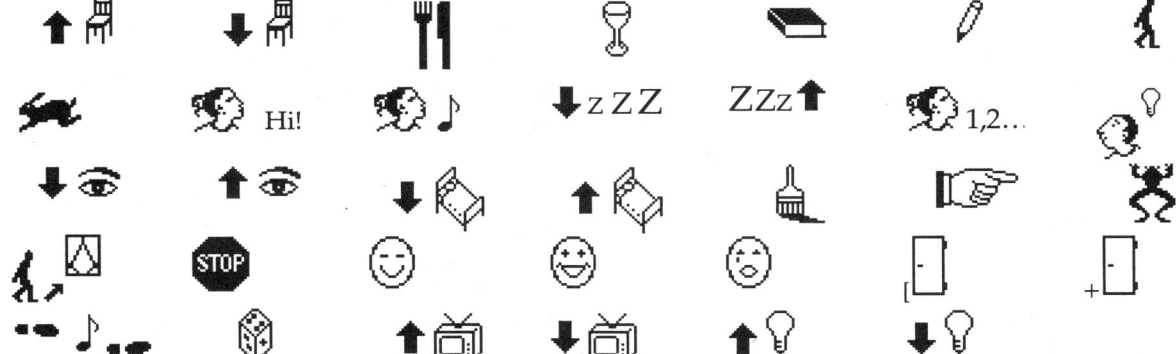

200

103

The Story of the Pig at the Stile
La Historia del Cerdo en el Portillo

An old woman was sweeping her floor and found a
   coin.
"What shall I do with it?" she thought.
"I'll go to the marketplace and buy a pig."
And this she did.

On her way home she came to a stile,
   but the pig would not jump over it.
So the woman went on.
Soon she came upon a dog.
She said to him:
"Dog, Dog, bite Pig.
   Pig won't jump over the stile,
   and I'll not get home tonight."
"No," said the dog. "I won't bite Pig."
So the woman went on her way.

Soon she came upon a stick.
She said to the stick:
"Stick, Stick, beat Dog.
   Dog won't bite Pig,
   Pig won't jump over the stile,
   and I'll not get home tonight."
"No," said the stick. "I won't beat Dog."
So the woman went on her way.

Soon she came to a fire.
She said to the fire:
"Fire, Fire, burn Stick,
   Stick won't beat Dog,
   Dog won't bite Pig,
   Pig won't jump over the stile,
   and I'll not get home tonight."
"No," said the fire. "I won't burn Stick."
So the woman went on her way.

Soon she came to a well.
She said to the water:
"Water, water, quench Fire.

*Una anciana estaba barriendo el piso y encontró una
   moneda.*
"¿Qué haré con esta moneda?" pensaba ella.
"Iré al mercado y compraré un cerdo."
Y así lo hizo.

De regreso a casa llegó a un portillo,
   pero el cerdo no quería saltarlo.
Así que la mujer siguió su camino.
Pronto encontró a un perro.
Ella le dijo al perro:
"Perro, Perro, muerde al cerdo.
   El cerdo no quiere saltar el portillo,
   y no llegaré a casa esta noche."
"¡No!" dijo el perro. "Yo no morderé al cerdo."
Así que la mujer siguió su camino.

Pronto encontró un palo.
Ella le dijo al palo:
"Palo, palo, pegale al perro.
   El perro no quiere morder al cerdo,
   el cerdo no quiere saltar el portillo,
   y no llegaré a casa esta noche."
"¡No!" dijo el palo. "Yo no le pegaré al perro."
Así que la mujer siguió su camino.

Pronto llegó a un fuego.
Ella le dijo al fuego:
"Fuego, Fuego, quema al palo.
   El palo no quiere pegarle al perro,
   el perro no quiere morder al cerdo,
   el cerdo no quiere saltar el portillo,
   y no llegaré a casa esta noche."
"¡No!" dijo el fuego. "No quemaré al palo."
Así que la mujer siguió su camino.

Pronto encontró un pozo de agua.
Ella le dijo al agua:
"Agua, agua, apaga al fuego.

Fire won't burn Stick,
Stick won't beat Dog,
Dog won't bite Pig,
Pig won't jump over the stile,
and I'll not get home tonight."
"No," said the water. "I won't quench the fire."
So the woman went on.

Soon she came to an ox.
She said to the ox:
"Ox, Ox, drink Water.
  Water won't quench Fire,
  Fire won't burn Stick,
  Stick won't beat Dog,
  Dog won't bite Pig,
  Pig won't jump over the stile,
  and I'll not get home tonight."
"No," said the ox. "I won't drink Water."
So the woman went on.

Soon she came to a butcher.
She said to the butcher:
"Butcher, Butcher, kill Ox.
  Ox won't drink Water,
  Water won't quench Fire,
  Fire won't burn Stick,
  Stick won't beat Dog,
  Dog won't bite Pig,
  Pig won't jump over the stile,
  and I'll not get home tonight."
"No," said the butcher. "I won't kill Ox."
So the woman went on.

Soon she came to a rope.
She said to the rope:
"Rope, Rope, hang Butcher.
  Butcher won't kill Ox,
  Ox won't drink Water,
  Water won't quench Fire,
  Fire won't burn Stick,
  Stick won't beat Dog,
  Dog won't bite Pig,
  Pig won't jump over the stile,
  and I'll not get home tonight."
"No," said the rope. "I won't hang butcher."
So the woman went on.

Soon she came to a mouse.
She said to the mouse:

El fuego no quiere quemar al palo,
el palo no quiere pegarle al perro,
el perro no quiere morder al cerdo,
el cerdo no quiere saltar el portillo,
y no llegaré a casa esta noche."
"¡No!" dijo el agua. "No apagaré al fuego."
Así que la mujer siguió su camino.

Pronto encontró un buey.
Ella le dijo al buey:
"Buey, Buey, bebe el agua.
  El agua no quiere apagar al fuego,
  el fuego no quiere quemar al palo,
  el palo no quiere pegarle al perro,
  el perro no quiere morder al cerdo,
  el cerdo no quiere saltar el portillo,
  y yo no llegaré a casa esta noche."
"¡No!" dijo el buey. "No beberé el agua."
Así que la mujer siguió su camino.

Pronto encontró a un carnicero.
Ella le dijo al carnicero:
"Carnicero, Carnicero, mata al buey.
  El buey no quiere beber el agua,
  el agua no quiere apagar al fuego,
  el fuego no quiere quemar al palo,
  el palo no quiere pegarle al perro,
  el perro no quiere morder al cerdo,
  el cerdo no quiere saltar el portillo,
  y no llegaré a casa esta noche."
"¡No!" dijo el carnicero. "No mataré al buey."
Así que la mujer siguió su camino.

Pronto encontró una soga.
Ella le dijo a la soga:
"Soga, soga, ahorca al carnicero.
  El carnicero no quiere matar al buey,
  el buey no quiere beber el agua,
  el agua no quiere apagar al fuego,
  el fuego no quiere quemar al palo,
  el palo no quiere pegarle al perro,
  el perro no quiere morder al cerdo,
  el cerdo no quiere saltar el portillo,
  y yo no llegaré a casa esta noche."
"¡No!" dijo la soga. "No ahorcaré al carnicero."
Así que la mujer siguió su camino.

Pronto encontró un ratón.
Ella le dijo al ratón:

"Mouse, Mouse, gnaw Rope.
  Rope won't hang Butcher.
  Butcher won't kill Ox,
  Ox won't drink Water,
  Water won't quench Fire,
  Fire won't burn Stick,
  Stick won't beat Dog,
  Dog won't bite Pig,
  Pig won't jump over the stile,
  and I'll not get home tonight."
"No," said the mouse. "I won't gnaw Rope."
So the woman went on.

Soon she came to a cat.
She said to the cat:
"Cat, Cat, catch Mouse.
  Mouse won't gnaw Rope,
  Rope won't hang Butcher.
  Butcher won't kill Ox,
  Ox won't drink Water,
  Water won't quench Fire,
  Fire won't burn Stick,
  Stick won't beat Dog,
  Dog won't bite Pig,
  Pig won't jump over the stile,
  and I'll not get home tonight."

Then the cat said to the old woman:
"If you'll go to the cow and get me a little milk, then
  I'll catch the mouse."
So the old woman went to the cow to get some
  milk.
But the cow said:
"If you'll go to the haystack
  and get me a handful of hay,
then I'll give you some milk."

So the old woman went to the haystack and brought
  a handful of hay to the cow.
As soon as the cow had eaten the hay,
she gave milk to the old woman,
and the old woman took the milk to the cat.

So Cat caught Mouse,
Mouse gnawed Rope,
Rope hanged Butcher,
Butcher killed Ox,
Ox drank Water,
Water quenched Fire,

"Ratón, Ratón, roe a la soga.
  La soga no quiere ahorcar al carnicero,
  el carnicero no quiere matar al buey,
  el buey no quiere beber el agua,
  el agua no quiere apagar al fuego,
  el fuego no quiere quemar al palo,
  el palo no quiere pegarle al perro,
  el perro no quiere morder al cerdo,
  el cerdo no quiere saltar el portillo,
  y yo no llegaré a casa esta noche."
"¡No!" dijo el ratón. "No roeré a la soga."
Así que la mujer siguió su camino.

Pronto encontró un gato.
Ella le dijo al gato:
"Gato, Gato, atrapa al ratón.
  El ratón no quiere roer a la soga,
  la soga no quiere ahorcar al carnicero,
  el carnicero no quiere matar al buey,
  el buey no quiere beber el agua,
  el agua no quiere apagar al fuego,
  el fuego no quiere quemar al palo,
  el palo no quiere pegarle al perro,
  el perro no quiere morder al cerdo,
  el cerdo no quiere saltar el portillo,
  y yo no llegaré a casa esta noche."

Entonces el gato le dijo a la anciana:
"Si vas a la vaca y me traes un poco de leche,
  entonces atraparé al ratón."
Así que la anciana fue a la vaca para conseguir algo
  de leche.
Pero la vaca dijo:
"Si vas al pajar y me consigues
  un manojo de paja,
entonces te daré un poco de leche."

Así que la anciana fue al pajar y le llevó un manojo
  de paja a la vaca.
Tan pronto como la vaca hubo comido la paja,
le dio leche a la anciana,
y ella le dio la leche al gato.

Así que el gato atrapó al ratón,
el ratón royó la soga,
la soga ahorcó al carnicero,
el carnicero mató al buey,
el buey bebió el agua,
el agua apagó al fuego,

Fire burned Stick,	*el fuego quemó al palo,*
Stick beat Dog,	*el palo le pegó al perro,*
Dog bit Pig,	*el perro mordió al cerdo,*
Pig jumped over the stile,	*el cerdo saltó el portillo,*
and the old woman got home that night.	*y la anciana llegó a casa esa noche.*

THE ADVENTURE CONTINUES

As you enter the cavernous chamber that is cell 41 on your maps, you are startled by a sound far below you: kerPLUNK!, as if a heavy rock had fallen—or been tossed—into the water. You freeze in your steps and hold your breath, then cautiously radio, "Stump, where are you?" you whisper. No response. You repeat the question louder. Again no response.

"Has something happened to Stump?" you wonder, realizing your helpless situation without your partner. Then another kerPLUNK! Taking a risk, you pick up a big rock, heave it and hear it hit the water below with a loud kerPLUNK!

"Hey! Cut that out!" a familiar voice rings out.

"Hey, Stump! What are you doing here?" You both laugh. You shake hands and congratulate each other: "Hey, we've made it to this point. It will be easier now if we can stay together." Little do you imagine the adventure and the challenges that face you.

You report, "We are now in chamber 41...TOGETHER! One step from Target."

You are surprised to find out that all that is required to make it through chamber 42 to the threshold of the innermost chamber, and then step into that last chamber, is to spend time reviewing and practicing what you have learned. You settle back and do this assignment conscientiously. It is nice to be working together. You continue to do tasks 104 (Openers and Rejoinders) to 110 (Second Meeting at the University).

104

📼 Openers and Rejoinders

I'm outta here.
Good-bye.

Tomorrow I take my exams.
Good luck!

Thanks a lot.
No problem.

Congratulations!
For what? I haven't done anything.

We're there!
Finally!

It's going to rain.
So it seems. (It seems so.)

I have a question.
What is it?

I'm going to the fair.
Me too.

Good luck.
Thanks. Same.

Excellent! Remarkable!
Yes. Marvelous! Fantastic!

Thanks for your time.
Any time.

See you tomorrow then.
Till then.

It's getting late.
Yes, let's go home.

Bring me a drink, please.
Right away.

Please carry my coat.
With pleasure.

I like this.
Me too.

Your suitcase is heavy. Let me help you.
There's no need. It's light.

And another thing, you owe me $5.
Since when?

Ya me voy.
¡Qué te vaya bien!

Mañana tomo mis exámenes.
¡Buena suerte!

Muchas gracias.
No hay porqué.

¡Felicitaciones!
¿Por qué? No he hecho nada.

¡Ya llegamos!
¡Por fin!

Va a llover.
Así parece. (Parece que sí.)

Tengo una pregunta.
¿Cuál es?

Yo voy a la feria.
Yo también.

Que le vaya bien.
Gracias. Igualmente.

¡Excelente! ¡Fantástico!
Sí. ¡Maravilloso! ¡Fantástico!

Gracias por su tiempo.
Cualquier hora.

Nos vemos mañana entonces.
Hasta entonces.

Ya es tarde.
Sí. Vamos a casa.

Tráeme un refresco, por favor.
En seguida.

Por favor, lleve mi saco.
Con mucho gusto.

Me gusta ésto.
A mí también.

Su maleta es pesada. Permítame ayudarle.
No hay necesidad. Es ligera.

Y otra cosa. Me debes cinco dólares.
¿Desde cuándo?

105

📼 Storytime: Little Red Riding Hood

La Caperucita Roja

Here is a little girl.	*Aquí está una niñita.*
She is called Red Riding Hood.	*Se llama caperucita roja.*
Here is her mother.	*Aquí está su mamacita.*
Here is her grandma.	*Aquí está su abuelita.*
Here is her mother's house.	*Aquí está la casa de su mamacita.*
Here is her grandma's house.	*Aquí está la casa de su abuelita.*
Here is the forest.	*Aquí está el bosque.*
Here is a wolf.	*Aquí está un lobo.*
Well.	*Bueno.*
The grandma is sick.	*La abuelita está enferma.*
Mother sends Red Riding Hood with a basket of cookies.	*La mamacita manda a caperucita roja con una canasta de galletas.*
In the woods the wolf asks her:	*En el bosque el lobo le pregunta:*
"Where are you going? What is your name?"	*"¿Adónde vas? ¿Cómo te llamas?"*
Red Riding Hood tells him, and he goes away.	*Caperucita roja le contesta, y él se aleja.*
He runs to the grandma's house.	*Corre a la casa de la abuelita.*
He knocks on the door.	*Toca a la puerta.*
The grandma asks:	*La abuelita pregunta:*
"Who is it?"	*"¿Quién es?"*
The wolf answers:	*El lobo responde:*
"Red Riding Hood."	*"Caperucita roja."*
"Come in."	*"Adelante."*
Grandma sees the wolf and runs from the house.	*La abuelita ve al lobo, y corre de la casa.*
The wolf gets in bed.	*El lobo se mete en la cama.*
Red Riding Hood comes.	*Caperucita roja viene.*
She enters and sees the wolf.	*Entra y ve al lobo.*
She thinks it's her grandma.	*Piensa que es su abuelita.*
She asks: "Why do you have such big ears?"	*Pregunta: "¿Por qué tienes las orejas tan grandes?"*
The wolf answers: "To hear you better."	*El lobo responde: "Para oirte mejor."*
"Why do you have such big teeth?"	*"¿Por qué tienes los dientes tan grandes?"*
"To eat you better."	*"Para comerte mejor."*
Red Riding Hood screams:	*Caperucita roja grita:*
"Oh, it's the wolf!"	*"¡Ay, es el lobo!"*
At that moment the grandma enters with a dog.	*En ese momento entra la abuelita con un perro.*
The wolf runs out and escapes.	*El lobo sale corriendo y se escapa.*
Then Red Riding Hood and the grandma and the dog eat the cookies.	*Entonces caperucita roja y la abuelita y el perro se comen las galletas.*

106

A Spanish Lesson
Spanish Only
Una Lección de Español

Take your pencil. Take it.	*Toma tu lápiz. Tómalo.*
Put your pencil here. Put it here.	*Pon tu lápiz aquí. Ponlo aquí.*
Take your white paper. Take it.	*Toma tu papel blanco. Tómalo.*
Put your paper here. Put it here.	*Pon tu papel aquí. Ponlo aquí.*
Take my red pencil. Take it.	*Toma mi lápiz rojo. Tómalo.*
Put my pencil here. Put it here.	*Pon mi lápiz aquí. Ponlo aquí.*
Take my red paper. Take it.	*Toma mi papel rojo. Tómalo.*
Put my red paper here.	*Pon mi papel rojo aquí.*
Excellent!	*¡Excelente!*
Here there is a pencil.	*Aquí hay un lápiz.*
And here there are two pencils.	*Y aquí hay dos lápices.*
How many pencils? Two.	*¿Cuántos lápices? Dos.*
Put this one in the box.	*Pon este en la caja.*
Put it in.	*Pónlo.*
Put these in the box too.	*Pon estos en la caja también.*
Put them in.	*Pónlos.*
Take a paper and put it in this box.	*Toma un papel y ponlo en la caja.*
Take another paper and put it in the same box.	*Toma otro papel y ponlo en la misma caja.*
Take two pencils and put them in this sack.	*Toma dos lápices y ponlos en esta bolsa.*
Take another pencil and put it in the same sack.	*Toma otro lápiz y ponlo en la misma bolsa.*
In the sack there is a pencil.	*En la bolsa hay un lápiz.*
Take it out.	*Sácalo.*
Take one pencil from the sack and put it in the box.	*Toma un lápiz de la bolsa y ponlo en la caja.*
Take one paper from the box and put it in the sack.	*Toma un papel de la caja y ponlo en la bolsa.*
I take the red paper out and put it in the box.	*Yo saco el papel rojo y lo pongo en la caja.*
Pick up the box. Pick it up.	*Toma la caja. Tómala.*
Give it to me.	*Dámela a mí.*
Pick up the pencil. Pick it up.	*Toma el lápiz. Tómalo.*
Give it to me.	*Dámelo a mí.*
Pick up your pencils. Pick them up.	*Toma tus lápices. Tómalos.*
Give them to me.	*Dámelos a mí.*
Pick up the sack. Pick it up.	*Toma la bolsa. Tómala.*
Give it to me.	*Dámela a mí.*
Pick up the sheets. Pick them up.	*Toma las hojas. Tómalas.*
Give them to me.	*Dámelas a mí.*
Yes, give them to me, please.	*Sí, dámelas a mí, por favor.*

107

📼 Chatter at a Royal Ball

🔘 GETTING READY FOR CONVERSACIÓN

Some words

To buy	*Comprar*	To continue, keep on	*Seguir*
To sell	*Vender*	Leave, abandon, quit	*Dejar*
To remember	*Acordarse* (remind <u>self</u>)	To let, allow	*Dejar*
To call oneself (be named)	*Llamarse*	To doubt	*Dudar*
To write	*Escribir*	I doubt it.	*Lo dudo.*
To forge checks	*Falseficar cheques*	Recently	*Recién*

Some Sentences

Leave me in peace.	*Déjeme en paz.*
Let me think.	*Déjeme pensar.*
He buys a cat.	*El compra un gato.*
He buys him/her a cat.	*El le compra un gato.*
He buys himself a cat.	*El se compra un gato.*
What do you call yourself (what's your name)?	*¿Cómo se llama Ud.?*
I am called (my name is) Carlos.	*Me llamo Carlos.*
He calls himself Jose.	*El se llama José.*
He was called Jose.	*El se llamaba José.*
What do you call yourself, sonny?	*¿Cómo te llamas, hijito?*
Maria, do you remember that?	*¿María, te acuerdas de eso?*
I remember that I was with you.	*Me acuerdo que yo estaba contigo.*
I don't remember when.	*No me acuerdo cuando.*
He remembers that.	*El se acuerda de eso.*
He lived in Madrid.	*El vivía en Madrid.*
He lived there for two years.	*El vivió allá por dos años.*
(He) must be crazy.	*Tiene que estar loco.*
She had to speak Spanish there.	*Ella tenía que hablar español allá.*
She had to sell the dog?	*¿Ella tuvo que vender el perro?*
She wrote me two bad checks.	*Ella me escribió dos cheques falsos a mí.*
Just go ahead/go right ahead/continue, please	*¡Siga, no más!*
She keeps on doing that: buying and selling cats...and writing checks.	*Ella sigue haciendo eso: comprando y vendiendo gatos...y escribiendo cheques.*
Now (she) has quit doing that.	*Ya ha dejado de hacer eso.*

CONVERSACIÓN

•: What has happened to the queen that lived in Ventura and bought and sold cats?

••: Bought and sold cats?

•: †† This sentence is not read on the tape but should be: One time she sold her cat and bought <u>herself</u> an enormous dog, don't you remember?

••: Just a moment...let me think...

•: I think she was called Anita...the queen, not the dog.

••: Anita...yes, now I remember her. She lived there ten years I think.

•: And now?

••: She doesn't live there now. And now she doesn't sell cats anymore.

•: So what does she do now?

••: I'm not sure. For many years she forged checks, that I know.

•: She forged checks?

••: Wrote false checks.

•: And has she left off doing that?

••: I doubt it. A year ago...more or less...she wrote me two bad checks.

•: What did she do?

••: She wrote me two bad checks.

•: And why did she do that?

••: Who knows why? She had to do it. She's crazy.

•: She must be crazy.

••: Do you think she's going on doing that...writing bad checks?

•: I doubt it.

·¿Qué le ha pasado a la reina que vivía en Ventura y compraba y vendía gatos?

¿Compraba y vendía gatos?

Una vez vendió su gato y <u>se</u> compró un perro enorme, ¿no te acuerdas?

Un momento...déjame pensar...

Creo que se llamaba Anita...la reina, no el perro.

Anita...sí, ahora me acuerdo de ella. Ella vivió allá diez años, creo.

¿Y ahora?

Ya no vive allá. Y ya no vende gatos.

¿Pues qué hace ahora?

No estoy seguro. Por muchos años ella falsificaba cheques, eso sé.

¿Falsificaba cheques?

Escribía cheques falsos.

¿Y ya ha dejado de hacer eso?

Lo dudo. Hace un año...más o menos...ella me escribió dos cheques falsos a mí.

¿Qué hizo?

Me escribió dos cheques falsos.

¿Y por qué hizo eso?

¿Quién sabe por qué? Tuvo que hacerlo. Está loca.

Tiene que estar loca.

¿Crees que ella sigue haciendo eso...escribiendo cheques falsos?

Lo dudo.

 Focus on the Language 17–18

FOCUS 17

The use of *le:*

¿Qué le ha pasado a ella?	What (to her) has happened to her?
¿Qué ha pasado a ella?	What has happened to her?
¿Qué le ha pasado a él?	What (to him) has happened to him?
¿Qué ha pasado a él?	What has happened to him?
¿Qué le ha pasado?	What has happened to him\her?

NOTE: It is usual to include the word *le* before the verb as well as the *a* + pronoun after the verb. If context is clear and no particular emphasis is intended, the *a* + pronoun is left off the end.

Observation and Practice

What (to her) has happened <u>to</u> the queen?	*¿Qué le ha pasado <u>a</u> la reina?*
And the prince, what (to him) has happened <u>to</u> him?	*Y el príncipe, ¿qué le ha pasado <u>a</u> él?*
What (to him) has happened <u>to</u> the king?	*¿Qué le ha pasado <u>al</u> rey?*
And the princess, what (to her) has happened <u>to</u> her?	*Y la princesa, ¿qué le ha pasado <u>a</u> ella?*
And what has happened <u>to</u> the cat?	*¿Y qué le ha pasado al gato?*

Translate Orally from and into Spanish

What has happened to the queen?	*¿Qué le ha pasado a la reina?*
What has happened to the princess?	*¿Qué le ha pasado a la princesa?*
What has happened to her?	*¿Qué le ha pasado a ella?*
What has happened to him?	*¿Qué le ha pasado a él?*
What has happened to the king?	*¿Qué le ha pasado al rey?*
What has happened to the prince?	*¿Qué le ha pasado al príncipe?*
The princess has suffered a lot.	*La princesa ha sufrido mucho.*
Now she's eaten the chocolates.	*Ahora ella ha comido los chocolates.*
She's already eaten the chocolates.	*Ella ya ha comido los chocolates.*
But she has cried a lot.	*Pero ha llorado mucho.*
And the queen has cried with her.	*Y la reina ha llorado con ella.*

PERFORMANCE TEST

Instructions: Translate the following sentences into English, then check your answers. Then translate from English into Spanish.

•:	¿Qué le ha pasado a la reina?	What has happened to the queen?
••:	La reina que vivía en Ojai y vendía gatos...	The queen that lived in Ojai and used to sell cats...
•:	Ella está escribiendo cheques falsos.	She is writing false checks.
••:	Y el rey, ¿qué le ha pasado a él?	And the king, what has happened to him?
•:	¿A aquel que tenía una pistola?	To the-one who used to have a pistol?
••:	Está viviendo una vida santa.	He is living a saintly life.
•:	También está dirigiendo el coro de madres.	He is directing the mothers' choir.
••:	¿Qué le ha pasado al príncipe?	What has happened to the prince?
•:	El príncipe tuvo un ataque.	The prince had an attack.
••:	El comió demasiado chocolate.	He ate too much chocolate.
•:	Ahora el lo come con los angelitos.	Now he eats it with the angels.
••:	¿Y la princesa? ¿Qué le ha pasado a ella?	And the princess? What has happened to her?
•:	¿A cuál princesa?	To which princess?
••:	A aquella que sabía hablar ruso.	To the one who knew how to speak Russian.
•:	Ella también escribía tonterías.	She also used to write foolish stories.
••:	Ella está viviendo en Siberia.	She is living in Siberia.

FOCUS 18

The use of *se* meaning "for himself (herself, themselves)"

She bought me a cat.	*Ella me compró un gato.*
She bought herself a cat.	*Ella se compró un gato.*
He bought himself a cat.	*El se compró un gato.*
They have bought themselves a cat.	*Ellos se han comprado un gato.*
He wants to buy himself a cat.	*El quiere comprarse un gato.*

Practice

He bought himself a dog.	*El se compró un perro.*
He ate all of it for himself.	*El se comió todo.*
They have eaten all of it for themselves.	*Ellos se han comido todo.*
He takes a swallow.	*El se toma un trago.*

109

📼 A Hungry Giant
Un Gigante Hambriento

Have you ever seen a giant?

Do you know how big a giant is?

Do you know how much a hungry giant can eat?

Well I haven't ever seen a giant, but one time my father saw one.

Anyway he told me he saw one.

This happened when he was a boy just my age.

One morning before breakfast, he took a walk and saw a fly caught in a spider's web.

He watched as the spider came and ate the fly.

Good, thought my father. The spider ate the fly. I don't like flies.

A moment later there came a bird and ate the spider.

Good, thought my father. The bird ate the spider. I don't like spiders.

But the next moment a cat came along and ate the bird.

And my father thought: Too bad, the cat ate the bird. I like birds.

But the next moment a snake came along and ate the cat.

And my father thought: Too bad. I like cats.

But the next moment a pig came along and ate the snake.

And my father thought: Good, the pig ate the snake. I don't like snakes.

Before long a leopard came along and ate the pig.

And my father thought: Wow! A leopard ate the pig. This is exciting!

A while later a crocodile came along and ate the leopard.

And my father thought: Wow! A crocodile ate the leopard. This is really exciting. What will happen next?

Before long a hippopotamus came along and ate the crocodile.

And my father thought: Wow! A hippopotamus ate the crocodile. What will happen next?

¿Has visto alguna vez a un gigante?

¿Sabes lo grande que es un gigante?

¿Sabes lo mucho que puede comer un gigante hambriento?

Bueno, yo nunca he visto a un gigante, pero una vez mi padre vió a uno.

Como quiera, me dijo que vió a uno.

Esto pasó cuando él era un niño justo mi edad.

Una mañana antes del desayuno, daba un paseo y vio una mosca que estaba atrapada en una telaraña.

Observó como la araña vino y se comió la mosca.

Qué bueno, pensó mi papá. La araña se comió la mosca. No me gustan las moscas.

Un momento después vino un pájaro y se comió la araña.

¡Qué bueno!, pensó mi papá. El pájaro se comió la araña. No me gustan las arañas.

Pero poco después vino un gato y se comió el pájaro.

Y mi papá pensó: ¡Qué lástima que el gato se comió al pájaro! Me gustan los pájaros.

Pero poco después vino una serpiente y se comió al gato.

Y mi papá pensó: ¡Qué lástima! Me gustan los gatos.

Pero poco después vino un chancho y se comió la serpiente.

Y mi papá pensó: ¡Qué bueno que el chancho se comió la serpiente! No me gustan las serpientes.

Poco después vino un leopardo y se comió el chancho.

Y mi papá pensó: ¡Caramba! Un leopardo se comió el chancho. ¡Qué emocionante!

Más tarde vino un cocodrilo y se comió el leopardo.

Y mi papá pensó: ¡Caramba! Un cocodrilo se comió el leopardo. Esto sí que es emocionante. ¿Qué más pasará?

Poco después vino un hipopótamo y se comió el cocodrilo.

Y mi papá pensó: ¡Caramba! Un hipopótamo se comió el cocodrilo. ¿Qué más pasará?

A moment later a whale came along and ate the
     hippopotamus.
And my father thought: Wow! This is too much.
     Just imagine:
A whale has eaten a hippopotamus,
     the hippopotamus had eaten a crocodile,
     the crocodile had eaten a leopard,
     the leopard had eaten a pig,
     the pig had eaten a snake,
     the snake had eaten a cat,
     the cat had eaten a bird,
     the bird had eaten a spider,
     and the spider had eaten a fly.
     That's amazing. I've never seen such a thing.
Just then a hand reached down from the sky and
     picked up the whale.
My father looked up just as the giant swallowed it
     whole.
And he thought: Wow! This is the first time I've
     seen a giant.
Maybe he's still hungry. I'd better get out of here.
And he ran home as fast as he could.
And there, as he ate a big bowl of oatmeal,
     he thought of the fly
     and the spider
     and the bird
     and the cat
     and the snake
     and the pig
     and the leopard
     and the crocodile
     and the hippopotamus
     and the whale.
But most of all he thought of the giant and how
     hungry he must have been.

*Después de un momento vino una ballena y se comió
     el hipopótamo.*
*Y mi papá pensó: ¡Caramba! Esto ya es demasiado.
     ¡Imagínate!:*
*Una ballena se ha comido un hipopótamo, el
     hipopótamo se había comido un cocodrilo,
     el cocodrilo se había comido un leopardo,
     el leopardo se había comido un chancho,
     el chancho se había comido una serpiente,
     la serpiente se había comido un gato,
     el gato se había comido un pájaro,
     el pájaro se había comido una araña,
     y la araña se había comido una mosca.
     ¡Es increíble! Jamás había visto tal cosa.*
*En ese preciso momento una mano bajó del cielo y
     levantó a la ballena.*
*Mi papá miró hacia arriba en el momento justo en
     que el gigante se la tragaba entera.*
*Y él pensó: ¡Caramba! Es la primera vez que veo a
     un gigante.*
Tal vez todavía tenga hambre. ¡Mejor me voy!
Y corrió a su casa tan rápido como pudo.
*Y allí, mientras comía un tazón de avena,
     pensaba en la mosca
     y la araña
     y el pájaro
     y el gato
     y la serpiente
     y el chancho
     y el leopardo
     y el cocodrilo
     y el hipopótamo
     y la ballena.*
*Pero más que nada pensaba en el gigante y en lo
     hambriento que debía haber estado.*

110

📼 Second Meeting at the University
Segundo Reunión en la Universidad

It is spring. April.	*Es la primavera. Abril.*
N: Vincent?	N: *¿Vicente?*
V: Rose, hello.	V: *Rosa, hola.*
N: Hi, Vincent.	N: *Hola, Vicente.*
You forgot my name. It's Nancy.	*Olvidaste mi nombre, me llamo Nancy.*
V: Nancy, forgive me.	V: *Nancy, perdóneme.*
I suppose I have Rose in my head.	*Supongo que tenía Rosa en mi mente.*
N: Who is this Rose?	N: *¿Quién es esta Rosa?*
V: She's just a friend…	V: *Ella es una amiga no más…*
many years ago.	*hace muchos años.*
So be it. How are things?	*Bueno pues, ¿cómo van las cosas?*
N: Quite well, thanks.	N: *Bastante bien, gracias.*
V: And how is your husband?	V: *¿Y cómo está su esposo?*
N: Fine. Everything's fine with us.	N: *Bien, Todo está bien con nosotros.*
How're you doing? Everything okay?	*Ud. ¿Cómo le va? ¿Está todo bien?*
I haven't seen you for a long time.	*No le he visto por mucho tiempo.*
V: I haven't seen you since fall.	V: *No le he visto desde el otoño.*
And it's already 1993.	*¡Y ya es 1993!*
By the way, happy new year!	*A propósito, ¡feliz año nuevo!*
N: Same to you.	N: *Igualmente.*
Are you coming from work?	*¿Vienes del trabajo?*
V: No, from a singing lesson.	V: *No, de una lección de cantar.*
I'm going to the library.	*Voy a la biblioteca.*
N: Still working at the post office?	N: *¿Todavía está trabajando en el correo?*
V: No. I quit in February.	V: *No, renuncié de allí en Febrero.*
To tell the truth, they fired me.	*Para decir la verdad, me echaron.*
N: That's too bad!	N: *¡Qué lástima!*
What happened?	*¿Que pasó?*
Why did they fire you?	*¿Por qué le echaron?*
V: Because I couldn't come on time.	V: *Porque no podía llegar a tiempo.*
N: How so?	N: *¿Como que no podía llegar a tiempo?*
V: I always study till midnight in the library.	V: *Siempre estudio hasta la media noche en la biblioteca.*
I can't get up at five in the morning.	*No puedo levantarme a las cinco en la mañana.*
N: I understand that.	N: *Entiendo eso.*
V: But now my father is angry with me.	V: *Pero ahora mi padre esta enojado conmigo.*
N: Why is that?	N: *¿Por qué?*
V: He says I'm a fool.	V: *Dice que soy tonto.*
I should've bought an alarm clock.	*Debía de haber comprado un despertador.*
N: In my opinion, it would have been better to go to bed earlier.	N: *En mi opinión, hubiera sido mejor acostarse más temprano.*
V: And get poor grades in my courses?	V: *¿Y sacar malas calificaciones en mis cursos?*

N: Such is life!
    Are you looking for a job?
	N: *¡Así es la vida!*
	    ¿Estas buscando un trabajo?

V: Of course. Otherwise I'd have no money.	V: *Por supuesto, de otro modo no tendría dinero.*
N: Where do you work now?	N: *¿Donde trabajas ahora?*
V: At the bookstore.	V: *En la libreria.*
N: That's where my sister works.	N: *Allí trabaja mi hermana.*
V: Really. I didn't know. What is her name?	V: *De veras, no lo sabía. ¿Cómo se llama?*
N: Rose. Her name is Rose, believe it or not!	N: *Rosa, su nombre es Rosa, ¡créalo o no!*
V: You're kidding!	V: *¡Está bromeando!*

N: No, I'm not kidding. I'm telling the truth.
    She works in the computer section.
	N: *No, no estoy bromeando. Digo la verdad.*
	    Ella trabaja en la sección de computadoras.

V: Is she as beautiful as you?	V: *¿Es ella tan hermosa como usted?*
N: Oh, she's much, much more beautiful than me.	N: *Oh, ella es muchísimo mas hermosa que yo.*
V: Introduce me to her, will you?	V: *¿Preséntemela por favor?*
N: I will do that some day.	N: *Lo haré algún dia.*

V: Gotta go now. I'm going to a piano lesson. Nice
    to see you again.
	V: *Tengo que irme ahora. Voy a una lección de*
	    piano. Tanto gusto verle de nuevo.

N: So long.	N: *Hasta luego.*

The same conversation again, this time in Spanish only.

THE ADVENTURE CONTINUES

You report that you are together and have just crossed the threshold into the Target Chamber. It is dark and forbidding. You don't know how you can proceed into the blackness. You end the transmission and step into the dark cavern.

One step into the chamber and your foot plunges to the knee in ice cold water. You stumble to catch your balance. "You okay?" calls out Stump. "Yeah, I didn't fall. How cold do you think this water is?"

"Darn cold, I'd say." You feel your Mitron buzz. You put it to your ear to listen, but can barely discern its soft voice. "Sorry," you tell it, "the noise of a waterfall here makes it hard to hear."

The Mitron raises its voice level. The water is two degrees Celsius. Our sensors are picking up what appears to be a person approaching you from the right.

"Do you mean Stump?"

No. Stump is in front of you. You need to have more light.

"And just how do we get some light in here, can you tell me that?"

That's no big problem. Use the flashlight feature of your Mitrons and work through tasks 111 (Observing Closely How Spanish Works) to 113 (Questions and Answers).

111

Observing Closely How Spanish Works

Take plenty of time to closely observe the workings of the language in the following. The first time through go from Spanish to English; then from English to Spanish.

The queen knows how to sell cats.	*La reina sabe vender gatos.*
She sold me a cat.	*Me vendió un gato.*
She used to sell cats in Ojai.	*Vendía gatos en Ojai.*
She quit selling cats.	*Dejó de vender gatos.*
Now she has to sell chocolates?	*¿Ahora tiene que vender chocolates?*
The king knows how to direct hymns.	*El rey sabe dirigir himnos.*
He directed the national anthem.	*Dirigió el himno nacional.*
He quit directing the men's choir.	*Dejó de dirigir el coro de hombres.*
He began to direct the mothers' choir.	*Comenzó a dirigir el coro de madres.*
He's going to direct a funeral song.	*Va a dirigir un canto fúnebre.*
He did it. He already did it.	*Lo hizo. Ya lo hizo.*
He didn't want to do it.	*No quizo hacerlo.*
He had to do it.	*Tuvo que hacerlo.*
And then an angel appeared to him.	*Y entonces le apareció un angel.*
That princess speaks Russian.	*Aquella princesa habla ruso.*
She learned it in Siberia.	*Lo aprendió en Siberia.*
She learned Arabic there also.	*Aprendió el árabe allá también.*
She knew the Arabs.	*Conocía a los arabes.*
She met King Hussein.	*Conoció al rey Hussein.*
She used to write nonsense to him.	*Le escribía tonterías.*
She has to do it. She's crazy.	*Tiene que hacerlo. Está loca.*
She's going to live in Siberia.	*Va a vivir en Siberia.*
She prefers to live there, I think.	*Prefiere vivir allá, creo.*
That prince eats too much.	*Aquel príncipe come demasiado.*
He likes to eat.	*Le gusta comer.*
He has to quit eating too much.	*Tiene que dejar de comer demasiado.*
He has to begin eating only a little.	*Tiene que comenzar a comer sólo un poco.*
He didn't want to eat it, but he ate it.	*No quizo comerlo, pero lo comió.*
He had to eat the chocolates.	*Tuvo que comer los chocolates.*
Then he sang one hymn with her.	*Entonces cantó un himno con ella.*
And he suffered a fatal attack.	*Y sufrió un ataque fatal.*
Now he has to eat chocolates with the angels.	*Ahora tiene que comer chocolates con los angelitos.*
Poor thing. What a pity! Really!	*¡Pobrecito! ¡Qué lástima! ¡De veras!*

216

MAKING DISTINCTIONS

By getting a sense of the meaning of these verb forms, you'll cross a major threshold into Spanish. Practice saying them outloud.

buys it	*lo compra*
(he) used to buy it	*lo compraba*
(he) bought it	*lo compró*
wants to buy it	*quiere comprarlo*
has bought it	*lo ha comprado*
sells them	*los vende*
(he) used to sell them	*los vendía*
(he) sold them	*los vendió*
wants to sell them	*quiere verderlos*
has sold them	*los ha vendido*
sings hymns	*canta himnos*
(he) used to sing hymns	*cantaba himnos*
(he) sang a hymn yesterday	*cantó un himno ayer*
knows how to sing hymns	*sabe cantar himnos*
has to sing hymns	*tiene que cantar himnos*
has sung hymns	*ha cantado himnos*
(he) lives in Ojai	*vive en Ojai*
used to live in Ojai	*vivía en Ojai*
lived in Ojai two years	*vivió en Ojai dos años*
wants to live in Ojai	*quiere vivir en Ojai*
has to live in Ojai	*tiene que vivir en Ojai*
has lived in Ojai	*ha vivido en Ojai*
is living in Ojai	*está viviendo en Ojai*
used to attend church	*asistía a la iglesia*
attended church (one occasion)	*asistió a la iglesia*
has attended church	*ha asistido a la iglesia*
has to attend church	*tiene que asistir a la iglesia*
is attending church	*está asistiendo a la iglesia*
used to direct the hymns	*dirigía los himnos*
directed the hymns	*dirigió los himnos*
has directed the hymns	*ha dirigido los himnos*
knows how to direct the hymns	*sabe dirigir los himnos*
is directing the hymns	*está dirigiendo los himnos*
eats too much	*come demasiado*
used to eat too much	*comía demasiado*
ate too much	*comió demasiado*
has eaten too much	*ha comido demasiado*
is going to eat too much	*va a comer demasiado*
writes to him	*le escribe*
used to write to him	*le escribía*
wrote to him	*le escribió*
has to write to him	*tiene que escribirle*

is writing to him	le está escribiendo
quit writing to him	dejó de escribirle
likes to write to him	le gusta escribirle

happens to him	le pasa
used to happen to him	le pasaba
happened to him	le pasó
has happened to him	le ha pasado
is going to happen to him	le va a pasar
is happening to him	le está pasando

talks with her	habla con ella
used to talk with her	hablaba con ella
had a talk with her	habló con ella
has talked with her	ha hablado con ella
didn't want to talk with her	no quizo hablar con ella
had to talk with her	tuvo que hablar con ella
was having to talk with her	tenía que hablar con ella

is going to do it	va a hacerlo
is doing it	lo está haciendo
did it	lo hizo
does it	lo hace
used to do it	lo hacía
had to do it	tuvo que hacerlo
has to do it	tiene que hacerlo
wants to do it	quiere hacerlo

enjoys buying a cat	le gusta comprar un gato
used to enjoy buying one	le gustaba comprar uno
enjoyed (once) buying one	le gustó comprar uno
will enjoy buying one	le va a gustar comprar uno
has enjoyed buying one	le ha gustado comprar uno

Note the similarities in the use of the infinitive in Spanish and English.

To eat is to live.	Comer es vivir.
To eat it is to live.	Comerlo es vivir.
He likes to eat and drink.	Le gusta comer y tomar.
wants to eat	quiere comer
is going to eat	va a comer
has to eat	tiene que comer
had to eat	tuvo que comer
knows how to eat	sabe comer
started to eat	comenzó a comer
prefers to eat	prefiere comer

Sometimes the Spanish infinitive is not rendered by an English infinitive:

| He quit eating. | Dejó de comer. |

Practice

Cover the English and translate the Spanish, then do the reverse.

She doesn't speak Spanish.	*Ella no habla español.*
She doesn't know how to speak.	*No sabe hablar.*
He prefers to speak Spanish.	*El prefiere hablar español.*
She prefers not to speak.	*Ella prefiere no hablar.*
He started talking.	*El comenzó a hablar.*
He quit talking.	*El dejó de hablar.*
She is now going to talk Spanish.	*Ella ahora va a hablar español.*
Going to start talking Spanish.	*Va a comenzar a hablar español.*
She has to speak Spanish.	*Ella tiene que hablar español.*
She had to speak Spanish.	*Ella tuvo que hablar español.*
She has to know how to speak.	*Ella tiene que saber hablar.*
She has to start talking.	*Ella tiene que comenzar a hablar.*
She had to start talking.	*Ella tuvo que comenzar a hablar.*
She has to quit talking.	*Ella tiene que dejar de hablar.*
She had to quit talking.	*Ella tuvo que dejar de hablar.*
He had to quit talking.	*El tuvo que dejar de hablar.*
He used to have to talk Spanish.	*El tenía que hablar español.*
She didn't used to have to talk.	*Ella no tenía que hablar.*
She didn't know how.	*Ella no sabía.*
She was beginning to talk Spanish.	*Ella comenzaba a hablar español.*

112

📼 The Skillful Calculator
El Calculador Hábil

A poor man passes by a bakery.	*Un pobre pasa por una panadería.*
He sees and smells the bread rolls.	*El ve y huele los pancillos.*
He is hungry, but he has no money.	*Tiene hambre, pero no tiene dinero.*
He enters the bakery and asks a new employee:	*Entra en la panadería y le pregunta a una empleada nueva:*
Say, how much are the rolls?	*Este...¿A cómo son los pancillos?*
A dozen for eleven pesos.	*A una docena por once pesos.*
Mm, a dozen for eleven pesos. Could you give me eleven for ten pesos?	*Mm, una docena por once pesos. ¿Me puede dar once por diez?*
Mm, surely.	*Mm, claro.*
Then ten for nine?	*Entonces, ¿diez por nueve?*
Well...uh...yes, it's possible.	*Pues...este...sí, se puede.*
Then nine for eight?	*¿Entonces, nueve por ocho?*
All right.	*Está bien.*
Then eight for seven?	*¿Entonces, ocho por siete?*
But of course.	*Claro pues.*
Then seven for six?	*¿Entonces siete por seis?*
Yes.	*Sí.*
How about six for five?	*¿Qué tal seis por cinco?*
Why not?	*¿Por qué no?*
And five for four?	*¿Y cinco por cuatro?*
I think so.	*Pienso que sí.*
Perhaps four for three?	*¿Tal vez cuatro por tres?*
Fine.	*Está bien.*
How about three for two?	*¿Qué tal tres por dos?*
Why yes.	*Sí pues.*
Then two for one peso?	*¿Entonces dos por un peso?*
Yes.	*Sí.*
Then just give me one.	*Entonces, déme solo uno.*

113

🔲 Questions and Answers
Preguntas y Respuestas

May I?	*¿Puedo?*
Yes, you may.	*Sí, puede.*
May I come in?	*¿Puedo entrar?*
Come in, please.	*Adelante, por favor.*
Understood?	*¿Entendido?*
Yes, understood.	*Entendido.*
What happened?	*¿Qué pasó?*
Nothing of importance.	*Nada de importancia.*
What's happening here?	*¿Qué pasa aquí?*
Nothing is happening.	*No pasa nada.*
What's new?	*¿Qué hay de nuevo?*
Nothing much.	*No mucho.*
What's new?	*¿Qué hay de nuevo?*
Nothing.	*Nada especial.*
Don't you believe it?	*¿No lo crees?*
No, I can't believe it.	*No, no puedo creerlo.*
May I come in?	*¿Puedo entrar?*
Surely. Please come in.	*Sí, claro. Pase adelante.*
Shall we go on?	*¿Seguimos?*
Of course. Go right ahead.	*¿Cómo no? Siga, nomás.*
Can it be done?	*¿Se puede?*
It certainly can. Of course.	*Sí se puede. Claro que sí.*

THE ADVENTURE CONTINUES

You report, "Now in Target Chamber. Can see nothing. No idea where or how to find the treasure."

On completion of your tasks, the high vaulted ceiling of the cavern begins to creek and ping as an enormous skylight scrolls open. Luckily it is daylight outside. Pebbles and sand fall into the water and a widening beam of sunlight cuts through the darkness and projects a rainbow before your eyes. Now you see the two armed guards approaching on your right in a canoe. They remove their night vision goggles and fix their eyes on the two of you. There are nasty expressions on their faces as they growl: *"Invasores."* They take you to be invaders. *"¿Invasores? No, nosotros no somos los invasores!"* you insist. They don't believe you. They tell the two of you to get in the canoe.

As you step into the canoe, they quickly handcuff you and start to tie a gag around your mouth. Before they can secure the gags, however, you say, *"Un momento, señor. Permítame contarle un cuento."*

Surprised by your offer to tell a story, the guard says: *"¿Un cuento?"*

He shoots a glance at his fellow guard, who nods almost imperceptibly. *"Sí, un cuento, por favor."*

Stump blurts out, *"Yo también tengo un cuento."*

"Muy bien," the other guard agrees, *"dos cuentos, entonces."*

They untie the gags but leave the handcuffs on. You and Stump each tell a story. The guards listen and even crack a faint smile, but then they shake their heads, as if to indicate your stories are not the right ones. Could there be a particular story that would convince them that you are not the enemy?

Although you are both still in handcuffs, you whisper a report to your Mitron, "Still in Target Chamber. Arrested by guards. Now can see, but don't know what's ahead. No idea where or how to obtain the treasure. Spanish stories may be the key."

Going on the hunch that they want original stories, you take on tasks 114 (Focus on the Language) and 115 (Wrap-up Activities) in preparation for creating your own stories.

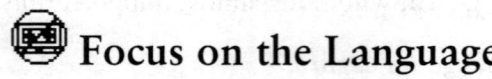 Focus on the Language

Look at the following verbs in the imperfect. Note the parallel between the endings *-aba* and *-ía* (shortened from *-iba*)

Infinitive	Imperfect	English	Infinitive	Imperfect	English
hablar	*hablaba*	used to speak	*asistir*	*asistía*	used to attend
tomar	*tomaba*	used to drink	*saber*	*sabía*	used to know
amar	*amaba*	used to love	*conocer*	*conocía*	used to know

Have you noticed any patterns? What type of verbs take *-aba* as the ending? What type of verbs take *-ía* as the ending?

Infinitives ending in *-ar*, take *-aba* to indicate the imperfect, whereas infinitives ending in *-er* or *-ir* take *-ía* to indicate the imperfect.

STUDY TASK

Take a few unhurried minutes now to review the key vocabulary presented in the sentences below. Make three passes through each of these sentences.

1st pass: Compare the Spanish forms and their meaning with the English. (Suggestion: read the Spanish out loud, then look away and say it, thinking of its meaning and form.)

2nd pass: Cover the English and see if you can translate the Spanish into English.

3rd pass: Cover the Spanish and see if you can translate the English into Spanish.

Group A

1. (He) knows things and knows Tarzan. — *Sabe cosas y conoce a Tarzán.*
2. (They) know things and (they) know Tarzan. — *Saben cosas y conocen a Tarzán.*
3. (He) used to know things and (he) used to know Tarzan. — *Sabía cosas y conocía a Tarzán.*
4. (They) used to know things and (they) used to know Tarzan. — *Sabían cosas y conocían a Tarzán.*
5. (He) knows it; (he) knows her. — *Lo sabe; la conoce.*
6. (He) doesn't know much yet. Only a little. — *El todavía no sabe mucho. Sólo un poco.*

Group B

1. Used to attend, but no longer attends. — *Asistía, pero ya no asiste.*
2. She used to attend and used to speak Chinese a little. — *Ella asistía y hablaba Chino un poco.*
3. Still attends and still knows Tarzan. — *Todavía asiste y todavía conoce a Tarzan.*
4. Ana doesn't know the queen yet. — *Ana todavía no conoce a la reina.*
5. Doesn't know the king either. — *Tampoco conoce al rey.*
6. I believe (she) doesn't know them. — *Creo, que no los conoce.*
7. But they know her. — *Pero ellos la conocen a ella.*

Group C

1.	He is with her talking.	*El está con ella hablando.*
2.	The princess is not drinking juice.	*La princesa no está tomando jugo.*
3.	She doesn't drink it yet.	*Ella todavía no lo toma.*
4.	She is only drinking water.	*Ella está tomando agua no más.*
5.	He alone is drinking it.	*Sólo él lo está tomando.*
6.	He alone drinks them.	*Sólo él los toma.*
7.	They drink it.	*Ellos lo toman.*

Group D

1.	Does the prince speak Chinese?	*¿Habla el príncipe chino?*
2.	No, only the princess speaks it.	*No, sólo la princesa lo habla.*
3.	Doesn't speak it much.	*No lo habla mucho.*
4.	Speaks it only in church.	*Lo habla solo en la iglesia.*
5.	She knows many (people).	*Ella conoce a muchos.*
6.	Knows the Chinese (people).	*Conoce a los chinos.*
7.	Knows a lot (of things).	*Sabe mucho.*
8.	The Chinese (people) attend church.	*Los chinos asisten a la iglesia.*

Group E

1.	(They) live there in the castle.	*Viven allá en el castillo.*
2.	The Chinese used to live in China.	*Los chinos vivían en China.*
3.	Does the prince live there in the tavern?	*¿Vive el príncipe allá en la cantina?*
4.	Where do the king and queen live?	*¿Dónde viven el rey y la reina?*
5.	It pleases me to sing.	*Me gusta cantar.*
6.	It doesn't please me to smoke.	*No me gusta fumar.*
7.	It pleases him to play the drum.	*Le gusta tocar el tambor.*
8.	What is it pleases her?	*¿Qué es lo que le gusta a ella?*
9.	It used to please her to sing with the dog.	*Le gustaba cantar con el perro.*

PERFORMANCE TEST

Instructions: Match the lettered Spanish phrases with the numbered English phrases, placing the letter in the blank before the corresponding number.

___ 1. They used to drink water. A. *Están tomando agua.*
___ 2. They drink water. B. *Tomaban agua.*
___ 3. They are drinking water. C. *Toman agua.*

___ 4. Is speaking Chinese well. A. *Hablaban chino bien.*
___ 5. They speak Chinese well. B. *Hablan chino bien.*
___ 6. They used to speak Chinese well. C. *Están hablando chino bien.*

___ 7. Attends church there. A. *Asistí allá la iglesia.*
___ 8. He used to attend church there. B. *Asiste allá la iglesia.*
___ 9. They used to attend church a lot. C. *Asistían mucho la iglesia.*
___ 10. They attend church little. D. *Asisten un poco la iglesia.*

___ 11. Knows many things. A. *Sabía muchas cosas.*
___ 12. He used to know many things. B. *Sabe muchas cosas.*
___ 13. They know many things. C. *Saben muchas cosas.*

___	14. They used to know many things.	D.	*Sabían muchas cosas.*
___	15. Knows many Chinese there.	A.	*Conocen muchos chinos allá.*
___	16. They know many Chinese there.	B.	*Conocían los chinos.*
___	17. He used to know the Chinese.	C.	*Conoce muchos chinos allá.*
___	18. They used to know the Chinese.	D.	*Conocía los chinos.*
___	19. It didn't please me to sing.	A.	*Me gusta cantar.*
___	20. It pleases me to sing.	B.	*No me gustaba cantar.*
___	21. It doesn't please her to eat it.	C.	*No le gustar comerlo.*
___	22. It didn't please him to eat it.	D.	*No le gustaba comerlo.*
___	23. She didn't used to speak it.	A.	*Ella no lo hablaba.*
___	24. Didn't used to understand it.	B.	*No lo entendía.*
___	25. Now (she) understands it.	C.	*Ahora lo entiende.*

115

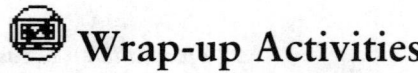 Wrap-up Activities

You are encouraged now to create more of your own mini-story plots, to write them out or, better, just to plan them so you can give them orally.

NEW VOCABULARY

Persons and Samples of Associated Verbs

The chief...	*El jefe chef...*
is the one who commands.	*es él que manda.*
The assistant...	*El ayudante...*
needs help.	*necesita ayuda.*
The old nurse...	*El enfermera vieja...*
helps the assistant.	*ayuda al ayudante.*
The young lawyer (advocate)...	*El abogado joven...*
falls in love with her.	*se enamora de ella.*
The surgeon...	*El cirujano...*
condemns the general.	*condena al general.*
The commander...	*El comandante...*
wins the battle.	*gana la batalla.*
rescues the nurse.	*rescata a la enfermera.*
saves the young lawyer.	*salva al abogado joven.*

Places and associated verbs

the circus	*el circo*
Diverts himself in the circus.	*Se divierte en el circo.*
the battle field	*el campo de batalla*
Leaves the battle field.	*Sale del campo de batalla.*

225

Concrete Objects and Associated Verbs

suitcase	*maleta*
Carries a suitcase.	*Lleva una maleta.*
coat	*saco*
Wears a white coat.	*Lleva un saco blanco.*
weapons	*armas arms.*
Carries weapons.	*Llevan armas.*
tools instruments.	*instrumentos*
Contains tools.	*Contiene instrumentos.*
battle	*batalla*
Wins (gains) the battle.	*Gana la batalla.*

Adverbs and Adjectives

suddenly	*de repente*
Suddenly gets up.	*De repente se levanta.*
at times	*a veces*
At times he talks Japanese.	*A veces él habla japonés.*
many times / often	*muchas veces*
Often he comes alone.	*Muchas veces él viene solo.*
day and night	*día y noche*
Sings day and night.	*Canta día y noche.*
especially	*especialmente*
I especially like to sing.	*Especialmente me gusta cantar.*
famous	*famosa*
A very famous surgeon.	*Un cirujano muy famoso.*
therefore (lit. for this)	*por eso*
Therefore he works alone.	*Por eso él trabaja solo.*

Verbs and Associated Nouns

carries, carried	*lleva, llevaba / llevó*
He carries a suitcase.	*El lleva una maleta.*
contains, contained	*contiene / contenía*
The suitcase contains a bomb.	*La maleta contiene una bomba.*
is hidden, was hidden (ensconced)	*está escondido, estaba escondido*
He is hidden in the kitchen.	*El está escondido en la cocina.*
shouts, shouted	*grita, gritaba / gritó*
The queen shouts: HELP!	*La reina grita: ¡SOCORRO!*
finds, found encounter.	*encuentra, encontraba / encontró*
Finds the queen in the park.	*Encuentra a la reina en el parque.*
saves, saved salvation.	*salva, salvaba / salvó*
The surgeon saves the princess.	*El cirujano salva a la princesa.*
falls in love, fell in love	*se enamora en amor., -aba / ó*
The soldier falls in love with her.	*El soldado se enamora de ella.*
marries, married	*se casa, se casaba / se casó*
He marries (with) her.	*Se casa con ella.*
is known, was known	*se sabe, se sabía*
It's not known that he's a general.	*No se sabe que él es un general.*
stops, stopped ceased from.	*cesa de, cesaba de / cesó de*
Stops (from) singing.	*Cesa de cantar.*
wins, won (gain)	*gana, ganaba / ganó*

wins the hand of the young lady.	gana la mano de la jovencita.
returns, returned (regress)	regresa, regresaba / regresó
leaves and doesn't return.	sale y no regresa.

SAMPLE MINI-STORY PLOT

(In present tense)

Hay un soldado que viene del campo de batalla. Es un soldado viejo...de hecho, un general—pero no se sabe que él es un general. Y hay una reina, una reina vieja, que vive en el castillo con el rey. El soldado viejo se enamora de la reina vieja, pero no habla nada de su amor. El sabe que el rey es cruel y que el rey detesta a la reina. El rey detesta a la reina por que ella siempre está cantando. Día y noche ella canta. Al comandante le gusta cuando la reina canta. Le gusta escucharla cantando. De hecho, le gusta cantar él mismo. Muchas veces el canta en el campo de batalla. A veces el canta con los soldados. Ahora él quiere cantar con la reina. El quiere cantar con la reina en el castillo. Pero el soldado viejo es un hombre muy bueno. La reina no conoce al soldado viejo, y él no habla nada con la reina.

Un día el rey muere. Ahora la reina está sola en el mundo. ¿Cesa la reina de cantar? No, no cesa de cantar. Un día el soldado viejo encuentra a la reina en un parque. Es el parque de un gigante—un gigante que de hecho es un cirujano muy famoso. La reina está escondida en un árbol. ¿Qué está haciendo en el árbol? De hecho, está cantando. El soldado viejo viene donde la reina y dice: «¿Por qué está Ud. escondida en este árbol?» Y ¿Por qué está cantando? Y la reina responde: «Me gusta cantar. Especialmente me gusta cantar en un árbol en el parque.» El soldado viejo dice: «Pero éste es el parque del gigante, y él es un gigante cruel, ¿no?» La reina no responde. Por eso, el soldado viejo sale y no regresa. Eso es todo. (If you don't like this ending, write a continuation of the story yourself.)

(The same story told in past tense)

Había un soldado que había venido (had come) *del campo de batalla. Era un soldado viejo...de hecho, un general—pero no se sabía que él era un general. Y había una reina, una reina vieja, que vivía en el castillo con el rey. El soldado viejo se enamoró de la reina vieja, pero no hablaba nada de su amor. El sabía que el rey era cruel y que el rey odiaba a la reina. El rey odiaba a la reina por que ella siempre estaba cantando. Día y noche ella cantaba. Al general le gustaba cuando la reina cantaba. Le gustaba escucharla cantar. De hecho, le gustaba cantar él mismo. Muchas veces el cantaba en el campo de batalla. A veces el cantaba con los soldados. Ahora él quería cantar con la reina. El quería cantar con la reina en el castillo. Pero el soldado viejo era un hombre muy bueno. La reina no conocía al soldado viejo, y él no hablaba con la reina.*

Un día el rey murió. Ahora la reina estaba sola en el mundo. ¿Cesó la reina de cantar? No, no cesó de cantar.

Un día el soldado viejo encontró a la reina en un parque. Era el parque de un gigante—un gigante que de hecho era un cirujano muy famoso. La reina estaba escondida en un árbol. ¿Qué estaba haciendo en el árbol? De hecho, estaba cantando. El soldado viejo venía donde la reina y dijo: «¿Por qué estába escondida en este árbol y por qué estaba cantando?» Y la reina respondió: «Me gusta cantar. Especialmente me gusta cantar en un árbol en el parque.» El soldado viejo dijo: «Pero éste es el parque del gigante, y él es un gigante cruel, ¿no?» La reina no respondió. Por eso, el soldado viejo salió y no regresó. Eso es todo.

THE ADVENTURE CONTINUES

When you are ready, you invite them to listen as you weave words into little stories of your own fabrication. The guards cheer in appreciation, but then look at each other and shake their heads—which you take to indicate that none of those stories is the right password.

Your report, "Little change, but now strongly suspect that story-telling will provide the key to the successful outcome of our mission."

Reasoning that a certain story—or certain stories—must serve as the password (the *consigna*) you request again: *"Por favor, permítan-nos contarles unos otros cuentos."*

"Sí, hay tiempo para más cuentos," they respond. They stop the canoe, and as you set out to prepare your next performance, they offer you sandwiches. Up to now you have been sustained by the *jugo de fuerza* in your canteens. You graciously accept their offering and in turn offer your canteens for them to have the last bit of your precious juice. On tasting the juice, they look at each other quizzically and nod. You can't even guess what is meant by that. Certainly more than that they liked the taste.

They take a three-hour rest while you prepare your stories, still shackled with the handcuffs. The first half of the time Stump takes on task 116 (The Dream of a Little Girl) to 119 (A Geography Lesson) while you prepare stories 120 (The Arab and His Camel) to 123 (A Spanish Lesson). The second half you do the reverse.

116

📼 Dream of a Little Girl

Un Sueño de una Niñita

This I saw in a dream:
  a little girl, walking down the street came to my
  house.
She came up to the door, opened it, and went in.
She entered the kitchen,
  went up to the table,
  sat on a chair,
  put her hands on the table,
  laid her head in her hands,
  and cried and cried.
And as I looked at her,
  I cried also.
Then she stood up,
  wiped her tears,
  went to the door,
  opened it, and went out.
I watched her go down the street.
Why she was crying I'd like to know.
Perhaps she had lost a kitten?
Perhaps she had lost a friend?
Only she knows.
I think that I'll never find out.

Esto es lo que ví en un sueño:
  una niñita, que caminaba por la calle vino a mi
  casa.
Vino a mi puerta, la abrió, y entró.
Entró a la cocina,
  fue a la mesa,
  se sentó en una silla,
  puso sus manos sobre la mesa,
  apoyó su cabecita en sus manos,
  y lloró y lloró.
Y mientras yo la miraba,
  también lloré.
Después se puso de pie,
  secó sus lágrimas,
  fue a la puerta,
  la abrió, y salió.
Yo la miré ir por la calle.
Me gustaría saber por qué lloraba.
¿Habrá perdido un gatito?
¿Habrá perdido un amigo?
Sólo ella sabe.
Pienso que nunca lo sabré.

117

🔊 **The Story of the Three Billygoats**

Spanish Only

Los Tres Cabritos

There were three goats that lived in the mountains.	*Habían tres cabritos que vivían en las montañas.*
They were brothers.	*Eran hermanos.*
There was a big goat, a middle-sized goat, and a little goat.	*Había un cabrito grande, un cabrito mediano, y un cabrito chiquito.*
The goats liked very much to eat green grass in the mountains, and they never went down to the valley.	*A los cabritos les gustaba mucho comer zacate verde en las montañas, y nunca bajaron al valle.*
They never had crossed the bridge.	*Nunca habían cruzado el puente.*
One day the small goat noticed that on the other side of the bridge there was a lot of green grass.	*Un día el cabrito chiquito observó que al otro lado del puente había mucho zacate verde.*
Then the small goat thought about crossing the bridge and descending to the valley to eat that green grass.	*Entonces el cabrito chiquito pensó en cruzar el puente y bajar al valle para comer de aquel zacate verde.*
He didn't know that beneath the bridge there lived a dwarf very ugly and very fierce.	*No sabía que abajo del puente vivía un enano muy feo y muy feroz.*
Well, the little goat neared the bridge and soon began to cross it.	*Bueno, el cabrito chiquito se acercó al puente y pronto comenzó a cruzarlo.*
But when he was crossing the bridge, his footsteps sounded:	*Pero cuando iba cruzando el puente, se oían sus pisadas:*
Tip, tap, tip, tap…	*Trip, trip, trip, trip…*
Upon hearing the footsteps of the small goat, the dwarf jumped from the water and yelled with a fierce voice:	*Al oír las pisadas del cabrito pequeño, el enano feo brincó del agua y gritó con voz feroz:*
"Who is crossing my bridge?"	*"¿Quién va cruzando mi puente?"*
"It's me, the little goat."	*"Soy yo, el cabrito chiquito."*
"¡¿$#! And why do you come here?"	*"¡¿$#! ¿Ya qué vienes aquí?"*
"I am going to go down to the valley to eat the green grass over there."	*"Voy a bajar al valle para comer el zacate verde que está allá."*
"Get off of my bridge! If not, I will eat you."	*"¡Fuera de mi puente! Si no, te como."*
"Oh, please, don't eat me. I am very small. Better wait until my brother passes by here.	*"Oh, por favor, no me coma a mí. Yo soy muy chiquito. Espérese mejor hasta que pase mi hermano por aquí.*
He is bigger and fatter than me."	*El es más grande y más gordo que yo."*
"Okay, go ahead then this time."	*"Bueno, entonces pasa esta vez."*
A little later, the middle-sized goat saw that his little brother was in the valley below and was happy there, eating green grass.	*Poco tiempo después, el cabrito mediano vió que su hermanito estaba en el valle abajo y estaba feliz allí comiendo zacate verde.*
Now he thought of crossing the bridge to go down into the valley where there was a lot of green grass.	*Ahora él pensó en cruzar el puente para bajar al valle donde había mucho zacate verde.*
He neared the bridge and began to cross without knowing of the dwarf that lives below.	*Se acercó al puente y comenzó a cruzar sin saber del enano feo que vive abajo.*

But when he went crossing the bridge, his footsteps sounded:

Tip, tap, tip, tap…

Upon hearing the footsteps of the middle-sized goat on the bridge, the ugly dwarf jumped from the water and yells with a fierce voice:

"Who is crossing my bridge?"

"I am, the middle-sized billygoat."

"¡¿$#, and why do you come here?"

"I am going to go down to the valley to eat the green grass there with my brother."

"Get off of my bridge! If not, I will eat you."

"Oh, please, don't eat me.

I am still very small.

Better wait until my big brother passes by here.

He is bigger and fatter than me."

"Okay, then, pass this time."

A little time later the big billygoat (the big brother) sees that his little brothers are in the valley below happily eating green grass.

Now he thinks of crossing the bridge and going down to the valley to eat that grass.

He nears the bridge and begins to cross without knowing of the ugly dwarf.

But as he was crossing the bridge, his footsteps were heard:

Tope, tope, tope, tope…

and the bridge rocked from such weight.

Upon hearing the footsteps and feeling the bridge sway, the ugly dwarf jumped from the water and yelled with a fierce voice:

"Who is crossing my bridge?"

"I am, the big billygoat."

"¡¿$, and why did you come here?"

"I'm going to go down to the valley to eat some green grass there with my little brothers."

"Get off my bridge.

Otherwise, I'm going to eat you."

"Well, come ahead."

The ugly dwarf moved up close, but the big billygoat lowered his head, and with his horns he gave a tremendous blow to the ugly dwarf.

He fell into the water and sank.

And from that day onward, the ugly dwarf hasn't bothered the billygoats.

The billygoats can cross the bridge whenever they want, and they can eat the grass in the valley as well as in the mountains.

Pero cuando iba cruzando el puente, se oyeron sus pisadas:

Trap, trap, trap, trap…

Al oír las pisadas del cabrito mediano en el puente, el enano feo brincó del agua y grita con voz feroz:

"¿Quién va cruzando mi puente?"

"Soy yo, el cabrito mediano."

"¡¿$#, ¿y a qué vienes aquí?"

"Voy a bajar al valle para comer del zacate verde que está allí con mi hermano."

"¡Fuera de mi puente! Si no, te voy a comer."

"Oh, por favor, no me coma a mí.

Yo soy muy chico todavía.

Espérese mejor hasta que pase por aquí mi hermano mayor.

El es más grande y más gordo que yo."

"Bueno, entonces pasa esta vez."

Poco tiempo después el cabrito grande (el hermano mayor) ve que sus hermanitos están en el valle abajo comiendo felices zacate verde.

Ahora él piensa cruzar el puente y bajar al valle para comer del zacate.

Se acerca al puente y comienza a cruzar sin saber del enano feo.

Pero cuando iba cruzando el puente, se oyeron sus pisadas:

Trop, trop, trop, trop…

y el puente se mecía de tanto peso.

Al oír las pisadas y sentir que el puente se mecía, el enano feo brincó del agua y gritó con una voz feroz:

"¿Quién va cruzando mi puente?"

"Soy yo, el cabrito grande."

"¡¿$#!, ¿y a qué viniste aquí?"

"Voy a bajar al valle para comer del zacate verde allá con mis hermanitos."

"¡Fuera de mi puente!

Si no, te voy a comer."

"Muy bien, adelante."

El enano feo se acercó, pero el cabrito grande bajó la cabeza, y con sus cuernos le dió un golpe tremendo al enano feo.

Este se cayó en el agua y se hundió.

Y desde ese día en adelante, el enano feo no ha molestado a los cabritos.

Los cabritos pueden cruzar el puente cuando quieren y pueden comer zacate en el valle así como en las montañas.

Vincent and Isabelle
Vicente e Isabel

V: Hi.

I: Hello.

V: How are things?

I: Very well, thanks.

V: We met at the concert last week, remember?

I: Yes, I remember. Of course I remember. Nice to see you again.

V: Forgive me, I forgot your name.

I: My name is Isabel. And yours is Vincent, right?

V: Yes. Tell me, what's that?

I: That's my dog!

V: Your dog?! He looks like a wolf.

I: Yes. Actually his father was a wolf.

V: By the way, where is your home?

I: On the other side of the park. And yours?

V: On this side of the park.

I: By the university?

V: Exactly. I was told that you are a pianist.

I: No, I'm not a pianist. I'm a Russian spy.

V: Hmm, how interesting! And I'm an American secret agent.

I: I know that.

V: How did you find out?

I: My husband is also a secret agent. He told me that.

V: How about that!

I: Well, I gotta go.

V: Wait a second, I've got one last question.

I: What is it?

V: Tell me, what's your dog's name?

I: Napo. His name is Napo.

V: Why do you call him Napo?

I: Hard to say. Napoleon…

V: Well, gotta go. Good-bye, Napo. Good-bye Isabelle.

I: Good luck!

V: *Hola.*

I: *Hola.*

V: *¿Como va todo?*

I: *Muy bien, gracias.*

V: *Nos conocímos en el concierto en la semana pasada, ¿se acuerda?*

I: *Sí, me acuerdo, por supuesto que me acuerdo. ¡Que bueno verle otra vez!*

V: *Perdóneme, me he olvidado su nombre.*

I: *Me llamo Isabel. Y su nombre es Vicente, ¿no?*

V: *Sí. Dígame, ¿que es esto?*

I: *¡Es mi perro!*

V: *¿Su perro? Pero parece lobo.*

I: *Sí. En verdad su padre era lobo.*

V: *A propósito, ¿dónde está su casa?*

I: *Al otro lado del parque. ¿Y la suya?*

V: *En este lado del parque.*

I: *¿Por la universidad?*

V: *Exactamente. Se me ha dicho que Ud. es pianista.*

I: *No, yo no soy pianista. Soy una espía Rusa.*

V: *Hmm, ¡Qué interesante! Y yo soy un agente secreto Americano.*

I: *Lo sé.*

V: *¿Cómo lo supo?*

I: *Mi esposo también es un agente secreto. El me lo dijo.*

V: *¡Qué cosa!*

I: *Bueno, tengo que irme.*

V: *Espere un segundo, tengo una pregunta final.*

I: *¿Sí?*

V: *¿Cómo se llama su perro?*

I: *Napo. Su nombre es Napo.*

V: *¿Por qué lo llamas Napo?*

I: *Es dificil decir. Napoleon…*

V: *Bueno, tengo que ir. Adiós Napo. Adiós Isabel.*

I: *¡Buena suerte!*

The same conversation again, this time in Spanish only.

119

🎞️ **A Geography Lesson** (A City Map)

Una Lección de Geografía

Today we are going to look at a different map.	*Hoy vamos a mirar un mapa diferente.*
It isn't a map of continents, countries, oceans, and seas but a simple city-map.	*No es un mapa de continentes, paises, océanos, y mares, sino un simple mapa de una ciudad.*
A city map can be very useful when you travel and can prevent you from getting lost if you know how to read one.	*El mapa de una ciudad puede ser muy útil cuando uno viaja y puede ayudarlo a uno a no perderse si uno sabe leerlo.*
Like all maps, the north is at the top and the south at the bottom.	*Como en todos los mapas, el norte está en la parte de arriba y el sur en la parte de abajo.*
Once you orient yourself, the rest is easy.	*Una vez que uno se orienta, el resto es fácil.*
Let's look at the map we have right here.	*Miremos el mapa que tenemos aquí.*

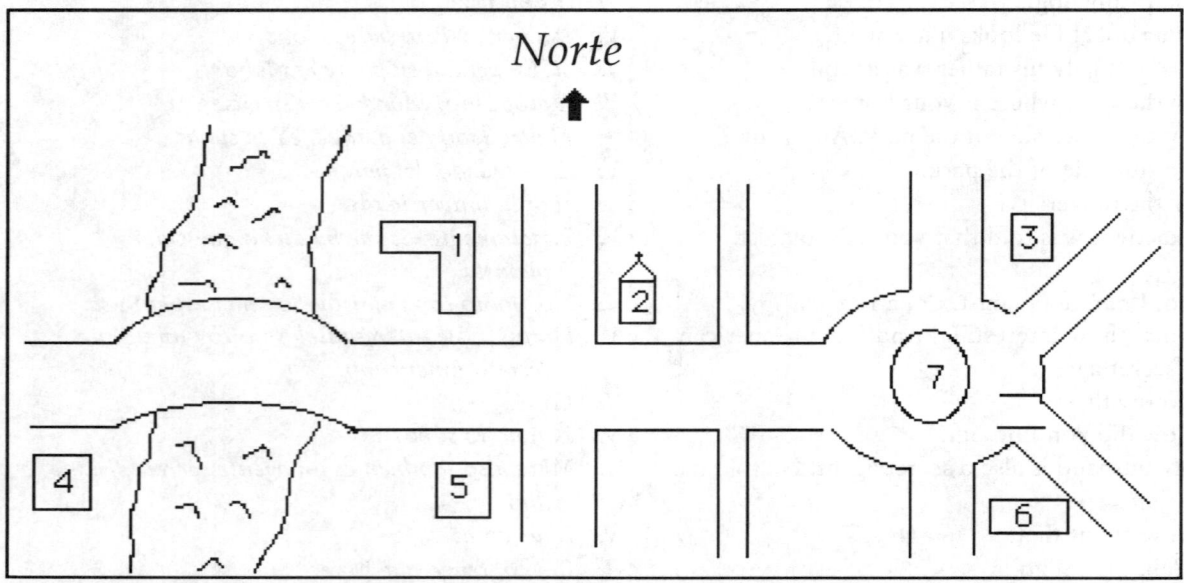

Norte

At the center of the map, you can see two wide streets crossing.	*Al centro del mapa, puedes ver dos calles anchas que se cruzan.*
The street that runs north and south is called Center Street.	*La calle que va de norte a sur se llama Center Street.*
The street that runs east and west is called Main Street.	*La calle que va de este a oeste se llama Main Street.*
At the north-west corner of this intersection is a department store (1), and right across the street from the department store there is an old church (2).	*En la esquina noroeste de esta intersección hay un negocio (1), y justo al frente del negocio, al otro lado de la calle, hay una iglesia antigua (2).*
So the old church is at the northeast corner of the intersection, right?	*Entonces la iglesia está en la esquina noreste de la intersección, ¿no?*
Across the street directly south of the department store is the city library (5).	*Al otro lado de la calle, directamente al sur del negocio está la biblioteca de la ciudad (5).*

What is this? Yes, it is a river.

It is a wide river that crosses the city from north to south.

There is a bridge on the map.

On the west side of the bridge is the city hall. What number is it?

On the east side (the right side) of the map, we have a roundabout with a big statue in the center (7) and a couple of buildings on either side (3, 6).

How do you go from the department store (1) to the city library (5)?

It is simple. Go down Center Street straight through the intersection. The library is on your right.

Tell me, how do you go from the old church to the train station (6)?

First, cross Main Street and turn left.

Walk until you see the roundabout with the statue in the middle.

Take the second street on your right and continue to walk until you see a long blue building.

That's the train station.

How do you go from the train station to city hall?

Go back through the roundabout and take Main Street.

Go straight past the church and the department store.

You'll come to a bridge. Cross it, and you'll see the city hall on your left.

¿Qué es esto? Sí, es un rio.

Un rio ancho que cruza la ciudad de norte a sur.

Hay un puente en el mapa.

Al lado oeste del puente está la municipalidad. ¿Qué número es?

Al lado este (lado derecho) del mapa, verá una rotonda con una gran estatua en el centro (7) con un edificio a cada lado (3, 6).

¿Cómo se va del negocio (1) a la biblioteca (5)?

Simple. Vaya por Center Street derecho por la intersección. La biblioteca estará a su derecha.

Dígame, ¿Cómo se va desde la iglesia a la estación de trenes (6)?

Primero, cruce Main Street y doble a la izquierda.

Camine haste que vea la rotonda con la estatua en el centro.

Tome la segunda calle de la derecha y siga caminando hasta que vea un edificio azúl largo.

Esa es la estación de trenes.

¿Cómo se va de la estación de trenes a la municipalidad?

Vuelva a la rotonda y tome Main Street.

Vaya derecho pasando la iglesia y el negocio.

Va a llegar a un puente. Crúcelo y verá la municipalidad a su izquierda.

120

 The Arab and His Camel

El Arabe y Su Camello

(A Fable from Ancient Greece)

Once on a cold winter night there was an Arab
sleeping in his tent.

Suddenly his camel stuck his nose into the tent and
said:

"Master, may I come in to warm myself?"

After hesitating a moment, the Arab said, "You may."

In a little while the camel stretched his neck into the
tent and said:

"I still feel cold. May I put my neck in?"

"Yes, you may," the Arab said.

In a little while the camel said: "I'm still very cold.
May I put my forelegs in?"

"You may," the Arab said.

Now the Arab had to move back himself to make
more room.

The camel spoke again: "Standing like this I keep the
tent open, and it's cold for both of us.

Let me enter and close the curtain. Then it'll be warm
for both of us."

"All right," said the Arab.

And the camel stepped inside and closed the curtain.

But now there was not room enough for both of them.
The tent was too small.

After a moment the camel said:

"There's not room enough for both.
You are smaller than I.
It would be better for you to leave.
Then there will be room for me.
At least one of us will be comfortable."

Then the camel pushed his master out of the tent.

The Arab said to himself: "I was wrong.
I should never have let him stick his head inside in
the first place."

(Una Fábula de la Grecia del Antiguo)

En una fría noche de invierno se encontraba un
árabe durmiendo en su tienda.

De repente su camello metió su naríz en la tienda y
dijo:

"Amo, ¿podría entrar para calentarme?"

Después de dudar por un momento el árabe dijo:
"Está bien."

Luego el camello estiró su cuello dentro de la tienda
y dijo:

"Todavía siento frío. ¿Podría meter mi cuello?"

"Sí, está bien," dijo el árabe.

Luego el camello dijo: "Todavía siento mucho frío.
¿Podría meter mis patas delanteras?"

"Está bien," dijo el árabe.

Ahora el árabe tenía que retroceder para hacer más
lugar.

El camello habló otra vez: "En esta posición
mantengo la tienda abierta, y ambos sentimos
frío.

Déjame entrar y cerrar la cortina. Así ambos
podemos calentarnos."

"Bueno," dijo el árabe.

Y el camello entró y cerró la cortina.

Pero ya no había suficiente espacio para ambos. La
tienda era demasiada pequeña.

Despúes de un momento el camello dijo:

"No hay suficiente espacio para ambos.
Tú eres más pequeño que yo.
Sería mejor que tú salieras.
Entonces habrá espacio para mí.
Por lo menos uno de nosotros estará cómodo."

Despúes el camello sacó a su amo de la tienda de un
empujón.

El árabe se dijo a sí mismo: "Estaba equivocado.
En el primer lugar, no le hubiera dejado meter la
cabeza."

📼 The Critical Mother

La Mamá Criticadora

Reynaldo's mother sent him a gift for Christmas: she sent two silk ties, one red and one green.

And she wrote him that she was coming to see him next Sunday and asked him to please come to the airport to meet her.

Reynaldo knows that his mother is very critical.

He decides to wear the red tie.

Arriving at the airport, he receives his mother with an embrace.

She says: "So you didn't like the green tie, eh?"

La mamá de Reynaldo le mandó un regalo de navidad: dos corvatas de seda, una roja y una verde.

Entonces ella le mandó una carta diciendo que va a visitar el próximo domingo y que por favor venga al aeroporto recibirla.

Reynaldo sabe que su madre es muy criticadora.

El decide ponerse la corvata roja.

Al llegar al aeropuerto, él recibe a su madre con un abrazo.

Ella le dice: "No te gustó la corvata verde, ¿no es cierto?"

122

📼 Chicken Little
Pollito Chico

This is the story of Chicken Little, a chickie that became alarmed and set itself to believe that the sky was falling.

One day this chickie was in the garden eating, when a leaf, a very large leaf, fell on her head.

The poor chickie was startled and imagined that the sky was falling.

It started to run, screaming: "Peep, peep, Mommy, where are you Mommy?"

"Cluck, cluck, here I am Chickie. What is it?"

"The sky is falling! The sky is falling!"

"How do you know, Chickie?"

"I saw it with my very eyes, and a piece fell BOOM! on my head. I tell you the truth."

"Let's flee!" screamed the hen. "Let's flee, run! Duck, Duck, where are you, Duck?"

"Quack, quack, here I am.
   What happened? What happened?"

"The sky is falling! The sky is falling!"

"How do you know, Hen?"

"The chickie told me."

"How do you know, Chickie?"

"I saw it with my very eyes, and a piece fell BOOM! on my head. I tell you the truth."

"Let's flee!" screamed the duck. "Let's flee, run!"

"Goose, Goose, where are you, Goose?"

"Honk, honk, here I am, Duck. What happened?"

"The sky is falling! The sky is falling!"

"How do you know, Duck?"

"The hen told me."

"How do you know, Hen?"

"The chickie told me."

"How do you know, Chickie?"

"I saw it with my very eyes, and a piece fell BOOM! on my head. I'm telling you the truth."

"Let's flee!" screamed the goose. "Let's flee, run!"

"Turkey, Turkey, where are you, Turkey?"

"Gobble, gobble. Here I am, Goose. What happened? What happened?"

"The sky is falling! The sky is falling."

"How do you know, Goose?"

Esta es la historia de Pollito Chico, un pollito que se alarmó y se puso a creer que el cielo se estaba cayendo.

Un día este pollito estaba comiendo en el jardín cuando una hoja, una hoja muy grande, le cayó en la cabeza.

El pobre pollito se asustó y se puso a creer que el cielo se estaba cayendo.

Se puso a correr, gritando: "Pío, pío, Mami, ¿dónde estás Mami?"

"Clo, clo, aquí estoy, Pollito. ¿Qué pasa?"

"¡El cielo se está cayendo! ¡El cielo se está cayendo!"

"¿Cómo lo sabes, Pollito?"

"Lo vi con mis propios ojos, y un pedazo del cielo cayó ¡BUM! sobre mi cabeza. Te digo la verdad."

"¡Huyamos!" gritóla gallina. "¡Huyamos, corre! Pato, Pato, ¿dónde estás, Pato?"

*"Cuac, cuac, aquí estoy.
   ¿Qué pasó? ¿Qué pasó?"*

"¡El cielo se está cayendo! ¡El cielo se está cayendo!"

"¿Cómo lo sabes, Gallina?"

"Me lo dijo el pollito."

"¿Cómo lo sabes, Pollito?"

"Lo vi con mis propios ojos, y un pedazo del cielo cayó ¡BUM! sobre mi cabeza. Les digo la verdad."

"¡Huyamos!" gritó el pato. "¡Huyamos, corran!"

"Ganso, Ganso, ¿dónde estás, Ganso?"

"Uank, uank, aquí estoy, Pato. ¿Qué pasa?"

"¡El cielo se está cayendo! ¡El cielo se está cayendo!"

"¿Cómo lo sabes, Pato?"

"Me lo dijo la gallina."

"¿Cómo lo sabes, Gallina?"

"Me lo dijo el pollito."

"¿Cómo lo sabes, Pollito?"

"Lo vi con mis propios ojos, y un pedazo del cielo cayó ¡BUM! sobre mi cabeza. Les estoy diciendo la verdad."

"¡Huyamos!" gritó el ganso. "¡Huyamos, corran!"

"Pavo, Pavo, ¿dónde estás, Pavo?"

"Gabul, gabul. Aquí estoy, Ganso. ¿Qué pasó? ¿Qué pasó?"

"¡El cielo se está cayendo! ¡El cielo se está cayendo!"

"¿Cómo lo sabes, Ganso?"

"The duck told me."
"How do you know, Duck?"
"The hen told me."
"How do you know, Hen?"
"The chickie told me."
"How do you know, Chickie?"
"I saw it with my very eyes, and a piece fell BOOM! on my head. I'm telling you the truth."

"Let's flee!" screamed the turkey. "Let's flee, run!"
"Fox, Fox, where are you, Fox?"
"Yif, yif. Here I am. What's happening?"
"The sky is falling! The sky is falling!"
"How do you know, Turkey?"
"The goose told me."
"How do you know, Goose?"
"The duck told me."
"How do you know, Duck?"
"The hen told me."
"How do you know, Hen?"
"The chickie told me."
"How do you know, Chickie?"
"I saw it with my very eyes, and a piece fell BOOM! on my head. I'm telling you the truth."

The fox thought a little and said: "Don't be afraid. I will save you. Come with me to my cave."
And all the animals went with the fox into her den.

Poor animals!

"Me lo dijo el pato."
"¿Cómo lo sabes, Pato?"
"Me lo dijo la gallina."
"¿Cómo lo sabes, Gallina?"
"Me lo dijo el pollito."
"¿Cómo lo sabes, Pollito?"
"Lo vi con mis propios ojos, y un pedazo del cielo cayó ¡BUM! sobre mi cabeza. Les estoy diciendo la verdad."

"¡Huyamos!" gritó el pavo. "¡Huyamos, corran!"
"Zorra, Zorra, ¿dónde estás, Zorra?"
"Yif, yif. Aquí estoy. ¿Qué pasa?"
"¡El cielo se está cayendo! ¡El cielo se está cayendo!"
"¿Cómo lo sabes, Pavo?"
"Me lo dijo el ganso."
"¿Cómo lo sabes, ganso?"
"Me lo dijo el pato."
"¿Cómo lo sabes, Pato?"
"Me lo dijo la gallina."
"¿Cómo lo sabes, Gallina?"
"Me lo dijo el pollito."
"¿Cómo lo sabes, Pollito?"
"Lo vi con mis propios ojos, y un pedazo del cielo cayó ¡BUM! sobre mi cabeza. Les estoy diciendo la verdad."

La zorra pensaba un poco y dijo: "No tengan miedo. Yo les salvaré. Vengan conmigo a mi cueva."
Y todos los animales se fueron con la zorra en la cueva.

¡Pobres animales!

123

📼 A Spanish Lesson
Una Lección de Español

Mine. My pencil. My pencil.	*Mío. El lápiz mío. Mi lápiz.*
Yours. Your pencil. Your pencil.	*(El) suyo. El lápiz suyo. Su lápiz.*
I have a yellow pencil.	*Tengo un lápiz amarillo.*
This is my yellow pencil.	*Este es mi lápiz amarillo.*
Do you have a pencil too?	*¿Tiene usted también un lápiz?*
Yes, you have a red pencil.	*Sí, Ud. tiene un lápiz rojo.*
This is my pencil.	*Este es el lápiz mío.*
Is this your pencil?	*¿Es éste el lápiz suyo?*
I have yellow paper.	*Tengo papel amarillo.*
Do you have white paper?	*¿Tiene usted papel blanco?*
Yes, this is your paper.	*Sí, este es el papel suyo.*
This is my paper.	*Este es el papel mío.*
To give. To give me. To give it to me.	*Dar. Darme. Dármelo.*
You want. You don't want.	*(Ud.) quiere. (Ud.) no quiere.*
Is this pencil yours or mine?	*¿Este lápiz es suyo o mío?*
I believe it's yours.	*Creo que es suyo.*
This sheet of paper isn't yours.	*Esta hoja de papel no es suyo.*
It's mine, right?	*Es mío, ¿verdad?*
Yes, I believe it's mine.	*Sí, creo que es mío.*
You want to give me your paper.	*Ud. quiere darme el papel suyo.*
Oh, you don't want to give me it.	*Oh, Ud. no quiere dármelo.*
Do you want to give me a pencil?	*¿Quiere darme un lápiz?*
Thank you. You're very kind.	*Gracias. Ud. es muy amable.*
That pencil. That paper.	*Ese lápiz. Ese papel.*
This pencil is mine.	*Este lápiz es mío.*
That one is yours.	*Ese es suyo.*
That paper is yours.	*Ese papel es suyo.*
Your paper is here.	*El papel suyo está aquí.*
My paper is here.	*El papel mío está aquí.*
Is it clear? I hope so.	*¿Está claro? Espero que sí.*
There. Where?	*Allí. ¿Donde?*
It's here. It's there.	*Está aquí. Está allí.*
The white paper is here.	*El papel blanco está aquí.*
Where is the yellow paper?	*¿Dónde está el papel amarillo?*
It's there.	*Está allí.*
The yellow pencil is there.	*El lápiz amarillo está allí.*
Where is the white pencil?	*¿Dónde está el lápiz blanco?*
It's here.	*Está aquí.*
Will you give me it?	*¿Quiere dármelo?*
With pleasure.	*Con mucho gusto.*

Many thanks.	*Muchas gracias.*
Your pencil. Your paper.	*Su lápiz. Su papel.*
Big or small?	*¿Grande o pequeño?*
Short or long?	*¿Corto o largo?*
Your pencil is long.	*Su lápiz es largo.*
Your paper is long too.	*Su papel es largo también.*
This pencil is short.	*Este lápiz es corto.*
Is it yours?	*¿Es suyo?*
That paper is small.	*Ese papel es pequeño.*
Is it mine?	*¿Es mío?*
Your paper is long.	*Su papel es largo.*
Is your pencil long?	*¿Es largo su lápiz?*
My yellow pencil is long.	*Mi lápiz amarillo es largo.*
Is my black pencil long too?	*¿Es largo también mi lápiz negro?*
Longer than. The longest.	*Más largo que. El más largo.*
I have three pencils: a red one, a black one, and a yellow one.	*Yo tengo tres lápices: uno rojo, uno negro, y uno amarillo.*
The black pencil is longer than the red one.	*El lápiz negro es más largo que el rojo.*
The yellow pencil is longer than the black one.	*El lápiz amarillo es más largo que el negro.*
So the yellow pencil is the longest, and the red one is the shortest.	*Entonces el lápiz amarillo es el más largo, y el rojo es el más corto.*
Is it clear? I hope so.	*¿Está claro? Espero que sí.*
You have three sheets of paper: a white one, a black one, and a red one.	*Usted tiene tres hojas de papel: una blanca, una negra, y una roja.*
The black paper is longer than the red, and the white is longer than the black.	*El papel negro es más largo que el rojo, y el blanco es más largo que el negro.*
So the white paper is the longest, and the red is the shortest.	*Entonces el papel blanco es el más largo, y el rojo es el más corto.*
Is it clear? I think so.	*¿Está claro? Creo que sí.*
Your red paper is shorter than my red pencil.	*Su papel rojo es más corto que mi lápiz rojo.*
My black pencil is longer than your black paper.	*Mi lápiz negro es más largo que su papel negro.*
My yellow pencil is longer than your white paper.	*Mi lápiz amarillo es más largo que su papel blanco.*
So my things are longer than yours.	*Entonces las cosas mías son más largas que las suyas.*
Understand? I hope so.	*¿Entiende? Espero que sí.*

End Tape 5, Side A

THE ADVENTURE CONTINUES

After three hours you perform your stories. They nod approvingly and remove the handcuffs. *"Gracias. Muchas gracias."* you say. You do not know where you are headed, but, relieved to be free of the handcuffs, you go along without resisting.

You report, "Hands free. Moving down river. Destination unknown. Stories helping."

Seeking guidance from your map, you take out the glasses and look again at the shaded square at the center of your map. It shows the key, but now you notice a tiny number 3 at its tip. "What do you think that represents, Stump?" you ask. "Could it be pointing to the third cell to the north, the last shaded cell?"

You look at that cell and see the faint outline of a town, and underneath it the words *CAFÉ PARQUE DE LAS GIRAFAS*. "Good thinking, Stump." you respond, "and notice that that completes all the places or items found in the poem *La Llave del Reino del Rey: el reino, el pueblo, el parque, la casa, el cuarto, el florero, la flor.*"

"Hey, I think we're getting the final pieces to a puzzle," says Stump. "What it seems we need now is the key. Where can we find a little key in a giant place like this?"

As the canoe moves through the deep, narrow cavern, you are captivated by the brilliantly colored murals that create a veritable garden of Eden. In one section of the giant mural you see a park with giraffes grazing in the trees. That jars your senses. You look for other familiar signs, and soon they appear. A king standing over his kingdom. A room. A vase. A rose…"That's it," you cry out. "That must be the password they have been waiting for—and the proof we are not invaders."

"What are you talking about?" asks Stump.

"Stump, why haven't we seen it before? It's the poem, The Keys of the King's Kingdom. *That's* the key; that's the story they are waiting for. If we can recite that poem, they will know we are not invaders, and we can enter the next chamber.

After reviewing the poem you recite it to them. Great job! The guards stop paddling and look at you with big smiles and thumbs up. Obviously you passed their test—and just in time. The canoe has reached the threshold of the next chamber. What would have happened if you hadn't found the "key?"

You report, "Found the 'key' just in time; it worked! Now entering first chamber north of 'key chamber.'"

Waiting on the other side of the threshold are two new guards who get in the canoe with you and start off again downstream. In the distance ahead you hear the sound of rushing water. You feel the canoe rise and drop in an increasingly swift current as you enter a winding tunnel so narrow that the canoe can barely squeeze through. You see only darkness ahead. Told by the guards that it will take a couple of hours to get through the tunnel, you decide to invest the time in learning. Your Mitron's flashlight feature would enable you to use your notebook as you glide through the tunnel, but you ask the guards what it would take to have lighting. He indicates that if you will undertake four respectable learning tasks, he can get lighting for you. Wanting a change of pace, you propose to take a first look at three extraordinary pieces: 124 (A Helpful Way to Reference Spanish Endings), 125 (Aspects of Past Time), and 126 (Simple Verb Tenses). He approves and gets the lighting system turned on. You spend an interesting two hours to explore some of the crucial differences between Spanish and English grammar. You don't expect it to increase your fluency, but you know it will raise your awareness about some features of Spanish.

124

⊞ The Spanish Endings *-aba, -ó* and *-ado*
The Imperfect, Perfect, and Past Participle

You are going to learn how to speak of past events. To reap the benefits of this section, pay close attention now and come back and review it later.

As you are aware, each of the following forms of the verb *viajar* has its own distinct meaning, yet each can be translated into English as "traveled." In other words, each of the endings *-aba, -ó* and *-ado* can be rendered as -ed in English.

Technical Term	Spanish	Explanation
Imperfect	*viaj-aba*	Viewed not as a single, unbounded event: traveled (not at specified time to given place).
Preterite (or perfect)	*viaj-ó*	Viewed as a single, bounded event: traveled (at specified time(s) to given place).
Past Participle	*viaj-ado*	Viewed as a resultant state: has traveled.

Since all three endings are translated into English generally by the ending -ed, but since each signals a different meaning, it will be useful to indicate each in a distinctive way when we reference Spanish to English. We will do this as follows:

-ed[1] IMPERFECT

-ed[2] PRETERITE

-ed[3] PAST PARTICIPLE

Travel-ed[1]	*Juan viaj-aba en Méjico.*	Juan traveled in Mexico.
Travel-ed[2]	*Juan viaj-ó a Méjico.*	Juan traveled to Mexico (referring to a single trip).
Travel-ed[3]	*Juan ha viaj-ado mucho.*	Juan has traveled a lot.
	Juan ha viaj-ado a Méjico.	Juan has traveled (made a trip) to Mexico.

The "past tense marker" of an English verb such as travel-ed contains more information than just placing the action in the past. By itself, the *-ed* marker does not reveal whether that action is to be viewed "generically" or as a particular instance. Only when an *-ed* verb is used in actual context can its meaning be known. For example, the statement

(a) John travel<u>ed</u> in Mexico.

we would think refers not to just a single act of traveling from one place to another, but rather as something which John did repeatedly over a period of time. But the statement

(b) John travel<u>ed</u> to Mexico.

most likely refers to one particular instance of travel—a single act viewed and presented by the speaker as bounded by both a beginning and end.*

Note that the past-tense marker -ed occurs in both (a) and (b) even though the meaning "completed, particular, one-time occurrence" (sentence b) contrasts sharply with the meaning "non-particular, non-one-time occurrence" (sentence a). If the context of a verb marked with -ed is too unclear, we have different ways to clarify it. For example, to clarify sentence (a), we could say

(c) John traveled <u>repeatedly</u> in Mexico.

(d) John <u>used to</u> travel in Mexico.

(e) John <u>was</u> traveling in Mexico.

(f) John <u>went about</u> traveling in Mexico.

Now look at some Spanish sentences and see how these meanings are handled.

(1a) *Juan viaj-aba en Méjico.*	John traveled in Mexico.
(1b) *Juan enseñ-aba inglés.*	John taught (teach-ed) English.

Here, the Spanish ending -*aba* corresponds to the English ending -*ed* in designating what the action was and in placing it in the past. But beyond that -*aba* contains certain information that -*ed* does not contain: it presents a view of that action NOT as a particular instance, NOT as something the speaker wants you to see as a single bounded action, carried through from beginning to end, but as an *unbounded action*.

Contrast (1a) and (1b) above with (2a) and (2b) below.

(2a) Juan viaj-ó a Méjico.	John traveled to Mexico.
(2b) Juan enseñ-ó una lección.	John taught a lesson.

Here, the stressed ending -*o* corresponds to the ending -*ed* in placing the action in the past, but beyond that it contains certain information that the -*ed* does not contain. It presents a view of a particular instance of an action, something the speaker wants you to see as *a bounded action*, carried through from beginning to end.

You should see from the above that in talking about someone else's action in the past, a Spanish speaker must present to his audience how he wishes them to view the action: he may present it as a single particular act carried through from start to finish, or designate the act without this particular aspect of meaning. To do this with -*ar* verbs (*"viaj-ar," "enseñ-ar,"* etc.) the speaker MUST choose either -*aba* or -*ó*: *viajaba* or *viajó*. (With -*er* and -*ir* verbs such as *comer* and *dormir* the same contrast in aspect is signaled by -*ía* and *ió*.)

Look closely. What would the following mean?

Juan viaj-aba a Méjico.

Juan enseñ-aba una lección.

Eva com-ía y comía.

Eva com-ió un limón.

Construct the proper form of the Spanish verb *visitar* to fit the following situations:

Manuel <u>visited</u> with his friend often.

He <u>was visiting</u> his friend when lightning struck him.

He <u>visited</u> his friend once when it was winter.

125

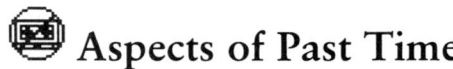 Aspects of Past Time

Acts that occurred in past time can be spoken of from different perspectives or different points of view. For example: *lo comía* "he ate it (from time to time)" vs. *lo comió* he ate it (on a given occasion)." The former simply names a customary or unbounded action, the latter refers to a specific act, a bounded event carried through to completion. This is a crucial distinction that speakers of Spanish must make every time they refer to action in the past.

A closer look at what is meant by *cantaba* vs. *cantó*

In English there are several ways of referring to customary, recurring, or ongoing behavior in the past. For example:

When he was young...

> a) he sang a lot

> b) he used to sing a lot

> c) he would sing a lot

> d) he did a lot of singing

The one Spanish equivalent of these is:

Cuando él era joven...

> a) *cantaba mucho.*

When a Spanish speakers use the form *cantaba*, they are not indicating a single, completed act of singing; rather they are viewing the singing as a customary, recurring or ongoing action in the past. If they wish to indicate a single completed act of singing, as in: "She sang a song," (or specifically numerable completed acts of singing, as in: "She sang five songs," then they will use the form *cantó*: *Ella cantó un canto. Ella cantó cinco cantos.*

El cantaba un canto is how to say "He was singing a chant." Note that this freezes the action, looks at its middle rather than its end, views it as ongoing. This in contrast to *El cantó un canto*, in which the speaker views a given action as carried through to completion.

These contrasting views of the action as *completed* or *not completed* we will call the "aspectual" meaning. A marker of "aspectual" meaning always accompanies the designation of an action in the past. Verbal "aspect" is different from verbal "tense." Grammarians refer to the form *cantó* (and analogous forms of all other Spanish verbs) as the perfect or preterite—which indicates both *past tense* and *completive aspect*. They refer to the form *cantaba* (and analogous forms of all other Spanish verbs) as the imperfect—which indicates both *past tense* and *incompletive aspect*. We will use the symbol $\Rightarrow$ | to represent the view of an action brought to completion, and the symbol $\Rightarrow$ ... to represent the view of an ongoing action in the past.

English	Imperfect	Preterite
He sang	*El cantaba*	*El cantó*

PERFORMANCE TEST 1

Instructions. Identify the meaning of the following forms by encircling the symbol $\Rightarrow$ | or $\Rightarrow$ ... for each. Check your answers in the appendix.

ate	*comió*	$\Rightarrow$ |	$\Rightarrow$ ...	lived	*vivió*	$\Rightarrow$ |	$\Rightarrow$ ...
ate	*comía*	$\Rightarrow$ |	$\Rightarrow$ ...	lived	*vivía*	$\Rightarrow$ |	$\Rightarrow$ ...
did	*hacía*	$\Rightarrow$ |	$\Rightarrow$ ...	met	*conoció*	$\Rightarrow$ |	$\Rightarrow$ ...
did	*hizo*	$\Rightarrow$ |	$\Rightarrow$ ...	spoke	*hablaba*	$\Rightarrow$ |	$\Rightarrow$ ...
directed	*dirigió*	$\Rightarrow$ |	$\Rightarrow$ ...	spoke	*habló*	$\Rightarrow$ |	$\Rightarrow$ ...
directed	*dirigía*	$\Rightarrow$ |	$\Rightarrow$ ...	wrote	*escribió*	$\Rightarrow$ |	$\Rightarrow$ ...
knew	*conocía*	$\Rightarrow$ |	$\Rightarrow$ ...	wrote	*escribía*	$\Rightarrow$ |	$\Rightarrow$ ...

PERFORMANCE TEST 2

Instructions. Write the (preterite or imperfective) ending called for to render the meaning indicated in the non-verbal symbol. The answers are in the appendix.

1. *llor-*	$\Rightarrow$ |	5. *sufri-*	$\Rightarrow$ |	9. *vivi-*	$\Rightarrow$ |
2. *llor-*	$\Rightarrow$ ...	6. *sufr-*	$\Rightarrow$ ...	10. *viv-*	$\Rightarrow$ ...
3. *cant-*	$\Rightarrow$ |	7. *habl-*	$\Rightarrow$ ...		
4. *cant-*	$\Rightarrow$ ...	8. *habl-*	$\Rightarrow$ |		

Note that the simple past tense in English (he traveled, he ate) is ambiguous: to the Spanish mind it could refer to either ⟹ | or ⟹ ...

A closer look at what is meant by *ha cantado* vs. *cantó* or *cantaba*

In English we make an important distinction between "has sung" and "sang." We use "sang" to indicate a past action not specified as relevant or connected to the present state of affairs. One might well look back on the London Blitz of 1940 and say: "Hitler ordered air raids on London." To say: "Hitler has ordered air raids on London," indicates that the statement has some present moment. Similarly to say "Beethoven has composed a tenth symphony" makes our mind suppose that he must still be alive, or that in some odd way this statement has relevance to the present moment.

We can depict connectedness or relevance to the present as ⟹ —, where — represents the present moment or current state of affairs and the arrow represents a given action. Here are three views of past action:

1.	He has sung.	*El ha cantado.*
2.	He sang (at times in the past).	*El cantaba.*
3.	He sang (a song through to completion at a given time).	*El cantó.*

Ha cantado shows present relevance, so we can depict it in the same way as its English equivalent. Consider then these three ways of viewing past action: (1) Particularly relevant to the present state of affairs: *ha cantado*; or (2) not particularly relevant to the present state of affairs, but viewed as (a) completed (*cantó*) or (b) not completed (*cantaba*).

Practice

Identify which meaning component (⟹ ..., ⟹ —, or ⟹ |) depicts each of the following verb forms.

(-ar verbs)	(-er/-ir verbs)
tomaba	*comió*
tomó	*comía*
ha tomado	*ha comido*
lloraba	*tenía*
lloró	*tuvo*
ha llorado	*ha tenido*
jugaba	*sufría*
jugó	*sufrió*
ha jugado	*ha sufrido*

Review

Go back now over the sentences in Study Tasks 1 and 2 that refer to past action or state of being, only now visualize each action or state in the way the meaning of the three past forms has been described.

126

 Simple Verb Tenses (without an auxiliary verb)

Five "Indicative" Forms

	Name	Abbr.	Form	Example
(A)	Simple present	Pres.	[verb]s	He <u>speaks</u> English.
(B)	Imperfect past	Imp.	[verb]ED[1]	As a child, she <u>spoke</u> {unbounded} a lot.
(C)	Preterite past	Pret.	[verb]ED[2]	I <u>spoke</u> {bounded} with him yesterday.
(D)	Future	Fut.	will [verb]	She <u>will speak</u> at the conference tomorrow.
(E)	Conditional	Cond.	would [verb]	If he weren't shy, he <u>would speak</u> more.

Two "Subjunctive" Forms

	Name	Abbr.	Form	Example
(F)	Present Subjunctive	Pres. Sub.	that he [verb]	I insist that he speak.
(G)	Past Subjunctive	Past Sub.	that he [verb]ED[3]	I insisted that he spoke.
				I insisted that he speak.

EXAMPLES

Indicative Modes

Form	-ar	Spanish	English
Pres.	-a	*Sé que el niño habl-a.*	I know the child speaks.
		Insisto que el niño habl-a.	I insist that the child speaks.
Imp.	-a	*Sé que el niño habl-a.*	I know the child spoke (at times).
Pret.	-ó	*Sé que el niño habl-ó.*	I know the child spoke (on a given occasion).
Fut.	-ará	*Sé que el niño habl-ará.*	I know the child will speak.
Cond.	-aría	*Sé que el niño habl-aría.*	I know the child would speak.

Form	-er/ir	Spanish	English
Pres.	-e	*Sé que el niño com-e.*	I know the child eats.
		Insisto que el niño com-e.	I insist that the child eats.
Imp.	-ía	*Sé que el niño com-ía.*	I know the child ate (at times).
Pret.	-ió	*Sé que el niño com-ió.*	I know the child ate (on a given occasion).
Fut.	-erá	*Sé que el niño com-erá.*	I know the child will eat.
Cond.	-ería	*Sé que el niño com-ería.*	I know the child would eat.

Subjunctive

Subjunctive (*Irrealis*) is signaled by switching the thematic vowels from A to E and E/I to A:

Form	-ar	Spanish	English
Pres. Sub.	-e	*Insisto en que el niño habl-e.*	I insist that the child speak.
		Dudo que el niño habl-e.	I doubt the child speaks.
Past Sub.	-ara	*Insistaba que el niño habl-ara.*	I insisted that the child speak.
	-ase	*(or Insistaba que el niño habl-ase.)*	I insisted that the child speak.
		Dudaba que el niño habl-ara.	I doubted the child spoke.
		(or Dudaba que el niño habl-ase.)	I doubted the child spoke.

Form	-er/-ir	Spanish	English
Pres. Sub.	-a	*Insisto en que el niño com-a.*	I insist that the child eat.
		Dudo que el niño com-a.	I doubt the child eats.
Past Sub.	-iera	*Insistaba que el niño com-iera.*	I insisted that the child eat.
	-iese	*(or Insistaba que el niño com-iese.)*	I insisted that the child eat.
		Dudaba que el niño com-iera.	I doubted the child ate.
		(or Dudaba que el niño com-iese.)	I doubted the child ate.

There are two types of verbs in the independent clause: those that are affirmative (like insist) or negative (like doubt). Some examples of those verb types are listed below.

Affirmative Verbs
insisto...
digo que...
quiero que...
es necesario que...
es importante que...

Negative Verbs
dudo que...
no creo que...
no pienso que...
tengo dudas que...
etc.

Note that the subjunctive tense only affects the verb in the dependent clause. Note also that in English, the verb in the dependent clause is different depending on the nature of the verb in the independent clause. That difference, however, doesn't exist in the Spanish.

THE ADVENTURE CONTINUES

You delay your report until you have something more interesting to say.

While in the canoe, the Mitron says: Take advantage of this boat ride to further your comprehension of Spanish. You are to complete 5 tasks: 127 (A Little Boy and a Flower) through 131 (Minidialogues).

248

127

🖭 A Little Boy and a Flower
Un Niñito y una Flor

A little boy found a pretty flower.
"Because this is such a pretty flower,
and because I love my sister,
I'll pick it and give it to her."
So he picked the flower
and took it to his sister.
"Here," he said, "take it.
This flower is for you from me.
It says I love you."

The sister took the flower and said:
"Then we love each other.
Thank you, dear brother."

The sister took the flower to her father,
gave it to him, and said,
"Here, take it!
This flower is for you from me.
It says I love you."

The father took the flower and said:
"Then we love each other.
Thank you, dear daughter."

The father took the flower to his wife,
gave it to her, and said,
"Here, take it!
This flower is for you from me.
It says I love you."

The wife took the flower and said:
"Then we love each other.
Thank you, dear husband."

Un niñito halló una bonita flor.
"Porque ésta es una flor tan bonita,
y porque yo amo a mi hermana,
la voy a tomar y dársela."
Entonces el levantó la flor
y se la llevó a su hermana.
"Aquí," dijo, "tómala.
Esta flor es para tí de parte de mí.
Dice que te amo."

La hermana tomó la flor y dijo:
"Entonces nos amamos el uno al otro.
Gracias, querido hermano."

La hermana llevó la flor a su padre,
se la dió, y dijo:
"¡Aquí, tómala!
Esta flor es para tí de parte de mí.
Dice que te amo."

El padre tomó la flor y dijo:
"Entonces nos amamos el uno al otro.
Gracias, querida hija."

El padre llevó la flor a su esposa,
se la dió a ella, y dijo:
"¡Aquí, tómala!
Esta flor es para tí de parte de mí.
Dice que te amo."

La esposa tomó la flor y dijo:
"Entonces nos amamos el uno al otro.
Gracias, querido esposo."

128

 ## The Three Little Pigs

Los Tres Cochinitos

Cover the English and read the Spanish account of this popular story. See how much you can understand without looking at the English. Then compare the English and the Spanish.

Three little pigs.	*Tres cochinitos.*
Brothers.	*Hermanos.*
Three houses.	*Tres casas.*
One house of straw.	*Una casa de paja.*
One house of sticks.	*Una casa de leños.*
One house of bricks.	*Una casa de ladrillos.*
A wolf.	*Un lobo.*
He comes with hunger.	*Viene con hambre.*
He comes to the house of straw.	*Viene a la casa de paja.*
He blows.	*Sopla.*
The house of straw falls.	*La casa de paja se cae.*
But the little pig escapes.	*Pero el cochinito se escapa.*
The wolf comes another time.	*El lobo viene otra vez.*
He comes to the house of sticks.	*Viene a la casa de leños.*
He comes very hungry.	*Viene con mucha hambre.*
He blows.	*Sopla.*
The house of sticks falls.	*La casa de leños se cae.*
But the little pig escapes.	*Pero el cochinito se escapa.*
The wolf comes another time.	*El lobo viene otra vez.*
He comes to the house of bricks.	*Viene a la casa de ladrillos.*
He comes with MUCH hunger.	*Viene con MUCHA hambre.*
He blows.	*Sopla.*
He blows another time.	*Sopla otra vez.*
But the house of bricks doesn't fall.	*Pero la casa de ladrillos no se cae.*
And the wolf leaves with MUCH, MUCH hunger.	*Y el lobo sale con MUCHA, MUCHA hambre.*

129

📼 A Spanish Lesson
Lección de Español

Take your pencil and draw a line.	*Toma tu lápiz y dibuja una línea.*
Draw another line, a long line.	*Dibuja otra línea, una larga.*
Draw a line, a straight line.	*Dibuja una línea, una línea derecha.*
Draw a longer line.	*Dibuja una línea más larga.*
Draw a still longer line.	*Dibuja una línea aún más larga.*
Draw a vertical line.	*Dibuja una línea vertical.*
Draw a taller vertical line.	*Dibuja una línea vertical más larga.*
Draw a long horizontal line.	*Dibuja una línea horizontal larga.*
Draw two parallel horizontal lines.	*Dibuja dos líneas horizontales paralelas.*
Draw a vertical line in the middle of the page.	*Dibuja una línea vertical en el centro de la página.*

Draw a line from left to right in the middle of the page.	*Dibuja una línea de izquierda a derecha en el centro de la página.*
Draw a vertical line from top to bottom in the middle of the page.	*Dibuja una línea vertical de arriba hacia abajo en el centro de la página.*
Make a dot.	*Haz un punto.*
Draw a string of dots.	*Dibuja una línea de puntos.*
Draw a long curved line.	*Dibuja una larga línea curva.*
Draw a square, a large one.	*Dibuja un cuadrado, uno grande.*
Draw a rectangle, a small one.	*Dibuja un rectángulo, uno pequeño.*
Draw a face, the face of a girl.	*Dibuja una cara, la cara de una niña.*
Draw another face, that of a man.	*Dibuja otra cara, la cara de un hombre.*
Draw a stairway (some steps).	*Dibuja unas escaleras.*
Draw a line from left to right.	*Dibuja una línea de izquierda a derecha.*

Compare these two lines.	*Compara estas dos líneas.*
In what way are they similar?	*¿De qué manera son similares?*
Both are long, thin lines, aren't they?	*Ambas son líneas largas y finas, ¿no?*
Now contrast these similar lines.	*Ahora contrasta estas líneas similares.*
What kind of line is this?	*¿Qué tipo de línea es esta?*
Straight or curved?	*¿Derecha o curva?*
It's straight. It's a straight line.	*Es derecha. Es una línea derecha.*
With your finger draw a straight line.	*Con tu dedo dibuja una línea derecha.*
Below it draw a curved line.	*Debajo de esta dibuja una línea curva.*
On top draw another curved line.	*Encima dibuja otra línea curva.*

130

🔲 **The Crocodile**

El Cocodrilo

A pale, nervous man came into the office of a psychiatrist who was a personal friend.

The doctor said: "Paolo, my friend, I see you are under great stress. Tell me what your problem is."

"Oh Doctor, please help me. I am extremely frightened."

"What is it that's frightening you?"

"There's a crocodile under my bed."

"A crocodile under your bed?"

"Yes, there's a crocodile under my bed one meter long. I'm afraid it's going to eat me."

"Don't worry, Paolo," said the doctor. "It's only an illusion.

I have many patients who have a similar problem. It's really nothing serious.

I have some pills that will cure your ailment in a short time.

Here, take three of these little pills three times a day: three in the morning, three at noon, and three at night before going to bed.

I can assure you, you'll soon be well again.

Come back and see me in three weeks, will you?"

"Thank you doctor, thank you very much."

In three weeks the man came again to the office.

He was even paler and thinner than before.

He said: "Oh doctor, I still have the same problem. And it's getting worse.

The crocodile is still under my bed, only now it is one-and-a-half meters long.

I'm sure it's going to eat me.

Oh, what'll I do? You've gotta help me."

"Have you taken the three pills three times a day as I prescribed?"

"Yes, yes, of course, three in the morning, three at noon, and three at night before going to bed."

"Well then, I'll give you these other pills. They are more powerful than the others.

Take six of them, three times a day: six in the morning, six at noon, and six at night before going to bed.

Un hombre pálido y nervioso entró en la oficina de un siquiatra, de quien era amigo.

El doctor dijo: "Paulo, mi amigo, veo que estás bajo mucha presión. Díme cual es tu problema."

"Oh, doctor, por favor ayúdeme. Me siento extremadamente asustado."

"¿Qué es lo que te asusta?"

"Hay un cocodrilo debajo de mi cama."

"¿Un cocodrilo debajo de tu cama?"

"Sí, hay un cocodrilo debajo de mi cama, de un metro de largo. Tengo miedo que me va a devorar."

"No te preocupes, Paulo," dijo el doctor. "Es sólo una ilusión.

Tengo muchos pacientes que tienen problemas similares. En verdad no es muy serio.

Tengo unas píldoras que te van a curar la enfermedad en poco tiempo.

Mira, toma tres de estas píldoritas tres veces al día: tres en la mañana, tres al mediodía, y tres en la noche antes de acostarte.

Te aseguro que te mejorarás pronto.

Regresa a verme de nuevo en tres semanas."

"Muchas gracias, doctor, muchas gracias."

En tres semanas el hombre regresó de nuevo a la oficina.

Estaba aún más pálido y delgado que antes.

Dijo: "Oh doctor, todavía tengo el mismo problema. Y se está empeorando.

El cocodrilo todavía está debajo de mi cama, sólo que ahora mide metro y medio.

Estoy seguro que va a devorarme.

Oh, ¿Qué hago? Tiene que ayudarme."

"¿Has tomado las tres píldoras tres veces al día, tal como te lo prescribí?"

"Sí, sí, claro. Tres en la mañana, tres al mediodía, y tres en la noche antes de acostarme."

"Bueno entonces, te daré otras píldoras. Estas son más fuertes que las otras.

Toma seis de estas tres veces al día: seis en la mañana, seis al mediodía, y seis en la noche antes de acostarte.

I can assure you, you'll soon be well again.
  Come back and see me in six weeks, will you?"
"Thank you doctor, thank you very much."
In six weeks the man came again to the office.

He was even thinner, paler, and more nervous than
  before.
He said: "Oh doctor, I still have the same problem,
  and it's getting worse.
The crocodile is still under my bed, only now it is
  two meters long. I know it's going to eat me.
Oh, What shall I do? You've gotta help me."
"Have you taken the six pills three times a day as I
  prescribed?"
"Yes, yes, of course. Six in the morning, six at noon,
  and six at night before going to bed."
"Well then, I'll give you these new pills.
  They are extremely powerful. I want you to take
  nine of them three times a day: nine in the
  morning, nine at noon, and nine at night before
  going to bed.
I can assure you you'll be well again soon.
Come back and see me in nine weeks, will you?"
Nine weeks went by but the man didn't come.
Ten weeks, eleven weeks, twelve weeks.
After twelve weeks, the doctor by chance was
  walking along a street,
  and he passed the house of his sick friend.
He decided to stop and call on him.
He knocked on the door, and his friend's wife
  answered the door. She was crying.
"Good evening, Mrs. Lopez, I came to see how
  Paolo is doing."
"Oh doctor, haven't you heard?"
"What?"
"Paolo is dead."
"Dead?"
"Yes, he was eaten by the crocodile."

Te aseguro que te mejorarás muy pronto.
  Regresa a verme de nuevo en seis semanas."
"Gracias, doctor, muchas gracias."
En seis semanas el hombre regresó de nuevo a la
  oficina.

Estaba aún más delgado, pálido, y nervioso que
  antes.
Dijo: "Ay, doctor, todavía tengo el mismo problema,
  y se está empeorando.
El cocodrilo está todavía debajo de mi cama, sólo
  que ahora mide dos metros. Sé que va a devorarme.
Oh, ¿Qué haré? Tiene que ayudarme."
"¿Has tomado las seis píldoras tres veces al día como
  te lo prescribí?"
"Sí, sí, claro. Seis en la mañana, seis en la tarde, y
  seis en la noche antes de acostarme."
"Bueno, entonces te daré otras píldoras.
  Son bastante fuertes. Quiero que te tomes nueve
  tres veces al día: nueve en la mañana, nueve al
  mediodía, y nueve en la noche antes de acostarte.
Te puedo asegurar que pronto te mejorarás.
Regresa a verme en nueve semanas."
Nueve semanas pasaron, pero el hombre no regresó.
Diez semanas, once semanas, y doce semanas.
Después de doce semanas, por casualidad el doctor
  caminaba por la calle,
  y pasó por la casa de su amigo enfermo.
Entonces decidió visitarlo.
Golpeó la puerta, y la esposa de su amigo salió
  llorando.
"Buenas noches, señora López. Vengo para ver cómo
  está Paulo."
"Ay, doctor, ¿acaso no se enteró?"
"¿Qué?"
"Paulo está muerto."
"¿Muerto?"
"Sí, se lo comió un cocodrilo."

131

🖾 Minidialogues

I'm very proud of my son.	*Estoy muy orgulloso de mi hijo.*
Why?	*¿Por qué?*
He can spell his name backwards and forwards.	*El sabe escribir su nombre al derecho y al revés.*
What's his name?	*¿Cómo se llama él?*
Bob.	*Bob.*

I'm going to leave you.
Oh!
I'm never coming back.
Oh!
Good luck.
Farewell!

Te voy a dejar.
¡Oh!
Jamás volveré.
¡Oh!
Buena suerte.
¡Que le vaya bien!

How many cars do you have?
Cars? In America? Three. One big one and two small ones.
All are new?
No. One new one and two old ones.
How much does a new car cost in America?
About $20,000, $30,000.
    For this one I paid $20,000.
You must be very rich.
Not really.

¿Cuántos autos tiene usted?
¿Autos? ¿En América? Tres. Uno grande y dos pequeños.
¿Son nuevos ellos?
No. Uno nuevo y dos viejos.
¿Cuánto cuesta un auto nuevo en América?
Alrededor de 20,000, 30,000 dólares.
    Por éste pagué 20,000 dólares.
Usted debe ser muy rico.
En verdad no.

Nonsense!
No, it's absolutely true.
I don't believe it.
I'm telling the truth.
You're lying.
Believe me! I'm not lying to you.
Impossible!
I can prove it.

¡No puede ser!
No, es absolutamente verdad.
No lo creo.
Digo la verdad.
Está mintiendo.
¡Créame! No le miento.
¡Imposible!
Lo puedo comprobar.

It means I won the prize?
That's right.
Heavens! I can't believe it.

¿Quiere decir que gané el premio?
Es correcto.
¡Cielos! No lo puedo creer.

I have a headache.
And I have a toothache.
Where do we have aspirin?
Where is the dentist?

Me duele la cabeza.
Me duele un diente.
¿Dónde tenemos asipirina?
¿Dónde está el dentista?

We're proud of you.

Estamos orgullosos de usted.

No reason to be. I didn't do anything special.
There is reason. You're our hero (f).

Get out of bed! You're so lazy!
I'm sick. I can't budge!
Lazy! Lazy! Lazy!

Where's your daddy?
He is working today.
And your mother?
She's in town today.

Ha ha ha ha!
Don't make fun of me!
But you're so funny!

Are you married?
No, I'm single. Are you married?
No, I'm single too.

There's a letter on the table for you.
Oh, I hadn't noticed. Who from?
From your girlfriend.

What do you want from me?
Respect. Nothing more.
That shouldn't be too hard.

Sin razón. No hice nada en particular.
Hay una razón. Usted es nuestro héroína.

¡Quítate de la cama! ¡Eres tan perezoso!
Estoy enfermo. ¡No me puedo mover!
¡Perezoso! ¡Perezoso! ¡Perezoso!

¿Dónde está su papá?
Está trabajando hoy.
¿Y su mamá?
Está en el centro hoy.

¡Ha ha ha ha!
¡No te burles de mí!
¡Pero eres tan cómico!

¿Es casada?
No, soy soltera. ¿Es usted casado?
No, soy soltero también.

Hay una carta en la mesa para usted.
Oh, no me había fijado. ¿De quién?
De su novia.

¿Qué desea usted de mí?
Respeto. Nada más.
Esto no debe ser tan difícil.

THE ADVENTURE CONTINUES

You look up from studying and see that Stump has fallen asleep. You start to relax a little and listen to the sound of the water. You report that you are going to rest for a minute. Your Mitron says: Relaxing can facilitate your learning Spanish. Go ahead, take a few breaths, and listen to the next 7 sections: 132 (The Little Red Hen) to 138 (Poems and Ditties).

132

📼 The Little Red Hen

Spanish Only
La Gallina Muy Trabajadora

A hen found a grain of wheat.
"Let's plant it," she said.
"Who is going to help me?"
"Quack, quack. Not I," said the duck.
"Honk, Honk. Not I," said the goose
"Gobble, gobble. Not I," said the turkey.
"Then I'll plant it myself," said the hen.
And she planted it.
The wheat ripened.
"Who is going to help me harvest it?" said the hen.

"Not I," said the duck.
"Not I," said the goose.
"Not I," said the turkey.
"Then I'll do it myself," said the hen.
And she did.
"Who is going to help me take it to the mill?"
"Not I," said the duck.
"Not I," said the goose.
"Not I," said the turkey.
"Then I'll take it myself," said the hen.
And she did.
"Now who is going to help me make bread?"
"Not I," said the duck.
"Not I," said the goose.
"Not I," said the turkey.
"Then I'll make it myself," said the hen.
And she did.
"Now," said the hen, "who wants to eat bread?"
"Me," said the duck.
"Me," said the goose.
"Me," said the turkey.
"Oh no," said the hen.
"You didn't help me plant.
You didn't help me harvest.
You didn't help me carry it to the mill.
And you didn't help me make the bread."
Then the hen and her chicks ate all the bread.

Una gallina encontró un granito de trigo.
"Vamos a sembrarlo," dijo.
"¿Quién me va a ayudar?"
"Cuaac, cuaac. Yo no," dijo el pato.
"Uank, uank. Yo no," dijo la gansa.
"Gabul, gabul. Yo no," dijo el pavo.
"Entonces yo lo haré sola," dijo la gallina.
Y lo sembró.
El trigo se maduró.
"¿Quién me va a ayudar a cosecharlo?" dijo la gallina.
"Yo no," dijo el pato.
"Yo no," dijo la gansa.
"Yo no," dijo el pavo.
"Entonces yo lo haré sola," dijo la gallina.
Y lo hizo.
"¿Quién me va a ayudar a llevarlo al molino?"
"Yo no," dijo el pato.
"Yo no," dijo la gansa.
"Yo no," dijo el pavo.
"Entonces yo lo haré sola," dijo la gallina.
Y lo hizo.
"Ahora ¿quién me va a ayudar a hacer el pan?"
"Yo no," dijo el pato.
"Yo no," dijo la gansa.
"Yo no," dijo el pavo.
"Entonces yo lo haré sola," dijo la gallina.
Y lo hizo.
"Ahora," dijo la gallina, "¿quién quiere comer pan?"
"Yo," dijo el pato.
"Yo," dijo la gansa.
"Yo," dijo el pavo.
"Ah no," dijo la gallina.
"Ustedes no me ayudaron a sembrar.
No me ayudaron a cosechar.
No me ayudaron a llevarlo al molino.
Y no me ayudaron a hacer el pan."
Entonces la gallina y sus pollitos se comieron todo el pan.

133

🖭 Nobody Cares about Me
Spanish Only
A Nadie le Importo

(D: Medical doctor, P: Patient)
M: Please come in. Sit down.
P: Thank you, doctor.
M: Tell me, what is your problem?
P: Oh, doctor. Please help me.
    Tell me what to do.
    I feel I am worthless.
    I feel no one cares about me.
    No one pays attention to me.
    Everyone treats me as if I didn't matter.
    Everyone treats me as if I didn't even exist.
M: Next!

(M: Médico, P: Paciente)
M: Entre por favor. Siéntese.
P: Gracias, doctor.
M: Dígame, ¿cuál es su problema?
P: Oh, doctor, por favor ayúdeme.
    Dígame que puedo hacer.
    Siento que no valgo nada.
    Siento que a nadie le importo.
    Nadie me presta atención.
    Todos me tratan como si yo no valiera nada.
    Todos me tratan como si yo no existiera.
M: ¡El siguiente!

134

🖭 A Geometry Lesson
Una Lección de Geometría

A rectangle, like a square has four straight lines and four right angles, is that not so?

Then what is the difference between a rectangle and a square?

Listen. I will explain it to you.

A square is one kind of rectangle.

Like any rectangle, a square has four sides.

But different from other rectangles, the four sides of a square are equal in length.

Each side is parallel with the opposite side.

This is a rectangle.

This is one side.

This is the opposite side.

This side and the opposite side are parallel.

Also the top side and the bottom side are parallel.

What's the difference between a circle and an oval?

In what way are a circle and an oval alike?

Can you explain?

Un rectángulo, como un cuadrado, tiene cuatro líneas y cuatro ángulos rectos, ¿no?

Entonces, ¿cuál es la diferencia entre un rectángulo y un cuadrado?

Escucha. Yo te lo voy a explicar.

Un cuadrado es un tipo de rectángulo.

Como todo rectángulo, un cuadrado tiene cuatro lados.

Pero a diferencia de otros rectángulos, los cuatro lados de un cuadrado son del mismo largo.

Cada lado es paralelo al lado opuesto.

Este es un rectángulo.

Este es un lado.

Este es el lado opuesto.

Este lado y el lado opuesto son paralelos.

También el lado de arriba y el de abajo son paralelos.

¿Cuál es la diferencia entre un círculo y un óvalo?

¿En qué manera son similares el círculo y el óvalo?

¿Puedes explicar?

135

 ## Unity
La Unidad

"Unity is Strength"
A man had several sons who often quarreled with
  each other.
The father tried to teach them to live in peace, but
  they would not listen.
Finally he hit on an idea:
  he gathered several sticks
  and tied them together in a bundle.
Then he called his sons to him and said:
"Let's see if you can break this bundle of sticks."
Each of the sons took the bundle of sticks and tried
  with all his might to break it, but they could not.

After they had tried and given up, the father said:

"Now I'll untie the bundle, and each of you take one
  stick and see if you can't break it."
This they did without difficulty.
Then the father said: "When the sticks were bound
  together you saw that they were strong. You
  couldn't break them.
But one stick at a time you could break easily.

If you stop quarreling and live in peace with each
  other you'll be like the bundle of sticks.
But if you quarrel with each other and live in
  disunity you will be as weak as one of the sticks all
  by itself."
Unity is strength.

"La Unidad hace la Fuerza"
Un hombre tenía varios hijos, los cuales se peleaban
  mucho entre.
El padre trató de enseñarles a vivir en paz, pero no le
  hacían caso.
Finalmente se le ocurrió un idea:
  juntó varios palillos
  y los ató.
Entonces llamó a sus hijos y les dijo:
"Veamos si pueden romper este atado de palillos."
Cada uno de los hijos tomó el atado de palillos y
  intentó con todas sus fuerzas romperlo, pero no
  pudieron.
Después de que habían tratado y se habían dado por
  vencidos, el padre les dijo:
"Ahora desataré los palillos y cada uno de ustedes va
  a tomar uno para ver si lo puede romper."
Lo cual hicieron sin ninguna dificultad.
Entonces les dijo el padre: "Cuando los palillos
  estaban unidos, se dieron cuenta que eran muy
  fuertes. No los pudieron romper.
Sin embargo, a un solo palillo lo pudieron romper
  fácilmente.
Si dejan de pelear y viven en paz el uno con el otro
  serán fuertes como este atado de palillos.
Pero si pelean el uno con el otro y viven en desunión,
  serán tan debiles como un solo palillo."

La unidad hace la fuerza.

136

📼 Openers and Rejoinders

Give me an example.
Well, for example…

Deme un ejemplo.
Bueno, por ejemplo…

Tomorrow is Saturday.
Thank the Lord!

Mañana es sábado.
¡Gracias al Señor!

Please. After you.
You're very kind.

Por favor, después de usted.
Ud. es muy amable.

Let's take a walk in the park.
Why not?

Vamos a dar una vuelta en el parque.
¿Por qué no?

We'll arrive at the meeting late.
Better late than never.

Llegaremos tarde a la reunión.
Mejor tarde que nunca.

Edy Gourmé was a very popular singer.
And now she's hardly known. How can it be?

Edy Gourmé era una cantante muy popular.
Y ahora casi no se conoce. ¿Cómo puede ser?

We did it ourselves.
You've done well.

Lo hicimos nosotros mismos.
Lo han hecho bien.

Try not to move so much.
But it hurts so much.

Procure no moverse tanto.
Pero me duele mucho.

He should not complain.
That's just what I told him.

El no debe quejarse.
Eso mismo le dije yo.

So, you're from Barcelona.
It's true.

De modo que Ud. es de Barcelona.
Es cierto.

I can't! I can't!
Yes you can. Try!

¡No puedo! ¡No puedo!
Sí, puedes. ¡Esfuérzate!

Good news for you.
Well tell me!

Buenas noticias para tí.
¡Dígame pues!

We reached the top.
Well now let's rest a bit.

Alcanzamos la cumbre.
Pues ahora descansemos un poco.

I can't leave until Friday.
Me neither.

No puedo salir hasta el viernes.
Yo tampoco.

They say a cow jumped over the moon.

Dicen que una vaca saltó sobre la luna.

[Incredible!]	¡Increíble!
These papers are worthless. Throw them out.	*Estos papeles no valen nada. ¡Tíralos!*
As you say.	*Como Ud. diga.*
I have lived here five months.	*Hace cinco meses que vivo aquí.*
A very short time.	*Muy poco tiempo.*
I'm mistaken. Excuse me.	*Me equivoqué. Disculpe Ud.*
No reason.	*No hay porqué.*
I'd like to talk with Mr. Perez.	*Quisiera hablar con el Señor Perez.*
Who is calling?	*¿De parte de quién?*
Stay with me.	*Quédate conmigo.*
I can't. I have to go.	*No puedo. Tengo que irme.*

137

The Silent Fishermen
Los Pescadores Callados

Early one Saturday morning a fisherman and his son went out fishing.	*Temprano un sábado por la mañana, un pescador y su hijo salieron a pescar.*
Because fishermen don't like to talk a lot, the men in our story were quiet as fish.	*Puesto que a los pescadores no les gusta hablar mucho, los hombres en nuestro cuento estaban tan callados como los peces.*
Only at noon, when clouds appeared on the horizon, did the son say to his father:	*Solamente al mediodía, cuando las nubes aparecieron en el horizonte, el hijo le dijo al padre:*
"Looks like it's gonna rain."	*"Parece que va a llover."*
The father looked up for a while and nodded to the son. But he did not say a word.	*El padre levantó la vista hacia el cielo y movió la cabeza en señal de aprobación. Pero no dijo ni una palabra.*
A day went by like that.	*Un día pasó de esa manera.*
On Sunday they took a rest. But as usual, they said nothing to each other.	*El domingo tomaron un descanso. Pero como de costumbre, no se dijeron nada.*
On Monday they went fishing again. But they were still in silence.	*El lunes fueron de nuevo a pescar, pero todavía en silencio.*
Tuesday, Wednesday, Thursday, Friday, all passed in the same way.	*Así pasaron el martes, el miércoles, el jueves, y el viernes, todos pasaron de la misma manera.*
It was only on Friday evening when it was raining hard, the father wiped his forehead with his hand and said: "Yes, you're right."	*No fue sino hasta el viernes por la noche, cuando empezó a llover fuerte, que el padre se secó la frente con su mano y dijo: "Sí, tienes razón."*

Here are some more poems ands ditties for you to enjoy.

138

📼 Poems and Ditties

No sé...	I don't know...
Por una mirada...un mundo.	For a glance...a world.
Por una sonriza...el cielo.	For a smile...the sky.
Por un beso...	For a kiss...
¡Ay, no sé que te diera por un beso!	I don't know what I'd give thee for a kiss!
Veo la luna,	I see the moon,
Y la luna ve a mi.	And the moon sees me.
¡Que Dios bendiga la luna, y bendiga también a mi!	God bless the moon, and also bless me!

Hola Johnny,   Hi there, Johnny,
Gringo boy,   Gringo boy,
¿Qué estás haciendo?   What are you doing?
Ya me voy.   I'm just leaving.

Tengo hambre,   I am hungry,
¿Qué hay de comer?   What is there to eat?
Sanwiches y sopa.   Sandwiches and soup.
Pues, a ver.   Well, let me see.

Tengo sed,   I am thirsty,
¿Qué bebidas hay?   What drinks are there?
Té, café, y Pepsi.   Coffee, tea, and Pepsi.
¡Ay ay ay!   Ay ay ay!

Tengo sueño,   I am sleepy,
Voy a dormir,   I'm gonna go to sleep,
No me digas nada,   Don't say anything to me,
Ahora quiero ir.   I want to go now.

Vamos Berta.   Let's go, Bertha.
¿A dónde, pues?   Where to then?
Vamos a la luna,   Let's go to the moon,
Esta vez.   This time.

¿Que tal Carlos?   How's it going, Carlos?
¿A dónde va?   Where are you going?
Voy con mi banquero.   I'm going to my banker.
¡Ojalá!   I hope so!

Tengo frio,   I am cold,

Sábanas,	Blankets,
Si no, me muero pronto.	Otherwise I'll die soon.
¿Donde estás?	Where are you?
Dame hielo,	Give me ice,
Hace calor,	It's hot (weather),
Aquí en esta casa,	Here in this house,
¡Qué dolor! Sí, señor.	What pain! Yes, sir.

End Tape 5, Side B

THE ADVENTURE CONTINUES

You report, "Both in canoe continuing to study."

As you are traveling, you note that the water seems to be getting a little rough. The Mitron tells you and Stump that the ride is smoother if Spanish is being spoken. You both begin telling each other stories. You continue to progress through tasks 139 (The Story of the Three Bears) to 146 (Useful Words and Phrases).

This is a tape only activity. Close your eyes and listen, trying to understand the Spanish.

139

📼 The Story of the Three Bears
Spanish Only
El Cuento de los Tres Osos

If you had difficulty understanding this, review the account of the *Three Bears* on Tape 4, Side A.

140

📼 Openers and Rejoinders

Juan Gonzalez is an acquaintance of mine. I don't know him.	*Juan Gonzalez es un conocido mío.* *Yo no lo conozco.*
I'm sorry, but I have to go now. Come and see me soon.	*Lo siento, pero tengo que salir ahora.* *Venga a verme pronto.*
It was nice talking with you. Same here.	*Ha sido un placer hablar con Ud.* *Igualmente.*
Thank you for helping me. Thank you.	*Gracias por haberme ayudado.* *Gracias a usted.*
You remind me of my brother. How can that be?	*Usted me hace acordar de mi hermano.* *¿Cómo puede ser eso?*
I have something special I want to give you. Thanks, but you don't owe me anything.	*Tengo una cosa especial que quiero presentarle.* *Gracias, pero Ud. no me debe nada.*
Come at once. Right away. I'm coming.	*Venga pronto.* *Ahorita. Ya vengo.*
Evidently I was mistaken. You should have known.	*Evidentemente yo me equivoqué.* *Debería de haber sabido.*
You're driving me crazy.	*Me vas a volver loco.*

But you don't give me what I want.

I know you're busy with the exams.
Yes, and in view of this, I can't see you.

Perhaps we can see each other tomorrow.
I hope so.

It's been a long time since we've seen each other.
Too long.

Everybody is contributing but the rich.
That I don't understand.

I'm sorry for having run over you!
It's nothing. Such things happen.

Point out the way.
I don't know the way myself.

I was ashamed of you.
I'm ashamed of myself.

This time it's my turn to pay the bill.
Don't even think of it!

I noticed a mistake here.
Yes, I'm aware of it.

I must go now.
I'm going to miss you a lot.

If today is Monday, this must be Madrid.
It must be.

It turns out they're going to kick you out of here.
That doesn't matter. It's nothing.

I'm going to the beach.
Look out for the sharks...and the girls.

Pero tú no me das lo que quiero.

Sé que Ud. está ocupada con los exámenes.
Sí, y en vista de esto, no puedo verle hoy.

Tal vez mañana podamos vernos.
Espero que sí.

Hace mucho tiempo que no nos vemos.
Demasiado tiempo.

Todos contribuyen menos los ricos.
No comprendo eso.

¡Siento mucho que la pisé!
No es nada. Tales cosas suceden.

Muéstrame el camino.
Ni yo misma sé el camino.

Yo estaba avergonzada de tí.
Yo estaba avergonzado de mí mismo.

Esta vez me toca a mí pagar la cuenta.
¡Ni pensar!

Me dí cuenta de un error aquí.
Sí, estoy enterado.

Ahora me tengo que ir.
Te voy a extrañar mucho.

Si hoy es lunes, ésta ha de ser Madrid.
Ha de ser.

Resulta que te van a echar de aquí.
Eso no importa. No es nada.

Voy a la playa.
Cuidado con los tiburones...y las chicas.

141

📼 The House of Chuchurumbel
Spanish Only
La Casa de Chuchurumbel

This is the house of Chuchurumbel.
This is the door of the house of Chuchurumbel.
This is the key of the door of the house of Chuchurumbel.
This is the cord of the key of the door of the house of Chuchurumbel.
This is the rat that ate the cord of the key of the door of the house of Chuchurumbel.
This is the cat that killed the rat that ate the cord of the key of the door of the house of Chuchurumbel.
This is the dog that chased the cat that killed the rat that ate the cord of the key of the door of the house of Chuchurumbel.
This is the club that beat the dog that chased the cat that killed the rat that ate the cord of the key of the door of the house of Chuchurumbel.
This is the fire that burned the club that beat the dog that chased the cat that killed the rat that ate the cord of the key of the door of the house of Chuchurumbel.
This is the water that put out the fire that burned the club that beat the dog that chased the cat that killed the rat that ate the cord of the key of the door of the house of Chuchurumbel.
This is the farmer that brought the ox that drank the water that put out the fire that burned the club that beat the dog that chased the cat that killed the rat that ate the cord of the key of the door of the house of Chuchurumbel.
This is the ox that drank the water that put out the fire that burned the club that beat the dog that chased the cat that killed the rat that ate the cord of the key of the door of the house of Chuchurumbel.
This is the house of Chuchurumbel where lives the farmer who brought the ox that drank the water that put out the fire that burned the club that beat the dog that chased the cat that killed the rat that ate the cord of the key of the door of the house of Chuchurumbel.

Esta es la casa de Chuchurumbel.
Esta es la puerta de la casa de Chuchurumbel.
Esta es la llave de la puerta de la casa de Chuchurumbel.
Esta es el cordón de la llave de la casa de Chuchurumbel.
Este es el ratón que se comió el cordón de la llave de la puerta de la casa de Chuchurumbel.
Este es el gato que mató al ratón que se comió el cordón de la llave de la puerta de la casa de Chuchurumbel.
Este es el perro que persiguió al gato que mató al ratón que se comió el cordón de la llave de la puerta de la casa de Chuchurumbel.
Este es el garrote que le pegó al perro que persiguió al gato que mató al ratón que se comió el cordón de la llave de la puerta de la casa de Chuchurumbel.
Este es el fuego que quemó el garrote que le pegó al perro que persiguió al gato que mató el ratón que se comió el cordón de la llave de la puerta de la casa de Chuchurumbel.
Este es el agua que apagó el fuego que quemó el garrote que le pegó al perro que persiguió al gato que mató el ratón que se comió el cordón de la llave de la puerta de la casa de Chuchurumbel.
Este es el campesino que acarreó el buey que tomó el agua que apagó el fuego que quemó el garrote que le pegó al perro que persiguió al gato que mató el ratón que se comió el cordón de la llave de la puerta de la casa de Chuchurumbel.
Este es el buey que tomó el agua que apagó el fuego que quemó el garrote que le pegó al perro que persiguió al gato que mató el ratón que se comió el cordón de la llave de la puerta de la casa de Chuchurumbel.
Esta es la casa de Chuchurumbel donde vive el campesino que acarreó el buey que tomó el agua que apagó el fuego que quemó el garrote que le pegó al perro que persiguió al gato que mató el ratón que se comió el cordón de la llave de la puerta de la casa de Chuchurumbel.

142

📼 A Geometry Lesson
Spanish Only
Una Lección de Geometría

There are lines that have no end.
For example, the equator is a line that has no end.
Of course such lines also have no midpoint.
That's logical, isn't it?
But if a line has one end, a beginning, then it must
    also have an end.
There is no line that has only one end.
Nor is there a line that has three ends.
Here is a line, a line with two ends.
Therefore this line has a midpoint.
Here is the approximate midpoint.
Locate the left end.
Label it A.
Label the other end B.
This line can then be called AB.

Hay líneas que no tienen fin.
Por ejemplo, el ecuador es una línea que no tiene fin.
Claro que tales líneas tampoco tienen punto central.
Eso es lógico, ¿verdad?
Pero si una línea tiene un extremo, un principio,
    entonces también debe tener otro extremo.
No hay línea que tenga sólo un extremo.
Tampoco hay línea que tenga tres extremos.
Aquí hay una línea, una línea con dos extremos.
Luego esta línea tiene un punto central.
Aquí está el punto central aproximado.
Localiza el extremo izquierdo.
Márquelo A.
Marque el otro extremo B.
Entonces esta línea puede llamarse AB.

143

📼 Five Blind Men Describe an Elephant
Cinco Ciegos Describen un Elefante

One day five blind men were chatting
and the subject turned to elephants.
One of them said: "I've grown this old, and I still
don't know what an elephant looks like."
"Neither do I."
"Me, I haven't seen one either."
"Same here."
"What in fact does an elephant look like?"
All five had the same feeling, so they at once
decided to ask someone to take them to an
elephant so they could feel it.
One day the group of blind men finally got the
chance to "see" what an elephant was.
With great delight they went up to the elephant and
attentively began to feel it.
"Aha! Now I know, an elephant is the shape of a
wall."
"No! An elephant has the shape of a thick rope."

"No! No! An elephant looks like a big fan."
"You are all wrong! An elephant looks like a pillar."

"All of you are wrong. An elephant looks like a
snake."
Each thought only his own opinion was right.
Since each thought the part he felt constituted the
whole elephant,
they would not listen to one another or accept one
another's opinions.
It finally ended in a quarrel.

Un día cinco ciegos conversaban
y el tema resultó ser los elefantes.
Uno de ellos dijo: "Yo he llegado a esta edad y
todavía no sé como es un elefante."
"Ni yo tampoco."
"Yo tampoco he visto uno."
"Ni yo tampoco."
"En realidad, ¿cómo es un elefante?"
Los cinco tenían el mismo deseo, por lo que
decidieron pedirle a alguien que los llevara cerca de
un elefante para poder tocarlo.
Un día el grupo de ciegos lograron ir a "ver" qué era
un elefante.
Con gran deleite se dirigieron hacia el elefante y
atentamente empezaron a tocarlo.
"¡Ajá! Ya sé, un elefante es como una pared."

"¡No! Un elefante tiene la forma de una soga
gruesa."
"¡No! ¡No! Un elefante se parece a un gran abanico."
"¡Todos ustedes están equivocados! Un elefante se
parece a una columna."
"Todos ustedes están equivocados. Un elefante se
parece a una serpiente."
Cada uno creía solamente en su propia opinión.
Ya que cada uno de ellos pensaba que la parte que
había tocado era el elefante entero,
no escuchaban el uno al otro ni aceptaban las
opiniones de los demás.
Y todo terminó en una pelea.

📼 A Geometry Lesson
Una Lección de Geometría

We've seen many kinds of lines.	*Hemos visto muchas clases de líneas.*
For example, vertical lines like this one.	*Por ejemplo, líneas verticales como ésta.*
Diagonal lines like this one.	*Líneas diagonales como ésta.*
Solid lines like this one.	*Líneas sólidas como ésta.*
Broken lines like this one.	*Líneas quebradas como ésta.*
What kind of line is this?	*¿Qué clase de línea es ésta?*
It's different from the lines already seen.	*Es diferente de las líneas ya vistas.*
It's different from line AB.	*Es diferente de la línea AB.*
This section, from point A to point B, is called a wave.	*Esta sección, del punto A al punto B, se llamada onda.*
A wave has essentially three parts:	*Una onda tiene tres partes esenciales:*
the crest, the trough, and the slope.	*la cima, la artesa, y la inclinación.*
This is the crest of the wave.	*Esta es la cima de la onda.*
This is the trough of the wave.	*Esta es la artesa de la onda.*
This is the slope of the wave.	*Esta es la inclinación de la onda.*
This line resembles a snake, doesn't it?	*Esta línea parece una culebra, ¿verdad?*
So it can be called a "serpentine line."	*Así que puede llamarse una "línea serpentina."*
In what way are these lines alike?	*¿En qué se parecen estas líneas?*
Both are long, thick lines.	*Ambas son líneas largas y gruesas.*
Is either of them curved?	*¿Es alguna de ellas curva?*
Which is longer, the top one or the bottom one?	*¿Cuál es mas larga, la de arriba o la de abajo?*
This line is different from those lines.	*Esta línea es diferente de esas líneas.*
For one thing it's longer.	*Por una parte es mas larga.*
Also it's thicker.	*También es mas gruesa.*
The other lines are all short and thin.	*Las otras líneas son cortas y delgadas.*

The Shepherd Boy Who Cried Wolf!

El Muchacho Pastor Mentiroso

There was once a shepherd boy who liked to play tricks on people.

Every day he herded his sheep to the hillside to graze.

One day with nothing to do he felt bored, so he decided to play a trick on the villagers.

He cried out: "Wolf! Wolf! Help!"

The villagers heard the cry and rushed up the mountain with stones and sickles.

But when they got there and looked around, there was simply no wolf to be seen.

In anger the villagers scolded the boy: "Don't ever play such tricks again.

It's very dangerous. Do you understand?"

The boy said: "I'm sorry. I won't do it again."

A week went by. With nothing to do, the boy was bored,

so he decided to play the trick again. He cried: "Wolf! Wolf! Help!"

Hearing the desperate cries of the shepherd boy, the villagers rushed up the mountain to save the sheep.

When they again found there was no wolf but only a laughing boy playing tricks, they were extremely angry.

They severely scolded him again.

Finally he said: "I'm sorry. I won't do it again." And the villagers returned home, shaking their heads.

Not long after this, wolves really did come and attack the sheep.

The shepherd boy was desperate. He shouted at the top of his voice: "Wolf! Wolf! Help!"

But the villagers only shook their heads and said: "The foolish chap is playing tricks again."

So no one went to help the poor boy.

No one trusted his word.

So the wolves killed many many sheep.

Había una vez un pastorcillo a quien le gustaba bromear con la gente.

Cada día llevaba sus ovejas a la ladera a pastar.

Un día que no tenía nada que hacer, se sentía aburrido, así que dicidió bromear con los aldeanos.

Gritó: "¡Lobo! ¡Lobo! ¡Socorro!"

Los aldeanos oyeron los gritos y subieron con piedras y guadañas.

Pero cuando llegaron allá y miraron alrededor, simplemente no había ningún lobo a la vista.

En su enojo los aldeanos reprendieron al niño: "Nunca hagas esa clase de bromas.

Es muy peligroso. ¿Entiendes?"

El niño dijo: "Lo siento. No lo volveré a hacer."

Una semana pasó. No teniendo nada que hacer, el muchacho estaba aburrido,

entonces decidió jugar la broma nuevamente. El gritó: "¡Lobo! ¡Lobo! ¡Socorro!"

Escuchando los gritos desesperados del pastorcillo, los aldeanos corrieron subiendo la montaña a salvar las ovejas.

Cuando encontraron una vez más que no había ningún lobo, sólo un niño riendo que le gustaba hacer bromas, estuvieron extremadamente enojados.

Le regañaron fuertemente una vez más.

Finalmente el niño dijo: "Lo siento. No lo volveré a hacer." Los aldeanos regresaron a sus casas, moviendo sus cabezas en señal de desaprovacíon.

No pasó mucho tiempo y los lobos de verdad vinieron y atacaron las ovejas.

El pastorcillo estaba desesperado. Gritaba a toda voz: "¡Lobo! ¡Lobo! ¡Socorro!"

Pero los aldeanos, sólo moviendo sus cabezas y dijeron: "Ese chico tonto vuelve a hacer bromas."

Así que nadie fué para ayudar al pobre pastorcillo.

Nadie creyó en sus palabras.

Así que los lobos mataron muchas muchas ovejas.

146

📼 Useful Words and Phrases

A bit faster.	*Un poco más rápido.*
A bit slower.	*Un poco más lento.*
A little bit.	*Un poquito.*
A long time ago.	*Hace mucho tiempo.*
A table for two.	*Una mesa para dos.*
About 100 pesetas.	*Más o menos 100 pesetas.*
About ten minutes ago.	*Hace como diez minutos.*
Above or below?	*¿Arriba o abajo?*
According to him, I made an error.	*Según él yo cometí un error.*
Accustomed. He's accustomed to it.	*Acostumbrado. Esta acostumbrado.*
After breakfast.	*Después de desayuno.*
After they came, we left.	*Después que llegaron, salimos.*
After you, ma'am.	*Después de usted, señora.*
Again he spoke.	*Otra vez habló.*
Again you're late.	*Otra vez estás tarde.*
All at once.	*De una vez.*
All day and all night.	*Todo el día y toda la noche.*
All of the time.	*Todo el tiempo.*
All week long.	*Toda la semana.*
Already you speak well.	*Ya hablas bien.*
Although he doesn't have a car...	*Aunque él no tenga carro...*
Although he is sick...	*Aunque esté enfermo...*
I'll always help you.	*Yo siempre te ayudaré.*
And now what will she do? Do you know?	*Y ahora, ¿que hará ella? ¿Sabes?*
And so? (So what?)	*¿Y entonces?*
Another cup, please.	*Otra tasa, por favór.*
Anyone want my sandwich?	*¿Alguien quiere mi sandwich?*
Anything but this!	*¡Cualquier cosa menos esto!*
Anyway...	*De todos modos...*
Are you angry with me?	*¿Estás enojado conmigo?*
Are you comfortable?	*¿Estás cómodo?*
Are you hungry?	*¿Tienes hambre?*
Are you sleepy?	*¿Tienes sueño?*
Are you thirsty?	*¿Tienes sed?*
Are you tired?	*¿Está cansado?*
Are you upset?	*¿Estás ajitado?*
As soon as possible.	*Lo antes posible.*
As you like.	*Cómo quieras.*
At first she wrote often.	*Al princípio, ella me escribía a menudo.*
At what time does the party begin?	*¿A qué hora comienza la fiesta?*
Be careful not to fall.	*Cuidado con caerse.*
Be careful! Don't break the cups.	*¡Cuidado! No rompas las tasas.*
Be careful. Watch out!	*Tenga cuidado. ¡Ojo!*

Before he left he was crying.	*Antes de salir estaba llorando.*
Before Christmas or after New Year's.	*Antes de navidad o después del año nuevo.*
Before dinner.	*Antes de la cena.*
Before he comes, let's talk.	*Antes que venga, hablemos.*
Before leaving we'll have to…	*Antes de salir tendremos que…*
Believe me.	*Créame.*
Besides that.	*Además de eso.*
Besides that, I like to read.	*Además de eso, me gusta leer.*
Besides this one, also that one.	*Además de eso, ese.*
Better and better.	*Mejor y mejor.*
Bring anyone you like.	*Traiga a quien quiera.*

THE ADVENTURE CONTINUES

Just before you come to the end of the tunnel you detect the perfumed fragrance of fruit—the unmistakable fragrance of the *jugo de fuerza* you carried in your canteens. The tunnel turns a corner and opens into a very large and palatial room, all white with gold trim. Your guards leave you alone and you walk in wonder around the room. In its center, under a huge chandelier, is a fountain from which liquid is flowing—but the liquid is apparently not water. It is silver-colored. On a white panel directly in front of you is a glass-like plate, whose intricate central design is dazzling in its colors and its artistic complexity. Its borders are filled with a series of dots, lines and figures that you assume is some type of pictographic written language that the ancient inhabitants of the island used.

The thing that first rivets your attention is that on the head of the central figure is a bright red rose on a green cactus, very similar to the Mexican flag! Your eyes focus on the rose. "Look at that, Stump!" you exclaim. "I think we've hit pay dirt! There's your cactus rose. What do you make of those other things that look like various fruits?"

Stump answers, "I think they might be the fruits that went into making the juice that has sustained our lives. I agree, Rump, we are looking at the makings of the legendary *jugo de fuerza*: the goal of our quest. I can't figure what the two items there on the right are, can you?"

"They don't look like anything I've ever seen before, but they could possibly stand for the horseradish and aloe vera oil."

"Yeah, that's possible. What I don't see is the combination formula, the proportions of each ingredient needed to make up the proper formula. Maybe it is all there, written in the pictographs. We'd better take pictures of the stele."

"Good idea, only I lost my camera back there a couple of days ago. So now what?"

"Let's make a report."

You report, "Have made it to the object of our quest. It is very large and heavy. Our camera is gone, so we cannot take pictures. Could bring some juice. Please advise."

A minute later your Mitron buzzes: Don't worry. The cameras in your glasses have already sent the image to us. You will need to get us a sample of the juice, however. Please do the following tasks: 147 (Mercury and the Woodcutters) to 149 (Afanti and the Clown) and then await instruction.

147

🔲 Mercury and the Woodcutters

Mercurio y los Leñadores

A woodcutter was cutting wood along the riverside.

By accident he let his ax fall into the river.

Because he had lost his work tool, he sat down on the riverbank and contemplated his misfortune.

To his astonishment, Mercury suddenly appeared before him and asked:

"What happened? Why are you grieving?"

After the woodcutter told of his misfortune, Mercury jumped into the river and came up holding a golden ax.

He said: "Is this yours?"

"No, it's not mine. Mine is made of iron."

Then Mercury jumped again into the river and this time came up with a silver ax.

"Is this one yours?" "No, it's not mine. Mine is made of iron."

A third time Mercury dove into the river.

This time he brought up the woodcutter's lost ax.

"Is this one yours?" "Yes, that's mine. Thank you!"

Mercury said: "You are an honest man.
Therefore I will give you the golden ax and the silver ax as well as your iron ax."

Back home, the woodcutter told his strange experience to his relatives and neighbors.

One of them thought he would try his luck, so he took his ax and went to the river.

He threw his ax into the water and then sat down on the riverbank and pretended to bemoan his misfortune.

Just as he had hoped, Mercury appeared before him and asked: "What happened? Why are you grieving?"

The woodcutter said: "My ax accidentally fell in the river.

Would you dredge it up for me?"

Mercury said: "I will try and see."

He dove to the bottom of the river and came up with a golden ax.

"Is this yours?" he asked.

"Yes, it's mine. And last week I lost another ax.

Would you see if you can find it?"

Un leñador estaba cortando madera a lo largo del río.

Por accidente, se le cayó el hacha en el río.

Porque había perdido su herramienta de trabajo, se sentó en el banco del río a contemplar su desgracia.

Para sorpresa del leñador, Mercurio de pronto se le apareció y le preguntó:

"¿Qué pasó? ¿Por qué estás afligido?"

Después que el leñador le contó de su desgracia, Mercurio saltó al río y salió sosteniendo una hacha de oro.

El dijo: "¿Es ésta tu hacha?"

"No, no es la mía. La mía está hecha de hierro."

Entonces Mercurio se metió al río de nuevo, y esta vez sacó una hacha de plata.

"¿Es ésta hacha la tuya?" "No, no es la mía. La mía está hecha de hierro."

Por tercera vez, Mercurio se metió al río.

Esta vez, sacó el hacha de hierro del leñador.

"¿Es ésta la tuya?" "Sí, ésa es la mía. ¡Gracias!"

*Mercurio dijo: "Tú eres un hombre honesto.
Por lo tanto, te daré el hacha de oro, la de plata, y la de hierro."*

De regreso a casa, el leñador contó la extraña experiencia a sus familiares y vecinos.

Uno de ellos pensó que podría probar su suerte, así que tomó su hacha y fue al río.

Tiró el hacha en el agua y se sentó y fingió llorar su desgracia.

Tal como lo había esperado, Mercurio se le apareció y le preguntó: "¿Qué pasó? ¿Por qué te lamentas?"

El leñador dijo: "Mi hacha cayó accidentalmente en el río.

¿Me la podrías sacar?"

Mercurio dijo: "Voy a ver."

Se metió al fondo del río y sacó una hacha de oro.

"¿Es ésta tu hacha?" preguntó.

"Sí es la mía. Y la semana pasada, perdí otra hacha.

¿Puedes ver si la encuentras?"

Mercury dove into the water and soon came back with a silver ax.

"Is this your lost ax?"

"Yes, yes," the woodcutter said greedily.

Then Mercury said to him: "You have lied to me. You are both greedy and dishonest.

Therefore I will give you neither the golden ax nor the silver ax.

And I will not fetch up the iron ax you threw into the river either."

Mercurio se metió al agua de nuevo y sacó una hacha de plata.

"¿Es ésta tu hacha perdida?"

"Sí, sí," dijo el leñador codiciosamente.

Entonces Mercurio le dijo: "Me has mentido. Eres codicioso y deshonesto.

Por lo tanto, no te daré el hacha de oro ni la de plata.

Ni tampoco voy a sacar el hacha de hierro que tiraste al río."

148

📼 Questions and Answers

Preguntas y Respuestas

Which of the two do you prefer?	*¿Cuál de los dos prefiere Ud.?*
I like this one better.	*Me gusta más este.*
Can I drop by Saturday morning?	*¿Puedo pasar el sábado por la mañana?*
Please do.	*Con todo gusto.*
How was the film?	*¿Cómo fué la película?*
Marvelous! I loved it.	*¡Maravillosa! Me gustó muchísimo.*
Is today Saturday?	*¿Hoy es sábado?*
Yes, if I'm not mistaken.	*Sí, si no me equivoco.*
Then tomorrow is Sunday, right?	*Entonces mañana es domingo, ¿verdad?*
Right.	*Correcto.*
Who can do it?	*¿Quién puede hacerlo?*
I can do it.	*Yo puedo hacerlo.*
Can you take care of my dog?	*¿Puedes cuidar a mi perro?*
Trust me.	*Confía en mí.*
At what window do they sell stamps?	*¿En qué ventanilla venden sellos?*
At window five.	*En la ventanilla cinco.*
Whose turn is it now?	*¿A quién le toca ahora?*
Let's see. Seems like it's mine.	*A ver. Parece que me toca a mí.*
How does tomorrow seem to you?	*¿Qué le parece mañana?*
Sure, that's fine. Why not?	*Pues sí, está bien. ¿Por qué no?*
How can I be of service to you?	*¿En qué puedo servirle?*
Thanks, you're very kind, but there's no need.	*Gracias, muy amable, pero no hay necesidad.*
Did you understand what I told you?	*¿Entendió lo que le dije?*
Yes, I understood more or less.	*Sí, entendí más o menos.*
May I ask you some questions?	*¿Me permite hacerle unas preguntas?*
Oh yes. As you like.	*Pues sí, como quiera.*
Is this yours?	*¿Es suyo ésto?*
Yes, it's mine. And that is mine too.	*Sí, es mío. Y eso también es mío.*

Didn't you like it?	¿No te gustó?
Not that much.	No tanto.
Who is in charge here?	¿Quién es la persona responsable aquí?
It's me.	Soy yo.
Are you sure of that?	¿Está segura de eso?
[Absolutely.]	Absolutamente.
You're from California, right?	Ud. es de California, ¿verdad?
Yes, from Santa Barbara.	Sí, de Santa Bárbara.
Where were you born?	¿Dónde nació Ud.?
In Buenos Aires.	En Buenos Aires.
Can I eat some of your bread?	¿Puedo comer un poco de tu pan?
Go right ahead.	Con toda confianza.
How do you like the climate here?	¿Le gusta el clima aquí?
I like it very much. It's very nice.	Me gusta muchísimo, muy agradable.
Why isn't there any gas today?	¿Por qué no hay gasolina hoy?
It's all gone (used up).	Ya se acabó.
Do you remember I loaned you $1000?	¿Se acuerda que yo le presté $1000?
No sir, I don't remember. When was it?	No, señor, no me acuerdo. ¿Cuándo fue eso?
Have you paid the fine already?	¿Ya has pagado la multa?
Not yet. I'll pay it on Monday.	Todavía no. La pagaré el lunes.
Do you feel better now?	¿Te sientes mejor ahora?
Yes, a bit. But my head still aches.	Sí, un poco. Pero todavía me duele la cabeza.
How do you feel?	¿Cómo te sientes?
I'm hungry, thirsty, and sleepy.	Tengo hambre, tengo sed, y tengo sueño.
You'll win the prize, don't you think?	Vas a ganar el premio, ¿no crees?
I doubt it.	Lo dudo.
Are you going already?	¿Ya te vas?
I'll be right back.	Ahorita vuelvo.

149

🔲 Afanti and the Clown

Afanti y el Payaso

Afanti had a dye shop.
One day a clown came in.
In his hand was a cloth.
"What can I do for you?" said Afanti.
"I'd like to have you dye this cloth," said the clown.
"What color do you want?" Afanti asked.
"I want it a non-existent color."
Obviously the clown was joking.
"And what is a non-existent color?" asked Afanti.
"It's one that's ...
    neither black nor gray
    nor red nor brown
    nor blue nor green
    nor purple nor white
    nor yellow nor orange.
    Do you understand?"
"I understand. Okay, I'll do as you ask."
"When shall I come to pick it up?" the clown asked.
"Come and get it on a non-existent day."
"And what is a 'non-existent' day?" the clown asked.
"It is neither Monday,
    nor is it Tuesday,
    nor is it Wednesday,
    nor is it Thursday,
    Friday, Saturday,
    or Sunday.
    Do you understand?"

Afanti tenía una tintorería.
Un día entró un payaso.
En su mano llevaba una tela.
"¿En qué puedo servirle?" dijo Afanti.
"Me gustaría que tintieras esta tela," dijo el payaso.
"¿Qué color quiere?" Afanti preguntó.
"La quiero de un color no existente."
Obviamente el payaso estaba bromeando.
"Y ¿qué es un color no existente?" preguntó Afanti.
"Es uno que...
    no es negro ni gris
    ni rojo ni café
    ni azul ni verde
    ni púrpura ni blanco
    ni amarillo ni anaranjado.
    ¿Entiendes?"
"Entiendo. Bueno, haré lo que pides."
"¿Cuándo vengo a buscarla?" preguntó el payaso.
"Venga a buscarla en un día no existente."
"¿Y qué es un día no existente?" preguntó el payaso.
"No es el lunes,
    ni es el martes,
    ni es el miércoles,
    el jueves,
    el viernes, el sábado,
    ni domingo.
    ¿Entiendes?"

THE ADVENTURE CONTINUES

After you finish the tasks, you notice a small chest. You open it and see that is filled with seeds! Could these be the seeds for the cactus and its fruit? You take the seeds and divide them in half, hoping that at least one of you can take the seeds to the submarine. You also fill your canteens with the *jugo* in the fountain.

You report, "Tasks accomplished. We have the juice and seeds and are just entering the cell to the north. Being careful. Should make rendezvous on time."

You read the next instructions: **To reach the exit, you are to complete the following tasks: 150 (Useful Words and Phrases) to 154 (Needle Soup).**

Here are some more useful words and phrases.

150

🔲 Useful Words and Phrases

Bring the boxes here.	*Traiga las cajas aqui.*
But of course.	*Pero por supuesto.*
By boat.	*Por barco.*
By plane or by train?	*¿Por avión o por tren?*
By the way.	*A propósito.*
Call me tomorrow.	*Llámeme mañana.*
Can you help me?	*¿Me puedes ayudar?*
Can you see the sign?	*¿Puede usted ver la señal?*
Can you tell me where the café is located?	*¿Me puede decir dónde está el café?*
Can't anything be done?	*¿No se puede hacer algo?*
Close the door.	*Cierre la puerta.*
Come and eat.	*Vén a comer.*

End Tape 6, Side A

151

 Past Participle

(corresponding to English -en/-ed in beaten, ended...)

INFINITIVE ENDING -AR: -ADO

TOMAR: *tom-Ado;* FUMAR: *fum-Ado;* CANTAR: *cant-Ado*

Practice:

1. (He) has smoked.	*H-a fumado.*
2. (He) has sung.	*H-a cantado.*
3. I have drunk the water.	*H-e tomado el agua.*

INFINITIVE ENDING -ER, -IR: -IDO

VENDER: *vend-Ido;* SALIR: *sal-Ido;* LEER: *le-Ido;* DORMIR: *dorm-Ido*

Practice:

1. (He) has left.	*H-a salido.*
2. (He) has sold the house.	*H-a vendido la casa.*
3. I have read the book.	*H-e leido el libro.*
4. You have slept two hours.	*H-as dorm-ido dos horas.*

IRREGULAR PAST PARTICIPLES

The following list shows irregular past participles that end in -to rather than -do.

Verb	Infinitive	1000 A.D.	Current	English	
to die	*MORir*	*MORto*	*MUERto*	has	died
to return[1]	*VOLVer*	*VOLto*	*VUELto*	has	returned
to resolve	*reSOLVer*	*reSOLto*	*reSUELto*	has	resolved
to open	*ABRir*	*ABIRto*	*ABIERto*	has	opened
to cover	*CUBRir*	*CUBIRto*	*CUBIERto*	has	covered
to write[2]	*eSCRIBir*	*eSCRIBto*	*eSCRIto*	has	written
to position[3]	*PONer*	*POSto*	*PUESto*	has	positioned
to see	*VEr*	*VESto*	*VISto*	has	seen
to say	*DECir*	*DICto*	*DICHo*	has	said
to do	*FACer/HACer*	*FACto/HACto*	*HECHo*	has	done
to break	*ROMPer*	*ROMPto*	*ROto*	has	broken

1. *deVOLVer* (return something), *reVOLVer* (revolve), *desenVOLVer* (develop)

2. *deSCRIBir* (describe), *preSCRIBir* (prescribe), *proSCRIBir* (proscribe), *subSCRIBir* (subcribe)

3. *dePONer* (deposit), *rePONer* (put back), *comPONer* (compose), *descomPONer* (discompose)

152

🎞 The Story of Little Red Riding Hood

Spanish Only
La Caperucita Roja

Here is a little girl.	*Aquí está una niñita.*
She is called Red Riding Hood.	*Se llama Caperucita Roja.*
Here is her mother.	*Aquí está su mamacita.*
Here is her grandma.	*Aquí está su abuelita.*
Here is her mother's house.	*Aquí está la casa de su mamacita.*
Here is her grandma's house.	*Aquí está la casa de su abuelita.*
Here is the woods.	*Aquí está el bosque.*
Here is a wolf.	*Aquí está un lobo.*
Well.	*Bueno.*
The grandma is sick.	*La abuelita está enferma.*
Mother sends Red Riding Hood with a basket of cookies.	*La mamacita manda a Caperucita Roja con una canasta de galletas.*
In the woods the wolf asks her:	*En el bosque el lobo le pregunta:*
"Where are you going?	*"¿Adónde vas?*
What is your name?"	*¿Cómo te llamas?"*
Red Riding Hood tells him, and he goes away.	*Caperucita Roja le dice, y él se aleja.*
He runs to the grandma's house.	*Corre a la casa de la abuelita.*
He knocks on the door.	*Toca a la puerta.*
The grandma asks:	*La abuelita pregunta:*
"Who is it?"	*"¿Quién es?"*
The wolf answers:	*El lobo responde:*
"Red Riding Hood."	*"Caperucita Roja."*
"Come in."	*"Adelante."*
Grandma sees the wolf and runs from the house.	*La abuelita ve al lobo y corre de la casa.*
The wolf gets in bed.	*El lobo se mete en la cama.*
Red Riding Hood comes.	*Viene Caperucita Roja.*
She enters and sees the wolf.	*Entra y ve al lobo.*
She thinks it's her grandma.	*Piensa que es su abuelita.*
She asks: "Why do you have such big ears?"	*Pregunta: "¿Por qué tienes las orejas tan grandes?"*
The wolf answers: "To hear you better."	*El lobo responde: "Para oírte mejor."*
"Why do you have such big teeth?"	*"¿Por qué tienes los dientes tan grandes?"*
"To EAT YOU better."	*"Para COMERTE mejor."*
Red Riding Hood screams:	*Caperucita Roja grita:*
"Oh, it's the wolf!"	*"¡Ay, es el lobo!"*
At that moment the grandma enters with a dog.	*En ese momento entra la abuelita con un perro.*
The wolf runs out and escapes.	*El lobo sale corriendo y se escapa.*
Then Red Riding Hood and the grandma and the dog eat the cookies.	*Entonces Caperucita Roja y la abuelita y el perro se comen las galletas.*

153

📼 Here Are Some More Openers and Rejoinders

We lost the game.	*Perdimos el juego.*
How can that be?	*¿Cómo puede ser (eso)?*
I'm sorry for having run over you.	*Siento mucho haberle atropellado.*
Well, so it goes from time to time.	*Pues así sucede de vez en cuando.*
Life gets harder and harder.	*La vida está siempre más y más dura.*
Keep the faith, brother.	*Mantenga la fe, hermano.*
I'm looking for a person who knows how to draw.	*Yo busco a una persona que sepa dibujar.*
And I'm looking for someone who can read Chinese.	*Y yo busco a alguien que pueda leer chino.*
I'm looking for a Mr. Juan Gonzalez.	*Busco a un señor Juan Gonzalez.*
There's no such person here.	*No hay tal persona aquí.*
You must be a millionaire.	*Ud. ha de ser millonario.*
On the contrary, I'm not even rich.	*Al contrario, ni siquiera soy rico.*
For sure you told me 2 + 2 = 5.	*Seguro que me dijiste que 2 + 2 = 5.*
Then I was mistaken.	*Entonces me equivoqué.*
I flunked the exam.	*Fallé en el examen.*
Don't worry. For sure the sun will come out tomorrow.	*No te preocupes. Seguro que el sol saldrá mañana.*
You collided with a tree.	*Chocaste con un árbol.*
I didn't realize it.	*No me di cuenta.*
This is a very important matter.	*Esto es un asunto muy importante.*
I'll do it as soon as possible.	*Lo haré cuanto antes.*
This is a robbery. Hands up!	*Este es un asalto. ¡Manos arriba!*
Get out of here.	*Fuera de aquí.*
The most important thing in the world is money.	*La cosa más importante en el mundo es el dinero.*
I doubt it. I don't believe that.	*Lo dudo. Yo no creo eso.*
A little piece of bread is better than none.	*Un pedacito de pan es mejor que nada.*
You're right.	*Tienes razón.*

I feel sad. Then cheer up!	*Me siento triste.* *¡Pues anímese!*
They're going to kick him out of the country. What a relief!	*Lo van a sacar del país.* *¡Menos mal!*
I can't attend the meeting. What a shame! It'll be interesting.	*No puedo asistir a la reunión.* *¡Qué lástima! Va a ser interesante.*
Now I feel very well. I'm glad of that.	*Ahora me siento muy bien.* *Me alegro por eso.*
You have to do it every day. From now on I will.	*Tienes que hacerlo cada día.* *De aquí en adelante lo haré.*
Come without fail at six in the evening. I assure you I'll be on time.	*Venga Ud. sin falta a las seis de la tarde.* *Te aseguro que estaré a tiempo.*
It's necessary to do it as soon as possible. I'll do it for sure. Don't worry.	*Hay que hacerlo lo más pronto posible.* *Sí lo haré. No se preocupe.*
There is no remedy for this. What do you mean no remedy!	*Esto no tiene remedio.* *¡¿Cómo que no tiene remedio?!*

154

🎞️ Needle Soup

Sopa de Aguja

(An old Czech tale)

There was once a boy named Sasha.

His mother was a poor widow.

One day her house caught on fire.

She managed to save her son, but she died in the
fire,
leaving Sasha alone in the world.

The only thing he found in the ashes of the house
was his mother's needle.

Poor Sasha was only ten years old.

He had no brother or sister, no grandmother or
grandfather.

Where could he go? What could he do?

He decided to leave the village to make his way in
the world.

Besides the clothes he was wearing and his mother's
needle,
he took nothing with him.

He wrapped the needle in paper and placed it in his
pocket.

Because I have no money, I'll just have to live by my
wits, he thought.

For two days he wandered, cold and hungry.

At last, he came to a village.

Weak and tired, he knocked on the door of a pretty
house near the village gate.

A lady opened the door.

When she saw the ragged little boy, she thought:

Such a ragged child must be a beggar.

I don't like beggars. I won't give him a thing.

She was quite selfish and greedy, don't you think?

"Please, ma'am, have you a small crust of bread for
a hungry child?" Sasha asked.

"No," the lady said. "Beggars and thieves have taken
all my food."

"Don't you have anything left to eat?"

"I already told you, I haven't even a crumb of
bread."

"Very well," said Sasha with a sigh. "Then I shall
have to have needle soup."

The selfish lady was about to close the door,
but the little boy's words made her hesitate.

"Needle soup?" she said, wrinkling her brow.

(Un viejo cuento de Checoslovaquia)

Había una vez un muchacho llamado Sasha.

Su madre era una pobre viuda.

Un día la casa se incendió.

*La madre pudo salvar a su hijo, pero ella murió en el
incendio,
dejando a Sasha solo en el mundo.*

*La única cosa que encontró entre las cenizas de su
casa fue la aguja de su madre.*

El pobre Sasha tenía sólo diez años.

*No tenía ni hermanos, ni hermanas, tampoco abuela
o abuelo.*

¿A dónde podría ir? ¿Qué podría hacer?

*Decidió irse de la aldea y buscar su camino en el
mundo.*

*Además de la ropa que llevaba puesta y la aguja de
su madre,
no llevó nada más consigo.*

*Envolvió la aguja en un papel y se la guardó en el
bolsillo.*

*Ya que no tengo dinero, tendré que vivir por mi
ingenio, pensó.*

Por dos días anduvo errante, con hambre y sed.

Al fin llegó a una aldea.

*Débil y cansado, tocó a la puerta de una hermosa
casa a la entrada de la aldea.*

Una dama abrió la puerta.

Cuando ella vio al pequeño harapiento [niño] pensó:

Este niño harapiento debe ser un mendigo.

A mí no me gustan los mendigos. No le daré nada.

Ella era bastante egoísta y codiciosa, ¿no te parece?

*"Por favor, señora, ¿tiene un pedazo de pan, para un
niño hambriento?" preguntó Sasha.*

*"No," dijo la dama. "Los mendigos y ladrones se han
llevado toda mi comida."*

"¿No le queda nada de sobra para comer?"

"Ya te dije, que ni siquiera tengo una migaja de pan."

*"Muy bien," Sasha dijo con un suspiro. "Entonces
tendré que tomar sopa de aguja."*

*La egoísta mujer estaba a punto de cerrar la puerta,
pero las palabras del niño la hicieron vacilar.*

"¿Sopa de aguja?" dijo, frunciendo el ceño.

"Yes, it's really quite tasty, only I've had it three
   nights in a row now.
I'd rather have a bit of bread tonight."
The lady started to think:
Wouldn't it be nice to know how to make soup
   from needles?
Then I would never want for food.
She smiled at the boy and opened the door.
"I'm sorry I don't have any food for you,
   but if you like you may come inside and cook
   some needle soup in my pot."
Sasha smiled too and thought: I may not have food,
   but I have my wits.
Soon a large pot of water was boiling on the fire.

Sasha carefully took the package from his pocket.

He unfolded the paper, took the needle, and held it
   up for the lady to see.
He said: "This needle has an especially good flavor."

Then he dropped the needle into the pot.
The lady watched, her eyes wide open, as Sasha
   busied himself stirring the pot.
After a moment Sasha said: "With salt and pepper
   it's especially good.
Did the thieves and beggars take all your salt and
   pepper?"
"No. I still have plenty of salt and pepper. Here!"

"Marvelous!" Sasha said, pouring some salt and
   pepper into the boiling water.
Then he stirred the pot some more, smacked his lips
   and said:
"Hmm, smell it! Doesn't it smell good already!
It's a pity the thieves and beggars took all of your
   food.
An onion would have given extra flavor to the
   soup."
The lady said: "Come to think of it, I did save one
   onion. I'll go get it."
When she returned, she had not one but three
   onions.
"Marvelous!" Sasha said, and he peeled them and
   sliced them and dropped them into the boiling
   water.
Then he continued stirring the pot. After a little
   while he said:

"Sí, es realmente sabrosa, sólo que ya la he comido
   durante tres noches seguidas.
Me preferiría comer un poco de pan esta noche."
La dama empezó a pensar:
¿No sería bueno saber hacer sopa de agujas?

Entonces nunca me faltaría comida.
Ella le sonrió al muchacho y abrió la puerta.
"Lo siento que no tengo comida para tí,
   pero si deseas puedes entrar y cocinar la sopa de
   aguja en mi olla."
Sasha sonrió también, y pensó: tal vez no tenga
   comida, pero sí tengo mi ingenio.
Rápidamente una inmensa olla de agua estaba
   hirviendo en la estufa.
Con mucho cuidado, Sasha sacó el paquetito de su
   bolsillo.
Desenvolvió el papel, tomó la aguja, y la sostuvo en
   lo alto para que la dama la viera.
El dijo: "Esta aguja tiene un sabor especialmente
   bueno."
Despúes él tiró la aguja en la olla.
La dama miraba con sus ojos bien abiertos, a medida
   que Sasha se ocupaba en revolver la sopa.
Despúes de un momento Sasha dijo: "Con sal y
   pimienta tiene un sabor especialmente bueno.
¿Llevaron los mendigos y ladrones toda su sal y
   pimienta?"
"No, todavía tengo mucha sal y pimienta. Aquí
   tienes."
"¡Maravilloso!" dijo Sasha al poner algo de sal y
   pimienta en el agua hirviendo.
Entonces él revolvió la olla un poco más y
   lamiéndose los labios dijo:
"¡Uhm! Huela. ¿Verdad que bien huele?
Es una lástima que los ladrones y méndigos se
   llevaron toda su comida.
Una cebolla le habría dado un sabor más exquisito a
   la sopa."
La dama dijo: "Ahora que me acuerdo, guardé una
   cebolla que la voy a traer."
Cuando regresó no tenía solo una, sino tres cebollas.

"¡Maravilloso!" dijo Sasha, y las peló, las cortó, y las
   echó en la olla de agua hirviendo.

Entonces siguío revolviendo la olla. Después de un
   rato dijo:

"A bit of cabbage would have really added a good taste.

What a pity the beggars and thieves took all of your food."

The lady exclaimed: "Come to think of it, they said they didn't like cabbage, so they left two heads of it."

As soon as she had spoken, she was off to get the cabbage.

"Marvelous!" Sasha said, and he sliced it with a knife and dropped it into the soup.

Soon, delicious smells filled the room where the soup was cooking.

"What a pity that all of your food was stolen," said Sasha.

"If it hadn't all been stolen
we could have added a carrot or two.

Then it would have been most delicious."

"Oh, I nearly forgot about my garden.

Just this morning I noticed two carrots ready to pull."

She went outside and in a moment came back with two big carrots and a nice big potato.

"Marvelous!" Sasha said as he peeled and washed them off.

Then he cut them up and dropped them into the soup, and as he stirred he said:

"If the beggars and thieves hadn't taken all your food,
we could have had some meat in our needle soup."

"Come to think of it," said the lady, "I hid a tiny scrap of meat from them."

In a moment she was back with a nice big chunk of beef.

"Marvelous!" Sasha said as he cut up the meat and dropped the pieces into the soup.

Soon the kitchen was filled with a delicious aroma.

Sasha kept stirring the soup.

In a while he said: "Ma'am, it will soon be ready.

Perhaps you have a nice tablecloth and porcelain bowls and spoons for this special occasion."

"Indeed I do." The woman put a linen cloth on the table and set her china bowls and glass spoons on top.

In a few minutes the soup was served in the fine china bowls.

"Un poco de col le hubiera dado buen sabor de verdad.

Qué lástima que los mendigos y ladrones se llevaron toda su comida."

La dama exclamó: "Ahora que me acuerdo, dijeron que no les gustaba la col, así que dejaron dos cabezas."

Tan pronto como terminó de hablar, se fué para conseguir la col.

"¡Maravilloso!" dijo Sasha, y cortó la col con un cuchillo y la echó a la sopa.

Muy pronto aromas deliciosas comenzaron a llenar el cuarto donde se estaba cocinando la sopa.

"Qué lástima que toda su comida se la robaron," dijo Sasha.

*"Si no hubiera sido toda robada,
hubiéramos podido agregar una zanahoria o dos.*

Y así la sopa hubiera sido riquísima."

"Oh, casi olvidé mi jardín.

Justamente esta mañana noté que había dos zanahorias que estaban listas para arrancarlas."

Ella salió afuera y al momento regresó con dos zanahorias y una papa buena y grande.

"¡Maravilloso!" dijo Sasha al pelarlas y lavarlas.

Después las cortó en pedazos y las echó en la sopa, y revolviéndola, dijo:

*"Si los mendigos y los ladrones no se hubieran llevado su comida,
hubiéramos tenido un poco de carne en nuestra sopa de aguja."*

"Ahora que me acuerdo," dijo la dama, "Escondí un pedacito de carne."

En un momento ella regresó con un buen pedazo de carne.

"¡Maravilloso!" dijo Sasha al ir cortando la carne, y echó los pedazos en la olla.

Muy pronto la cocina estaba llena de una aroma deliciosa.

Sasha seguía revolviendo la sopa.

Luego él dijo: "Señora, esto estará listo muy pronto.

Quizás tenga usted un mantel bonito, platos de porcelana y cucharas para esta ocasión especial."

"Tienes razón." La mujer puso un mantel de lino sobre la mesa, con los platos de porcelana y las cucharas de vidrio.

En unos pocos minutos la sopa estaba servida en los finos platos soperos de porcelana.

And the two sat down together and enjoyed the tasty soup.

But the story does not end here.

The woman saw that Sasha was a very fine boy.

"What is your name, little boy?"

"Sasha."

"And where do you live?"

"I have no place to live. My mother and father are dead."

"So where will you go now?"

"Out into the cold, dark night."

Now the woman saw her own selfishness.

"I live alone here. I don't have any children.

I apologize for being unkind to you.

Here there is a warm fire. Won't you stay inside and keep warm?"

Sasha stayed. In the morning the woman gave him chores to do.

Sasha was very clever, and he was a willing worker.

He liked the village and found the woman to be really very kind.

When he was twenty he was elected to be a member of the town council.

People came to him for advice. And do you know what he told them?

"If you use your wits, you can find a solution to every problem."

Even today, Sasha keeps his mother's needle.

He wears it on his shirt.

And when people ask him why he wears a needle on his shirt,

he says: "One never knows what tomorrow will bring,

but as long as I have my wits and this needle, I know I will never go hungry."

Y se sentaron los dos juntos y gozaron de la sabrosa sopa.

Pero la historia no termina aquí.

La mujer vio que Sasha era un muchacho excelente.

"¿Cuál es tu nombre, niñito?"

"Sasha."

"¿Y dónde vives?"

"No tengo donde vivir. Mi padre y mi madre han muerto."

"¿Y a dónde vas ahora?"

"Afuera a la noche oscura y fría."

Ahora la mujer vio su propio egoísmo.

"Vivo sola aquí. No tengo ningún hijo.

Perdóname por haber sido tan descortés contigo.

Aquí hay un fuego caliente. ¿Te gustaría quedarte adentro y calentarte?"

Sasha se quedó. A la mañana siguiente, la mujer le dio unas tareas para hacer.

Sasha era muy listo, y muy trabajador.

Le gustaba la aldea y encontró que la mujer era realmente muy bondadosa.

Cuando él tenía viente años, fue elegido para ser un miembro del consejo municipal del pueblo.

La gente venía a él para pedirle consejo. ¿Y saben lo que él les decía?

"Si ustedes usan su ingenio, pueden hallar una solución para todo problema."

Aún hoy en día Sasha guarda la aguja de su madre.

El la lleva en su camisa.

Y cuando las personas le preguntan por qué lleva una aguja en su camisa,

él dice: "Nunca se sabe lo que el mañana le traerá,

pero mientras tenga mi ingenio y esta aguja, yo sé que nunca tendré hambre."

THE ADVENTURE CONTINUES

To enter the last chamber you are instructed that you must dive deep down in a pool of water, enter a narrow opening to an underwater tunnel, then swim through the tunnel a few meters before surfacing inside a cave that ascends steeply to a hidden opening at the surface. Measuring the terrors of this against the difficulty of returning by the long routes that brought you this far, you and Stump give each other a thumbs up, take a deep breath, dive into the pool and make your way through the underwater tunnel that leads you to the outside. Emerging a few minutes later through the hidden opening of the cave, you breathe deep breaths of sweet-scented air. "Well, Stump, we made it," you say, "and we have what we came for."

"We're not there quite yet, Rump. Come on, let's maintain concentration."

You see in the distance the lights of a town. Searchlights are crisscrossing in the night sky. You are met by a guide who demands a *consigna*. You weren't told you would have a guide at this point. Stump quickly recites *"La Llave del Reino del Rey"* and the man nods, smiles and shakes hands with each of you. You feel you are safe and within a three hour hike to the rendezvous point. It is five hours before midnight—enough time and to spare.

You report, "Safely out of the labyrinth. Will proceed with guide to rendezvous point."

Your Mitron buzzes softly. You put it to your ear and hear the words: Beware. You are not supposed to have a guide.

Walking down the mountain, Stump is a few yards in front of you and the guide a few yards in front of him. Detecting footsteps behind you, you whisper to Stump on your Mitron. He doesn't respond. You try again. No response. Yet you see him walking in front of you. You call out in a stage-whisper, "Stump!"

He turns and answers: "What is it?"

"Are you all right?"

"Yeah, sure."

"Then answer my call on your Mitron!" A three-second pause sends shivers down your back. Then Stump shouts: "My Mitron is gone!"

You quickly report on your Mitron: "Stump's Mitron has been taken!"

The words are scarcely out of your mouth before you hear the guide yell. *"Aquí! Aquí!"* And promptly three men appear out of the dark.

You shout, "Make a run for it, Stump!"

He quickly adds, "Meet at the park!"

Stump runs off to the right, you to the left, the men pursuing you. You are both fleet of foot, and evade the invaders in the dim light of the evening. You enter the town and look for a park. There is no park. Then you see a sign: *CAFÉ PARQUE DE LAS GIRAFAS*. Taking a chance, you run in, look about, and not seeing Stump, are about to run out again. Suddenly you hear: "Rump, I'm here."

You see him hiding behind a curtain. You go to him and plan your strategy together. You first report: Escaped enemy. Ready to run to rendezvous point. Should be right on time.

A message comes back. Your completion of four more tasks will make rendezvous possible: 155 (Past Participle) to 158 (The Most Beautiful Thing in the World).

155
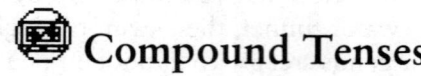 Compound Tenses

NAMES OF FIVE INDICATIVE FORMS

A.	Present perfect	has [verb]ed	he has spoken
B1.	Imperfective past perfect	had [verb]ed	he had spoken
B2.	Preterite past perfect	had [verb]ed	he had spoken
C.	Future perfect	will have [verb]ed	he will have spoken
D.	Conditional	would have [verb]-ed	he would've spoken

Examples in Spanish (realis)

A.	*Sé que el niño h-a hablado.*	I know the child has spoken.
B1.	*Sé que el niño hab-ía hablado.*	I know the child had spoken.
B2.	*Sé que el niño hub-o hablado.*	I know the child had spoken.
C.	*Sé que el niño habr-á hablado.*	I know the child will have spoken.
D.	*Sé que el niño habría hablado.*	I know the child would have spoken.

NAMES OF TWO SUBJUNCTIVE FORMS

E.	Present subjunctive perfect
F.	Past subjunctive perfect

Examples in Spanish (irrealis)

E.	*Dudo que el niño haya hablado.*	I doubt the child has spoken.
F.	*Dudaba que el niño hubiera hablado.*	I doubted the child had spoken.

CONJUGATING THE VERB *HABER*

Because of its use as an auxiliary in forming so-called compound tenses, the verb *haber* is very important.

Note that this verb has various stems: *h-, hab-, hub-*

	Present	Future	Imperfect	Preterite	Conditional
yo	*h-e*	*h-aré*	*hab-ía*	*hub-e*	*habr-ía*
tú	*h-as*	*h-arás*	*hab-ías*	*hub-iste*	*habr-ías*
él	*h-a*	*h-ará*	*hab-ía*	*hub-o*	*habr-ía*
nosotros	*h-emos*	*h-aremos*	*hab-íamos*	*hub-imos*	*habr-íamos*
ustedes	*h-an*	*h-arán*	*hab-ían*	*hub-ieron*	*habr-ían*
ellos	*h-an*	*h-arán*	*hab-ían*	*hub-ieron*	*habr-ían*

(English counterparts)

I have	I'll have	I had	I had	I'd have

you	have	you'll have	you had	you had	you'd have
he	has	he'll have	he had	he had	he'd have
we	have	we'll have	we had	we had	we'd have
you	have	you'll have	you had	you had	you'd have
they	have	they'll have	they had	they had	they'd have

A. Present Perfect (have or has [verb]ed)

h-e
h-as
h-a   *tom-Ado*   *com-Ido*   *dorm-Ido*
h-emos   tak-en   eat-en   slep-t
h-an
h-an

B1. Preterite Past Perfect (had [verb]ed)

hub-e
hub-iste
hub-o   *tom-Ado*   *com-Ido*   *dorm-Ido*
hub-imos   tak-en   eat-en   slep-*t*
hub-ieron
hub-ieron

B2. Imperfect Past Perfect (had [verb]ed)

hab-ía
hab-ías
hab-ía   *tom-Ado*   *com-Ido*   *dorm-Ido*
hab-íamos   tak-en   eat-en   slep-*t*
hab-ían
hab-ían

C. Future Perfect (will have [verb]ed)

habr-é
habr-ás
habr-á   *tom-Ado*   *com-Ido*   *dorm-Ido*
habr-emos   tak-en   eat-en   slep-t
habr-án
habr-án

(E) Conditional (would have [verb]ed)

habr-ía
habr-ías
habr-ía   *tom-Ado*   *com-Ido*   *dorm-Ido*
habr-íamos   tak-en   eat-en   slep-*t*
habr-ían
habr-ían

(F) Present Subjunctive Perfect (have [verb]ed {irrealis})

hay-a			
hay-as			
hay-a	tom-Ado	com-Ido	dorm-Ido
hay-amos	tak-en	eat-en	slep-t
hay-áis			
hay-an			

(G) Past Subjunctive Perfect (had [verb]ed {irrealis})

hub-iera			
hub-ieras			
hub-iera	tom-Ado	com-Ido	dorm-Ido
hub-iéramos	tak-en	eat-en	slep-t
hub-ieran			
hub-ieran			

156

📼 A Geometry Lesson
Una Lección de Geometría

These three lines are parallel.	*Estas tres líneas son paralelas.*
They are also equally long.	*También son del mismo tamaño.*
Lines AB and CD are far apart.	*Las líneas AB y CD están muy separadas.*
Line AB is next to line EF.	*La línea AB está junto a la línea EF.*
Line AB is between lines CD and EF.	*La línea AB está entre las líneas CD y EF.*
What's the difference between these two lines and these two?	*¿Cuál es la diferencia entre estas dos líneas y estas dos?*
These lines touch but don't cross.	*Estas líneas se tocan, pero no se cruzan.*
This line touches that one but doesn't cross it.	*Esta línea toca esa pero no la cruza.*
These lines are very close to each other but do not touch.	*Estas líneas están muy cerca, la una a la otra pero no se tocan.*
Line AB crosses line CD at point X.	*La línea AB cruza la línea CD en el punto X.*
These lines touch at point Y.	*Esas líneas se tocan en el punto Y.*
Draw a diagonal line about this long.	*Dibuje una línea diagonal más o menos así de larga.*
Then draw a curved line that crosses the diagonal two times.	*Despues dibuje una línea curva que cruza dos veces la diagonal.*
Then draw another line that crosses both the diagonal and the curved line.	*Entonces dibuje otra línea que cruza y la línea diagonal y la línea curva.*

157

Maliang and His Magic Brush

Malián y Su Pincel Mágico

(A Story from China)

Once there was a boy named Maliang.

Since the time he was small, he liked to draw but his family was too poor to have even a brush.

One day as he was herding cows home,
  he passed by a school and saw a painter inside
  with a brush, painting a picture for a magistrate.

The magistrate and his attendants were by his side watching.

Maliang was so fascinated that without stopping to think he went in.

He said to the magistrate and the painter:

"Could you let me use one of your brushes? I'd like to learn to draw."

Hearing this the magistrate and teacher roared with laughter and said:

"A poor boy wants to learn to draw too."

Maliang said in a huff: "Well I think a poor boy could learn to draw."

After that Maliang practiced drawing with heart and soul.

When he went into the hills to gather wood, he would use a stick to draw birds of the sky.

When he went to the riverside to cut straw, he'd use his finger to draw fish in the sand.

Whatever he saw, he would draw.

A person asked him: "Maliang, when you've learned to draw will you go and draw for the magistrates?"

Maliang shook his head and said: "No. Never! I'll only draw for the poor."

Day followed day and Maliang progressed rapidly in his talent.

But he still had no brush.

How he longed to have a brush!

One night he was lying in bed.

All of a sudden a golden shaft of light illuminated the room.

An old man with a white beard appeared before him.

(Un Cuento de China)

Había una vez un muchacho llamado Malián.

Desde pequeño le gustaba dibujar, pero su familia era tan pobre que no tenía ni siquiera para comprar un pincel.

Un día mientras arreaba las vacas hacia su casa, pasó por una escuela y vio a un pintor adentro que con un pincel, pintaba un cuadro para un magistrado.

El magistrado y sus ayudantes se encontraban a su lado observando.

Malián estaba tan fascinado que sin pensarlo entró.

Le preguntó al magistrado y al pintor:

"¿Me permiten usar uno de sus pinceles? Me gustaría aprender a dibujar."

Al escuchar ésto el magistrado y el maestro rompieron en carcajadas y dijeron:

"Un muchacho pobre quiere aprender también a dibujar."

Malián dijo con enfado: "Bueno, creo que un muchacho pobre puede aprender a dibujar."

Después de ese incidente, Malián se dedicó a practicar el dibujo con alma y corazón.

Cuando iba a las montañas a recoger la leña, usaba una varilla para dibujar las aves del cielo.

Cuando iba a la orilla del río a cortar paja, usaba su dedo para dibujar peces en la arena.

Dibujaba todo lo que él veía.

Una persona le preguntó: "¿Malián, cuando aprendas a dibujar, dibujarás para los magistrados?"

Malián sacudió la cabeza y dijo: "No. ¡Nunca! Sólo dibujaré para los pobres."

Pasaron los días y Malián progresaba rápidamente en su talento.

Pero aún no tenía un pincel.

¡Cómo anhelaba tener un pincel!

Una noche él se encontraba acostado en su cama.

De pronto un rayo de luz dorada iluminó el cuarto.

Un anciano de barba blanca apareció ante él.

The old man handed him a brush and said:

"Maliang, now that you have a brush, remember your own words: draw only for the poor."

Maliang was truly happy.

He immediately took the brush and drew a rooster on the wall.

Miraculously, the rooster came alive, flew down from the wall, jumped onto the window sill, and began to crow: "Cock-a-doodle-doo."

It turned out that the brush the old man gave him was magic.

Having this magic brush, every day Maliang drew pictures for the poor people.

Whatever they wanted he would draw.

Whatever he drew they would have.

One day while he was passing by a field, he saw a farmer and child pulling a plow to till the soil.

The ground was so hard they could barely move the plow.

Maliang took his magic brush out and drew a big ox for them.

"Moo." The ox went to work plowing.

A magistrate heard Maliang had a magic brush and sent his soldiers to fetch him and bring him to the court.

He wanted him to draw some gold bricks.

Maliang hated the magistrate and standing motionless, he cried out: "I can't draw."

The magistrate got extremely angry and locked him in prison.

When midnight came, the guard fell fast asleep.

Maliang, with his magic brush, drew a door on the wall, and when he gave it a push it opened.

He said: "Fellow villagers, let's get out of here."

And all the poor prisoners followed him and escaped.

When the magistrate heard that Maliang had escaped he sent his soldiers to catch him.

But earlier Maliang had drawn a fast horse.

He mounted the horse and rode far off where they could not catch up with him.

One day he arrived at a place where the ground was parched.

El anciano le dió un pincel y dijo:

"Malián, ahora que ya tienes un pincel, recuerda tus propias palabras: dibuja sólo para los pobres."

Malián estaba en verdad feliz.

Inmediatamente tomó el pincel y dibujó un gallo en la pared.

Milagrosamente el gallo tomó vida, bajó volando de la pared, brincó la ventana, y comenzó a cantar: "Qui-quiri-quí."

Resultó que el pincel que el anciano le había dado era mágico.

Teniendo este pincel mágico, todos los días Malián dibujaba cuadros para la gente pobre.

Cualquier cosa que querían se las dibujaba.

Cualquier cosa que dibujaba era para ellos.

Un día mientras él pasaba por un campo, vio a un granjero y a su hijo jalando el arado para labrar la tierra.

La tierra estaba tan dura que apenas podían mover el arado.

Malián sacó su pincel mágico y les dibujó un gran buey.

"Muu." El buey empezó a trabajar arando.

Un magistrado oyó que Malián tenía un pincel mágico y envió a sus soldados para que lo apresaran y lo llevaran a la corte.

Quería que él dibujara unos ladrillos de oro.

Malián aborrecía al magistrado, y parado totalmente inmóvil gritó: "Yo no puedo dibujar."

El magistrado se enojó en extremo y lo encerró en la prisión.

Cuando llegó la medianoche, el guardia se quedó profundamente dormido.

Malián, con su pincel mágico, pintó una puerta en la pared y cuando la empujó se abrió.

Dijo: "Compañeros, vámonos de aquí."

Todos los prisioneros pobres lo siguieron y escaparon.

Cuando el magistrado supo que Malián había escapado, envió a sus soldados para que lo apresaran.

Pero más antes Malián había dibujado un caballo muy veloz.

Montó al caballo y se alejó para que no lo pudieran alcanzar.

Un día llegó a un lugar en donde la tierra estaba seca.

The peasants had no waterwheel, so they had to
  carry water in buckets.
"Hang yow, hang yow," they chanted as they
  strained.
Maliang said: "Let me draw you some
  waterwheels."
Getting water wheels, the peasants were happy.

Just then, several guards stepped out of the crowd,
  put chains around Maliang's neck, and took him
  away.
The magistrate, seated in the great court, shouted
  repeatedly:
"Take Maliang and tie him up.
  Take his brush away from him and send at once
  for the painter."
When the painter came, the magistrate asked him to
  draw a precious coin tree.
The painter took Maliang's brush and painted a
  precious coin tree.
The magistrate was overjoyed.
He ran hastily to the tree but only hit his head on
  the wall,
  giving himself a bruise on his forehead.
The painting was still a painting.
It had not turned into a real precious coin tree.

The magistrate came over to Maliang, untied him,
  and in a voice that feigned sweetness said:
"Maliang, good Maliang, wouldn't you draw a nice
  picture for me?"
Intending to get his magic brush back, Maliang
  replied in one breath:
"All right. I'll draw you a picture one time."
The magistrate, seeing Maliang agree, gladly took
  the magic brush and gave it back, asking him to
  draw a gold mountain.

Maliang didn't say anything,
  but on the wall with his magic brush he drew a sea
  with no end.
The magistrate furiously said: "Who asked you to
  draw a sea?
Draw me a gold mountain. Now!"
Maliang made some strokes with his brush.
In the middle of the sea, a gold mountain appeared.
A mountain of glittering gold.
The magistrate jumped straight up and said over and
  over:

Los campesinos no tenían una aspas de molino, así
  que tenían que llevar agua en baldes.
"Jon-yo, Jon-yo," cantaban a medida que se
  esforzaban.
Malián dijo: "Déjenme dibujarles unas aspas de
  molino."
Al tener sus aspas de molino, los campesinos se
  alegraron.

En ese momento, varios guardias salieron de entre la
  multitud, le pusieron cadenas a Malián en su
  cuello, y se lo llevaron.
El magistrado, sentado en la gran corte, exclamó
  repetidas veces:
"Llévense a Malián y amárrenlo.
  Quítenle el pincel y llamen de inmediato al
  pintor."
Cuando el pintor llegó, el magistrado le pidió que
  dibujara un árbol de monedas precioso.
El pintor tomó el pincel de Malián y pintó un árbol
  de monedas preciosas.
El magistrado estaba muy contento.
Corrió apresuradamente hacia el árbol, mas sólo
  consiguió golpearse la cabeza en la pared,
  y recibió una magulladura en la frente.
La pintura seguía siendo una pintura.
No se había convertido en un verdadero árbol de
  monedas preciosas.

El magistrado vino a Malián, lo desató, y en una voz
  que fingía dulzura le dijo:
"Malián, buen Malián, ¿podrías dibujar un bonito
  cuadro para mí?"
Con intenciones de recobrar su pincel, Malián replicó
  con un suspiro:
"Está bien. Voy a dibujarte una pintura una vez."
El magistrado, viendo que Malián aceptaba,
  gustosamente tomó el pincel mágico y se lo
  devolvió, pidiéndole que dibujara una montaña de
  oro.

Malián no dijo nada,
  pero en la pared dibujó con su pincel mágico un
  mar sin fin.
El magistrado dijo furiosamente: "¿Quién te pidió
  que dibujaras un mar?
¡Dibuja una montaña de oro, ahora mismo!"
Malián dio varias pinceladas.
En medio del mar apareció una montaña de oro.
Una montaña llena de reluciente oro.
El magistrado saltó y dijo una y otra vez:

"Quick, draw a big boat—draw a big boat.

I want to climb the gold mountain and carry off the
gold."
Maliang drew a big boat.
Taking his soldiers, the magistrate jumped on board
and said:
"Quick, set sail, set sail!"
Maliang drew some gusts of wind, and the sails
picked it up.
The boat started sailing out to the sea.
The magistrate thought the boat too slow.

So, standing on the bow, he shouted:
"More wind. More wind."
Again Maliang drew several fierce gusts of wind.

The sea's waters became rough and the boat began
to rock.
The magistrate became frightened and said, begging
for mercy: "Enough wind, enough wind."
But Maliang paid no attention to him and continued
to draw more wind.
The wind got still fiercer and the sea began to roar.

Finally the waters became like mountains striking
against the boat.
The boat capsized.
The magistrate and all the others sank to the bottom
of the sea.
Maliang went back to the poor people, drawing
whatever thing they needed.

"Rápido, dibuja un gran barco—dibuja un gran
barco.
Quiero escalar la montaña para recoger el oro."

Malián dibujó un gran barco.
Guiando a sus soldados, el magistrado se subió a
bordo y dijo:
"¡Apúrense, zarpemos, zarpemos!"
Malián dibujó unas ráfagas de viento que empujaban
a las velas.
El barco comenzó a navegar entrando al mar.
El magistrado pensó que el barco iba demasiado
lento.

Así que parándose en la proa, gritó:
"¡Más viento, más viento!"
Otra vez Malián dibujó algunas fuertes ráfagas de
viento.

Las aguas del mar se enfurecieron y el barco comenzó
a tambalear.
El magistrado se asustó, y suplicando misericordia
dijo: "¡Basta de viento! ¡Basta de viento!"
Pero Malián no le prestó atención y continuó
dibujando más viento.
El viento se pusó más furioso y el mar comenzó a
rugir.

Finalmente las aguas se volvieron como montañas
que azotaban al barco.
El barco naufragó.
El magistrado y todos los demás se hundieron hasta
el fondo del mar.
Malián regresó a los pobres, dibujándoles cualquier
cosa de la cual ellos tuvieran necesidad.

End Tape 6, Side B

158

🔲 The Most Beautiful Thing in the World
La Cosa Más Bella en el Mundo

Cover the English and read the story. Don't worry if you can't understand everything. After you have read the story in Spanish, look at the English.

Once there was a young artist who wanted to paint the most beautiful thing in the world.	*Había una vez un joven artista que quería pintar la cosa más hermosa del mundo.*
Not knowing what it was or where to find it, he left his family and went out into the world to search for it.	*Sin saber qué era o dónde encontrarla, dejó a su familia y salió al mundo a buscarla.*
As he traveled about, he saw an old priest.	*Mientras viajaba, vio a un viejo*
He said to him: "Father, you have lived very long and you look wise.	*sacerdote y le dijo: "Padre, usted ha vivido muchos años y parece ser sabio.*
Can you tell me what the most beautiful thing in the world is?"	*¿Puede decirme cuál es la cosa más bella del mundo?"*
The old priest replied: "That is very simple. Surely faith is the most beautiful thing in the world."	*El viejo sacerdote le contestó: "Eso es muy sencillo: Obviamente la fe es la cosa más bella del mundo."*
Pondering the priest's answer, but unsure how to paint faith, the young artist traveled on until he came to an old farmer.	*Meditando la respuesta del sacerdote, pero sin estar seguro de cómo pintar la fe, el joven artista siguió viajando hasta que llegó con un viejo granjero.*
"Kind sir," he said to the farmer, "you have lived close to nature.	*"Respetable señor," le dijo al granjero, "usted ha vivido cerca de la naturaleza.*
Can you tell me what the most beautiful thing in the world is?"	*¿Podría decirme cuál es la cosa más bella del mundo?"*
The farmer replied: "That is easy. Surely hope is the most beautiful thing in the world."	*El granjero contestó: "Eso es sencillo: Definitivamente la esperanza es la cosa más bella del mundo."*
Pondering the answers of the farmer and the priest, yet not knowing how he could depict faith and hope, the artist traveled on until he came to a young bride.	*Meditando las respuestas del granjero y del sacerdote, pero sin saber cómo podía pintar la fe y la esperanza, el artista siguió viajando hasta que llegó a una novia joven.*
He said to her: "How happy you look! Can you tell me what is the most beautiful thing in the world?"	*Le dijo: "¡Qué feliz luces! ¿Puedes decirme cuál es la cosa más bella del mundo?"*
The bride replied: "That is easy. Surely love is the most beautiful thing in the world."	*La novia le respondió: "Eso es muy fácil: Sin duda el amor es la cosa más bella del mundo."*
Not knowing how he could depict love, the artist traveled on until he came to a wounded soldier limping home from war.	*Sin saber cómo podía pintar el amor, el artista siguió viajando hasta que se encontró con un soldado que regresaba cojeando de la guerra.*

He asked him: "Can you tell me what is the most beautiful thing in the world?"
The soldier replied: "That is easy.
    Surely peace is the most beautiful thing in the world."

The young artist pondered what the priest,
    the farmer, the bride, and the soldier had said,
    but thought: How can I depict faith, hope, love, and peace in one picture?
Thinking there was nothing further he could learn, he turned back and returned home.

The moment he entered his home, he saw the following:
In the forehead of his mother he saw faith.
In the eyes of his children he saw hope.
In the smile of his wife he saw love.
And around his house he saw peace.

At once the young artist set about to paint the picture of the most beautiful thing in the world.
And that picture was nothing more than his own home and family.
Let us not forget that in our own home we find faith, hope, love, and peace,
    and these are surely the most beautiful things in the world.

Le preguntó al soldado: "¿Puedes decirme cuál es la cosa más bella del mundo?"
El soldado le contestó: "Eso es fácil:
    Estoy seguro de que la paz es la cosa más hermosa del mundo."

El joven artista meditó lo que el sacerdote,
    el granjero, la novia, y el soldado habían dicho,
    pero pensó: ¿Cómo puedo yo pintar la fe, la esperanza, el amor, y la paz en una sola pintura?
Pensando que ya no había nada más que pudiera aprender, dió la vuelta y regresó a su casa.

Al momento de entrar a su casa, vió lo siguiente:

En la frente de su madre vió la fe.
En los ojos de sus hijos vió la esperanza.
En la sonrisa de su esposa vió el amor.
Y alrededor de su casa vió la paz.

Sin perder tiempo el joven artista empezó a hacer la pintura de la cosa más bella del mundo.
Y la pintura no era más que el retrato de su propio hogar y de su familia.
No olvidemos que en nuestro propio hogar encontramos la fe, la esperanza, el amor, y la paz,
    y estas son verdaderamente las cosas más hermosas del mundo.

THE ADVENTURE CONTINUES

You report: "Tasks accomplished. Just entered the cell to the north. Being careful. Should make rendezvous on time."

You breathe easier as you approach the North point of the Island and see the submarine surface. You know it's there to meet you. As you and Stump climb aboard you are debriefed by the captain as well as the panel of experts. You hand the seeds to one of the botanists and go to your quarters to rest. As you think back on the past few days, you realize all that you've accomplished.

The next day the captain calls you into his ready room. "Congratulations! Those seeds you found were the missing ingredient!"

He then pours each of you a champagne glass of *jugo de fuerza*, you have a toast to your success. *El jugo* goes down smoothly and tastes sweeter than ever—but you almost choke on it when you hear your captain's orders: "You've proven you can learn a language, so choose your next adventure: France for *l'île de Providence* or Germany for *Flucht nach Deutschland*?"

Appendix (Answer Keys)

Chapter 1
(1) d. (2) h. (3) i. (4) b. (5) g. (6) c. (7) j. (8) f. (9) e. (10) a. (11) e. (12) d. (13) i. (14) j. (15) a.
(16) f. (17) b. (18) h. (19) g. (20) c. (21) h. (22) j. (23) i. (24) a. (25) d. (26) g. (27) f. (28) b. (29) c.
(30) e.

Chapter 2   Puzzle Part 1
1. *Pablo y María.* 2. *Pablo es un muchacho.* 3. *María es una muchacha.* 4. *Pablo tiene dos hermanas.* 5. *María tiene tres hermanos.* 6. *Pablo es el hermano de María.* 7. *María es la hermana de Pablo.* 8. *Ella es una de las hermanas de Pablo.* 9. *La madre y el padre de Pablo y María.* 10. *Las hermanas y los hermanos de Pablo.*

Chapter 2   Exercise 1
un padre, el padre, una madre, la madre, un hermano, el hermano, los hermanos, una hermana, la hermana, las hermanas, un muchacho, el muchacho, una muchacha, la muchacha, él tiene, ella tiene, una de (las hermanas), de Pablo, de María.

Chapter 2   Puzzle Part 2
1. *Este muchacho es alto...muy alto.* 2. *El otro no es tan alto.* 3. *Este es rico; el tiene mucho dinero.* 4. *El otro no es rico; el no tiene dinero.* 5. *Esta hermana no es rica.* 6. *Pero ella es muy bonita.* 7. *Esa (la otra hermana) no es tan bonita.* 8. *Pero ella tiene más encanto.*

Chapter 2   Exercise 2
esta muchacha, (ella es) alta y rica, (él es) alto y rico, el dinero de Pablo, ese muchacho, El no es muy rico. Ella no es tan alta. El tiene mucho dinero.

Chapter 2   Puzzle Part 3
1. *Esta serpiente. Esa paloma.* 2. *Estas serpientes y esas palomas.* 3. *Una serpiente. La serpiente. La otra serpiente.* 4. *Unas serpientes. Las otras serpientes.* 5. *Las palomas. Unas otras palomas.* 6. *Unas serpientes duermen mucho.* 7. *Unas serpientes no duermen.* 8. *Esta paloma duerme; esa serpiente come.* 9. *Estas palomas duermen; esas serpientes comen.* 10. *Cuando las otras palomas duermen...* 11. *Una serpiente <u>las</u> ve.* 12. *Si la serpiente duerme las palomas <u>la</u> ven.* 13. *La serpiente oye la paloma.* 14. *Pero las palomas no oyen la serpiente.* 15. *Las palomas <u>la</u> ven pero no <u>la</u> oyen.* 16. *Las palomas <u>las</u> oyen pero no <u>las</u> ven.*

Chapter 2   Verb Practice
1. *come*   2. *oye*   3. *ve*   4. *no come*   5. *no oye*   6. *no ve*   7. *comen*   8. *oyen*   9. *ven*   10. *no comen*   11. *no oyen*   12. *no ven*   13. *la oye*   14. *la ve*   15. *no la oye*   16. *no la ve*

Chapter 3   Understanding Basic Sentences
1. The dove eats when the snake sleeps. 2. If the snakes eat, the doves sleep. 3. Those doves don't hear the snakes. 4. But these snakes see the doves and hear them. 5. Some doves sleep when the snakes eat. 6. If this dove doesn't hear, that snake doesn't see. 7. If some doves sleep, the snakes see (watch) them. 8. If these doves don't sleep, the snakes see (watch) the others. 9. Some snakes and some doves eat a lot, but these snakes and those doves don't eat much.

Chapter 5   Self–Quiz
1. *¿A dónde va?* 2. *¿Habla usted español?* 3. *¿Habla usted inglés?* 4. *¿Cuánto?* 5. *¿Qué es esto?* 6. *Gracias.* 7. *No, gracias.* 8. *¿Entiende usted?* 9. *Si.* 10. *¡Muy bien!* 11. *¿De dónde es usted?* 12. *De Cuba.* 13. *¿E a dónde vamos?* 14. *Pase usted.* 15. *¿Dónde está la puerta?* 16. *¿Cuál (de las puertas)?* 17.

Esta. 18. *Entiendo.* 19. *Siéntese, por favor.* 20. *¿Entiende usted?* 21. *Gracias.* 22. *¿Cómo se dice gimme a break en español?* 23. *No sé.* 24. *Hasta la vista.* 25. *¿Por qué?* 26. *No sé por qué.* 27. *¿Quién?* 28. *No sé quién.* 29. (Spanish ditty from chapter 4: *No sé cuándo,* etc..) 30. *¡Muy bien!*

Chapter 7   Script to Multiple-Choice

A	*cuatro* (a)	*dos* (b)	*tres* (d)
B	*seis* (b)	*cinco* (c)	*cuatro* (d)
C	*cinco* (b)	*dos* (d)	*seis* (c)
D	*cuatro* (b)	*tres* (c)	*dos* (d)
E	*tres puntos y una línea* (b)	*dos puntos* (a)	*un punto y una línea* (d)
F	*dos puntos y un número* (c)	*dos líneas y un número* (b)	*dos puntos y una línea* (a)
G	*dos puntos y una línea* (d)	*tres puntos y una línea* (c)	*cuatro puntos* (a)
H	*dos números* (a)	*dos puntos* (b)	*dos líneas* (c)
I	*los números 1, 2, y 4* (b)	*los números 1, 3, y 4* (d)	*los números 1, 3, y 2* (c)
J	*seis números* (a)	*cuatro números y cuatro puntos* (c)	*tres líneas y cinco puntos* (d)

Chapter 7   Listen and Draw

1. •• 2. _____ 3. 2 5 6 4. •__4 5. ••• __ __

Chapter 7   Read for Meaning

A line and the number one. A point and the number five. Two numbers, the numbers three and four. Six points, three lines, and two numbers; the numbers three and one.

Chapter 9   Rapid Oral Translation 1

1. *¿Quién es Pedro?* 2. *¿Y quién es Julio?* 3. *Entonces, ¿quién es Alberto?* 4. *Alberto es Juan.* 5. *¿Pero quién es Juan?* 6. *¿Quién es?* 7. *¿Es Jorge?* 8. *No, no es Jorge.* 9. *¿Es Manuel?* 10. *No es Manuel.* 11. *Es Amado, ¿no?* 12. *No, no es Amado.* 13. *Entonces ¿quién es?* 14. *Es Jaime.* 15. *¿Jaime?* 16. *Sí, Jaime.* 17. *O, Jaime.*

Chapter 9   Rapid Oral Translation 2

1. *José es un amigo.* 2. *El es un príncipe.* 3. *Josefina es una princesa, ¿no?* 4. *Sí, ella es una princesa y una amiga también.* 5. *¿Y Matilda?* 6. *Ella es una enemiga.* 7. *Pero ella es una princesa, ¿no?* 8. *Sí, ella es una princesa, pero también es una enemiga.* 9. *Una enemiga muy formidable.* 10. *Alfonzo es un príncipe, pero es un enemigo también.* 11. *El es un príncipe terrible, pero un enemigo formidable.* 12. *Entonces, ¿quién es un bobo?* 13. *Usted es un bobo.* 14. *El no es un príncipe, es un bobo.*

Chapter 10   Sample Story Plot

1. *Una señora va a la tienda.* 2. *Ella compra una botella de limonada.* 3. *Ella lleva la botella a una maestra.* 4. *La maestra va a la farmacia.* 5. *Ella compra una botella de medicina.* 6. *Ella trae la medicina a la señora.* 7. *La medicina es buena.* 8. *La limonada no es buena.* 9. *La maestra lleva la botella de limonada a la tienda y dice, «La limonada no es buena.»* 10. *La señora en la tienda dice, «La botella es buena.»* 11. *La maestra dice, «No, la limonada no es buena. La botella es buena, pero la limonada en la botella no es buena.»* 12. *La señora en la tienda dice, «Oquei, la limonada en la botella no es buena.»* 13. *La maestra dice, «Oquei», y lleva una botella de naranjada.* 14. *Ella dice, «La naranjada es buena.»*

Chapter 14 Multiple-Choice Frames

A	*un punto pequeño* (a)	*un número pequeño* (b)	*un punto grande* (c)	*un número grande* (d)
B	*el número 6 y un punto pequeño* (a)	*una línea gruesa* (b)	*un punto grande* (c)	*una línea delgada* (d)
C	*una línea gruesa y dos líneas delgadas* (a)	*una línea delgada y dos líneas gruesas* (b)	*un punto pequeño y una línea gruesa* (c)	*dos puntos grandes y un punto pequeño* (d)

D	*el número dos* (a)	*el número siete* (c)	*dos líneas* (d)
E	*el número ocho* (b)	*el número siete* (a)	*el número cinco* (d)
F	*seis puntos* (c)	*el número ocho* (b)	*el número nueve* (a)
G	*diez* (d)	*ocho* (c)	*nueve* (a)
H	*ocho* (a)	*once* (b)	*nueve* (c)
I	*diez, ocho* (b)	*nueve, diez* (d)	*diez, nueve* (c)
J	*doce, once* (a)	*doce, siete* (d)	*doce, nueve* (c)

Chapter 14   Listen and Draw

1.   • 11 ___   2.   __ __ __9   3.   • • • • • • • _____   4.   12, 11, 10, 9, 8

Chapter 14   Read for Meaning

1. Two lines: a thick one and a thin one.   2. Two plus two is four (2+2=4). Two points plus two points is four points.   3. Three lines plus two lines are 5 lines.   4. These lines are thick; these two lines are thin.   5. These are big points, and these are small points.   6. These two points are small, and these two are big. These are small points and big points. 7. These two lines are long, and these two are short.

Chapter 15   Key to Part 1

1. *Este hombre es un rey.*   2. *Este hombre es este rey.*   3. *Este rey es un hombre.*   4. *Este servidor es un rey.*   5. *Este servidor es este rey.*   6. *Este rey es un servidor.*   7. *¿Quién es este rey?*   8. *Un hombre es un rey.*   9. *Un rey es un hombre.*

Chapter 15   Key to Part 2

1. *¿Quién es una reina?*   2. *Esta reina es una servidora.*   3. *Ella es una reina.*   4. *Aquella mujer es una reina.*   5. *Ella es esta mujer.*   6. *¿Quién es una servidora?*   7. *Ella es una servidora.*   8. *¿Quién es aquella mujer?*   9. *Una reina es una servidora.*

Chapter 16   Rapid Oral Translation Exercise 1

1. *¿De dónde es José? ¿De Méjico?*   2. *No, él es de Chile.*   3. *María es de Chile también.*   4. *¿Y es Matilda de Chile también?*   5. *No, ella es de España, de Sevilla.*   6. *¿Y quién es ésta?*   7. *Esta es mi madre.*   8 *¿Y éste?* 9. *Es mi padre.*   10. *¿De dónde es su padre?*   11. *De aquí.*   12. *Mi madre es de aquí también.*   13. *Su padre es de aquí, y su madre es de aquí, también.*   14. *Su padre es su amigo, y su madre es su amiga también.*

Chapter 16   Rapid Oral Translation Exercise 2

1. *¿Quién es éste? Yo no sé quien es.*   2. *No sé si él es un amigo o un enemigo.*   3. *¿Es usted mi amigo?*   4. *Claro. ¿No es usted mi amiga?*   5. *[Yo] soy una amiga de Alberto. Yo también.*   6. *Pero no soy una amiga de Roberto. Yo tampoco.*   7. *¿Sabe usted si Pancho es un amigo de Anita?*   8. *Es cierto que él es un amigo de María, pero no sé si es amigo de Anita también.*   9. *¿Quién es Francisco? No sé quién es.*   10. *Claro que no somos príncipes.*   11. *Pero es cierto que somos amigos.*   12. *Sé que usted es mi amigo, Carlos.*   13. *¿Sabe Ud. (standard abbreviation for usted) si Pancho es un amigo del príncipe?*   14. *No, no sé.*

Chapter 21

1. *Un vendedor vende dulces en el mercado.*   2. *Su amigo Manuel viene al (a + el) mercado.*   3. *Manuel pregunta si los dulces son buenos.*   4. *El vendedor responde que los dulces son muy buenos.*   5. *El da un dulce a su amigo.*   6. *El amigo toma el dulce.*   7. *El prueba el dulce y dice, «Mmm, sí, los dulces son muy buenos.»*   8. *El vendedor vende un kilo de dulces a su amigo.*   9. *Manuel lleva los dulces a un comedor.*   10. *Un amigo en el comedor prueba los dulces.*   11. *El dice, «Mmm, muy dulce.»*   12. *El prueba otro y dice: «¡Mmm, muy, muy dulce!»*   13. *Manuel da los dulces a su amigo.*   14. *El amigo come más dulces.*   15. *El come más y más.*   16. *El come el kilo de dulces.*   17. *Manuel pregunta, «Muy dulce, ¿no?»*   18. *Su amigo no responde.*   19. *Manuel pregunta, «Muy dulce, ¿no?»*   20. *Su amigo responde, «No, los dulces no son buenos.»*   21. *El amigo va al mercado y compra un kilo de dulces.*   22. *El trae los dulces a Manuel.*   23. *El da los*

dulces a Manuel. 24. Manuel toma los dulces. 25. El prueba los dulces. 26. El come los dulces. 27. El dice, «Los dulces son muy buenos.»

Chapter 26 Multiple-Choice Frames

A *Un punto y una línea vertical (a)*   *un punto y una línea horizontal (c)*   *un punto y una línea diagonal (d)*

B *dos líneas diagonales (b)*   *dos líneas horizontales (d)*   *una línea vertical y una diagonal (a)*

C *dos líneas largas y horizontales y una línea corta horizontal (a)*   *cuatro líneas cortas diagonales y una línea vertical (d)*   *cuatro líneas cortas diagonales y una línea horizontal (b)*

D *un número grande, una línea vertical, y un número pequeño (d)*   *un número grande, una línea horizontal, y un número pequeño (a)*

E *un punto delante de una línea (c)*   *un número delante de un punto (a)*   *un punto delante de un número (d)*

F *una línea horizontal delante de una línea diagonal (b)*   *una línea vertical delante de una línea diagonal (c)*   *una línea diagonal delante de una línea vertical (a)*

G *el número doce delante de un punto (a)*   *el número dos delante de una línea horizontal (d)†*   *el número dos delante de una línea diagonal (c)*

H *un número pequeño delante de un punto grande (d)*   *un número pequeño delante de un número grande (b)*   *un número grande delante de un número pequeño (a)*

I *un punto pequeño delante de un punto grande (a)*   *un punto grande delante de un punto pequeño (b)*   *un número pequeño delante de un punto pequeño (d)*

J *una línea horizontal y una línea diagonal delante de un número grande (c)*   *una línea horizontal y una línea diagonal delante de un número pequeño (d)*   *una línea vertical delante de una línea diagonal delante de un punto grande (b)*

Chapter 26 Listen and Draw
1. _____ | 2. /\ | | | __ __   3. 9 7   4. • ● \/\\

Chapter 34 Translation of Ministory Plot

1. There are three persons: a trombonist, a violinist, and a drummer. 2. The trombonist loves the violinist. 3. But the violinist doesn't love the trombonist. 4. She hates...detests the trombonist. 5. The violinist loves the drummer. 6. But the drummer doesn't love the violinist. 7. He loves an actress. 8. The drummer sings and dances with the actress. 9. He sends letters to the actress, and the actress sends letters to the drummer. 10. One day the trombonist sends a letter to the violinist. 11. The violinist receives the trombonist's letter. 12. The violinist attacks the trombonist.

Chapter 35 Rapid Oral Translation Exercise 1 in Appendix

1. Rolando <u>era</u> (un) príncipe y <u>es</u> (un) príncipe. 2. Ricardo no <u>era</u> (un) príncipe y no <u>es</u> (un) príncipe. 3. José es (un) amigo de Juanita, que es una princesa. 4. La amiga de Josefina no es una princesa. 5. El amigo de Pedro era un príncipe, sí. 6. El era de España, y era amigo de la madre de Ud. María también, ¿no? 7. ¿Quién es Juanita? Es la princesa que era amiga de José. 8. Usted era amigo de José, ¿no? Sí, yo era amigo del príncipe y de la princesa, pero no era amigo de Josefina. 9. ¿Era enemiga ella? Sí, era. 10. Sí, somos enemigos. Ella <u>era</u> mi enemiga y todavía <u>es</u> mi enemiga.

Chapter 35 Rapid Oral Translation Exercise 2 in Appendix

1. ¿Dónde está el príncipe? ¿De dónde es? 2. ¿Sabe Ud. si él es de España? 3. ¿Sabe Ud. si él está en casa ahora? 4. ¿Está el señor en la casa? 5. ¿Estaba el señor en la casa? 6. ¿Está el señor en casa? 7. ¿Estaba el señor en casa? 8. ¿Dónde está la señora? ¿Está en el jardín? 9. ¿Dónde estaba la señora? ¿Estaba en el

hospital?   10. *La señorita que estaba aquí no es mi amiga.*   11. *Roberto es mi amigo, pero él no estaba aquí.*
12. *¿Quién estaba aquí y quién estaba allá?*   13. *¿Quién era su amigo y quién era su enemigo?*

Chapter 39   Translation Exercise

1. *Comer es vivir.*   2. *Es imposible dormir allá.*   3. *Es imposible trabajar allá sin estar contento.*   4. *Comer mucho para dormir bien es estupido.*   5. *Es imposible dormir sin reposar, pero es posible reposar sin dormir.*
6. *Es posible trabajar sin reposar, pero es estupido.*

Chapter 42   Self-Test Part 1

(1) E.   (2) B.   (3) N.   (4) F.   (5) I.   (6) C.   (7) D.   (8) J.   (9) A.   (10) K.   (11) M.   (12) L.
(13) O.   (14) F.   (15) N.   (16) C.   (17) E.   (18) A.   (19) J.   (20) B.   (21) L.   (22) D.   (23) M.

Chapter 47 Multiple-Choice Frames

A	*Una línea diagonal entre dos puntos* (a)	*un número entre dos líneas diagonales* (d)	*un punto entre dos líneas verticales* (b)
B	*una flecha negra indicando hacia la izquierda* (b)	*una flecha negra y una flecha blanca indicando hacia la derecha* (c)	*una flecha blanca indicando hacia la derecha* (a)
C	*dos flechas negras indicando hacia la izquierda* (b)	*dos flechas negras indicando hacia la derecha* (c)	*dos flechas negras indicando hacia arriba* (d)
D	*un punto arriba de una línea horizontal* (a)†	*una línea horizontal debajo de un punto* (a)†	*una línea vertical debajo de un punto* (b)†
E	*trés puntos entre dos líneas diagonales* (d)	*trés puntos entre dos líneas verticales* (c)	*trés puntos arriba de una línea horizontal* (b).

Chapter 47   Key to Listen and Draw

1. | • | 2.   +   3.   / ⇒ /   4. $\frac{4}{5}$ 5.   ⇒ ⇒   ⇐ ⇐

Chapter 47   Read for Meaning

1. Two arrows: one pointing up and the other down.   2. A white arrow pointing toward a small point and a black arrow pointing to a large point.   3. A long horizontal line next to a short vertical line.   4. Two lines: A long, thick, horizontal line; and a short, thin, vertical line.   5. The horizontal line is next to the vertical line.   6. A number and a small point between two diagonal lines.   7. The number five and two large points between two vertical lines.   8. A white arrow pointing toward the right and a black arrow pointing toward the left.   9. The point is to the right side of the vertical line.   10. Two points are to the left side of the diagonal line.

Chapter 58   Sample Plot One

1. In this story there's a palace.   2. The king is in the palace.   3. The king has a treasure.   4. He has jewels.   5. He adores his jewels.   6. It's a secret where he keeps the jewels.   7. But the secretary knows the secret.   8. And the duke also knows where the king keeps the jewels.   9. In this story there's also a thief.   10. The thief also is in the palace.   11. He doesn't know where the jewels are.   12. But he thinks they are in the bathroom.   13. He enters the bathroom.   14. He searches and searches, but he finds nothing. He doesn't find the jewels.   15. He thinks that the jewels are in the tower.   16. He climbs up the tower.   17. He searches and searches, but doesn't find the jewels. He doesn't find anything.   18. He thinks that the jewels are in the chamber of the queen.   19. He enters the queen's chamber.   20. He searches and searches, and finally finds the jewels.

Chapter 59   Self-Quiz

sit down, stand up, eat, drink, read, write, talk, sing, walk, run

Chapter 63 Multiple-Choice Frames

A   *Un triángulo (c)*   *un cuadrado (d)*   *una estrella (b)*

B   *Un triángulo al lado de un*   *un triángulo arriba de un*   *un triángulo debajo de un*
    cuadrado (a)   *cuadrado (d)*   *cuadrado (c)*

C   *Un círculo al lado de otro círculo*   *un círculo arriba de otro círculo* *un triángulo al lado de otro*
    (c)   *(b)*   *triángulo (d)*

D   *Un cuadrado al lado de otro (c)*   *dos figuras pequeñas (b)*   *un círculo y una figura pequeña*
                                                                               (a)

E   *Un cuadrado y una cruz arriba de*   *una cruz y un triángulo debajo de* *una cruz y un triángulo arriba de*
    una línea (a)   *una línea (d)*   *una línea (b)*

Chapter 63   Listen and Draw

1.    2.   W V   3.

4.    5.   ☆ ☆ ☆ ☆ ☆ ✚ ✚

Chapter 63   Read for Meaning

1. Which letter is this? Is it the letter "D" or the letter "O"? It's a "D."   2. What type of figure is this? Is it a circle or a square?   3. All these triangles point up and all these arrows point down.   4. These two figures are between two vertical lines.   5. What type of figure precedes the letter F?   6. What type of figure follows the letter F?   7. Which letter follows the big triangle, and which precede the big circle?   8. Doesn't the letter B follow the big triangle?

Chapter 71   Reading Activity

1. In this picture you can see a park.   2. In the park you can see some tables and benches.   3. Also in the park there are soldiers from two countries.   4. This is a North American soldier.   5. The others are from Cuba.   6. These are the Cuban soldiers.   7. The park is situated in a town in a country of Central America.   8. What were the Cubans doing in the park, working or relaxing? 9. And what were the Yankees doing?   10. Working or playing?   11. Who is listening to music on the radio, the Yankees or the Cubans?

Chapter 71   Comprehension Questions

1. In Central America. *En Centro America.* 2. In Cuba. *En Cuba.* 3. Cuban soldiers. *Soldados cubanos.* 4. They are playing baseball. ***Están jugando beisbol.*** *5.* They are eating lunch and listening to music. *Están commiendo almuerzo y escuchando musica.* 6. No, they are eating fruit and sandwiches. *No, Están commiendo frutas y sandwiches.* 7. Cuban music. *Musica cubana.* 8. No. *No.* 9. One of the Cubans. *Uno de los cubanos.* 10. The Cuban *el cubano* 11. To the North Americans. *A los norteamericanos.*

Chapter 81   Practice A

(1) S.   (2) C.   (3) S.   (4) S.   (5) C.   (6) C.   (7) S.   (8) S.   (9) C.   (10) S.

Chapter 82 Mini-Story Plot

There is a parrot. It is the parrot of the princess. The parrot always tells the truth. The princess never tells the truth. The parrot says that the king is coming. The princess says that the king isn't coming. In fact, the king is coming. He is coming with the queen. The princess hates the parrot because the parrot always tells the truth. The princess is in the kitchen with the cook. The cook is preparing tomato soup to give to the parrot. The secret agent 007 sees that the princess puts something in the soup. The princess gives a little of the soup to the parrot. Do you think the parrot drinks the soup? Do you think agent 007 comes?

Chapter 93 Focus on Scene

In this picture, there are various things. In the center of the picture, there is a suitcase. And on one side of the suitcase we see two adults: a man and a woman. On the other side there are two children. To the left on the extreme side of the picture, there are two things. To the right on the other extreme, there are four big buildings. Perhaps it's the center of the city. Above there is an alarm clock. The alarm clock reads 9:05. Below there is a street, and on the street there is a car and a driver. In front of the car, there is a stoplight.

Chapter 100 Focus on Scene

In this picture, there are various objects. On the top of the picture, there is a train that is going from the left to the right. Beneath the train and in the center of the picture, there are three instruments used to communicate over long distances. The instrument to the left of the three is a letter. The instrument to the right is a television. And the instrument in the middle is a telephone. Under the horizontal line, we see two modes of transportation. One is faster than the other. They are an airplane and a truck. The airplane is to the left of the truck and is pointing to the left. The truck is pointing to the right. On the bottom left, we see two types of arms (weapons); a pistol and a knife. The pistol is to the left of the knife. On the opposite side of the weapons, we see two types of animals; a turtle and a dinosaur. The latter is to the right.

Chapter 114 Performance Test

(1) B. (2) C. (3) A. (4) C. (5) B. (6) A. (7) B. (8) A. (9) C. (10) D. (11) B. (12) A. (13) C. (14) D. (15) C. (16) A. (17) D. (18) B. (19) B. (20) A. (21) C. (22) D. (23) A. (24) B. (25) C.

Chapter 121 Performance Test 1

Those ending in -*aba* or -*ía* are imperfective forms and have an aspectual meaning represented by $\Rightarrow$ …; Those ending in -*ó* or -*o* are preterite forms and have an aspectual meaning represented as $\Rightarrow$ | .

Chapter 121 Performance Test 2

1. *llor-ó* 2. *llor-aba* 3. *cant-ó* 4. *cant-aba* 5. *sufri-ó* 6. *sufr-ía* 7. *hablaba* 8. *habl-ó* 9. *vivi-ó* 10. *viv-ía*